Defining Civil and Political Rights

The Jurisprudence of the United Nations Human Rights Committee

Second Edition

ALEX CONTE
Consultant on Security and Human Rights, France

RICHARD BURCHILL
University of Hull, UK

ASHGATE

Published by
Ashgate Publishing Limited
Wey Court East
Union Road
Farnham
Surrey, GU9 7PT
England

Ashgate Publishing Company
Suite 420
101 Cherry Street
Burlington
VT 05401-4405
USA

www.ashgate.com

British Library Cataloguing in Publication Data
Conte, Alex, 1971-
Defining civil and political rights : the jurisprudence of the United Nations Human Rights Committee. - 2nd ed.
1. United Nations. Human Rights Committee 2. Human rights - Philosophy
I. Title II. Burchill, Richard
341.4'8

Library of Congress Cataloging-in-Publication Data
Conte, Alex, 1971-
Defining civil and political rights : the jurisprudence of the United Nations Human Rights Committee / by Alex Conte and Richard Burchill.
p. cm.
Includes bibliographical references and index.
ISBN 978-0-7546-4927-4 (hardback)
ISBN 978-0-7546-7656-0 (pbk)
1. United Nations. Human Rights Committee. 2. Human rights--Cases. I. Burchill, Richard. II. Title.

K3241.C66 2009
341.4'8--dc22

2008041948

ISBN 978 0 7546 4927 4 (Hbk)
ISBN 978 0 7546 7656 0 (Pbk)
eISBN 978 0 7546 9131 0 (ebook)

FSC Mixed Sources
Product group from well-managed forests and other controlled sources
www.fsc.org Cert no. SA-COC-1565
© 1996 Forest Stewardship Council

Printed and bound in Great Britain by
MPG Books Ltd, Bodmin, Cornwall.

Contents

Table of Contents

Table of Cases

By Case Name

By Communication Number

About the Authors

Alex Conte LLB (Cant), LLM (Hons)(VUW), PhD (Cant)
Barrister of the High Court of New Zealand
Consultant on Security and Human Rights (www.alexconte.com)
Series Editor, *Ashgate International Law Series*

Richard Burchill BA (Maine), LLM (Hull), PhD (Nottingham)
Senior Lecturer in Law, University of Hull, England
Director, McCoubrey Centre for International Law

Preface

The objective of this work is to provide an examination and commentary on the jurisprudence of the United Nations Human Rights Committee, an independent and quasi-judicial international body established under the International Covenant on Civil and Political Rights (ICCPR). It has an international focus, examining the Committee's decisions (technically referred to as 'views') and comments on the substantive rights and freedoms set out in Parts I and II of the Covenant, rather than focusing on communications against any one State party. Those views and comments are analysed within this text, with the aim of establishing a comprehensive reference point for civil and political rights practitioners, judiciary and academics.

The work should hold domestic as well as international appeal. Within the domestic context, Ministries of Foreign Affairs, human rights commission offices, and practitioners in the human rights arena (including the judiciary and other State agencies) will benefit from reference to this text, given that the rights and freedoms set out in many municipal human rights statutes are founded upon, or at least set out to incorporate international obligations under, the ICCPR. Universities are likely to find the work useful in the areas of public/constitutional law, international law, international human rights, civil liberties and international institutions. Non-parties should find use in the text too, with American and European human rights bodies often making reference to Human Rights Committee views and comments.

The first edition of this work considered the views and comments of the Human Rights Committee since its establishment and up to the conclusion of its 77th session, ending 4 April 2003. This second edition updates this earlier work by taking into account views of the Committee since then and up to the conclusion of its 92nd session in March and April 2008. It includes discussion of the Committee's General Comments 31 and 32 on the nature of obligations under the ICCPR (see Chapter 2) and the right to a fair trial (see Chapter 6). Attention has also been paid in this second edition to the question of derogations under article 4 of the ICCPR, and the general rules concerning the application of limitations upon rights and freedoms guaranteed under the Covenant (by inclusion of a new Chapter 3). Views and comments of the Human Rights Committee are accessible online. The authors have found two main web sites of considerable assistance: that of the United Nations High Commissioner for Human Rights at URL <http://tb.ohchr.org/default.aspx>; and the University of Minnesota Human Rights Library at URL <http://www1.umn.edu/humanrts/undocs/undocs-index.html>.

The first edition of this title was written by me with two fellow authors: Professor Scott Davidson of the University of Canterbury in New Zealand, and Dr Richard Burchill of the University of Hull in the United Kingdom. Due to his role as Pro-Vice-Chancellor (Law, Student Services and International), Professor Davidson had to withdraw from this second edition project. Dr Burchill and I have updated his earlier work (Chapters 1, 2 and 11) and we acknowledge the contribution to those chapters made by Professor Davidson's earlier work. We would finally express our thanks for the help and courtesy of the staff at Ashgate Publishing. Neither the work for nor the publication price of the present book has been subsidized by any official source or private foundation.

Dr Alex Conte
Consultant on Security and Human Rights
2009

Chapter 1
Introduction

Alex Conte and Richard Burchill[1]

The purpose of this book is to provide a narrative account of how the United Nations Human Rights Committee (HRC) has developed and continues to develop its jurisprudence under the individual communication procedure contained in the Optional Protocol to the International Covenant on Civil and Political Rights (ICCPR).[2] As mentioned in the Preface to this title, its focus is limited to an examination of the Committee's decisions (technically referred to as 'views'), and its General Comments on the application and interpretation of the substantive rights and freedoms set out in Parts I and II of the Covenant. Attention is paid to these two areas of the Committee's work in a manner which examines the meaning of rights and freedoms, rather than focusing upon communications against any one State party, or upon observations and conclusions on State party reports under article 40 of the ICCPR. The views and comments of the Human Rights Committee are thus analysed with the aim of establishing a comprehensive reference point for civil and political rights practitioners, judiciary and academics. Before doing this, however, it is necessary to provide some background to the emergence and development of the ICCPR and its related instruments, and to give some explanation of terms, as well as the overall context within which the HRC functions.

Introduction

A Brief History of the ICCPR

The ICCPR is one of three instruments which constitute what is sometimes known as the 'International Bill of Rights'.[3] The other instruments which comprise the

---

1 This chapter is based substantially upon its first edition equivalent, written by Professor Scott Davidson of the University of Canterbury, New Zealand.

2 International Covenant on Civil and Political Rights, opened for signature 16 December 1966, 999 UNTS 171 (entered into force 23 March 1976).

3 There is an extensive literature dealing with the origins of the ICCPR and its sibling instruments. Among the more recent literature see, for example, Dominic McGoldrick, *The Human Rights Committee: Its Role in the Development of the International Covenant on Civil and Political Rights* (Oxford: Clarendon Press, 1990) Chapter 1; Philip Alston (ed.), *The United Nations and Human Rights: A Critical Appraisal* (Oxford: Clarendon

Bill of Rights are the Universal Declaration of Human Rights (UDHR) and the International Covenant on Economic Social and Cultural Rights (ICESCR).[4] As recognized in the 1993 Vienna Declaration and Programme of Action, the UDHR is the parent of the two Covenants.[5] It was adopted as a non-binding resolution of the General Assembly of the United Nations on the 10 December 1948; a date now celebrated annually as International Human Rights Day. It contains a long catalogue of human rights which comprehends what have now come to be known as civil and political rights on the one hand and economic, social and cultural rights on the other. The terminology of 'first' and 'second' generation rights is also sometimes applied to these two categories of rights to signify the fact that civil and political rights are, by and large, concerned with freedom from State interference while economic, social and cultural rights represent objectives or aspirations for a State to pursue in promoting the well-being of its people.[6] There is some doubt whether it is possible to differentiate between the two categories of rights in such a hard and fast way, and the UN itself has always taken the view that *all* human rights are indivisible and mutually supportive.[7]

When it was adopted, it was envisaged that the UDHR would eventually be transformed from a non-binding resolution into a legally binding agreement.[8] This, however, did not occur, largely for two reasons. First, ideological disputes between the Western and Eastern Blocs over the priorities of the two sets of rights meant that agreement could not be reached over their inclusion in a single legally binding instrument. Second, the methods of implementing the two categories of rights were considered to be divergent: while it was thought that civil and political rights could be implemented with some immediacy, economic, social and cultural rights could only, it was argued by many, be implemented progressively

---

Press, 1992); and PR Ghandhi, *The Human Rights Committee and the Right of Individual Communication: Law and Practice* (Aldershot: Ashgate, 1998). McGoldrick, in particular, makes extensive reference to earlier literature on the subject.

4 Universal Declaration of Human Rights, adopted by the United Nations in 1948 under GA Res 217(III), UN GAOR, 3rd Sess, 183rd Plen Mtg, UN Doc A/Res/217(III) (1948); and International Covenant on Economic, Social and Cultural Rights, opened for signature 16 December 1966, 993 UNTS 3 (entered into force 3 January 1976).

5 See Vienna Declaration and Programme of Action, UN Doc A/CONF.157/23 (1993), preambular para 8, which states: '… the [UDHR] … is the source of inspiration and has been the basis for the [UN] in making advances in standard setting as contained in the existing international human rights instruments, in particular the [ICCPR] and the [ICESCR].'

6 For further explanation see Manfred Nowak, *UN Covenant on Civil and Political Rights* (2nd revised edn, Kehl, Germany: NP Engel, 2005) p XX; and Scott Davidson, *Human Rights* (Buckingham, Philadelphia, PA: Open University Press, 1993) pp 6–7.

7 Vienna Declaration and Programme of Action, above n 5, para 5, which states: 'All human rights are universal, indivisible and interdependent and interrelated.'

8 On the drafting of the two Covenants see Nowak, above n 6, pp XXII–XXIII; and McGoldrick, above n 3, pp 6–13.

and programmatically depending upon the resources available to each State. The result was the emergence of two instruments each designed to protect the different categories of rights. Furthermore, the methods of supervision envisaged for each of the Covenants also led to controversy. While States parties' obligations under the Covenants were to be monitored by way of periodic reports detailing the measures which they had taken to recognize and give effect to the rights protected, the Eastern Bloc objected to the creation of an independent Human Rights Committee to oversee the performance of obligations under the ICCPR. The ICESCR on the other hand was to be monitored by the Economic and Social Council (ECOSOC), a political organ of the UN and a forum in which States could effectively negotiate out any difficulties which might arise in their human rights records. A proposal by the Netherlands to incorporate a right of individual communication in order to police the ICCPR also met with hostility from a number of States, including the USA and the USSR. This particular problem was overcome in the Third Committee of the UN General Assembly by the proposal and ultimate adoption of an Optional Protocol which would allow States to accept the right of individual communication to the HRC through a separate international treaty.

The ICCPR was adopted by the United Nations General Assembly in December 1966 and entered into force on 23 March 1976, three months after it had received its thirty-fifth ratification.[9] Since the Covenant is of potentially worldwide application it is occasionally referred to as one of the UN's 'universal' instruments. At the time of writing this chapter, the ICCPR has 162 parties, with eight further States who are currently signatories only, representing adherence to the Covenant by a substantial majority of the world's States and self-governing territories.[10]

The Nature of Civil and Political Rights

As noted above, a distinction is often made between civil and political rights, or first generation rights, and economic, social and cultural rights, or second generation rights. Although it is clear that the modalities of their implementation are different, their interrelationship is far more complex than a simple statement of categories of rights would lead one to suppose. Furthermore, it might also be assumed that the term civil and political rights implies a distinction between two different, but related, sets of rights. While civil rights are those rights which are calculated to protect an individual's physical and mental integrity, to ensure that they are not the victims of discrimination, and to preserve their right to a fair trial, political rights are those which ensure that individuals are able to participate fully in civil society. Such rights include rights of democratic participation, such as the

9 ICCPR, article 49.

10 Office of the United Nations High Commissioner for Human Rights 'Status of Ratifications of the Principal International Human Rights Treaties'. For a breakdown of party status to the ICCPR and its Optional Protocol, see Appendix 3 herein.

right to vote and to participate in the public life of the State, freedom of expression and assembly, and freedom of thought, conscience and religion.

Some civil and political rights, however, have a dual or hybrid nature such as, for example, the right to marry and found a family. While the 'family' is regarded as the 'natural and fundamental unit of society',[11] it is clear that the changing nature of the family and its social role is not simply a civil right but can also be counted a social right. The evolutionary nature of such a right may thus not be well suited to the requirement that all aspects of the right must be implemented immediately. Furthermore, the right which prohibits discrimination has the capacity for application beyond civil and political rights alone, as the controversial jurisprudence of the HRC in this area has demonstrated.[12] The Committee has not established any strong distinctions when dealing with the different types of rights contained in the Covenant. Instead the approach has been to refer to article 2 of the ICCPR which establishes an 'obligation to respect and ensure the rights recognized by the Covenant' and this obligation has immediate effect for all States parties.[13]

General Characteristics of the ICCPR

The substantive rights protected by the Covenant are drafted with greater precision than their Universal Declaration counterparts. There are, however, some differences in the rights protected. Rights and freedoms protected by the ICCPR which are not included in the Universal Declaration are: minority rights; freedom from imprisonment for inability to fulfil a contractual obligation, such as the payment of a debt; the right to humane treatment while in detention; the right of children to acquire a nationality; and special measures of protection for minors. Amongst the rights referred to in the Universal Declaration, which are not included in the Covenant, are: the right to asylum; and the right to own property.

Furthermore, unlike the Universal Declaration, the ICCPR contains a derogation provision which allows States parties to temporarily suspend the application of certain rights 'in time of public emergency that threatens the life of the nation'.[14] Rights which are non-derogable, and thus not capable of suspension, are: the right to life; freedom from torture, cruel, inhuman or degrading treatment or punishment; freedom from slavery; freedom from imprisonment for failure to fulfil a contractual obligation; freedom from retroactive criminal laws; the right to recognition as a person before the law; and freedom of thought, conscience and religion.

---

11 ICCPR, article 23.

12 See Chapter 11 herein.

13 *General Comment 31: Nature of the General Legal Obligations Imposed on States Parties to the Covenant* UN Doc CCPR/C/21/Rev.1/Add.13 (2004), para 5.

14 See further Chapter 3 herein.

Obligations of States Parties

The General Nature of ICCPR Obligations

Under article 2(1) of the Covenant, States parties assume the following obligation:[15]

> Each State Party to the present Covenant undertakes to respect and to ensure to all individuals within its territory and subject to its jurisdiction the rights recognised in the present Covenant, without distinction of any kind, such as race, colour, sex, language, religion, political or other opinion, national or social origin, property, birth or other status.

The limits of this obligation have not been greatly analysed by the Human Rights Committee, but a number of preliminary points might be made about its content. First, the obligation to respect and ensure Covenant rights is owed to *individuals* within a State's territory and subject to its jurisdiction. The Covenant is thus concerned with the individual person and not collectives of individuals (despite the wording of article 1, which guarantees the right of peoples to self-determination)[16] or artificial legal persons such as corporations, charitable organizations or other similar legal foundations.[17] There are certain rights which appear to be collective in nature, such as the right of individuals to belong to ethnic, linguistic or religious minorities, but it is the right of the individual in question to belong to these pre-existing minorities which is of significance.[18] Second, individuals must be within the State's *territory or subject to its jurisdiction.* This does not mean that all individuals are treated exactly the same for the purposes of the attribution of various rights, since there are inevitably certain limitations on the rights of aliens and those who are not lawfully present within the territory of the State.[19] In other respects, however, all individuals, be they citizens or non-citizens, are on an equal footing as far as they are the subjects of the relevant civil and political right guaranteed

15 On the nature and effect of this obligation see Nowak, above n 6, pp 27–34 and 37–45; and David Harris, 'The International Covenant on Civil and Political Rights and the United Kingdom: An Introduction' in David Harris and Sarah Joseph (eds), *The International Covenant on Civil and Political Rights and United Kingdom Law* (Oxford: Clarendon Press, 1995) pp 3–4.

16 See Chapter 9 herein.

17 This has now become a well established part of the Committee's jurisprudence, see *Länsman et al v Finland*, Communication 1023/2001, UN Doc CCPR/C/83/D/1023/2001 (2005), para 6.1.

18 See Chapter 10 herein.

19 See, for example, article 25, the application of which is limited to citizens of the State.

by the ICCPR.[20] It is also possible that individuals who are not within a State's territory might be subject to its jurisdiction. As a number of communications have demonstrated, the personal relationship between a State based on ties of nationality may operate to impose responsibility on a State where it has violated the rights of one of its citizens, even though that citizen may be situated abroad.[21]

There is little doubt, according to the wording of article 2(1), that the primary obligation for ensuring the protection of rights is imposed upon the State, and in most circumstances there will be a more or less clear relationship between the organs of the State and the violation of human rights which imposes responsibility upon it for that violation.[22] This can be described as a vertical relationship between the State and the citizen. The wording of article 2(1) also raises the question of whether the State has a legal responsibility to ensure that the rights of its citizens are not violated by other private citizens. This may be called the enforcement of a horizontal relationship or, as it is known in German, *Drittwirkung*, or the protection by a State of third party rights. The Committee has explained that article 2 does not create any direct horizontal effects but that:[23]

> the positive obligations on States Parties to ensure Covenant rights will only be fully discharged if individuals are protected by the State, not just against violations of Covenant rights by its agents, but also against acts committed by private persons or entities that would impair the enjoyment of Covenant rights in so far as they are amenable to application between private persons or entities.

Certainly, there are particular rights espoused in the ICCPR which seem to imply the right of protection by the State from third parties.[24] Article 6(1), for example, requires the right to life to be protected by law. This would suggest, therefore, that a State which failed to criminalize the homicidal behaviour of 'private' death squads would fail in its obligation to protect the right to life. The Committee itself has directly referred to article 17 (right to privacy) and article 7 (freedom from torture) as particular areas of rights protection where the State will need to ensure that the actions of private persons or parties impair the ability of individuals to enjoy their rights under the Covenant.[25] Article 23, concerning family rights,

---

20 McGoldrick, above n 3, pp 20–21; Richard Lillich, *The Human Rights of Aliens in Contemporary International Law* (Manchester: Manchester University Press, 1984) p 145. General Comment 15 states: 'the general rule is that each one of the rights of the Covenant must be guaranteed without discrimination between citizens and aliens' – see *General Comment 15: The position of aliens under the Covenant*, UN Doc CCPR General Comment 15 (1986).

21 See further Chapter 2 herein.

22 Nowak, above n 6, pp 38–9.

23 General Comment 31, above n 13, para 8.

24 Nowak, above n 6, pp 39–40.

25 General Comment 31, above n 13, para 8.

recognizes that the exercise of family rights is subject to protection from both the State and society, the latter of which would include private parties.[26]

The final part of article 2(1) requires the rights recognized to be protected 'without distinction of any kind, such as race, colour, sex, language, religion, political or other opinion, national or social origin, property, birth or other status'. This is a broad non-discrimination provision which forbids all types of non-justifiable differentiation of individuals in the protection of their rights.[27] This broad prohibition is supported by the more specific prohibition of discrimination between men and women in the enjoyment of all civil and political rights set out in article 3 of the ICCPR. Furthermore, article 26 provides an autonomous prohibition on discrimination before the law which has been used in a creative, and not altogether universally approved, manner by the Human Rights Committee.[28]

Under article 2(2) States are also required to take the necessary legislative or other measures to give effect in their domestic law to the rights recognized in the ICCPR. It has been suggested by one former Committee member, Elizabeth Evatt, that the preference of the Human Rights Committee is for the rights protected by the Covenant to be constitutionally entrenched in domestic law rather than simply protected by the ordinary law of the land.[29] This, of course, raises some constitutional difficulties in States such as the United Kingdom and New Zealand where the concept of constitutional entrenchment is, in a formal sense, unknown. States are also required to provide effective remedies to those whose rights have been violated (article 2(3)). Such remedies may either be general remedies or remedies specifically designed to redress violations of rights protected by the ICCPR.

The Rights Guaranteed by the ICCPR

The full catalogue of rights contained in the ICCPR are: the right to life; the prohibition of torture or cruel, inhuman or degrading treatment or punishment; the prohibition of slavery, the slave trade, forced or compulsory labour; the right to liberty and security of the person and freedom from arbitrary arrest or detention; humane treatment of prisoners; no imprisonment for failure to fulfil a contractual obligation; freedom of movement, and freedom to choose a place of residence and freedom to leave a country; limitations upon the expulsion of aliens lawfully resident in a State; equality before all courts and tribunals and for due process guarantees in criminal and civil proceedings; prohibition on retroactive criminal laws; the right to recognition as a person; freedom from arbitrary or unlawful

---

26 See Chapter 8 herein.

27 Nowak, above n 6, pp 45–57.

28 See Chapter 11 herein.

29 See Elizabeth Evatt, 'The Impact of International Human Rights on Domestic Law' in Grant Huscroft and Paul Rishworth, *Litigating Rights: Perspectives from Domestic and International Law* (Oxford and Portland, OR: Hart Publishing, 2002) p 283.

interference with privacy, family home or correspondence and of unlawful attacks upon a person's honour or reputation; freedom of thought, conscience and religion; freedom of opinion and expression; prohibition of propaganda for war and of advocacy of national, racial or religious hatred that constitutes an incitement to discrimination, hostility or violence; the right of peaceful assembly; freedom of association; the right to marry and found a family; measures of protection for children; the right of every citizen to participate in the conduct of public affairs, to have the right to vote and be elected and to have equal access to public service in one's own country; equality of all persons before the law; and the protection of ethnic, religious or linguistic minorities.

Although the ICCPR implicitly recognizes that the death penalty is, in itself, not contrary to the right to life, nonetheless, the Second Optional Protocol to the ICCPR requires States not to execute anyone within their territories and to take necessary measures to abolish the death penalty.[30] The only reservation which may be made is to reserve the death penalty during time of war pursuant to a conviction for a most serious crime of a military nature.[31] The Second Optional Protocol also extends the competence of the Human Rights Committee to consider matters relating to the death penalty when reviewing States' periodic reports, and in relation to inter-State and individual communication procedures where these have been accepted.[32] The Protocol was adopted by the General Assembly on 15 December 1989 and entered into force on 11 July 1991 after receipt of its tenth ratification.[33] At the time of writing this chapter, the Protocol has 66 parties.[34]

The Human Rights Committee

Article 28 of the ICCPR establishes the Human Rights Committee to supervise States parties' compliance with the obligations under the Covenant, while article 1 of the Optional Protocol confers jurisdiction upon the Committee to consider individual communications. The Committee consists of 18 members who must be nationals of the States parties to the ICCPR. They must also be 'persons of high moral character and recognised competence in the field of human rights'.[35] Members of the Committee are elected for a four year term by secret ballot from among nominations by the States parties.[36] They serve in their personal capacity,

30 *Second Optional Protocol to the International Covenant on Civil and Political Rights, aiming at the abolition of the death penalty*, opened for signature 15 December 1989, 1642 UNTS 414 (entered into force 11 July 1991), article 1.

31 Ibid, article 2(1).

32 Ibid, article 3.

33 Ibid, article 8.

34 Above, n 12.

35 ICCPR, article 28(2).

36 ICCPR, article 32(1).

not as government representatives.[37] To reinforce this, members must, upon taking office, make a declaration that they will fulfil their functions impartially and conscientiously.[38] It was envisaged that the HRC should not simply be a 'legal' body in the sense of being composed entirely by lawyers.[39] Nonetheless, the majority of Committee members have been, and continue to be, lawyers of some distinction, although some past and present members have also come from diplomatic or governmental, rather than legal, backgrounds.

While there has been some discussion of the precise nature of the HRC, it now seems that there is a more or less general consensus of opinion that it is neither a judicial nor a quasi-judicial institution, even when acting in its capacity as the final agency for determining authoritatively whether or not there has been a violation of an individual's rights under the Optional Protocol procedure.[40] This view has been propounded by former member and authoritative commentator upon the ICCPR, Christian Tomuschat, and former member and chair, Nisuke Ando.[41] The Committee has itself declared that it is neither a court nor a quasi-judicial institution.[42] This view was endorsed by the European Court of Justice in *Grant v South-West Trains Ltd* in which it said that the HRC 'is not a judicial institution' and that its findings 'have no binding force in law'.[43] These comments leave open the question of the precise status of the HRC. It is tempting to suggest that the Committee is an institution *sui generis*, but this advances the issue little. What can be said with a high degree of certainty is that the Human Rights Committee is the sole body which is permitted to make authoritative interpretations of the ICCPR, thus when the Committee pronounces upon the content or the meaning of a right contained in the Covenant it does so with undeniable authority. Whether this makes its final 'views', the term used for the conclusion of the process of individual communication, either directly or indirectly binding is a matter of some

37 ICCPR, article 28(3).

38 Rule 16, Rules of Procedure of the Human Rights Committee.

39 Article 28(2), however, states that 'consideration [should be] given to the usefulness of the participation of some persons having legal experience'. In fact, since the Committee's inception, the majority of members have been legally qualified.

40 See, for example, Nowak, above n 6, p 75.

41 See: Christian Tomuschat, 'Evolving Procedural Rules: The United Nations Human Rights Committee's First Two Years of Dealing with Individual Communications' (1980) 1 *Human Rights Law Journal* 249; and Nisuke Ando, 'The Future of Monitoring Bodies – Limitations and Possibilities of the Human Rights Committee' [1991–1992] *Canadian Human Rights Yearbook* 169.

42 See *Selected decisions of the Human Rights Committee under the Optional Protocol. Volume 2*, UN Doc CCPR/C/OP/2 (1990), pp 1–2, where the Committee stated: '… the Committee is neither a court nor a body with a quasi-judicial mandate …'. For Further observations on the status of the Human Rights Committee, see: McGoldrick, above n 3, pp 53–4; and Ghandhi, above n 3, p 41.

43 *Grant v South-West Trains Ltd* [1998] ICR 449, ECJ case C-249/96, para 46.

controversy.[44] It also has implications for the concept of precedent or, perhaps more accurately in an institution of this nature, the development of a *jurisprudence constante*.[45]

The Functions of the Human Rights Committee

The Human Rights Committee is charged with four supervisory functions under the ICCPR and the Optional Protocol: the consideration of periodic reports by States parties; the making of General Comments; management of the inter-State complaints procedure; and management of the individual communication procedure.

Periodic reports Periodic reports are required from all States parties on the measures they have adopted to give effect to the rights recognized in the ICCPR and the progress made towards the enjoyment of those rights by individuals.[46] Such reports must be submitted by each State within one year of becoming party to the Covenant and at regular periods thereafter (normally about five years), as determined by the HRC.[47] These periodic reports are examined in public in the presence of a State party's representative. The Committee may request further details from a State party and may put questions to its representative. The Committee normally holds three sessions of three weeks each year, and reports annually to the General Assembly. While the HRC is supposed to undertake all of its work during this short period of time, including consideration of individual communications, the majority of the time is taken up by consideration of periodic reports. The principal objective of the Committee in considering periodic reports under the Covenant is not to treat States as if they were defendants in a criminal trial, but to develop a constructive dialogue with them.[48] The rationale here is that such a dialogue will be more effective in promoting State party compliance with the Covenant obligations. On completion of the reporting process, the Committee issues concluding statements which reflect the main areas of discussion. Here, the Committee may note its concerns regarding aspects of a State's implementation of obligations, or it may make suggestions and recommendations indicating ways in which the State's obligations might be fulfilled more effectively.

General Comments General Comments are statements made by the Human Rights Committee in which it conveys to States parties its understanding of the

44 See further Chapter 2 herein.

45 On the issue of precedent or *jurisprudence constante* see further Chapter 2.

46 ICCPR, article 40(1). On the reporting procedure see Nowak, above n 6, pp 712–52; and McGoldrick, above n 3, Chapter 3.

47 ICCPR, article 40(1)(a) and (b).

48 On this practice see Nowak, above n 6, pp 730–33.

meaning of the rights in the ICCPR, or sets out the methods of work.[49] Through its use of general comments, the HRC is able to develop its interpretation of the Covenant and thereby further assist States in the fulfilment of their obligations under it. The Committee has issued General Comments relating to a number of provisions of the Covenant including those relating to the right to life, torture, freedom of expression, treatment of detainees, war propaganda, the administration of justice, privacy, the rights of children and their families, sexual equality and public emergencies. Some of these General Comments, including the most recent on the right to a fair trial, are quite detailed, while others are exiguous and opaque.[50]

Inter-State complaint procedure The inter-State complaint machinery enables any State party to complain to the Committee that another party is failing to give effect to the provisions of the Covenant.[51] It is noticeable that this refers not just to the failure to give effect to the substantive rights contained in the ICCPR, but any of its obligations under that instrument. The inter-State complaint machinery is optional and depends upon reciprocal acceptance of the right of complaint by States.[52] State A may thus only bring a complaint against State B if both have accepted the optional procedure. The process for resolving inter-State disputes is conciliatory rather than adjudicative. Despite acceptance of this procedure by a number of States, it has never been used. The reason for this would appear to be the extreme political sensitivity which would necessarily attach to such complaints. Given the lack of use of this procedure under the ICCPR, and of similar procedures under other human rights instruments, the utility of this process must inevitably be open to serious question.[53]

Individual communications under the Optional Protocol As its title suggests, the procedures contained in the Optional Protocol to the ICCPR are only applicable to those States which have become party to the instrument.[54] It is proposed here to give only a brief outline of the functions and processes under the Optional Protocol, as this will be dealt with in detail in Chapter 2. States which become party to the Optional Protocol recognize the competence of the Committee to receive and consider communications from individuals subject to its jurisdiction

49 On the evolution of the practice of issuing General Comments see McGoldrick, above n 3, pp 89–96.

50 All of the Committee's General Comments may be found at http://www2.ohchr.org/english/bodies/hrc/comments.htm.

51 ICCPR, article 41. See also Nowak, above n 6, pp 753–76.

52 Ibid.

53 Scott Leckie, 'The Inter-State Complaint Procedure in International Human Rights Law: Hopeful Prospects or Wishful Thinking?' (1988) 10(2) *Human Rights Quarterly* 249.

54 Optional Protocol, article 1.

who claim to be a victim of a violation of one or more of the rights set forth in the ICCPR.[55] The corollary of this is that the Committee cannot receive complaints from individuals in States which have not become party to the Optional Protocol and which, as a consequence, are not subject to its jurisdiction. When the HRC receives a communication from an individual subject to the jurisdiction of one of the States parties, it then deals with the communication in two stages: first, it must determine whether or not the communication is admissible, that is whether it satisfies the formal requirements set out in the Protocol.[56] If it determines that the communication is admissible, it then proceeds to the second stage of determining whether or not there has been a substantive violation of any of the rights protected in the ICCPR.[57] In some circumstances the two stages are dealt with simultaneously, since it is at times impossible to separate the question of the merits of a communication with that of admissibility. This is particularly the case where there is some doubt about whether the ICCPR applies ratione materiae.[58] Furthermore, while the process is a two-stage procedure, the Human Rights Committee usually deals with the questions of admissibility and the merits of communications at the same sitting.[59]

All proceedings before the HRC take place on the written evidence before it.[60] The normal procedure is for the applicant to lodge their own complaint. There is a model complaint form by which this might be done, but it is not necessary to use this as long as the requisite information is made available to the HRC.[61] The State party concerned will then asked for its response, which it must make within six months.[62] The applicant is then given the opportunity to comment on the State's response. This process might be extended to further replies and responses until the Committee is satisfied that it has the information it requires. The entire process is concluded when the Committee issues its final views.[63] These are essentially a decision on the merits of the communication, but the precise legal status of final views is a matter of some ambiguity, perhaps deliberately so.[64] Where a State is found in breach of its obligations, it is normally required by the HRC to undertake remedial action, which may include modifying its domestic law and offering reparation to victims. In order to ensure compliance with its final views, the Committee has developed a follow-up procedure in which a *rapporteur* is appointed to investigate the measures which delinquent States have taken to

55 Ibid.

56 Optional Protocol, articles 2, 3 and 5.

57 Optional Protocol, article 1.

58 See further Chapter 2 herein.

59 Rule 91, Rules of Procedure.

60 Optional Protocol, articles 2 and 5.

61 See Appendix 4 for a copy of the Model Complaint Form.

62 Optional Protocol, article 4(2).

63 Optional Protocol, article 5(4).

64 See further Chapter 2 herein.

remedy their breaches of the ICCPR.[65] While this procedure is, like most of the Committee's activities, heavily underfunded, it has proved to be a useful measure of supervision. Another useful mode of supervision is the requirement that States, when making their periodic reports, indicate the measures which they have adopted to give effect to the HRC's final views in applicable communications.

Interim measures A further important mechanism which exists under the Protocol is the procedure under Rule 86, through which the Human Rights Committee has the power to order interim measures to avoid irreparable damage to an alleged victim of a violation of the rights protected by the ICCPR. This mechanism, which is similar to an injunction or interdict under domestic law, requires an individual to demonstrate prima facie satisfaction of the admissibility requirements contained in the Optional Protocol. This mechanism has been used, for example, in cases in which individuals have been sentenced to death in order to delay the execution of the sentence until the question of whether it has been imposed pursuant to the due process contained in the ICCPR have been satisfied.

The HRC and the Interpretation of the ICCPR

The HRC is the institution established by the ICCPR to interpret and supervise the operation of the ICCPR.[66] It is therefore the sole agency authorized to interpret the instrument of its creation. This being so, it is able to set limits on its own interpretative method. While the remainder of this book is concerned with the very issue of the interpretation of the Covenant rights, it is worth indicating some of the major features of the Committee's methods of interpretation.

While the Committee has been able to pronounce upon the meaning of most of the rights contained in the Covenant, it is worth indicating that it has been hampered in the development of a comprehensive jurisprudence by two main factors. First, many of the earlier communications originated from a limited number of States, particularly Uruguay and Zaire. Because of this, it was primarily concerned at that time with elaborating its rules of procedure and evidence. In most of these early cases, the HRC was faced with an obstructive attitude by the States concerned, and there was little need to proceed beyond establishing the veracity of the facts. Second, these early communications were concerned largely with gross and widespread human rights abuses primarily involving violations of article 7 (the right to be free from torture, inhuman and degrading treatment or punishment); article 9 (the right to liberty and security of the person and freedom from arbitrary arrest and detention); article 10 (the right of all persons deprived of their liberty to be treated with humanity and respect for the dignity of the human person); and article 14 (due process rights).

---

65 Rule 95, Rules of Procedure.

66 For an appraisal of the Human Rights Committee's approach to interpretation see Harris and Joseph, above n 15, pp 10–20.

Furthermore, there have been certain views in which the evident desire for consensus has led to less than satisfactory legal reasoning. Indeed, some views have been so brief as to be almost completely devoid of legal reasoning.[67] Although the General Comments of the Committee are designed to elucidate the meaning of the rights protected by the ICCPR, these too are of variable quality and not always current. The General Comment on non-discrimination was adopted in 1989 and has not taken account of developments in the Committee's jurisprudence since that time, whereas the General Comment of 2007 on the right to a fair hearing represents a generally excellent summary of the Committee's jurisprudence concerning article 14.

Despite these limitations on the development of its jurisprudence, however, the Committee has nonetheless grappled with a number of complex factual situations involving the development of other rights. The Committee has now been issuing views under the Optional Protocol for over thirty years and in this time it has developed a body of jurisprudence that may be incomplete in many respects, but it has also furthered our understanding of human rights protection in international law to a considerable degree. As will be demonstrated in this work some rights have received greater attention and elaboration than others. For example, the HRC has been reasonably active in the development of its jurisprudence concerning issues of discrimination.[68] Its jurisprudence under article 26, for example, has been particularly forward-looking and, it has to be said, not entirely greeted with universal acclaim. The Dutch government, for example, was disconcerted by the Committee's decisions which held that article 26 was an autonomous prohibition against discrimination which applied as much to social security rights (as a species of economic and social rights) as it did to civil and political rights. Also in the area of minority rights, while the Committee has not been particularly radical in its interpretation of article 27, its work in this area remains unique as it represents the only established legal framework that directly addresses the promotion and protection of minority rights.[69]

While the Human Rights Committee is not always explicit about the methods of interpretation it employs in individual communications, it has stated in a number of communications that it applies the canons of treaty interpretation which are contained in articles 31 and 32 of the Vienna Convention on the Law of Treaties 1969.[70] Article 31(1) of the Convention requires a treaty to be interpreted in good faith in accordance with the ordinary meaning to be given to the terms of the treaty

67 See *Tamihere v New Zealand*, Communication 891/1999, UN Doc CCPR/C/68/D/891/1999 (2000).

68 Chapter 11 herein.

69 See Chapter 10. There does exist the Council of Europe's Framework Convention for the Protection of National Minorities but this does not possess a petition procedure similar to the OP.

70 See, for example, *JB v Canada*, Communication 118/1982, UN Doc CCPR/C/28/D/118/1982 (1986).

in their context and in the light of the treaty's object and purpose. This places the emphasis on a literal interpretation of the ICCPR by reference to its object and purpose which can be derived from an examination of its preamble.[71] Elizabeth Evatt, a former Committee member, has confirmed this saying:[72]

> The Committee's approach to interpretation is that each Covenant right must be given its full scope in accordance with its ordinary meaning, and should not be cut down by reference to any other right, whether in the Covenant or any other instrument.

This is not to say that the interpretation of the Covenant is static. As Evatt again observes: '[c]hanges in the international climate since 1976 have opened the way for broader interpretations, bearing in mind the need to respect consistency of principle in the light of the Covenant's objectives.'[73] While the Committee has not elaborated the objectives and purposes of the Covenant in any detail, it observed in the West Indian capital punishment cases that:

> The provisions of the Covenant must be interpreted in the light of the Covenant's objects and purposes (article 31 of the Vienna Convention on the Law of Treaties). As one of these objects and purposes is to promote reduction in the use of the death penalty, an interpretation of a provision in the Covenant that may encourage a State party that retains the death penalty to make use of that penalty should, where possible, be avoided.

Relying upon article 32 of the Vienna Convention on the Law of Treaties, the Committee has also referred to *travaux préparatoires* in elucidating and elaborating the meaning of the rights protected by the ICCPR. While the *travaux* to the ICCPR are readily available,[74] they have not been extensively used by the Committee. While reference to the *travaux* in *JB and others v Canada* proved useful in resolving the question of whether article 22(1) includes a right to strike,[75] such reference has not normally appeared to have been particularly useful. An example of this can be seen in *Broeks v The Netherlands* where the Committee, in considering whether or not the application of article 26 was limited to substantive rights contained in the ICCPR said:[76]

---

71 On treaty interpretation in general see Sir Ian Sinclair, *The Vienna Convention on the Law of Treaties* (2nd edn, Manchester: Manchester University Press, 1984).

72 Evatt, above n 29, p 296.

73 Ibid, p 297.

74 Marc Bossuyt, *Guide to the Travaux Préparatoires of the International Covenant on Civil and Political Rights* (Dordrecht, Boston, MA: Nijhoff, 1987).

75 *JB v Canada*, above n 70: see discussion in Chapter 4 herein.

76 *Broeks v The Netherlands*, Communication 172/1984, UN Doc CCPR/C/29/D/172/1984 (1987), para 12.2. See also *Danning v The Netherlands*, Communication

> The discussions, at the time of drafting, concerning the question whether the scope of article 26 extended to rights not otherwise guaranteed by the Covenant, were inconclusive and cannot alter the conclusion arrived at by the ordinary means of interpretation referred to in paragraph 12.3 below.

Evatt suggests that the reason for the failure of the *travaux* to resolve issues of interpretation is that the political compromises involved in drafting the ICCPR mean that it is not always possible to discover why a particular term was used or what its meaning was supposed to be.[77]

The Committee has also eschewed the assistance of the jurisprudence of other international human rights bodies in interpreting the ICCPR. The reasons for this are not immediately apparent. There is a wealth of decided cases in the repertoire of the European Court of Human Rights, and the Inter-American Court of Human Rights has also begun to develop an interesting and instructive, if not yet substantial, jurisprudence. While the decisions of both these bodies could be used to support an interpretation of the ICCPR, and to develop a horizontally-integrated international human rights jurisprudence, it seems clear that the Human Rights Committee is not interested in pursuing this line of development. Could it be that the HRC has distanced itself from the regional human rights bodies because it wishes to forge a corpus of truly universal human rights law, or because it is afraid to open the door to arguments based on relativity of one kind or another? Support for this view might be derived from the way in which the HRC has also refused to explicitly endorse the doctrine of the margin of appreciation in the application of substantive rights, considered further in Chapter 3 herein.

When the jurisprudence of human rights institutions such as the European Court of Human Rights or, to a lesser extent, the Inter-American Court of Human Rights is examined, it is generally possible to see a trend in the mode or modes of interpretation employed by the judges. In the main it is perhaps fair to say that the ECHR and ACHR adopt a predominantly teleological or end-orientated approach to the interpretation of the rights which are contained in their respective instruments, that is to say they generally adopt a fair, large and liberal approach to interpretation designed to maximize the scope of the rights and thus the protection of the individuals who are their subjects.[78] Within the HRC, however, despite the observations of Evatt referred to above, it is difficult to perceive any general interpretative trends. There may be several reasons for this. First, the Committee

---

180/1984, UN Doc CCPR/C/29/D/180/1984 (1987), para 12.2; *Zwaan de Vries v The Netherlands*, Communication 182/1984, UN Doc CCPR/C/29/D/182/1984 (1987), para 12.2.

77 Evatt, above n 25, p 297.

78 This of course is a generalization. There are those judges who have been notoriously narrow in their interpretation of human rights instruments: see further David Harris, Michael O'Boyle and Colin Warbrick, *Law of the European Convention on Human Rights* (London: Butterworths, 1995) pp 5–19.

membership is diverse and frequently changing, factors which may militate against the forging of a common approach over a protracted period of time. Second, the Committee meets only three times each year for three weeks at a time, during which it must consider both periodic reports and individual communications. While this of itself may not inhibit the development of a common interpretative approach, it is unlikely to aid the cause. Third, the HRC is under-resourced which means that it does not have the level of support conducive to the development of a common jurisprudence. Fourth, the Committee's preferred *modus operandi* is consensus.[79] This, it would seem, has hindered the development of a more comprehensive jurisprudence and there are some decisions where their opaque, and arguably confused, nature indicates a lack of clear direction or disagreement within the Committee itself. In some of the article 26 decisions, for example, it is arguable that the Committee has shown a radical tinge, but even here there have been strong dissenting opinions which equate the application of article 26 to economic and social rights as requiring a progressive, programmatic approach to implementation rather than the immediate, unqualified approach which is normally the hallmark of civil and political rights.[80]

Governments have often been very critical of the Committee's views responding with outrage, disagreement[81] or attempts to redefine the legal status of the Covenant or the Optional Protocol.[82] There is also an increasing debate about the democratic legitimacy of an international monitoring body passing authoritative interpretations on what are essentially domestic constitutional practices. These matters may appear to highlight the inherent weaknesses of the Committee but at the same time they are also indications of the growth and development of international human rights law. States continue to accede to the Covenant and the OP; clearly indicating a willingness to accept the obligations of the Covenant and the role of the Committee in ensuring compliance. As with any human rights monitoring body the Committee will constantly face dissent and disagreement in its efforts to further the promotion and protection of human rights. But continual debate and discussion about the nature of the rights in the Covenant and how best to ensure their enjoyment is certainly a positive development. Despite the various shortcomings discussed above, the Committee has made considerable advances

---

79 McGoldrick, above n 3, pp 142–3.

80 See Chapter 11 herein.

81 See 'Response of the Australian Government to the Views of the Human Rights Committee in *A v Australia*, Communication 560/1993, reprinted in 9 *International Journal of Refugee Law* (1997) 674–8.

82 Guyana, Jamaica and Trinidad and Tobago have all withdrawn from the OP, then re-acceded to the Treaty with a reservation that the Committee is not competent to receive any individual communications from individuals who are facing the death penalty, see Declarations and Reservations to the Optional Protocol to the International Covenant on Civil and Political Rights, available at http://www2.ohchr.org/english/bodies/ratification/5.htm.

in developing the jurisprudence of rights protection under the Covenant. This has contributed not only to the wider UN system of human rights protection but also to the promotion and protection of human rights globally, making a study of the Committee's jurisprudence a necessary exercise.

Chapter 2
Procedure Under the Optional Protocol

Alex Conte[1]

Individual communications to the Human Rights Committee are governed by the (first) Optional Protocol (OP) to the International Covenant on Civil and Political Rights and the Committee's Rules of Procedure.[2] Since, by definition, the Protocol to the ICCPR is optional, only those States which have chosen to become party to it may be subject to the jurisdiction of the HRC for the purposes of individual communications. For the avoidance of doubt, article 1 of the OP provides that: 'no communication shall be received by the Committee if it concerns a State Party to the Covenant which is not party to the present Protocol'. This provision is reinforced by Rule 78(3) which states that any communication which is received in respect of a State which is not party to the OP shall not be registered by the Secretary-General. Not only does article 1 of the OP establish which States may be the subject of a communication, it also lays down certain requirements concerning the identity and status of those who may make a communication. First, the communication must be from 'individuals'. Second those individuals must be 'victims' of an alleged violation of the rights protected by the ICCPR. Third, these individual victims must be subject to 'the jurisdiction of the State'. Fourth, the rights which are claimed to have been violated must be those 'set forth in the Covenant'. Each of these specified indicia raise substantial issues of interpretation, but before this task can be undertaken, the relationship between article 1 of the OP and other articles in the Protocol must be examined. This will then provide a complete catalogue of the criteria which must be satisfied before an individual communication might be declared admissible and the substantive questions of alleged violation dealt with.

The criteria required for the receipt and admissibility of an individual communication are replicated and expanded upon in article 2 of the OP, which provides:

> Subject to the provisions of article 1, individuals who claim that any of their rights enumerated in the Covenant have been violated and who have exhausted

---

1 This chapter is based substantially upon its first edition equivalent, written by Professor Scott Davidson of the University of Canterbury in New Zealand.

2 The text of the Optional Protocol to the ICCPR is set out in Appendix 2 herein. For a comprehensive analysis of the individual communication procedure under the Optional Protocol, see PR Ghandhi, *The Human Rights Committee and the Right of Individual Communication: Law and Practice* (Brookfield, VT: Ashgate, 1998).

> all domestic remedies may submit a written communication to the Committee for consideration.

Again, it is clear that it is only 'individuals' who can be the subjects of communications and that it is only the violation of the rights which are 'enumerated in the Covenant' which can be a matter of complaint. Furthermore, article 2 of the OP requires that these individuals must have exhausted *all* domestic remedies before the Committee can consider the communication. Additionally, it appears that only a 'written communication' will be considered, thus excluding the possibility of an oral complaint being lodged. The criteria for admissibility are further elaborated in articles 3 and 5 of the OP. Article 3 states that the Committee shall consider inadmissible any communication which is: anonymous; or an abuse of the right of submission; or incompatible with the provisions of the ICCPR.

Article 5 provides further that the Committee shall not consider any communication from an individual if: the same matter is being examined under another procedure of international investigation or settlement; and all 'available' domestic remedies have not been exhausted, unless the application of such remedies is unreasonably prolonged.

From an accumulation of the criteria in each of the provisions examined above, it is possible to provide the following list of requirements which must be satisfied before a communication will be considered admissible by the Committee: (1) the communication must be by an *individual*; (2) that individual must be a *victim* of a rights violation; (3) the alleged violation must be of one of the rights and freedoms set forth in the ICCPR; (4) the communication must be in writing and must not be anonymous, abusive of the right of submission, or otherwise incompatible with the provisions of the ICCPR; (5) the violation must be committed by a State party; (6) the individual must be subject to the jurisdiction of the State; (7) the communication must not be the subject of another procedure of international investigation or settlement; and (8) all available domestic remedies must have been exhausted. If all these criteria are satisfied, the HRC will be able to proceed to a consideration of the substantive merits of the communication.

The Criteria for Admissibility

The Communication must be by an Individual who is a Victim of a Violation

Criterion 1: Individuals and their locus standi While there is no definition of who or what an individual is for the purposes of the OP, it is clear that an individual, in order to come within the terms of the ICCPR, must be a human being. This would therefore preclude the possibility of non-human legal persons being able to lodge communications under the OP. This position was made clear by the HRC in *A Publication and a Printing Company v Trinidad and Tobago.*

Here, the Committee held that:[3]

> … a company incorporated under the laws of a State Party to the [OP], as such, has no standing under article 1, regardless of whether its allegations appear to raise issues under the Covenant.

During the drafting of the OP the possibility of extending the right of communication to groups was mooted in the Third Committee of the UN General Assembly. This suggestion was ultimately rejected by the Commission on Human Rights since it was thought by some States that it would allow a right of class action (*actio popularis*) or communications by human rights NGOs on behalf of certain individuals.[4] Although some commentators have suggested that the Human Rights Committee should adopt a liberal interpretation to the requirement that communications can only be made by individual victims, it has, in fact, been quite strict in its approach. In *Kavanagh v Ireland*, for example, the author attempted to complain about Ireland's continued use of the Special Criminal Court which had been previously held by the Committee to violate article 26 of the ICCPR. The HRC observed that:[5]

> … this claim is in the nature of an *actio popularis*, relating as it does to further actions taken by the State party in respect of third parties rather than the author himself. It follows that the author is not personally a victim of these new alleged violations of the Covenant complained of, and this portion of the claim is inadmissible under article 1 of the Optional Protocol.

There is clearly no difficulty with the vast majority of communications where individuals are claiming to be the sole victim of a violation, but some problems have arisen where individuals who are not victims themselves claim to be representing others. That others are permitted to make a communication on behalf of an individual who is unable to do so is clear from the Committee's Rules of Procedure and its Model Complaint Form.[6] Rule 90(b) provides in the material part:

> Normally, the communication should be submitted by the individual personally or by that individual's representative; a communication submitted on behalf of

---

3 *A Publication and a Printing Company v Trinidad and Tobago*, Communication 361/1989, UN Doc CCPR/C/36/D/361/1989 (1989), para 3.2. See also *JRT and the WG Party of Canada v Canada*, Communication 104/1981, UN Doc CCPR/C/18/D/104/1981 (1983).

4 See Ghandhi, above n 2, pp 8–11.

5 *Kavanagh v Ireland*, Communication 1114/2002, UN Doc CCPR/C/76/D/1114/2002/Rev.1 (2002).

6 See Appendix 4 for a copy of the Model Complaint Form (available online at <http://www2.ohchr.org/english/bodies/docs/annex1.pdf>).

> an alleged victim may, however, be accepted when it appears that the individual in question is unable to submit the communication personally.

Where an individual is purporting to act on behalf of another, the Model Complaint Form requires such a person to state the capacity in which he or she is acting on behalf of the victim; why the person considers it appropriate to bring the communication on behalf of the person; and to provide information on why the victim is unable to submit the communication on his or her own behalf. In *Krausser v Austria*, the Committee determined that the applicant was not competent to lodge a communication on behalf of his mother where she had, together with the author, been convicted of aiding and abetting the author in the withholding of a child from the child's mother (who was entitled to have custody). The Committee expressed that it could only examine individual petitions presented by the alleged victims themselves or by 'duly authorised representatives'.[7]

While the absence of a 'link' between the petitioner and the victim will be fatal to the admissibility of a communication, there are nonetheless a number of circumstances in which the nature of the link may not be sufficiently substantial for the purposes of admissibility. The Committee has had occasion to examine the nature of these circumstances on a number of occasions. In a significant number of communications in which family members have been purporting to act on behalf of family members, the question of the appropriateness and sufficiency of the link to establish standing has proved neither controversial nor problematic. In *Massera v Uruguay*, the author lodged a communication not only on her own part, but also on behalf of her stepfather José Luís Massera who was being held incommunicado. The Committee had little difficulty in finding the communication admissible on the grounds that the 'author of the communication was justified by reason of close family connection in acting on behalf of the other alleged victims'.[8] This assumption of implicit authority also extends to representation by a victim's lawyer, who is taken to be acting on behalf of his or her client, even after that client has died.[9] Furthermore, where the victim's representative is given specific authority by the victim (for example, in the form of a power of attorney) or even an authorizing letter, the Committee will find an established link permitting standing.[10]

---

7 *Krausser v Austria*, Communication 890/1999, UN Doc CCPR/C/76/D/890/1999 (2002).

8 *Massera v Uruguay*, Communication 5/1977, UN Doc CCPR/C/7/D/5/1977 (1979).

9 *Marais v Madagascar*, Communication 49/1979, UN Doc CCPR/C/18/D/49/1979 (1983); *Croes v The Netherlands*, Communication 164/1984, UN Doc CCPR/C/34/D/164/1984 (1988); and *Burrell v Jamaica*, Communication 546/1993, UN Doc CCPR/C/57/D/546/1993 (1996).

10 See, for example, *Mpandanjila v Zaire*, Communication 138/1983, UN Doc CCPR/C/27/D/138/1983 (1986) (authorizing letter).

The Human Rights Committee has, however, taken a strict line against the lodging of complaints by NGOs. This is in stark contrast to the position under article 44 of the American Convention on Human Rights where NGOs are explicitly authorized to lodge individual petitions with the Inter-American Commission on Human Rights.[11] In *UR v Uruguay*, for example, the Human Rights Committee denied a member of Amnesty International the right to lodge a complaint on behalf of a prisoner in whom this person had taken an active interest for many years. The Committee held that 'a communication submitted by a third party on behalf of an alleged victim can only be considered if the author justifies his authority to submit the communication'.[12] In this case, the taking of an interest was not a sufficient basis on which to ground standing.

In communications in which the question of the right of representation has arisen, the Committee appears to have steered a judicious course between rigidity and flexibility. Too rigid an approach would have been injurious to the proper functioning of the OP individual communication system, since it would have precluded communications from those who, because of their circumstances, were unable to make their own petitions. The family nexus as a ground for standing is one way of ensuring flexibility in the system, but it leaves a number of questions unanswered. What, for example, is the degree of sanguinity required in such cases?[13] Would an estranged relative still have sufficient standing? Would a close friend have the necessary competence to act?[14] It may well be that a family member him or herself should be an indirect victim in order to gain *locus standi*, but the Committee has never articulated this as a necessary requirement.[15] Given the HRC's predilection for *ad hominem* decisions, the better view would seem that these are issues which would be decided on their individual merits.

In a number of communications, individuals have sought to represent groups of individuals or private organizations. The Committee has tended to reject as inadmissible those communications on behalf of organizations. Thus in *JRT v Canada* it rejected a communication lodged on behalf of an anti-Semitic political party on the grounds that such an association was not competent to submit a

---

11 See Scott Davidson, *The Inter-American Human Rights System* (Aldershot: Ashgate, 1997), pp 155–7.

12 *UR v Uruguay*, Communication 128/1982, UN Doc CCPR/C/18/D/128/1982 (1983).

13 As Nowak points out: '... the Committee has held communications to be admissible on behalf of spouses, parents, step-parents, non-custodial parents, parent-in-law, children, brothers, sisters, aunts and uncles, nephews and nieces and cousins': Manfred Nowak, *UN Covenant on Civil and Political Rights* (2nd revised edn, Kehl, Germany: NP Engel, 2005) p 836.

14 Nowak suggests that they would when the relationship is 'adequately substantiated': ibid.

15 See, however, *Quinteros v Uruguay*, Communication 107/1981, UN Doc CCPR/C/19/D/107/1981 (1983), in which the mother of the victim living in Sweden was also held to be a victim because of her constant fear over the events in question.

communication under the OP.[16] The same line of reasoning was employed in *Disabled and Handicapped Persons in Italy v Italy*, where an individual sought to represent an association of disabled persons:[17]

> … according to article 1 of the [OP], only individuals have the right to submit a communication. To the extent, therefore, that the communication originates for the Coordinamento, it has to be declared inadmissible because of lack of personal standing.

There may be cases, however, where an individual might be viewed as being the representative of other members of an organization. Such was the case in *Hartikainen v Finland* where the General Secretary of Free Thinkers in Finland was held competent to submit a communication on behalf of the other individual members, *qua* individuals rather than on behalf of the organization itself.[18]

There is a further group of communications in which individuals have sought to engage the OP procedure to vindicate the collective right of self-determination protected by article 1 of the ICCPR. This is a subject considered in substance in Chapter 9, but mention should be made here of the admissibility issues involved in such claims. In the first of such cases, *AD (Grand Captain of the Mikmaq) v Canada*, the author alleged that Canada had denied his tribe the right to self-determination.[19] At the admissibility stage, the main issue was whether the Grand Captain, AD, had the right to represent the tribe. It was ultimately found by the Committee that there was a lack of proof of the capacity of AD to act as the tribe's representative.[20] Although this decision might have suggested that the HRC would have been prepared to entertain a communication to vindicate the right of self-determination, had AD been able to establish proper representative authority on behalf of the tribe, decisions in subsequent communications have made it explicit that the OP *individual* communication procedure cannot be used to vindicate a right which is by its nature *collective*. This position was made clear in *Lubicon Lake Band v Canada* and has become part of the constant jurisprudence of the Committee.[21]

---

16 *JRT v Canada*, above n 3.

17 *Disabled and Handicapped Persons in Italy v Italy*, Communication 163/1984, UN Doc CCPR/C/21/D/163/1984 (1984), para 5.

18 *Hartikainen v Finland*, Communication 40/1978, UN Doc CCPR/C/12/D/40/1978 (1981).

19 *AD (Grand Captain of the Mikmaq) v Canada*, Communication 78/1980, UN Doc CCPR/C/22/D/78/1980 (1984).

20 Similar reasoning was used in *Kitok v Sweden*, Communication 197/1985, UN Doc CCPR/C/33/D/197/1985 (1988).

21 *Lubicon Lake Band v Canada*, Communication 167/1984, UN Doc CCPR/C/38/D/167/1984 (1990). See also *AB v Austria*, Communication 318/1988, UN Doc CCPR/C/39/D/318/1988 (1990), and *Mahuika et al v New Zealand*, Communication 547/1993, UN Doc CCPR/C/70/D/547/1993 (2000). For comment on *Mahuika* see Scott Davidson,

Criterion 2: Who is a victim? Individuals only have standing to submit a communication when they can demonstrate that they are victims of a violation by a State party of one or more of the rights protected by the ICCPR. In order to fall within the concept of 'victim' an individual must normally show that he or she has been directly and concretely affected by the alleged violation. The Committee will not entertain abstract claims of violation,[22] although it has indicated that it will admit communications in which an alleged victim's risk of being affected by a potential breach is 'more than a theoretical possibility'.[23]

The former situation has been considered in a number of cases. In the *Mauritian Women's Case* legislation which discriminated against the foreign spouses of Mauritian women, but not the foreign spouses of Mauritian men, was the subject of complaint. Despite the fact that the legislation had not been applied to any of the applicants, the Committee found a violation of the right to family life on the grounds of the uncertainty which the legislation engendered.[24] Similarly, in *Kindler v Canada* and *Ng v Canada*, the Committee was required to pronounce upon the situation in which the applicants concerned, if extradited, would face the death penalty in the USA. The Committee's views in *Ng v Canada* were that:[25]

> A State party would … be in violation of the Covenant if it handed over a person to another State in circumstances in which it was foreseeable that torture would take place. The foreseeability of the consequence would mean that there was a present violation by the State party, even though the consequences would not occur until later on.

'Fishing for Rights: *Mahuika v New Zealand* in the UN Human Rights Committee' in (2001) *International Journal of Marine and Coastal Law* 679. Note, however, *Gillot et al v France*, Communication 932/2000, UN Doc CCPR/C/75/D/932/2000 (2002), in which the HRC said at para 13.4: 'Although the Committee does not have the competence under the Optional Protocol to consider a communication alleging violation of the right to self-determination protected in article 1 of the Covenant, it may interpret article 1, when this is relevant, in determining whether rights protected in parts II and III of the Covenant have been violated. The Committee is of the view, therefore, that, in this case, it may take article 1 into account in interpretation of article 25 of the Covenant.'

22 See *Hertzberg v Finland*, Communication 61/1979, UN Doc CCPR/C/15/D/61/1979 (1982), where the HRC said at para 9.3 that 'it cannot review in the abstract whether national legislation contravenes the Covenant, although such legislation may, in particular circumstances produce adverse effects which directly affect the individual, making him this a victim in the sense contemplated by articles 1 and 2 of the [OP]'. See also *Disabled and Handicapped Persons in Italy v Italy*, above n 17; and *Lovelace v Canada*, Communication 24/1977, UN Doc CCPR/C/13/D/24/1977 (1981).

23 *Aumeeruddy-Cziffra and 19 other Mauritian Women v Mauritius*, Communication 35/1978.

24 Ibid.

25 *Ng v Canada*, Communication 469/1991, UN Doc CCPR/C/49/D/469/1991 (1994), para 6.2; and *Kindler v Canada*, Communication 470/1991, UN Doc CCPR/C/48/D/470/1991 (1993).

The Formal Requirements of Article 3 of the Optional Protocol

Criterion 3: Incompatibility ratione materiae The purpose of the communication procedure established by the OP is to protect 'the rights set forth in the Covenant'. It is thus apparent that if the rights in question which have allegedly been violated are not apparent on the face of the ICCPR, then there will be no cause of action under the OP. Not only is this made clear by articles 1 and 2 of the OP, but also by article 3 which requires the Committee to declare inadmissible any communication which is incompatible with the provisions of the Covenant. There have been a wide variety of cases in which substantive incompatibility has been identified, but the HRC has also examined issues going to the merits of a communication during the admissibility procedure.

In the area of substantive inadmissibility *ratione materiae*, the Committee has identified a number of communications which allege violations of rights not protected by the ICCPR. These have included the right to dispose of property,[26] discrimination in the application of income tax,[27] a claim to a right of asylum,[28] and the right to see another person prosecuted for a crime.[29] Circumstances in which decisions on the merits of a communication have been made during the admissibility process have been rather more controversial. In *LTK v Finland*, for example, the author of the communication was prosecuted for refusing to undertake military service on the grounds of conscientious objection and claimed that his rights under articles 18 and 19 had been violated. The HRC declared the communication inadmissible stating quite baldly that:[30]

> … the Covenant does not provide for the right to conscientious objection … neither article 18 or 16 of the Covenant, especially taking into account paragraph 3(c)(ii) of article 8 can be construed as implying that right.

It should be noted that the Committee has since changed its approach to whether the Covenant provides a right to conscientious objection, a matter considered in Chapter 4. Continuing with the question of dealing with the substance of rights during the admissibility phase of proceedings, the Committee has done the same in respect of article 26 of the ICCPR. This is a subject dealt with in Chapter 11, but it is relevant to note here that the Committee has held that article 26 is not a

26 *JJ v Denmark*, Communication 60/1979, UN Doc CCPR/C/9/D/60/1979 (1980).

27 *IM v Norway*, Communication 129/1982, UN Doc CCPR/C/18/D/129/1982 (1983).

28 *VMRB v Canada*, Communication 236/1987, UN Doc CCPR/C/33/D/236/1987 (1988).

29 *HCMA v The Netherlands*, Communication 213/1986, UN Doc CCPR/C/35/D/213/1986 (1989).

30 *LTK v Finland*, Communication 185/1984, UN Doc CCPR/C/25/D/185/1984 (1985), para 5.2.

parasitic provision but a substantive provision in its own right. In a line of cases beginning with *Broeks v The Netherlands* and *Zwaan de Vries v The Netherlands*, the Committee has held that freedom from discrimination applies not only to the civil and political rights protected by the ICCPR, but to any right, including social security rights.[31] It might be thought that since these were rights protected by the ICCPR's sibling instrument, the International Covenant on Economic, Social and Cultural Rights, and that their mode of implementation differs significantly from that of the ICCPR, such communications would be rejected on grounds of inadmissibility *ratione materiae*, but they were not. While in subsequent communications of a similar content have been the subject of profound differences of opinion, it seems that the Committee is wedded to this particular approach for the time being. There is some indication, however, that the HRC is prepared to apply limitations in its application. In a long line of decisions, the HRC has held that discrimination which is objectively justifiable and proportionate will be permitted.[32]

Criterion 4: Anonymity and non-abuse of process Article 3 of the OP states that the Human Rights Committee must consider inadmissible any communication which is anonymous. This places a mandatory obligation on the Committee. Despite this, the HRC accepted the communication in the *Mauritian Women's Case* where all the applicants, save one, had requested that their names be kept from the State party concerned.[33] The Committee found no difficulty in admitting the communication, because the names of all the applicants were known to the HRC. It is only in circumstances where the name of the applicant remains unknown to the Committee that a communication will be rejected on grounds of anonymity. In fact, even where an anonymous communication is received by the Secretary-General, it will be registered and further and better particulars concerning the applicant's identity and other personal details will be requested. Only if these are not subsequently forthcoming will the communication be rejected.

The HRC has rarely used the ground that a communication is abusive of the right of submission for rejecting a communication and has preferred instead to rely on incompatibility *ratione materiae* as a ground for rejection. Nevertheless, it could be used in circumstances in which an individual uses the communication process vexatiously or frivolously, or where he or she employs immoderate or intemperate language in the actual communication. Furthermore, since the OP does not place a time limit on the lodging of communications, a communication which has been delayed excessively might be dismissed on this ground.

---

31 *Broeks v The Netherlands*, Communication 172/1984, UN Doc CCPR/C/29/D/172/1984 (1987); and *Zwaan de Vries v The Netherlands*, Communication 182/1984, UN Doc CCPR/C/29/D/182/1984 (1987).

32 See the discussion on this point in Chapter 11.

33 *Aumeeruddy-Cziffra and 19 other Mauritian Women v Mauritius*, above n 23.

The Violation must be Committed by a State Party

The fact that the violation must be committed by a State party to the OP raises two issues. First, the State in question must, at the time of the violation, have been a party to both the ICCPR and the OP (inadmissibility *ratione temporis*). In addition, the State must be in breach of its obligation(s) to the individual concerned either through the action or inaction of its agents, that is, while the individual is subject to the jurisdiction of the State.

Criterion 5: Inadmissibility ratione temporis It is a rule of international law that a State is not bound by the terms of a treaty in respect of any dispute if the events in question occurred before the treaty entered into force or if the subject matter of the treaty ceased to exist before it entered into force for the State in question.[34] There is an exception to this rule where the effects of a violation of a treaty provision continue after the entry into force of the treaty for the State. These were the circumstances which occurred in *Massera v Uruguay*, the first case dealt with by the Human Rights Committee under the OP. Here, the Committee held that part of the communication was inadmissible in so far as it dealt with events which had allegedly occurred before the entry into force of the ICCPR. In the case of one of the victims who was allegedly still being detained, however, the HRC found that the continuing effects of the detention permitted the admissibility of the communication.[35] This has become the HRC's consistent approach. In *A et al v S*, the Committee stated:[36]

> ... as a rule the Committee can only consider an alleged violation of human rights occurring [on or] after the date of entry into force of the Covenant and the Protocol for the State Party concerned, unless the alleged violation is one which, although occurring before that date, continues or has effects which themselves constitute violations after that date.

There have been a significant number of cases in which communications have been rejected because the events complained of occurred before the entry into force of the Covenant for the State concerned. These have not caused difficulty. There have, however, also been communications in which the State allegedly in violation of its obligations while being party to the ICCPR had not, at the time of the alleged breaches, been party to the OP. While the doctrine of continuing effects

34 Article 28 of the Vienna Convention on the Law of Treaties, opened for signature 23 May 1969, 1155 UNTS 331 (entered into force 27 January 1980), states that: 'unless a different intention appears from the treaty or is otherwise established, its provisions do not bind a party in relation to any act or fact which took place or any situation which ceased to exist before the date of the entry into force with respect to that party'.

35 *Massera v Uruguay*, above n 8.

36 *A et al v S*, Communication 1/1976, UN Doc CCPR/C/OP/1 at 3 (1984), para (d).

clearly operates here, is it also possible that the OP may have retroactive effect? While some commentators have advocated the retroactive application of the OP in such circumstances, the HRC has rejected such an approach. In *MT v Spain* the Committee stated in respect of alleged acts of torture which took place after the entry into force of the ICCPR for Spain in 1977 but before its accession to the OP in 1985:[37]

> … the [OP] cannot be applied retroactively and concludes that the Committee is precluded *ratione temporis* from examining acts said to have occurred in March 1984, unless these acts continued after the entry into force of the [OP] and allegedly constituted a continued violation of the Covenant or had effects that themselves constitute a violation of the Covenant.

Nowak suggests that this *ratio* is out of line with the previous decisions of the Committee, but a number of subsequent communications seem to have reaffirmed the central principle of inadmissibility in cases bearing similar facts.[38]

Criterion 6: Inadmissibility ratione loci As noted above, the HRC only has competence to receive communications from individuals who are subject to the jurisdiction of the allegedly delinquent State. While article 2(1) of the ICCPR requires States parties to ensure the Covenant rights 'to all individuals within its territory and subject to its jurisdiction', the Committee has not felt itself constrained by a literal interpretation of this provision, that is, one which would limit communications to territorial jurisdiction alone. This is because there is a functional difference between the requirements of the Covenant and the object and purpose of the OP. It should be noted that there is no nationality requirement in these provisions. A foreigner who is thus subject to a State party's jurisdiction and whose rights are violated enjoys *mutatis mutandis* the same right of communication as a national of that State. Two issues arise concerning the limits of 'jurisdiction' under article 2(1) of the ICCPR: first, where individuals allege that their rights were violated within the territory of the State party, but their communication is being made from abroad; and second, where agents of the State allegedly commit violations of Covenant rights abroad.

In the first of these situations, the HRC has had little difficulty in finding that individuals are within the jurisdiction of the State within the meaning of the OP. In *Massiotti and Baritussio v Uruguay* the authors, who made their communication from the Netherlands, alleged that they had been the victims of arbitrary arrest and detention whilst in Uruguay. The Committee rejected Uruguay's contention that the communication was inadmissible since the individuals were not within the jurisdiction of the State at the time of making their communication, saying: 'the victims were under the jurisdiction of Uruguay while the alleged violations took

37 *MT v Spain*, Communication 310/1988, UN Doc CCPR/C/41/D/310/1988 (1991).

38 Nowak, above n 13, pp 855–6.

place.'[39] The HRC has consistently adopted this view in communications involving similar circumstances. This can only be correct, otherwise it would impair the protective function of the OP. One can envisage circumstances in which not only an individual has fled abroad to avoid further human rights violations by his or her State, but where the State expels individuals after violating their rights.

The second situation referred to above has arisen in a number of cases. In *López Burgos v Uruguay* and *Celiberti v Uruguay*, Uruguayan citizens who had fled abroad were kidnapped by State agents and returned to Uruguay where they were subjected to serious human rights abuses. The HRC noted that neither article 2(1) ICCPR nor article 1 OP was a bar to admissibility:[40]

> Article 2(1) of the Covenant places an obligation upon a State party to respect and ensure rights 'to all individuals within its territory and subject to its jurisdiction', but it does not imply that the State party concerned cannot be held accountable for violations of rights under the Covenant which its agents commit upon the territory of another State, whether with the acquiescence of the Government for that State or in opposition to it.

This holding, which clearly relies on the doctrine of imputability, is clearly consistent with general principles of international law in which the acts of a State's agents are taken to be the acts of the State itself. The Committee has explained this notion further in its General Comment 31:[41]

> States Parties are required by article 2, paragraph 1, to respect and to ensure the Covenant rights to all persons who may be within their territory and to all persons subject to their jurisdiction. This means that a State party must respect and ensure the rights laid down in the Covenant to anyone within the power or effective control of that State Party, even if not situated within the territory of the State Party. As indicated in General Comment 15 adopted at the twenty-seventh session (1986), the enjoyment of Covenant rights is not limited to citizens of States Parties but must also be available to all individuals, regardless of nationality or statelessness, such as asylum seekers, refugees, migrant workers and other persons, who may find themselves in the territory or subject to the jurisdiction of the State Party. This principle also applies to those within the power or effective control of the forces of a State Party acting outside its territory, regardless of the circumstances in which such power or effective control was obtained,

---

39 *Massiotti and Baritussio v Uruguay*, Communication 25/1978, UN Doc CCPR/C/16/D/25/1978 (1982).

40 *Celiberti v Uruguay*, Communication 56/1979, UN Doc CCPR/C/13/D/56/1979 (1981), para 10.3; and *Burgos v Uruguay*, Communication 52/1979, UN Doc CCPR/C/13/D/52/1979 (1981).

41 *General Comment 31: Nature of the General Legal Obligation on States Parties to the Covenant*, UN Doc CCPR/C/21/Rev.1/Add.13 (2004), para 10.

> such as forces constituting a national contingent of a State Party assigned to an international peace-keeping or peace-enforcement operation.

The International Court of Justice took the same approach concerning the extraterritorial application of the ICCPR and the Covenant on Economic, Social and Cultural Rights in its 2004 Advisory Opinion concerning the construction of the barrier in the occupied Palestinian territory.[42] The Committee has itself found a violation of the ICCPR concerning the conduct of State agents abroad in *Alzery v Sweden,* the circumstances of which are considered in Chapter 5.[43]

There are other circumstances in which the Committee has taken a reasonably liberal interpretation of the meaning of 'jurisdiction', exceeding any notion of territorial jurisdiction. In a number of cases, States' diplomatic or consular missions have failed to renew the passports of citizens resident overseas. In *Vidal Martins v Uruguay* the complainant alleged that a failure to renew her passport while she was resident in Mexico violated article 12(2) ICCPR. The Committee held:[44]

> The issue of a passport to a Uruguayan citizen is clearly a matter within the jurisdiction of the Uruguayan authorities and he is subject to the jurisdiction of Uruguay for that purpose. Moreover, a passport is a means of enabling him 'to leave any country, including his own', as required by article 12(2) of the Covenant. It therefore follows from the very nature of the right that, in the case of a citizen resident abroad it imposes obligation both on the State of residence and on the State of nationality. Consequently, article 2(1) of the Covenant cannot be interpreted as limiting the obligations of Uruguay under article 12(2) to citizens within its own territory.

Although this reasoning runs counter to a literal interpretation of article 2(1), it is arguable that the legal relationship established by the bond of nationality between a State and its citizens is a firm enough ground to give an extended meaning to the term jurisdiction both within article 2(1) ICCPR and article 1 OP.[45]

Criterion 7: Duplicate Procedure of International Investigation or Settlement

Under article 5(2)(a) a communication which is being examined under another procedure of international investigation or settlement cannot be considered by the

42 *Legal Consequences of the Construction of a Wall in the Occupied Palestinian Territories, Advisory Opinion* (2004) ICJ Reports 136, para 109.

43 *Alzery v Sweden,* Communication 1416/2005, UN Doc CCPR/C/88/D/1416/2005 (2006).

44 *Martins v Uruguay,* Communication 57/1979, UN Doc CCPR/C/15/D/57/1979 (1981), para 7.

45 Both Nowak, above n 13, p 861, and Ghandhi, n 2, pp 128–9, find the Committee's reasoning in this Communication unconvincing.

Human Rights Committee. The effect of this provision is not to render such a communication terminally inadmissible, but to prevent the HRC from considering the communication while another international body is seized of the matter. Nowak refers to this as a 'suspensive barrier to admissibility' rather than a bar to admissibility, as is the case in a variety of cognate international human rights instruments.[46] A complainant who withdraws his or her complaint from another international human rights body will thus avoid the suspending effect mandated by article 5(2)(a).

Given the large number of international human rights complaint procedures which now exist, the possibility of duplication of procedures is substantial. It seems reasonably clear, however, that the type of procedure to which article 5(2)(a) applies is limited to those procedures which can give rise to a remedy. It was thus held in *A et al v S* that the inclusion of an individual's name for the purposes of ECOSOC Resolution 1503 procedure did not preclude the admissibility of the communication, since that procedure was concerned with the examination of a general human rights situation and was not in any sense individualized. Furthermore, for article 5(2)(a) to apply, the matter under investigation must be the 'same matter'.[47] The degree of similarity which will act as a barrier to proceedings is not revealed by the OP, but in *Millán v Uruguay* a two-line reference to the applicant in a list of hundreds of other people allegedly imprisoned in Uruguay which was submitted to the Inter-American Commission on Human Rights was held to lack the similarity necessary to fall within the prohibition of article 5(2)(a).[48] It is also interesting to note that in *Broeks v The Netherlands*, the Committee found that the examination of State reports submitted to the Committee on Economic, Social and Cultural Rights under article 16 ICESCR did not amount to the 'same matter' within the meaning of article 5(2)(a).[49] In *Fanali v Italy* the HRC defined the 'same matter' as:[50]

> ... the same claim concerning the same individual, submitted by him or someone else who has standing to act on his behalf before the other international body.

This latter point deals with a number of communications in which the applicant has been unaware of applications or petitions made to another international human rights body other than the HRC on his or her behalf. In such cases the HRC has tended to treat such applications made without the alleged victim's knowledge as falling outside the prohibition of article 5(2)(a).

---

46 Nowak, above n 13, p 875.

47 *A et al v S*, above n 36.

48 *Millán v Uruguay*, Communication 6/1977, UN Doc CCPR/C/10/D/6/1977 (1980).

49 *Broeks v The Netherlands*, above n 31.

50 *Fanali v Italy*, Communication 75/1980, UN Doc CCPR/C/18/D/75/1980 (1983), para 7.2.

Criterion 8: Exhaustion of Domestic Remedies

Articles 2 and 5(2)(b) of the OP require applicants to have exhausted all available domestic remedies. The latter provision continues to provide that: 'this shall not be the rule where the application of the remedies is unreasonably prolonged.' Provisions similar to these are found in all international human rights instruments. The rationale behind this rule is to give States an opportunity to redress any wrongs that it may have committed before it is subjected to any international procedures.[51] In the context of the OP, the Committee has indicated that the exhaustion of domestic remedies rule is designed to allow a State party to remedy any violations 'before the Committee is seized of the matter'.[52] While the OP does not refer to the exhaustion of domestic remedies in accordance with the general principles of international law, as does the European Convention on Human Rights,[53] it is evident from the views of the Committee that this requirement is implicit in the provisions.[54]

In order to satisfy the obligation that domestic remedies be exhausted, applicants must attempt to secure redress in all appropriate domestic legal forums. This does not mean that they have to exhaust every possible remedy, no matter how theoretical. Rather, they need only exhaust remedies that are both available and effective.[55] It follows from this that the remedy must be a real legal remedy and not simply illusory. Thus 'remedies' which depend upon the application of discretion by a judicial or political official, such as the grant of a pardon or the non-binding decision of an ombudsman, will be regarded as being neither available nor effective. Furthermore, the remedy in question must afford the applicant a reasonable prospect of success.[56] Where, for example, it is unlikely that the settled jurisprudence of the highest court of the land will be overturned on an appeal by the applicant, she or he will not be required to pursue such an appeal.[57] Similarly,

51 *Interhandel Case (Switzerland v United States of America)* [1959] ICJ Rep 6.

52 *TK v France*, Communication 220/1987, UN Doc CCPR/C/37/D/220/1987 (1989), para 8.3; and *HK v France*, Communication 222/1987, UN Doc CCPR/C/37/D/222/1987 (1989), para 8.3.

53 (European) Convention on Human Rights and Fundamental Freedoms, opened for signature 4 November 1950, 213 UNTS 222 (entered into force 3 September 1953), article 35(1).

54 *NS v Canada*, Communication 26/1978, UN Doc CCPR/C/4/D/26/1978 (1979), penultimate (unnumbered) para.

55 See *Coronel et al v Colombia*, Communication 778/1997, UN Doc CCPR/C/76/D/778/1997 (2002), in which disciplinary and administrative proceedings were held not to provide effective domestic remedies.

56 *Patiño v Panama*, Communication 437/1990, UN Doc CCPR/C/52/D/437/1990 (1994); and *Thompson v Panama*, Communication 438/1990, UN Doc CCPR/C/52/D/438/1990 (1994).

57 See, for example, *Länsman v Finland*, Communication 511/1992, UN Doc CCPR/C/52/D/511/1992 (1994).

in common law states such as England and New Zealand in which parliamentary legislation cannot be overturned by the judiciary, it will not be necessary for an applicant to resort to litigation which will undoubtedly prove futile. In addition to this, there is one situation referred to explicitly in article 5(2)(b) where it is stated that exhaustion of domestic remedies will not be necessary if the relevant procedure is unreasonably prolonged. What amounts to unreasonable prolongation is not specified, but Ghandhi suggests that the average minimum period of delay which will excuse an applicant is around four to four and a half years, although there have been cases in which shorter periods have been held to apply.[58] In the application of this requirement, the Committee will undoubtedly take into account the circumstances of the case, including the characteristics of the victim. Despite these exceptions, however, it is quite strict on the requirement that domestic remedies be exhausted, and a good many communications have failed and continue to fail on this ground. Where, however, the HRC determines that domestic remedies have not been exhausted, this is not necessarily fatal to an applicant's cause since Rule 92(2) permits an applicant to resubmit his or her communication once the necessary defect had been rectified.

The initial burden of proving whether or not domestic remedies have been exhausted lies with the applicant who must make a *prima facie* case that either exhaustion has taken place or that the remedies available are illusory, ineffective or unreasonably prolonged. Once such a *prima facie* case has been made, the respondent State must then demonstrate with some specificity the actual remedies which the applicant has failed to exhaust if it wishes to argue for the inadmissibility of the communication on this ground. During the early days of the Committee, Uruguay attempted to make general denunciations of the fact that applicants had not exhausted remedies which were available to them, but the Committee insisted that the State provide full details of the remedies which remained to be exhausted.[59] Where the State is able to show that effective remedies remain available, the burden of proof is again reversed and placed upon the applicant who must show how she or he has attempted to exhaust these remedies or why they would not prove adequate to redress the violation in question.

58 See Ghandhi, above n 2, p 272; and contrast, for example, *Collins v Jamaica*, Communication 240/1987, UN Doc CCPR/C/43/D/240/1987 (1991). See also *Coronel et al v Colombia*, above n 55, where a complaint lodged with the Public Prosecutor's Office in February 1993 had not been dealt with by the time of the applicants' communication to the HRC in September 1996.

59 See, for example, *Lanza v Uruguay*, Communication 8/1977, UN Doc CCPR/C/9/D/8/1977 (1980).

Other Procedural Issues

Interim Measures

Rule 86 of the Committee's Rules of Procedure provides that the Committee may, before forwarding its final views to the State concerned, inform the State of its view that interim measures are desirable in order to avoid irreparable damage to an applicant.[60] The Rule further makes clear that its views on interim measures, which are similar to an interlocutory injunction or interdict in domestic law, do not imply a determination of the merits of the communication. Rule 86 is designed to deal with emergency situations in which the life or health of the applicant is threatened.[61] Like the HRC's final views, these interim measures have no legally binding effect, but failure on the part of the State to comply with them would clearly compound any delinquency and leave the State open to criticism by the Committee as well as the international community at large.

Post-Admissibility Procedure

Once the Human Rights Committee has decided that a communication is admissible, the respondent State is requested to furnish its observations on the merits of the complaint. The State is given a six month period for reply, although this may be extended by special request.[62] The State's response is then forwarded to the victim who is given six weeks to respond to any of the issues raised in the response. This exchange of views, between the victim and the respondent State may continue for some time until the HRC is satisfied that it has sufficient information on which to proceed. Although these further responses are not provided for in the Rules of Procedure, this is, as McGoldrick points out, 'in accordance with the general principle of procedural equality that the HRC seeks to apply to its considerations'.[63] When the HRC is of the opinion that it has all the information it needs, it will usually remit the communication to a rapporteur or working group of the Committee in order for an initial formulation of views to be made.[64] The communication is then considered by the full Committee in session where it adopts views on the merits.

60 For a thorough consideration of Rule 86 see Ghandhi, above n 2, pp 57–65.

61 See, for example, *Schedko v Belarus*, Communication 886/1999, UN Doc CCPR/C/77/D/886/1999 (2003), where Rule 86 was used to prevent the execution of the applicant's son. Unfortunately, he had been executed at a date prior to the transmission of interim measures.

62 Article 4(2) of the Optional Protocol.

63 Dominic McGoldrick, *The Human Rights Committee: Its Role in the Development of the International Covenant on Civil and Political Rights* (Oxford: Clarendon Press, 1991) p 141. This is sometimes referred to as 'equality of arms' in international proceedings.

64 Rule 89 of the Committee's Rules of Procedure.

Although in the past it was the practice of the Committee to consider questions of admissibility and merits separately, it now routinely considers them together.

The HRC's process is terminated by the delivery of what it terms 'final views'. Where possible the Committee attempts to formulate its views by consensus, but it is possible for dissenting and final views to be attached.[65] If the HRC takes the view that the respondent State has breached the ICCPR, it will give an indication of the remedial action required. Some of the remedies indicated by the Committee have been remarkably specific, including a direction that States repeal offending legislation, return property to a victim, undertake a proper investigation of a violation, or take steps to guarantee an individual enjoyment of his or her rights.[66] The most common form of remedy, however, is the traditional international law remedy of *restitutio in integrum*, or the payment of reparation. Although these requirements of specific redress appear to have a mandatory or legally binding quality about them, it is clear from the *travaux préparatoires* of the OP that final views were not intended to be legally binding.[67] In form, however, final views read like a court judgment and they are effectively decisions on the merits of the case.[68]

Despite the widely held view among commentators that final views are not legally binding, it seems that in communications over the past few years, the Committee has been attempting to enhance their status by seeking to endow them with greater authority.[69] Some commentators are also of the opinion that the Committee's final views are indirectly legally binding. Elizabeth Evatt, a former HRC member, has argued:[70]

> The Committee … is the only international body with the competence to form the view that there has been a violation of the Covenant. If it reaches this view, then under article 2(3) of the Covenant the State has undertaken to ensure that the person whose rights were violated has an effective and enforceable remedy. The Committee's competence to determine whether a remedy is effective is expressly recognised in the Optional Protocol itself. Failure to take action in respect of the Committee's views will leave the State in violation of its obligations under article 2(3).

---

65 Rules 93 and 94 of the Committee's Rules of Procedure.

66 Dinah Shelton, *Remedies in International Human Rights Law* (Oxford: Oxford University Press, 1999) pp 142–4.

67 Scott Davidson, 'Intention and Effect: The Legal Status of the Final Views of the Human Rights Committee' in Grant Huscroft and Paul Rishworth, *Litigating Rights: Perspectives from Domestic and International Law* (Portland, OR: Hart Publishing, 2002) p 305.

68 Nowak, above n 13, p 75.

69 Davidson, above n 67, pp 309–13.

70 Elizabeth Evatt, 'The Impact of Human Rights on Domestic Law', in Huscroft and Rishworth, above n 67, pp 300–301.

Although the HRC has in two cases against Barbados claimed legally binding status for its final views,[71] these have not been repeated, and there has been some disquiet expressed by some States about the Committee's attempts to claim an enhanced legal status for its views.[72] While Evatt's argument has much to commend it, it seems reasonably clear that it was not the original intention of States to grant the HRC's final views legally binding status, and that any attempt to elevate them in this way without formal amendment of the ICCPR would not be acceptable to the majority of States parties.

Follow-up Procedure

In July 1990, during its 39th Session, the HRC established a procedure to monitor States parties' compliance with its views by the development of a follow up procedure and the creation of a mandate for a Special Rapporteur for the Follow-Up on Views.[73] The mandate of the Special Rapporteur is set out in Rule 95 of the Rules of Procedure. The Special Rapporteur began to request follow-up information from States in 1991 and since then, follow-up information has been requested from States where the Committee's views have found a violation of the ICCPR. In particular, the Special Rapporteur seeks information on the measures that have been taken to give effect to the HRC's views and the remedies indicated therein. Unfortunately, the level of compliance has been low with only about 30 per cent of States responding satisfactorily to the follow-up procedure.[74] The majority of States found to be in violation of the HRC's views either challenge the HRC's findings or simply do not respond. In the absence of compliance, the HRC's power to act is limited.[75] It can send the Special Rapporteur to conduct an on-site investigation, but this is dependent upon the relevant State party's permission. Alternatively, it can include a State party's response to follow-up in its annual report to the General Assembly via the Secretary General of the United Nations. Despite the unwelcome notoriety which might accompany such an event, there are no available sanctions. As the HRC itself has reported, the lack of enforcement machinery under the OP is 'a major shortcoming in the implementation machinery established by the Covenant'.[76] It would seem therefore that continuous dialogue between a delinquent State, or the threat of adverse publicity, are the only real mechanisms available to the HRC to secure compliance.

71 *Bradshaw v Barbados*, Communication 489/1992, UN Doc CCPR/C/51/D/489/1992 (1994); and *Roberts v Barbados*, Communication 504/1992, UN Doc CCPR/C/51/D/504/1992 (1994).

72 Don Mackay, 'The UN Covenants and the Human Rights Committee' (1999) *Victoria University of Wellington Law Review* 11.

73 Ghandhi, above n 2, pp 335–53; and Nowak, above n 13, pp 710–12.

74 *Report of the Human Rights Committee, Volume 1*, UN Doc A/53/40 (1998), para 486.

75 Ibid.

76 Ibid.

Chapter 3
Limitations to and Derogations from Covenant Rights

Alex Conte

The nature of international human rights law is such that, other than in the case of a limited number of absolute rights, the guarantee of rights and freedoms incorporates a level of flexibility. This allows States to give effect to those rights and freedoms, while at the same time pursue important democratic objectives designed to protect society (such as national security) and to maintain a balance between conflicting rights (such as freedom of expression, balanced against privacy or the right to a fair hearing). In the context of the International Covenant on Civil and Political Rights, this accommodation is effected through two means: limitations which are permitted by virtue of the particular expression of the right or freedom; and the capacity under article 4 of the ICCPR to temporarily suspend the application of certain rights during a state of emergency which threatens the life of a nation. Two documents are of particular use to this chapter. The first is General Comment 29 of the Human Rights Committee which, while its primary focus is upon states of emergency, sets out principles of relevance to the entirety of this chapter.[1] Also worthy of consideration are the *Siracusa Principles on the Limitation and Derogation Provisions in the International Covenant on Civil and Political Rights*, which set out short but useful standards adopted by the United Nations Economic and Social Council in 1985.[2]

Absolute and Non-Derogable Rights

Before considering the means by which rights might be limited or suspended, it is important to note that certain rights are either expressed in a way which permits no limitation, or fall outside the derogations regime under article 4 of the ICCPR.

---

1 *General Comment 29: States of Emergency (Article 4)*, UN Doc CCPR/C/21/Rev.1/Add.11 (2001).

2 *Siracusa Principles on the Limitation and Derogation Provisions in the International Covenant on Civil and Political Rights*, UN Doc E/CN.4/1985/4, Annex (1985).

Absolute Rights

Certain rights within the ICCPR are expressed in such a way that they do not allow for any limitation. A good example of this is provided by article 7, the first sentence of which states: 'No one shall be subjected to torture or to cruel, inhuman or degrading treatment or punishment.' The prohibition is expressed in plain language which makes clear that no exception to it is permitted. The prohibitions against slavery and servitude, set out within article 8(1) and (2), are similarly expressed in clear, absolute terms.

The guarantee under article 10(1) that all persons deprived of their liberty are to be treated with humanity and with respect for the inherent dignity of the human person is also expressed in plain language which makes clear that no limitation is permitted. One's right to hold opinions is guaranteed under article 19(1) 'without interference' and without any wording which either expressly or impliedly allows any limitation upon the exercise of the right. Also expressed in absolute terms are the rights under articles 11 (imprisonment for failure to perform a contractual obligation), 15 (criminal law guarantees), 16 (recognition before the law) and 20 (the prohibitions against propaganda and incitement to discrimination, hostility or violence).

Non-Derogable Rights

The list of non-derogable rights Article 4 of the ICCPR allows temporary derogation from some rights during a state of emergency and, in establishing this regime, lists certain rights within paragraph 2 as being non-derogable. Article 4(2) identifies non-derogable rights as those under articles 6 (life), 7 (torture, or cruel, inhuman or degrading treatment), 8(1) and (2) (slavery and servitude), 11 (imprisonment for failure to perform a contractual obligation), 15 (criminal law guarantees), 16 (recognition before the law) and 18 (manifestation of religious belief). This list is not, however, an exhaustive one. The Human Rights Committee has made the point that provisions of the ICCPR relating to procedural safeguards, which often correspond to judicial guarantees, can never be made subject to measures if this would circumvent the protection of the non-derogable rights within article 4(2).[3] Thus, for example, any trial leading to the imposition of the death penalty must conform to all the procedural requirements of article 14 of the ICCPR. Indeed, even when derogation from article 14 is permissible, the Committee has explained that the extent of any such derogation is limited.[4]

The Committee has also noted that the full complement of 'non-derogable rights' includes rights applicable as part of obligations under international human rights law, international humanitarian law, and international criminal

3 General Comment 29, above n 1, para 15.

4 General Comment 29, above n 1, para 16. See also Chapter 5 herein, and the *Siracusa Principles*, above n 2, para 67.

law since article 4(1) requires that no measure derogating from the provisions of the ICCPR may be inconsistent with the State party's other obligations under international law.[5] Expanding upon this position, the Committee has identified certain rights under customary international law (applicable to all States) as being non-derogable. These include: the right of all persons deprived of their liberty to be treated with humanity and with respect for the inherent dignity of the human person (reflected within article 10 of the ICCPR); the prohibition against taking of hostages, abductions, or unacknowledged detention (also prohibited under article 9 of the Covenant); the international protection of the rights of persons belonging to minorities (corresponding to article 27); the deportation or forcible transfer of a population without grounds permitted under international law; and the prohibition against propaganda for war or in advocacy of national, racial or religious hatred that would constitute incitement to discrimination, hostility or violence (article 20 of the ICCPR).[6] Thus, for example, no declaration of a state of emergency under article 4 may be invoked as justification for a State party to engage itself in propaganda for war.[7] Nor could derogation from article 12 (freedom of movement) justify measures involving the forcible transfer of a population without grounds permitted under international law.[8]

'Absolute' versus 'non-derogable' rights Not all of the rights identified earlier in this chapter as being 'absolute' were also identified in the preceding section as being 'non-derogable', and vice versa. This raises fine but important distinctions between the notions of absolute versus non-derogable rights. The first is that most, but not all, absolute rights are also non-derogable. Of the rights identified as being absolute, those under articles 6, 7, 8, 11, 15 and 16 are also identified within article 4(2) of the Covenant as non-derogable, even during a state of emergency. The Human Rights Committee has furthermore recognized the rights under articles 10 and 20 as being norms of customary international law, thus also not capable of being derogated from in a state of emergency. It should further be noted that the prohibitions under articles 7 and 8 reflect peremptory norms of customary international law (*jus cogens*).[9] This means that the rights set out within these eight articles (6, 7, 8, 10, 11, 15, 16 and 20) are both *expressed* in absolute terms, which means that they cannot be interpreted in a way which permits any limitation upon them, *and* are not capable of being suspended, even temporarily during a state of emergency.

5 General Comment 29, above n 1, paras 9–13.

6 General Comment 29, above n 1, para 13.

7 General Comment 29, above n 1, para 13(e).

8 General Comment 29, above n 1, para 13(D).

9 International Law Commission, 'Commentary on the Vienna Convention on the Law of Treaties' (1966) 2 *Yearbook of the International Law Commission* 248. See also General Comment 29, above n 1, para 11.

The only right which is expressed in absolute language but is not either expressly or impliedly included in the list of non-derogable rights is article 19(1), concerning the right to hold opinions without interference. While this seems illogical at face value, it should be noted that the right to hold opinions is given effective protection during states of emergency since the freedom of thought (protected under article 18(1) of the ICCPR) *is* non-derogable under article 4(2).

The second distinction to be made between absolute and non-derogable rights concerns the ability of some non-derogable rights to be made subject to limitations. As explained by the Human Rights Committee in its General Comment 29, the status of a substantive right as non-derogable does not mean that limitations or restrictions upon such a right cannot be justified.[10] The Committee gives the example of the freedom to manifest one's religion or beliefs (article 18 of the ICCPR).[11] Article 18 is listed within article 4(2) and cannot therefore be derogated from under the article 4 procedure. This listing does not, however, remove the permissible limitations upon the right expressed within article 18(3) itself, that is, limitations as are prescribed by law that are necessary to protect public safety, order, health, or morals or the fundamental rights and freedoms of others. Thus, whereas an absolute right may not be the subject of any limitation at all, a non-derogable treaty right may be capable of limitation depending upon its particular expression.

Features Common to the Limitation or Suspension of Rights

As noted earlier, there are two principal means through which the ICCPR accommodates the limitation of, or temporary suspension from, the unrestricted enjoyment of rights and freedoms. The first, to be discussed in the section that follows, is through limitations which are permitted as a result of the particular expression of the right or freedom. The second involves the capacity under article 4 of the ICCPR to temporarily suspend the application of certain rights during a state of emergency which threatens the life of a nation. Relevant to both mechanisms are four matters to be discussed here: the doctrine of the margin of appreciation; the requirement that limitations be 'prescribed by law'; the principles of necessity and proportionality; and the principle of non-discrimination.

Margin of Appreciation

The doctrine of the margin of appreciation has been developed extensively by the European Court of Human Rights, and involves the idea that each society is entitled to certain latitude in resolving the inherent conflicts between individual rights and

10 General Comment 29, above n 1, paras 4 and 7.

11 Ibid, paras 7 and 11.

national interests or among different moral convictions.[12] It should be noted here that the notion of a margin of appreciation is capable of applying in two contexts: first, in determining the means of application of rights within the jurisdiction of one State party as opposed to another; and, secondly, in the degree of leniency, if any, to be accorded to a State party in the determination of the existence of a state of emergency for the purpose of applying article 4 of the Covenant.

Margin of appreciation in the application of substantive rights In the context of the application of substantive rights, the margin of appreciation doctrine posits that States have a certain amount of discretion in the conduct of their legislative, judicial or administrative action in so far as these impinge upon the enjoyment of human rights by those within its territory and jurisdiction.[13] While this is subject to oversight by the European Court to ensure objective compliance with the protected rights, it is designed primarily to allow States to take account of local conditions and sensibilities in their implementation of rights. It is a principle which may therefore impact upon the interpretation of words or provisions that are capable of justifying limits upon the exercise of rights and freedoms. The Human Rights Committee has flirted with the concept of a margin of appreciation in *Hertzberg v Finland*, where it was required to give consideration to the notion of 'public morals' under article 19(3), stating that: '[i]t has to be noted, first, that public morals differ widely. There is no universally applicable common standard. Consequently, in this respect, a certain margin of discretion must be accorded to the responsible national authorities.'[14] The Committee soon after pointed out, however, that each international treaty, including the ICCPR, has a life of its own and must be interpreted in a fair and just manner *by the body* entrusted with the monitoring of its provisions, rather than national authorities.[15] Even in the difficult context of 'morals', it took a much more robust approach in *Toonen v Australia* (some years after its views in *Hertzberg*):[16]

> The Committee cannot accept either that for the purposes of article 17 of the Covenant, moral issues are exclusively a matter of domestic concern, as this would open the door to withdrawing from the Committee's scrutiny a potentially

12 See: Eyal Benvenisti, 'Margin of Appreciation, Consensus, and Universal Standards' (1999) 31 *International Law and Politics* 843; and Yutaka Arai-Takahashi, *The Margin of Appreciation Doctrine and the Principle of Proportionality in the Jurisprudence of the ECHR* (Antwerp: Intersentia, 2002).

13 David Harris, Michael O'Boyle and Colin Warbrick, *Law of the European Convention on Human Rights* (London: Butterworths, 1995) pp 12–15.

14 *Hertzberg et al v Finland*, Communication 61/1979, UN Doc CCPR/C/15/D/61/1979 (1982), para 10.3.

15 *JB and others v Canada*, Communication 118/1982, UN Doc CCPR/C/28/D/118/1982 (1986), para 6.2.

16 *Toonen v Australia*, Communication 488/1992, UN Doc CCPR/C/50/D/488/1992 (1994), para 8.6.

> large number of statutes interfering with privacy. It further notes that with the exception of Tasmania, all laws criminalizing homosexuality have been repealed throughout Australia and that, even in Tasmania, it is apparent that there is no consensus as to whether Sections 122 and 123 should not also be repealed. Considering further that these provisions are not currently enforced, which implies that they are not deemed essential to the protection of morals in Tasmania, the Committee concludes that the provisions do not meet the 'reasonableness' test in the circumstances of the case, and that they arbitrarily interfere with Mr Toonen's right under article 17, paragraph 1.

Ghandhi has reported that former Committee member Judge Rosalyn Higgins has gone as far as suggesting that the Human Rights Committee does not apply a margin of appreciation doctrine.[17] Schmidt, on the other hand, has identified incipient elements of the doctrine in some of the Committee's jurisprudence, but most especially in the separate opinions relating to article 26 of the Covenant.[18] However, while it is apparent in cases involving article 26 that the Committee is prepared to excuse discrimination which is objectively justifiable, reasonable and proportionate, this cannot be regarded as being the same as the fully-fledged margin of appreciation doctrine in the European system. The contrast between the approaches of the European Court of Human Rights and the Human Rights Committee is most apparent in the context of national security. While the European Court has said that States are to be given a very wide margin of appreciation when the protection of national security is in issue, the Committee has taken the view that it is for it, not States parties, to determine whether any measures taken are in fact necessary for the protection of national security.[19]

Margin of appreciation in declaring a state of emergency Common to the ICCPR and the European Convention on Human Rights is the facility for States parties to derogate from certain rights during a state of emergency threatening the life of the nation. This mechanism is discussed in more detail below but, in the context of the margin of appreciation, it is notable that here too the approaches of the European Court and the Human Rights Committee differ. Taking the approach that a wide margin of appreciation must be afforded to States in determining whether a state of emergency exists, and that it should do no more than proclaim whether a

---

17 PR Ghandhi, *The Human Rights Committee and the Right of Individual Communication: Law and Practice* (Aldershot: Ashgate, 1998) p 14.

18 Markus Schmidt, 'The Complementarity of the Covenant and the European Convention on Human Rights – Recent Developments' in David Harris and Sarah Joseph (eds), *The International Covenant on Civil and Political Rights and United Kingdom Law* (Oxford: Clarendon Press, 1995) p 629.

19 Contrast *Hadjianastassiou v Greece* (1993) 16 EHRR 219 with *Park v Republic of Korea*, Communication 628/1995, UN Doc CCPR/C/64/D/628/1995 (1998).

government's decision is 'on the margin' of the powers conferred by a derogating provision, the European Court has said:[20]

> By reason of their direct and continuous contact with the pressing needs of the moment, the national authorities are in principle in a better position than the international judge to decide both on the presence of such an emergency and on the nature and scope of derogations necessary to avert it.

In contrast, the Human Rights Committee has taken the view that compliance with all aspects of article 4, including the determination of whether a state of emergency exists, is a matter in respect of which it has final say. Although article 4 allows a State party to unilaterally declare the existence of a state of emergency, the Committee has stressed the fact that article 4(1) may only be invoked if and to the extent that a situation constitutes a threat to the life of the nation.[21] Observing that '[n]ot every disturbance or catastrophe qualifies as a public emergency which threatens the life of the nation',[22] the Committee has on a number of occasions expressed its concern over States parties that appear to have derogated from rights protected under the ICCPR in situations not covered by article 4.[23] In its Concluding Observations in 1995 concerning a derogation by the United Kingdom, for example, the Committee recommended that:[24]

> [g]iven the significant diminution in terrorist violence in the United Kingdom since the cease-fire came into effect in Northern Ireland and the peace process was initiated, the Committee urges the Government to keep under the closest review whether a situation of 'public emergency' within the terms of Article 4, paragraph 1, of the Covenant still exists and whether it would be appropriate for the United Kingdom to withdraw the notice of derogation, in accordance with Article 4 of the Covenant, which it issued on 17 May 1976.

---

20 *Ireland v United Kingdom* [1978] ECHR 1, para 207. See Susan Marks, 'Civil Liberties at the Margin: The UK Derogation and the European Court of Human Rights' (1995) 15(1) *Oxford Journal of Legal Studies* 69.

21 General Comment 29, above n 1, para 2.

22 General Comment 29, above n 1, para 3.

23 See, for example, the Concluding Observations of the Committee concerning: Bolivia, UN Doc CCPR/C/79/Add.74 (1997), para 14; Colombia, UN Doc CCPR/C/79/Add.76 (1997), para 25; the Dominican Republic, UN Doc CCPR/C/79/Add.18 (1993), para 4; Israel, UN Doc CCPR/C/79/Add.93 (1998), para 11; Lebanon, UN Doc CCPR/C/79/Add.78 (1997), para 10; Peru, UN Doc CCPR/C/79/Add.67 (1996), para 11; the United Kingdom of Great Britain and Northern Ireland, UN Doc CCPR/C/79/Add.55 (1995), para 23; the United Republic of Tanzania, UN Doc CCPR/C/79/Add.12 (1992), para 7; and Uruguay, UN Doc CCPR/C/79/Add.90 (1998), para 8.

24 *Concluding Observations of the Human Rights Committee: United Kingdom of Great Britain and Northern Ireland*, UN Doc CCPR/C/79/Add.55 (1995), para 23.

In the context of derogations from human rights, it should be noted that the margin of appreciation has been applied by the European Court of Human Rights not only to the question of whether a state of emergency exists, but also to whether particular derogating measures are necessary. The degree of deference applied has been mixed. In *Ireland v United Kingdom*, the Court asked simply whether there was *some* basis, at the time of declaring the state of emergency, for the government to believe that the derogating measures were necessary.[25] The European Court noted in *Lawless v Ireland*, however, that this issue must be exercised carefully, in a manner which prevents abuse, or excessive use, of the derogating power.[26] Critics have nevertheless noted that the Court applied a very wide margin of appreciation to this issue in its 1993 decision concerning the United Kingdom's derogation from liberty rights under article 5 of the European Convention.[27] As discussed below, however, the approach of the Human Rights Committee has been to require States to justify in full that each derogating measure is necessary.[28] The *Siracusa Principles* further state that '[i]n determining whether derogation measures are strictly required by the exigencies of the situation the judgment of the national authorities cannot be accepted as conclusive'.[29]

Limitations 'Prescribed by Law'

Common to all mechanisms authorizing the limitation of rights, any measure seeking to limit a right or freedom must be prescribed by law.[30] The expression 'prescribed by law' has been subject to careful examination by the European Court of Human Rights, with commentary on the expression within the *Siracusa Principles* also. The term was considered by the European Court in the *Sunday Times* case of 1978, where the Court concluded that two requirements flow from it: (1) the law must be adequately accessible so that the citizen has an adequate indication of how the law limits his or her rights; and (2) the law must be formulated with sufficient precision so that the citizen can regulate his or her conduct.[31] In the particular context of derogations under article 4, General Comment 29 reaffirms that derogations must be based upon the principles of legality and the rule of law, said to be inherent in the ICCPR as a whole.[32]

---

25 *Ireland v United Kingdom*, above n 20, para 214.

26 *Lawless v Ireland (No 3)* [1961] ECHR 2, para 37.

27 *Brannigan and McBride v United Kingdom* [1993] ECHR 21, commented upon by Susan Marks, above n 20.

28 See General Comment 29, above n 1, para 5.

29 *Siracusa Principles*, above n 2, para 57.

30 *Siracusa Principles*, above n 2, para 5.

31 *Sunday Times v United Kingdom* (1978) 58 ILR 491, 524–7, reaffirmed by the European Court in *Silver v UK* [1983] 5 EHRR 347. The principles of clarity and accessibility are contained within the *Siracusa Principles* also, above n 2, para 17.

32 General Comment 29, above n 1, para 17.

It should be noted that limiting measures may, even if they are prescribed by law, involve the conferral of a discretionary power. This may be a practical requirement of the implementation of limiting measures and there is, in principle, no prohibition against the conferral of discretions. The *Siracusa Principles* provide, however, that limitations must not be arbitrary or unreasonable (terms which have been considered and defined by the Human Rights Committee, as discussed below).[33] The *Principles* also state that adequate safeguards must exist to protect against the illegal or abusive imposition or application of limitations on human rights, and that limitations must be subject to the possibility of challenge to and remedy against abusive application.[34] Translating these principles into practical requirements applicable to the conferral and exercise of discretionary powers which might restrict the enjoyment of rights and freedoms, one can say that: (1) any law authorizing a restriction upon rights and freedoms must not confer an *unfettered* discretion on those charged with its execution; and (2) any discretion must not be *arbitrarily or unreasonably* applied. Both requirements call for the imposition of adequate safeguards to ensure that discretionary powers are capable of being checked, with appropriate mechanisms to deal with any abuse or arbitrary application of the discretion.

Necessity and Proportionality

Necessity and proportionality are elements common to derogation and limitation powers.[35] While these principles are inherent to the exercise of such powers, they may also be activated by the particular words used to express a right or freedom. As discussed below, for example, the requirement of 'reasonableness' implies that any interference with a right must be proportional to the end sought and necessary in the circumstances of any given case. The Human Rights Committee has observed that the words 'necessary' and 'proportionate' are interlinked, stating in *de Morais v Angola*, for example, that the requirement of necessity itself implies an element of proportionality.[36] There are, nevertheless, some distinct features of each term.

Necessity In the context of derogations under article 4, the principle of necessity permits States parties to derogate from certain rights under the Covenant only 'to the extent strictly required by the exigencies of the situation'.[37] Necessity is also a

---

33 *Siracusa Principles*, above n 2, para 16.

34 *Siracusa Principles*, above n 2, paras 8 and 18.

35 General Comment 29, above n 1, para 4.

36 See: *Faurisson v France*, Communication 550/1993, UN Doc CCPR/C/58/D/550/1993(1996), para 8; and *de Morais v Angola*, Communication 1128/2002, UN Doc CCPR/C/83/D/1128/2002 (2005), para 6.8. See also the *Siracusa Principles*, above n 2, para 10(d).

37 General Comment 29, above n 1, paras 3–5; and the *Siracusa Principles*, above n 2, para 51.

key feature of rights-specific limitations, commonly calling on three requirements. Firstly, reliance upon a rights-specific limitation will always require a State to establish that the limiting measure is in pursuit of an objective which is permitted by the expression of the right concerned.[38] Limitation clauses include various express objectives, including the protection of national security or public morals. The nature and meaning of these express objectives is considered further below.

Once a link is established between the objective of the limiting measure and one of the objectives listed in the rights-specific limitation clause, the second common feature of necessity involves establishing a link between the objective of the measure and the notion of a free and democratic society.[39] Rights-specific limitation provisions often set out express objectives in the context of a 'democratic society', such as article 14(1) which states that '[t]he press and the public may be excluded from all or part of a trial for reasons of morals, public order (ordre public) or national security *in a democratic society*' (emphasis added). Article 21 similarly prohibits restrictions on the right of peaceful assembly, other than those imposed in conformity with the law and which are 'necessary in a democratic society in the interests of national security …' and the like. The Committee has stated that reference to 'democratic society' indicates, in these contexts, that the existence and operation of the particular right is a cornerstone of a democratic society.[40] In considering such a qualification upon limits to the freedom of association with others, for example, the Committee stated in *Lee v Republic of Korea* that the existence and functioning of a plurality of associations, including those which peacefully promote ideas not favourably received by the government or the majority of the population, is one of the foundations of a democratic society.[41]

The final component of necessity, which is often implicitly considered but almost never expressly referred to, entails the need for limiting measures to be rationally connected to the achievement of the objective being pursued, based upon objective considerations.[42] This component is relatively simple in its application and requires that limiting measures logically further the objective being pursued so that they can indeed be said to be necessary to achieve the permissible objective.

Proportionality Establishing the *need* for any limit upon rights, or derogation therefrom, will normally involve a reasonably mechanical exercise whereby a State will point to permitted objectives and draw links between the limiting measure and those objectives. Critically, however, the establishment of such a relationship does

38 *Siracusa Principles*, above n 2, paras 6 and 10(a).

39 On this point, see paras 19–21 of the *Siracusa Principles*, above n 2.

40 In the context of the right to freedom of association with others under article 22(2), see, for example, *Zvozskov et al v Belarus*, Communication 1039/2001, UN Doc CCPR/C/88/D/1039/2001 (2006), para 7.2.

41 *Lee v Republic of Korea*, Communication 1119/2002, UN Doc CCPR/C/84/D/1119/2002 (2005), para 7.2.

42 *Siracusa Principles*, above n 2, para 10(b) and 10(c).

not provide the State with the ability to limit the right or freedom to whatever extent it wishes. The limiting measure must also be shown to be proportionate, such that the State may not use more restrictive means than are required to achieve the purpose of the limitation.[43] Proportionality calls into question not only the validity of the measure as a prescription by law (for example, whether or not the criminalization of certain conduct is proportional to the need to dissuade the conduct in question), but also the way in which it is applied to each particular case (for example, whether a sentence imposed upon conviction is proportional to the severity of the conduct). Proportionality assessments must be based on a full consideration of all relevant issues,[44] although there are two common factors which are brought to bear in the evaluation of whether limiting measures are proportional, namely: (1) the negative impact of the limiting measure upon the enjoyment of the right; and (2) the ameliorating effects of the limiting measure.

The negative impact of limiting measures upon the enjoyment of the particular right or freedom is the obvious starting point in determining whether the measure is proportional. In the context of criminal defamation acting as a limit upon the freedom of expression, for example, the Committee has considered the severity of the sanction imposed as relevant to the proportionality of the limit upon expression.[45] It will be important in this regard to consider the importance of the right and the 'value' that might be prescribed to it. While all rights are said to be equal and indivisible, it has already been mentioned that some rights and freedoms, such as the freedom of association with others, have been recognized by the Human Rights Committee as part of the 'foundations of a democratic society'. Limitations imposed upon such rights will therefore be carefully scrutinized by the Committee.

In evaluating the negative impact of a limiting measure, it will also be important to establish that the limitation is not so severe or so broad in its application as to destroy the very essence of the right in question.[46] This has been treated as especially important to justifying any distinctions between individuals in the protection of their rights.[47] It is notable in this regard that the Committee has expressed the view that restrictions on Covenant rights, even where permissible

43 *Siracusa Principles*, above n 2, para 11.

44 See, for example, *Burgess v Australia*, Communication 1012/2001, UN Doc CCPR/C/85/D/1012/2001 (2005), para 4.13.

45 See, for example: *Pietraroia v Uruguay*, Communication 44/1979, UN Doc CCPR/C/OP/1 at 65 (1984), para 16; *Jong-Cheol v Republic of Korea*, Communication 968/2001, UN Doc CCPR/C/84/D/968/2001 (2005), para 8.3; and *de Morais v Angola*, above n 36, para 6.8.

46 *Siracusa Principles*, above n 2, para 2.

47 See Chapter 11 herein and, for example: *Jacobs v Belgium*, Communication 943/2000, UN Doc CCPR/C/81/D/943/2000 (2004), para 9.5; *Althammer et al v Austria*, Communication 998/2001, UN Doc CCPR/C/78/D/998/2001 (2003), para 10.2; and *Haraldsson and Sveinsson v Iceland*, Communication 1306/2004, UN Doc CCPR/C/91/D/1306/2004 (2007), para 8.10.

under a rights-specific limitation provision, must be interpreted narrowly and with careful scrutiny of the reasons advanced by way of justification.[48] The *Siracusa Principles* add that '[a]ll limitation clauses shall be interpreted strictly and in favour of the rights at issue'.[49]

Also central to proportionality will be the importance of the objective being pursued and the extent to which the limiting measure contributes to that objective, that is, its ameliorating effects. The Committee has thus said that the scope of any restriction imposed on a right or freedom must be proportional to the value which the restriction serves to protect.[50] When examining the reliance by States parties upon limitation provisions, the Committee has taken into account the importance of the limitation to the enjoyment of other rights under the Convention, as well as to other democratic principles. In the context of limits upon the right to freedom of expression, for example, the Committee has taken into account the importance of public debate in a democratic society, especially in the media, including that concerning figures in the political domain.[51]

Non-Discrimination

Measures limiting the exercise of rights and freedoms must be non-discriminatory in nature.[52] This is brought to bear through a combination of often overlapping features of international human rights law. Non-discrimination is a specific condition upon the ability to derogate from certain rights under article 4 of the Covenant, paragraph 1 expressly providing that any derogating measure must not involve discrimination solely on the ground of race, colour, sex, language, religion or social origin. When resorting to measures that derogate from the Covenant, the Committee has emphasized that this aspect of article 4 must be complied with if any distinctions are made between persons under the derogating measures.[53] As noted in Chapter 11 herein, this list is more limited than the prohibited grounds of discrimination contained in article 2(1), since it may be permissible, during war or national emergency, to discriminate against enemy aliens and their property.[54]

---

48 See, for example, *Sisters of the Holy Cross of the Third Order of Saint Francis in Menzingen of Sri Lanka v Sri Lanka*, Communication 1249/2004, UN Doc CCPR/C/85/D/1249/2004 (2005), para 7.2.

49 *Siracusa Principles*, above n 2, para 3.

50 See, for example, *de Morais v Angola*, above n 36, para 6.8.

51 See, for example, *Bodrožić v Serbia and Montenegro*, Communication 1180/2003, UN Doc CCPR/C/85/D/1180/2003 (2006), para 7.2. See also, in the context of South Africa's blanket ban on the use of cannabis, *Prince v South Africa*, Communication 1474/2006, UN Doc CCPR/C/91/D/1474/2006 (2007), para 4.6.

52 *Siracusa Principles*, above n 2, para 9.

53 General Comment 29, above n 1, para 8.

54 Manfred Nowak, *UN Covenant on Civil and Political Rights* (2nd revised edn, Kehl, Germany: NP Engel, 2005) pp 99–100.

Outside the context of article 4, the principle of non-discrimination becomes involved in the limitation of rights through concepts such as arbitrariness and proportionality. As discussed below, the Human Rights Committee has explained that the concept of arbitrariness is intended to guarantee that even reasonable conduct which is provided for by law should be in accordance with the provisions, aims and objectives of the ICCPR, including non-discrimination.[55]

Limitations Permitted by the Expression of Rights and Freedoms

The principal way in which the ICCPR facilitates the needs of States to accommodate competing rights or interests is through the *expression* of individual rights and freedoms, as articulated within each article and paragraph of the Covenant. This can in turn be broken down into two means by which the expression of rights can allow for limitations: either through the particular words used to define the right (limitations by interpretation); or through an accompanying sentence or paragraph which sets out permissible objectives, the pursuit of which can justify limitation (rights-specific limitation provisions).

Limitations by Interpretation

Limitations by interpretation are ones that rely upon the meaning of the words contained within the expression of the right itself. The ICCPR incorporates concepts such as 'fair' trial (article 14(1)); 'reasonableness' (articles 9(3) and 25); 'arbitrariness' (relating to various rights); the need to take 'prompt' action in the context of persons deprived of their liberty or subject to criminal proceedings (articles 9 and 14); and the provision of 'adequate' time and facilities for the preparation of one's defence (article 14(3)(b)). Common to all limitations by interpretation is the inherent flexibility involved in the need to interpret the particular term, a feature which can be equally negative through lack of certainty. The qualifications in the latter provisions (articles 9 and 14) have been interpreted in terms which are very specific to the exercise of those rights, and are considered in detail within Chapters 5 and 6 herein. Considered next in this chapter are the interpretative approaches taken to the terms 'fair', 'reasonable', and 'arbitrary'.

Fair and reasonable The existence of a 'fair trial' for the purpose of article 14(1) is one which incorporates a number of elements, including equality of arms between parties, attendance at hearings, the ability to hear from and examine witnesses, and the prompt disposal of proceedings. It is based upon the idea that parties should

55 See, for example, *General Comment 16: The right to respect of privacy, family, home and correspondence, and protection of honour and reputation (Art 17)*, UN Doc CCPR General Comment 16 (1988), para 4. See also the *Siracusa Principles*, above n 2, para 5.

not be prejudiced or otherwise disadvantaged in being able to put their case to a tribunal, and entails the absence of any direct or indirect influence, pressure or intimidation, or intrusion from whatever side and for whatever motive.[56] These notions of equality and lack of prejudice appear to lie at the heart of the term 'fair', and the use of that term enables the Human Rights Committee to assess each communication on its own facts, something that the Committee has stressed to be important to the evaluation of fairness.[57]

Reasonableness is a concept seen within article 9(3), guaranteeing an entitlement to trial within a reasonable time after arrest or detention, and article 25, which recognizes and protects the right of every citizen to take part in the conduct of public affairs, vote and be elected, and participate in the public administration of one's country 'without unreasonable restrictions'. As with the notion of fairness, the Committee has taken a case-by-case approach to assessing reasonableness, based upon the particular circumstances of each case.[58] In the context of determining what might or might not constitute 'reasonable restrictions' under article 25, the Committee has commented that it will be important that any restriction is based on *objective* criteria.[59] It may, for example, be reasonable to require a higher age for election or appointment to particular offices, or that established mental incapacity may be a ground for denying a person the right to vote or to hold office.[60] In *Toonen v Australia*, concerning interference with one's private life, the Committee interpreted the requirement of reasonableness 'to imply that any interference with privacy must be proportional to the end sought and be necessary in the circumstances of any given case'.[61] This link between reasonableness on the one hand, and necessity and proportionality on the other, is important, although it should be remembered that necessity and proportionality are essential elements in the limitation of all rights and freedoms, by whatever mechanism.

Arbitrary conduct A number of provisions within the Covenant guarantee that certain rights are to be enjoyed in the absence of arbitrary interference, namely: the right not to be arbitrarily deprived of life (article 6(1)); the prohibition against arbitrary arrest or detention (article 9(1)); the exclusion of arbitrary deprivation of the right to enter one's own country (article 12(4)); and the right to be free

---

56 See Chapter 5 herein.

57 See, for example, *De Polay v Peru*, Communication 575/1994, UN Doc CCPR/C/53/D/575/1994 (1995), para 8.8.

58 See, for example, *Van Alphen v The Netherlands*, 305/1988, UN Doc CCPR/C/39/D/305/1988 (1990).

59 *General Comment 25: The right to participate in public affairs, voting rights and the right of equal access to public service (Art 25)*, UN Doc CCPR/C/21/Rev.1/Add.7 (1996), para 4. See also *Sohn v Republic of Korea*, Communication 518/1992, UN Doc CCPR/C/54/D/518/1992 (1995), para 10.4.

60 General Comment 25, ibid, para 4. See further Chapter 4 herein.

61 *Toonen v Australia*, above n 16, para 8.3.

from arbitrary or unlawful interference with one's privacy (article 17(1)). Added to these express prohibitions against the arbitrary limitation of rights, the *Siracusa Principles* provide that no limitation at all may be applied in an arbitrary manner.[62] Common to the interpretation of the term 'arbitrary' are three features. The first is that arbitrary conduct may, but need not, involve an act or omission which is against the law. As an adjective, one of the ordinary meanings of the word 'arbitrary' is that the associated conduct is dependent on will or pleasure, rather than law.[63] The approach of the Human Rights Committee has been that arbitrariness is more, however, than just illegal conduct. It is interesting to note, in this regard, that article 17(1) prohibits 'arbitrary *or unlawful*' interference with privacy, which may represent recognition by the drafters of the ICCPR that illegality is not the defining feature or arbitrariness.

Drawn from this is the second common feature involved in defining or ascertaining the existence of arbitrary conduct: a link between arbitrariness and reasonableness, such that the Committee has treated arbitrary conduct as including elements of unreasonableness. In the context of the arbitrary deprivation of liberty, for example, the Committee has said that to be deemed arbitrary, the detention of a person must include elements of inappropriateness, injustice, lack of predictability, and lack of due process of law.[64] In the context of the ICCPR, the final feature of arbitrariness is rather novel and appears to be based on a desire by the Human Rights Committee to uphold the entirety of the Covenant. The Committee has considered that the concept of arbitrariness is intended to guarantee that even reasonable conduct which is provided for by law (the first two factors just identified) should be in accordance with the provisions, aims and objectives of the ICCPR.[65] The *Siracusa Principles* state rather more broadly that it is implicit that *any* restrictions upon rights recognized in the Covenant must be consistent with other rights within it.[66] As indicated earlier, this has been key to the rule that all measures which limit the enjoyment of rights must be in accordance with the principle of non-discrimination.

Rights-Specific Limitation Provisions

The mechanism most commonly relied upon to impose restrictions upon rights and freedoms under the ICCPR is reliance upon rights-specific limitation provisions.

---

62 *Siracusa Principles*, above n 2, para 7.

63 *Shorter Oxford English Dictionary* (5th edn, Oxford: Oxford University Press, 2002) p 109.

64 See, for example: *Mukong v Cameroon*, Communication 458/1991, UN Doc CCPR/C/51/D/458/1991 (1994), para 9.8; and *de Morais v Angola*, above n 36, para 6.1. See further Chapter 5 herein.

65 See: General Comment 16, above n 55, para 4; and *García v Colombia*, Communication 687/1996, UN Doc CCPR/C/71/D/687/1996 (2001).

66 *Siracusa Principles*, above n 2, para 13.

Rights-specific limitations are those that are authorized by a sentence or words, or a stand-alone paragraph, found within the article of the Covenant which enumerates the particular right in question. The provision explains the circumstances in which the right may be limited. In the context of the right to a fair and open hearing, for example, the first two sentences of article 14(1) express the substance of the right. The next sentence then sets out the circumstances in which it is permissible to limit the right to an 'open' hearing, allowing the exclusion of the press for reasons of morals, public order or national security. The third sentence of article 14(1) provides that: '[t]he press and the public may be excluded from all or part of a trial for reasons of morals, public order (*ordre public*) or national security in a democratic society, or when the interest of the private lives of the parties so requires, or to the extent strictly necessary in the opinion of the court in special circumstances where publicity would prejudice the interests of justice.'

It is notable, in this regard, that the drafters of the ICCPR took the approach of including rights-specific limitations, rather than adopting a general limitations clause applicable to all rights. The latter approach, in contrast, is the one taken under the Universal Declaration of Human Rights:[67]

> Article 29
>
> 1. Everyone has duties to the community in which alone the full and free development of his personality is possible.
> 2. In the exercise of his rights and freedoms, everyone shall be subject only to such limitations as are determined by law solely for the purpose of securing due recognition and respect for the rights and freedoms of others and of meeting the just requirements of morality, public order and the general welfare in a democratic society.
> 3. These rights and freedoms may in no case be exercised contrary to the purposes and principles of the United Nations.

Limited rights Rights-specific limitations can be further broken down into limitations applicable to 'limited' and 'qualified' rights. Limited rights are those which explain the precise and limited extent to which the right or freedom may be restricted. A particularly good example of such a right is contained in article 5(1) of the European Convention on Human Rights, which contains an exhaustive list of the circumstances in which a person's liberty may be deprived including, for example, the lawful detention of a person after conviction by a competent court (article 5(1)(a)). The ICCPR contains only one limited right, within the second sentence of article 7, which guarantees the right to be free from medical or scientific experimentation except in the case where a person gives his or her

67 Universal Declaration of Human Rights, adopted under General Assembly Resolution 217(III), UN GAOR, 3rd Session, 183rd Plenary Meeting (1948).

'free consent' to such experimentation. The advantage of limited rights is that they are precise in nature and do not call for any further consideration to be had. Thus, if a person gives their free consent to medical treatment, there is no need to consider the 'necessity' or 'proportionality' of the treatment involved, albeit that the Committee has the ability to have regard to just what amounts to 'free' consent under article 7. Special protection is necessary in this regard, the Committee has said, in the case of persons not capable of giving their consent.[68]

Qualified rights Qualified rights are those where the right is asserted as a general principle, but then qualified by stating that it is lawful to interfere with the right if it is necessary to achieve certain objectives. This involves a more detailed assessment of the legitimacy of the interference, requiring that the limit is: (1) prescribed by law; (2) in pursuit of one of the listed objectives; (3) necessary and proportional to that end; and (4) non-discriminatory. Rights-specific limitation provisions affecting qualified rights are found within the ICCPR in articles 12(3) (liberty of movement), 13 (expulsion of aliens), 14(1) (fair and public hearing), 18(3) (freedom of thought, conscience and religion), 19(3) (freedom of expression), 21 (peaceful assembly) and 22(2) (freedom of association with others). Each provision lists specific objectives, the pursuit of which may legitimize limitations upon the right or freedom if, as discussed above, the limit is also prescribed by law, necessary and proportionate, and non-discriminatory. The full complement of permissible objectives found in the articles mentioned includes the protection of national security, public order (*ordre public*), public safety, public health, public morals, or the rights and freedoms of others. Each of these objectives is considered in turn next.

National security The Committee has spoken of limitations for the protection of national security as ones which must be necessary to avert a real, and not only hypothetical, danger to the national security or democratic order of the State.[69] The *Siracusa Principles* similarly speak of national security being capable of being invoked to justify the limitation of rights only where taken to protect the existence of the nation or its territorial integrity or political independence against force or threat of force.[70] The *Principles* add that national security cannot be invoked to prevent merely local or relatively isolated threats to law and order.[71] Despite these restrictive approaches, the majority of the Committee took a wider view in *Peltonen v Finland*, where it considered that it was a reasonable legislative

68 *General Comment 7: Article 7*, UN Doc HRI\GEN\1\Rev.1 at 7 (1994), para 3. General Comment 7 was replaced by *General Comment 20: Prohibition of torture and cruel treatment or punishment (Art 7)*, UN Doc CCPR General Comment 20 (1992).

69 *Lee v Republic of Korea*, above n 41, para 7.2. See also *Belyatsky et al v Belarus*, Communication 1296/2004, UN Doc CCPR/C/90/D/1296/2004 (2007), para 7.3.

70 *Siracusa Principles*, above n 2, para 29.

71 *Siracusa Principles*, above n 2, para 30.

requirement to refuse to issue a passport to a person who had avoided military service.[72] This decision might, however, be treated as unique in light of the fact that the *travaux préparatoires* to the freedom of movement under article 12(3) reveal that it was agreed that the right to leave one's country could not be claimed in order to avoid national service.[73] As discussed earlier, it should also be noted that the Committee has normally taken a very robust approach to the determination of whether a situation is linked to the objective of protecting national security, rejecting any margin of discretion on the part of national authorities.[74] In the context of summaries of information used in judicial proceedings and redacted for security concerns, for example, the Committee has treated such summaries as compatible with article 14 only in circumstances where compensatory mechanisms are adopted to ensure that this does not prejudice the overall right of a litigant to a fair trial.[75]

Public order The protection of public order is an objective which may justify the limitation of a number of qualified rights. The Committee has again taken a generally strict approach to the application of this ground of limitation, careful to ensure that limits are both necessary for and proportional to the risk posed to public order by any given situation. The arrest of the author in *Joana v Madagascar* was found to be in violation of the ICCPR, for example, in circumstances where it was claimed that his public denunciation of elections as fraudulent endangered public order and security.[76]

While the meaning of 'public order' is one which, according to the *Siracusa Principles*, should be interpreted in the context of the purpose of the particular human right which is being limited, there are two principal features the protection of which fall under the umbrella of 'public order': (1) rules which ensure the functioning of society or the set of fundamental principles on which society is founded; and (2) respect for human rights.[77] Falling within the first category is the case of *Gauthier v Canada* where, although certain restrictions on the freedom of expression were ultimately found to be disproportionate, the Committee agreed that the protection of Parliamentary procedure could be seen as a legitimate goal

72 *Peltonen v Finland*, Communication 492/1992, UN Doc CCPR/C/51/D/492/1992 (1994), para 8.4. Contrast with the individual dissenting opinion of Committee Member Bertil Wennergren, as discussed in Chapter 4 herein.

73 See *Peltonen v Finland*, ibid, para 8.3.

74 As in the case of *Park v Republic of Korea*, above n 19, discussed above and in Chapter 4 herein.

75 *Ahani v Canada*, Communication 1051/2002, UN Doc CCPR/C/80/D/1051/2002 (2004), para 10.4.

76 *Jaona v Madagascar*, Communication 132/1982, UN Doc CCPR/C/24/D/132/1982 (1985), para 14.

77 *Siracusa Principles*, above n 2, paras 22–3.

of public order.[78] As for the second feature of public order, a controversial case which raised questions about the relationship between objective justifications for differential treatment, issues of human dignity, and limitations upon one's private life was *Wackenheim v France*. The author, who suffered from dwarfism, complained about a law which prohibited dwarf tossing, alleging that this prevented him from working and was thus an affront to his human dignity. The Committee accepted France's argument that the ban was necessary to protect public order and due respect for the human dignity of the individual concerned.[79]

Public health and safety The objectives of protecting 'public health' and 'public safety' are sometimes interlinked in nature. In *Malakhovsky and Pikul v Belarus*, for example, the Committee determined that it was necessary for public safety, and proportionate to this end, for the registration of a religious association to be conditional upon the use by it of premises which satisfied health and fire safety standards.[80] The two objectives do, however, have distinctive characteristics. Public safety is understood to refer to the protection against danger to the safety of persons, to their life or physical integrity, or serious damage to their property.[81] The protection of public safety is therefore often raised to justify the imposition of criminal convictions and sanctions which might interfere with the unlimited enjoyment of rights under the ICCPR. Public health is much narrower in its scope, said to be capable of being invoked as a ground of limitation only in order to allow a State to take measures dealing with a serious threat to the health of the population or individual members of the population. Such measures must be specifically aimed at preventing disease or injury or providing care for the sick and injured.[82]

Public morals The issue of public morals has already been referred to in the context of the margin of appreciation, where the Committee initially referred in *Hertzberg v Finland* to this ground as one calling for a margin of discretion to be applied, but later took a much more robust approach in *Toonen v Australia*. The *Siracusa Principles*, adopted by the Economic and Social Council in 1985, reflect

---

78 *Gauthier v Canada*, Communication 633/1995, UN Doc CCPR/C/65/D/633/1995 (1999), para 13.5.

79 *Wackenheim v France*, Communication 854/1999, UN Doc CCPR/C/75/D/854/1999 (2002), para 7.4, discussed further in Chapters 7 and 11 herein.

80 *Malakhovsky and Pikul v Belarus*, Communication 1207/2003, UN Doc CCPR/C/84/D/1207/2003 (2005), para 7.4.

81 *Siracusa Principles*, above n 2, para 33.

82 *Siracusa Principles*, above n 2, para 25.

the Committee's earlier position in *Hertzberg* and are somewhat out of step with the Committee's 1994 views in *Toonen*, stating at paragraph 27:[83]

> Since public morality varies over time and from one culture to another, a state which invokes public morality as a ground for restricting human rights, while enjoying a certain margin of discretion, shall demonstrate that the limitation in question is essential to the maintenance of respect for fundamental values of the community.

Rights and freedoms of others The balancing of one person's right against another is a difficult matter, but one based on the principle that one's membership in society involves not only rights but also special duties and responsibilities to others. Preambular paragraph 5 to the ICCPR recognizes that each person has responsibilities and duties 'to other individuals and to the community to which he belongs'.[84] In the context of the rights-specific limitation provision under article 19(3), it is there specifically mentioned that the exercise of the freedom of expression carries with it special duties and responsibilities. This is a matter which has been subject to much consideration before the European Court of Human Rights in the context of the responsibilities of the media,[85] although not in communications before the Human Rights Committee due to the fact that such communications may only be brought by individuals.[86] It should also be noted that, in a similar context, limitations based on the protection of the reputation of others (as provided for under article 17(2) of the ICCPR) cannot be used to protect the State and its officials from public opinion or criticism.[87]

Added to the notion of one's membership in society is a further basis for balancing competing rights, reflected in article 5(1) of the ICCPR:[88]

> Nothing in the present Covenant may be interpreted as implying for any State, group or person any right to engage in any activity or perform any act aimed at the destruction of any of the rights and freedoms recognized herein or at their limitation to a greater extent than is provided for in the present Covenant.

Rights Derogable during States of Emergency

The second mechanism under the ICCPR allowing for restrictions upon the enjoyment of rights and freedoms involves the capacity under article 4 to

83 *Siracusa Principles*, above n 2, para 27. See also para 28.

84 See also the Universal Declaration of Human Rights, above n 67, article 29(1).

85 See, for example, *De Haes and Gijsels v Belgium* [1997] ECHR 7.

86 See Chapter 2 herein.

87 See: the *Siracusa Principles*, above n 2, para 37; and Chapter 4 herein.

88 See also the Universal Declaration of Human Rights, above n 67, article 29(3).

temporarily suspend the application of certain rights during a state of emergency which threatens the life of a nation. Article 4(1) sets out the essence of this exceptional measure, in almost identical terms to the derogating provision found in article 15 of the European Convention on Human Rights:

> In time of public emergency which threatens the life of the nation and the existence of which is officially proclaimed, the States Parties to the present Covenant may take measures derogating from their obligations under the present Covenant to the extent strictly required by the exigencies of the situation, provided that such measures are not inconsistent with their other obligations under international law and do not involve discrimination solely on the ground of race, colour, sex, language, religion or social origin.

Unlike rights-specific limitations, which might be semi-permanent in nature, derogations involve: a suspension in the application of certain rights within the territory and jurisdiction of the State party; for a limited period (that is, during a state of emergency threatening the life of the nation). In more technical terms, article 4 allows a State to suspend the application to it of obligations under certain articles of the ICCPR. For a derogation under article 4 to be valid, two procedural conditions and four substantive conditions must be satisfied.

Procedural Conditions

Non-derogable rights Article 4(2) of the ICCPR explains that certain rights may not be derogated from, even during a state of emergency. This is a matter considered earlier in this chapter, in the context of distinguishing between 'absolute' and 'non-derogable' rights. The article 4 procedure cannot be engaged with respect to non-derogable rights, although this has not prevented States from claiming to do so. The Committee has on several occasions expressed its concern about non-derogable rights being either derogated from or under a risk of derogation owing to inadequacies in the legal regime of the State party.[89]

Notice of derogation The second procedural condition under article 4 is found in paragraph 3, which requires that a State party must officially proclaim the existence within its territory of a public emergency that threatens the life of the nation.

---

89 General Comment 29, above n 1, para 7. See, for example, the Concluding Observations of the Committee concerning: Armenia, UN Doc CCPR/C/79/Add.100 (1998), para 7; Colombia, UN Doc CCPR/C/79/Add.76 (1997), para 25; the Dominican Republic, UN Doc CCPR/C/79/Add.18 (1993), para 4; Gabon, UN Doc CCPR/C/79/Add.71 (1996), para 10; Israel, UN Doc CCPR/C/79/Add.93 (1998), para 11; Iraq, UN Doc CCPR/C/79/Add.84 (1997), para 9; Jordan, UN Doc CCPR/C/79/Add.35 (1994), para 6; Kyrgyzstan, UN Doc CCPR/CO/69/KGZ (2000), para 12; Mongolia, UN Doc CCPR/C/79/Add.120 (2000), para 14; Nepal UN Doc CCPR/C/79/Add.42 (1994), para 9; Russian Federation,

Through the intermediary of the UN Secretary-General, a derogating State must immediately inform other States parties to the ICCPR of the provisions from which it has derogated and the reasons for which it has done so. The Human Rights Committee has emphasized that notification should include full information about the measures taken and a clear explanation of the reasons for them, with full documentation attached concerning the relevant law.[90] The *Siracusa Principles* are even more detailed in setting out the requirements of a notification of derogation, stating that such notification must contain: (1) the provisions of the Covenant from which the State has derogated; (2) a copy of the proclamation of emergency, together with the constitutional provisions, legislation, or decrees governing the state of emergency in order to assist the States parties to appreciate the scope of the derogation; (3) the effective date of the imposition of the state of emergency and the period for which it has been proclaimed; (4) an explanation of the reasons which actuated the government's decision to derogate, including a brief description of the factual circumstances leading up to the proclamation of the state of emergency; and (5) a brief description of the anticipated effect of the derogation measures on the rights recognized by the Covenant, including copies of decrees derogating from these rights issued prior to the notification.[91] Explaining the rationale behind the need for detailed proclamations, the Committee has stated that this:[92]

> … is essential for the maintenance of the principles of legality and rule of law at times when they are most needed. When proclaiming a state of emergency with consequences that could entail derogation from any provision of the Covenant, States must act within their constitutional and other provisions of law that govern such proclamation and the exercise of emergency powers.

Article 4(3) requires a further communication on the date on which a State terminates such derogation.

Substantive Conditions

Article 4, paragraph 1, contains four substantive requirements applicable to the adoption by a State party of measures which derogate from the ICCPR: (1) the measures must be ones that are adopted during a 'time of public emergency which threatens the life of the nation'; (2) the derogating measures must be limited to those 'strictly required by the exigencies of the situation'; (3) the measures must not be 'inconsistent with [the State's] other obligations under international law';

UN Doc CCPR/C/79/Add.54 (1995), para 27; Uruguay, UN Doc CCPR/C/79/Add.90 (1998), para 8; and Zambia, UN Doc CCPR/C/79/Add.62 (1996), para 11.

90 General Comment 29, above n 1, paras 5, 16 and 17.

91 *Siracusa Principles*, above n 2, para 45.

92 General Comment 29, above n 1, para 2. See also the *Siracusa Principles*, above n 2, para 43.

and (4) they must not 'involve discrimination solely on the ground of race, colour, sex, language, religion or social origin'.

War or public emergency The ability under article 4 to derogate from certain rights is triggered only 'in a time of public emergency which threatens the life of the nation'. The Human Rights Committee has characterized such an emergency as being of an exceptional nature.[93] Not every disturbance or catastrophe qualifies as such, and the Committee has commented that even during an armed conflict, measures derogating from the ICCPR are allowed only if and to the extent that the situation constitutes a threat to the life of the nation.[94] Interpreting the comparable derogation provision in article 15 of the European Convention on Human Rights, the European Court of Human Rights has identified four criteria to determine whether any given situation amounts to 'a time of public emergency which threatens the life of the nation'. This list mirrors various aspects of General Comment 29 and the *Siracusa Principles*, although the European Court's itemization of these features is useful. The Court identified, in *Lawless v Ireland*, the following criteria:[95] (1) the situation in question should be a crisis or emergency that is actual or imminent;[96] (2) it must be exceptional, such that 'normal' measures are plainly inadequate;[97] (3) it must threaten the continuance of the organized life of the community;[98] and (4) it must affect the entire population of the State which is taking the derogating measures.[99]

On the latter point, early decisions of the European Court spoke of an emergency needing to affect the whole population, although it now appears to have been accepted that an emergency threatening the life of a nation might only materially affect one part of the nation at the time of the emergency.[100] This is consistent with the view expressed in the *Siracusa Principles* that the geographic scope of any derogating measure must be such as strictly necessary to deal with the threat to the life of the nation.[101] As to the question of an emergency constituting a threat to the continued existence of the community, the *Siracusa Principles* explain that this involves a threat to the physical integrity of the population, the political independence or territorial integrity of the State, or the existence or basic functioning of institutions indispensable to ensure and protect the rights recognized

93 General Comment 29, above n 1, para 2.

94 General Comment 29, above n 1, para 3.

95 *Lawless v Ireland*, above n 26, para 28. See also *The Greek Case* (1969) 12 *Yearbook of the European Court of Human Rights* 1, para 153.

96 Compare with: General Comment 29, above n 1, para 3; and the *Siracusa Principles*, above n 2, paras 40 and 54.

97 Compare with General Comment 29, above n 1, paras 2 and 4.

98 Compare with the *Siracusa Principles*, above n 2, para 39(b).

99 Compare with: General Comment 29, above n 1, para 4; and the *Siracusa Principles*, above n 2, para 39(a).

100 *Ireland* v *United Kingdom*, above n 20.

101 *Siracusa Principles*, above n 2, para 51.

in the Covenant.[102] They also explain that internal conflict or unrest that does not constitute a 'grave and imminent threat to the life of the nation' cannot justify derogations under article 4, and that economic difficulties cannot *per se* justify derogating measures.[103]

In light of the Committee's repeated emphasis upon the exceptional and temporary nature of derogating measures, which may continue only as long as the life of the nation concerned is *actually* threatened, it will be important for the derogating State to continually review the situation faced by it to ensure that the derogation lasts only as long as the state of emergency exists.[104] The *Siracusa Principles* call for such review to be independent and undertaken by the legislature of the State party concerned.[105] While this might assist to ensure a more objective assessment of the necessity of derogating measures, as opposed to one undertaken by the government which declares the state of emergency, it must be recognized that the extent to which this is possible may be hindered by the classified status of any information concerning the continuing or imminent nature of a threat to the life of the nation. Notwithstanding this, it is important to recall that General Comment 29 declares that the restoration of a state of normalcy, where full respect for the provisions of the ICCPR can again be secured, must be the predominant objective of a State party derogating from the Covenant.[106] While internal review is very important, it should be further recalled that the ultimate task of monitoring derogating measures and assessing their compliance with article 4 belongs to the Committee and, to facilitate this role, the General Comment has called on States parties to include in their periodic reports 'sufficient and precise information about their law and practice in the field of emergency powers'.[107]

Exigencies of the situation The extent to which a State derogates from any right must be limited 'to the extent strictly required by the exigencies of the situation'. Any derogating measure must therefore be both necessary and proportionate, principles which have been considered in more detail earlier in this chapter.[108] In practice, these requirements will act to ensure that no provision of the Covenant, however validly derogated from, will be entirely inapplicable to the behaviour of

102 *Siracusa Principles*, above n 2, para 39(b).

103 *Siracusa Principles*, above n 2, paras 40–41.

104 General Comment 29, above n 1, para 2. See also the *Siracusa Principles*, above n 2, paras 48–50.

105 *Siracusa Principles*, above n 2, para 55.

106 General Comment 29, above n 1, paras 1 and 2; *Siracusa Principles*, above n 2, para 48.

107 General Comment 29, above n 1, para 2.

108 General Comment 29, above n 1, paras 3–5; and *Siracusa Principles*, above n 2, para 51.

a State party.[109] Considering States parties' periodic reports, the Committee has expressed concern over insufficient attention being paid to these principles.[110]

States must, the Committee said in its General Comment 29, provide careful justification not only for their decision to proclaim a state of emergency but also for any specific measures based on such a proclamation, based on an objective assessment of the situation. If States purport to invoke the right to derogate from the Covenant during, for instance, a natural catastrophe, a mass demonstration including instances of violence, or a major industrial accident, they must be able to justify not only that such a situation constitutes a threat to the life of the nation, but also that all their measures derogating from the Covenant are strictly required by the exigencies of the situation.[111]

Fundamental to understanding the article 4 procedure, one must distinguish between measures capable of dealing with a crisis as might be permitted under the rights-specific limitation provisions of the Covenant on the one hand, and the exceptional measure of derogating from rights under article 4 and 'to the extent strictly required by the exigencies of the situation' on the other. Where a situation of crisis can be adequately addressed, or even partly addressed, by recourse to a rights-specific limitation provision, such recourse must be had and any action to derogate from the right(s) in question will be deemed to fall outside the exigencies of the situation and thus in violation of article 4(1).[112] In referring to the 1998 Conclusions and Recommendations of the Committee, for example, the Special Rapporteur on the promotion and protection of human rights and fundamental freedoms while countering terrorism stated in his 2007 mission report to Israel that:[113]

> ... recourse to derogations under article 4 must be temporary and exceptional in nature, and that the enunciation of certain rights within the International Covenant on Civil and Political Rights already provide for the proportionate limitation of rights as prescribed by law and necessary for the protection of national security or public order, including articles 12 (3), 19 (3) and 21, relating to the freedoms of movement and residence, opinion and expression, and peaceful assembly.

---

109 General Comment 29, above n 1, para 4.

110 See, for example, *Concluding Observations of the Human Rights Committee: Israel*, UN Doc CCPR/C/79/Add.93 (1998), para 11.

111 General Comment 29, above n 1, para 5.

112 *Siracusa Principles*, above n 2, para 53. See also General Comment 29, above n 1, para 4.

113 *Report of the Special Rapporteur on the promotion and protection of human rights and fundamental freedoms while countering terrorism, Martin Scheinin, Mission to Israel, including visit to occupied Palestinian Territory*, UN Doc A/HRC/6/17/Add.4 (2007), para 10.

Other international obligations Importantly, article 4(1) requires that any measure derogating from the ICCPR may not be inconsistent with the State party's other obligations under international law, whether based on treaty law, or customary international law. This principle is reflected in article 5(2) of the Covenant, according to which there may be no restriction upon or derogation from any fundamental rights recognized in other instruments on the pretext that the Covenant does not recognize such rights, or that it recognizes them to a lesser extent. It is a feature which has been important to the enumeration of the full list of non-derogable rights, as discussed earlier in this chapter, and the Human Rights Committee has emphasized that it is a requirement particularly relevant to the compliance of States with the rules of international humanitarian law during a state of emergency.[114]

Non-discrimination The final substantive condition, already discussed earlier in this chapter in the context of common features to the limitation or suspension of rights, is that any derogating measure must not involve discrimination.

114 General Comment 29, above n 1, para 9.

Chapter 4
Democratic and Civil Rights

Alex Conte

Various rights and freedoms fall within the ambit of democratic and civil rights. Strictly speaking, the entire Covenant enumerates civil and political rights, hence its name. For the purpose of this chapter, focus will be placed on nine provisions within the Covenant, assembled into the following categories: freedom of movement (articles 12 and 13); freedom of expression, thought, conscience and religion, and associated prohibitions against propaganda and incitement (articles 18, 19 and 20); freedom of assembly and association (articles 21 and 22); the right to be recognized as a person before the law (article 16); and electoral rights (article 25).

Freedom of Movement

Liberty of movement encompasses two sets of rights. First are the rights of persons within the territory of a State to move within the territory and choose their residence (article 12). Next are the rights of entry to and departure from a territory (expressed within both articles 12 and 13). There are permissible limitations upon these rights, set out in article 12(3), which must not nullify the *principle* of liberty of movement and are governed by the requirements of necessity and consistency with other rights recognized in the Covenant.

The Enjoyment of Article 12 and 13 Rights by Aliens

Article 13 applies to aliens alone, concerning their procedural rights in any expulsion proceedings against them. As to article 12, paragraph 1 of that article describes the rights therein as applying to those 'lawfully within the territory of a State'. In principle, citizens of a State are always lawfully within the territory of that State. The question of whether an alien is 'lawfully' within the territory of a State is a matter governed by domestic law, which may subject the entry of an alien to the territory of a State to restrictions, provided they are in compliance with the State's international obligations. If the answer is affirmative, then the provisions within article 12 will also apply to him or her. Once an alien is lawfully within a territory, then, his or her freedom of movement within the territory and right to leave that territory may only be restricted in accordance with article 12. Differences in treatment between aliens and nationals, or between different categories of aliens, need to be justified under article 12(3), which sets out the permissible bases upon which article 12 may be restricted (discussed below).[1]

In *Celepli v Sweden*, the Committee held that an alien who enters a State illegally, but whose status has been subsequently regularized, must be considered to be lawfully within the territory for the purposes of article 12. Celepli had arrived in Sweden, fleeing political persecution in Turkey in 1975, and obtained permission to stay in Sweden, although not by way of refugee status. Following the murder of a former member of the Workers Party of Kurdistan, suspicions of his involvement in terrorist activities arose, and an expulsion order against him and eight other Kurds was issued. The expulsion order was not, however, enforced as it was believed that the Kurds could be exposed to political persecution in Turkey in the event of their return. Instead, the Swedish authorities prescribed limitations and conditions concerning the Kurds' place of residence. The author claimed to be a victim of a violation of articles 12 and 13 of the Covenant. Sweden submitted that the author's claim under article 12 was incompatible with the provisions of the Covenant, since he could only be regarded as being 'lawfully within the territory of' Sweden to the extent that he complied with the restrictions imposed upon him. Sweden also successfully invoked the limitation within article 12(3), which provides that restrictions may be imposed upon the enjoyment of article 12 rights, if they are provided by law and necessary for the protection of national security and public order.[2]

Freedom of Movement within a Territory

Everyone lawfully within the territory of a State enjoys, within that territory, the right to move freely and to choose his or her place of residence.[3] The right to move freely relates to the whole territory of a State, including all parts of federal states. According to article 12(1), persons are entitled to move from one place to another and to establish themselves in a place of their choice. The enjoyment of this right must not be made dependent on any particular purpose or reason for the person wanting to move or to stay in a place. Any restrictions must be in conformity with article 12(3).

Non-interference with the freedom of movement In the context of freedom of movement within a country, the Committee addressed various concerns within General Comment 27. It criticized provisions requiring individuals to apply for permission to change their residence or to seek the approval of the local authorities of the place of destination, as well as delays in processing such written

1 *General Comment 15: The position of aliens under the Covenant*, UN Doc CCPR General Comment 15 (1986), para 8.

2 *Celepli v Sweden*, Communication 456/1991, UN Doc CCPR/C/51/D/456/1991 (1994), para 9.2.

3 Article 12(1).

applications.[4] The imposition of unlawful or arbitrary house arrest can likewise result in a violation of article 12(1), although such matters will normally be dealt with under article 9 of the Covenant.[5]

State duty to protect freedom of movement Article 12 encompasses an obligation upon States parties to refrain from interference with the liberty of movement, as well as an active duty to protect persons within their territory against private interference.[6] The Committee has emphasized the importance of the duty to protect in the context of the freedom of movement by women. It would be incompatible with article 12(1), the Committee said, for the right of a woman to move freely and to choose her residence to be made subject, by law or practice, to the decision of another person, including a relative.[7]

Displacement The right to reside in a place of one's choice includes protection against all forms of forced displacement. It also precludes preventing the entry or stay of persons in a defined part of the territory.[8] The case of *Mpandajila v Zaire* dealt with one such instance, where a group of parliamentarians in Zaire sent an open letter to President Mobutu. The letter was held by the Central Committee of the Mouvement Populaire de la Revolution to be improper both in form and content. The result was that their Party stripped them of their membership of parliament. Along with various other consequences, they were made subject to an 'administrative banning measure', the effect of which was to relocate them and their families to a different and distant region against their will. The Committee found this to be in violation of article 12(1).[9] *Mpaka-Nsusu v Zaire* dealt with comparable facts, where the author was banished to his village of origin for an indefinite period after submitting a proposal to the Government of Zaire requesting recognition of a second political party in Zaire.[10]

Restrictions on the Freedom of Movement

The freedom of movement and choice of residence (article 12(1)) and the right to leave any country (article 12(2)) are subject to the restrictions set out in paragraph 3.

4 *General Comment 27: Freedom of movement (Article 12)*, UN Doc CCPR/C/21/Rev.1/Add.9 (1999), para 17.

5 See: *Gorji-Dinka v Cameroon*, Communication 1134/2002, UN Doc CCPR/C/83/D/1134/2002 (2005), para 5.5; and *Madani v Algeria*, Communication 1172/2003, UN Doc CCPR/C/89/D/1172/2003 (2007), paras 8.5–8.6.

6 General Comment 27, above n 4, para 6.

7 Ibid.

8 General Comment 27, above n 4, para 7.

9 *Mpandajila v Zaire*, Communication 138/1983, UN Doc CCPR/C/27/D/138/1983 (1986), para 10.

10 *Mpaka-Nsusu v Zaire*, Communication 157/1983, UN Doc CCPR/C/27/D/157/1983 (1986), para 10. See also *Birhashwira/Tshisekedi v Zaire*, Communications 241/1987 and

This provision authorizes the State to restrict these rights only for the purpose of protecting national security, public order, public health or morals and the rights and freedoms of others. To be permissible, restrictions must be provided by law, must be necessary in a democratic society, and must be consistent with all other rights recognized in the Covenant.[11]

Various requirements must therefore be met by a party to ensure a valid restriction upon article 12(1) and (2) rights. The first is that any restriction must be one 'provided by law' which means that, when setting out the bases upon which restrictions might be applied, precise criteria must be used to prevent the conferring of an unfettered discretion on those charged with their execution.[12] The second requirement is that the restrictions must both serve the permitted purpose (protection of national security, public order, public health or morals or the rights and freedoms of others) and be *necessary* to achieve such protection. Intimately linked with this concept of necessity is that of proportionality: the restrictive measures must be appropriate to achieve their protective function; they must do so by the least intrusive means available; they must be measured against and proportionate with the interests to be protected; and they must not be so restrictive as to impair the essence of the rights within paragraphs 1 and 2.[13] The Committee has noted that these elements of proportionality must not solely exist within the legal framework permitting restrictions to be imposed, but must also be observed in the administrative and judicial application of such law.[14]

Finally, and once again borne out of the words of article 12(3), restrictions must be consistent with the other rights recognized in the ICCPR. Most commonly, this has impacted upon the practice of States restricting movement in contravention of the rights of equality and non-discrimination (engaging article 26 of the Covenant). In examining State reports, the Committee has on several occasions found that measures preventing women from moving freely or from leaving the country by requiring them to have the consent or the escort of a male person constitute a violation of article 12.[15]

Freedom of Movement between Territories

Two particular rights are considered under this heading: the freedom of every person to leave any country, including their own (article 12(2)); and the right to enter one's own country (article 12(4)).

242/1987, CCPR/C/37/D/241&242/1987 (1989), para 13.

11 General Comment 27, above n 4, paras 11, 12 and 18.

12 General Comment 27, above n 4, para 13.

13 General Comment 27, above n 4, paras 13 and 14.

14 General Comment 27, above n 4, para 15.

15 General Comment 27, above n 4, para 18.

The right to leave any country Article 12(2) covers the right of every person to travel abroad, as well as departure for permanent emigration. Every person is free to leave the territory of a State, whether or not he or she is lawfully in the territory of that State, and this freedom cannot be made dependent on any specific purpose or on the period of time the individual chooses to stay outside the country.[16] Equally, the right of the individual to determine the State of destination is part of the legal guarantee. In the context of aliens being expelled from a territory, such a person is likewise entitled to elect the State of destination, subject to the agreement of that State.

Since international travel usually requires documentation, in particular a passport, the right to leave a country must include the right to obtain the necessary travel documents. For this reason, the enjoyment of the rights guaranteed by article 12(2) necessarily imposes obligations both on the State of residence and on the State of nationality. The issuing of passports is normally incumbent on the State of nationality of the individual. Accordingly, refusal by a State to issue a passport or prolong its validity for a national residing abroad may be held to deprive the person of the right to leave the country of residence and to travel elsewhere, albeit that restrictions may apply by application of article 12(3) (discussed above),[17] including the confiscation of a passport as a condition of bail.[18] It is no justification for a State to claim that its national would be able to return to its territory without a passport.[19]

The Human Rights Committee has expressed concern over the particular practice of States parties in unnecessarily creating an array of obstacles that make it more difficult for a person to leave the country, in particular for their own nationals. By way of example, it identified rules and practices requiring persons to apply for special forms through which the proper application documents for the issuance of a passport can be obtained; the lack of access for applicants to the competent authorities and a lack of information regarding requirements; the need for supportive statements from employers or family members; exact description of the travel route; issuance of passports only on payment of high fees substantially exceeding the cost of the service rendered by the administration; unreasonable delays in the issuance of travel documents; restrictions on family

16 General Comment 27, above n 4, para 8.

17 *Montero v Uruguay*, Communication 106/1981, UN Doc CCPR/C/18/D/106/1981 (1983), para 9.4. See also: *Lichtensztejn v Uruguay*, Communication 77/1980, UN Doc CCPR/C/18/D/77/1980 (1983), para 6.1; *Nunez v Uruguay*, Communication 108/1981, UN Doc CCPR/C/19/D/108/1981 (1983), para 9.3; *Kalenga v Zambia*, Communication 326/1988, UN Doc CCPR/C/48/D/326/1988 (1993), para 6.4; *El Ghar v Libyan Arab Jamahiriya*, Communication 1107/2002, UN Doc CCPR/C/82/D/1107/2002 (2004), para 7.3; and *El Dernawi v Libyan Arab Jamahiriya*, Communication 1143/2002, UN Doc CCPR/C/90/D/1143/2002 (2007), para 6.2.

18 *De Morais v Angola*, Communication 1128/2002, UN Doc CCPR/C/83/D/1128/2002 (2005), para 6.9.

19 General Comment 27, above n 4, para 9.

members travelling together; requirement of a repatriation deposit or a return ticket; requirement of an invitation from the State of destination or from people living there; harassment of applicants, for example by physical intimidation, arrest, loss of employment or expulsion of their children from school or university; and refusal, in one case, to issue a passport because the applicant is said to harm the good name of the country.[20]

Peltonen v Finland concerned a refusal to issue a passport to a person that had avoided military service. The Committee's majority considered that this was a reasonable legislative requirement.[21] Committee member Bertil Wennergren, however, considered that it was inappropriate to interpret article 12(3) as entitling a State party to do so since this would allow States parties to abuse the refusal of a passport as a means of exerting pressure on conscripts, so as to induce them to perform military service. This was not necessary, in the member's view, either for the protection of national security, public order or public morals, and would be entirely incompatible with the object and purpose of article 12(3). He was therefore of the opinion that Finland had violated article 12(2) by refusing a passport to the author.

The right to enter one's own country This right also has various facets. To begin with, it recognizes the special relationship of a person with his or her country. It implies the right to remain in one's own country and includes not only the right to return after having left one's own country, but may also entitle a person to come to the country for the first time if he or she was born outside their country of nationality. It also implies prohibition of enforced population transfers or mass expulsions to other countries.[22] It is important to note that article 12(4) does not distinguish between nationals and aliens. The right belongs to all persons within and outside their own country, guaranteeing that entrance into one's own country will not be arbitrarily withheld.[23] Indeed, the right to return is of the utmost importance for refugees seeking voluntary repatriation.

In a classic example of the application of article 12(4), the author in *Vaca v Colombia* was a practising trial lawyer in the city of Medellín and was the legal adviser in the region to several trade unions and people's organizations. From 1980 he was a member of the various commissions set up by the Government to find a solution to the social and labour conflicts and the violence in the region, until his exile in 1988 because of his professional activities on behalf of the unions. Colombia proposed that it could not be held responsible for the loss of rights which may be indirectly affected as a result of violent acts. Taking the view that the

20 General Comment 27, above n 4, para 17.

21 *Peltonen v Finland*, Communication 492/1992, UN Doc CCPR/C/51/D/492/1992 (1994), para 8.4.

22 General Comment 27, above n 4, para 19.

23 *Stewart v Canada*, Communication 538/1993, UN Doc CCPR/C/58/D/538/1993 (1996), para 12.10.

right to security of person (article 9) was violated, and that no effective domestic remedies were provided to allow the author to return from involuntary exile in safety, the Committee also concluded that Colombia had violated article 12(4) by failing to ensure that the author had a right to remain in, return to, and reside in his own country.[24]

A difficult aspect of the right under article 12(4) concerns the meaning of the term 'own country'. The term is broader than the concept of one's nationality, and the Committee has taken the view that the language of article 12(4) embraces any individual who, because of his or her special ties to or claims in relation to a given country, cannot be considered to be a mere alien.[25] Consideration to this was given in *Stewart v Canada*, where the author was born in Scotland in 1960 but, at the age of seven, emigrated to Canada with his family. The author lived with his mother and younger brother, and himself had two young twin children. He claimed to consider himself a Canadian citizen and that it was only when he was contacted by immigration officials following a criminal conviction that he realized that, legally, he was only a permanent resident, as his parents had never requested Canadian citizenship for him during his youth. Amongst other claims within his communication to the Committee, he alleged violation of article 12(4) on the basis that, for all intents and purposes, Canada was his home country. In interpreting article 12(4), the Committee took the view that, in seeking to understand the meaning of article 12(4), account must also be had of the language of article 13 of the Covenant.

This position gives rise to two possibilities. The first involves the concept of 'his own country' applying to nationals of the country *or* individuals who, while not nationals in a formal sense, are also not aliens within the meaning of article 13. The Committee gave two examples of the latter situation: nationals of a country who have there been stripped of their nationality in violation of international law; or individuals whose country of nationality has been incorporated into or transferred to another national entity whose nationality is being denied them.[26] The second possibility in the interpretation of articles 12(4) and 13 involves the situation where, as in *Stewart*, a person enters a given State under that State's immigration laws, and whether that person can regard that State as 'his own country' when he or she has not acquired its nationality and continues to retain the nationality of his or her country of origin. Here, the Committee envisaged that the answer could possibly be positive, if the country of immigration placed unreasonable impediments on acquiring nationality by new immigrants. When, however, the country of immigration facilitates acquiring its nationality, and the immigrant refrains from doing so (either by choice or by committing acts that will disqualify him from acquiring that nationality), the country of immigration

---

24 *Vaca v Colombia*, Communication 859/1999, UN Doc CCPR/C/74/D/859/1999 (2002), para 7.4.

25 General Comment 27, above n 4, para 20.

26 *Stewart v Canada*, above n 23, paras 12.3–12.4.

does not become 'his own country' within the meaning of article 12(4) of the Covenant.[27] The Committee concluded:[28]

> Mr Stewart is a British national both by birth and by virtue of the nationality of his parents. While he has lived in Canada for most of his life he never applied for Canadian nationality. It is true that his criminal record might have kept him from acquiring Canadian nationality by the time he was old enough to do so on his own. The fact is, however, that he never attempted to acquire such nationality. Furthermore, even had he applied and been denied nationality because of his criminal record, this disability was of his own making. It cannot be said that Canada's immigration legislation is arbitrary or unreasonable in denying Canadian nationality to individuals who have criminal records.

The final aspect of article 12(4) is that it does not permit the *arbitrary* denial of entry into one's own country. While there is no explanation within article 12 of the basis upon which any denial of entry *might* be made, the Committee has interpreted this to mean that even interference provided for by law should be in accordance with the provisions, aims and objectives of the Covenant and should be, in any event, reasonable in the particular circumstances.[29] It has expressed the view that there would be few, if any, circumstances in which deprivation of the right to enter one's own country could be reasonable.[30]

Expulsion of Aliens

By virtue of article 2(1) of the ICCPR, each State party has an obligation to ensure that the rights in the Covenant are applied 'to all individuals within its territory and subject to its jurisdiction'. In general terms therefore, excluding permissible restrictions attaching to certain rights and freedoms, the rights set out in the Covenant apply to everyone within a State party's territory, irrespective of the person's nationality or statelessness.[31] As discussed earlier, this is reflected within the views and comments of the Human Rights Committee that, once an alien is lawfully within the territory of a State party, then his or her freedom of movement, and freedom to leave the country, may only be restricted in accordance with article 12(3).

The principal concern of article 13 of the Covenant is the basis upon which aliens may be removed from the territory of a State party. As aliens, such persons

27 Ibid, para 12.5.

28 Ibid, para 12.6. See also: *Toala et al v New Zealand*, Communication 675/1995, UN Doc CCPR/C/70/D/675/1995 (2000), para 11.5; and *Madafferi v Australia*, Communication 1011/2001, UN Doc CCPR/C/81/D/1011/2001 (2004), para 9.6.

29 General Comment 27, above n 4, para 21.

30 Ibid.

31 General Comment 15, above n 1, para 1.

may be the subject of refugee status applications, extradition claims or other bases upon which their removal from a territory might be effected. The possibility of removal of those persons places upon them an inherent imbalance of rights. Article 13 seeks to redress that imbalance by ensuring that removal is achieved in a manner having respect for the human dignity of those subject to expulsion orders, by providing that:

> Article 13
> An alien lawfully in the territory of a State Party to the present Covenant may be expelled therefrom only in pursuance of a decision reached in accordance with law and shall, except where compelling reasons of national security otherwise require, be allowed to submit the reasons against his expulsion and to have his case reviewed by, and be represented for the purpose before, the competent authority or a person or persons especially designated by the competent authority.

The wording of article 13 is such that it expresses the rights therein to apply to those that might be 'expelled' from a territory. The Committee has made it clear that, despite this wording, the rights apply equally to any procedures aimed at the obligatory departure of an alien, whether or not described within municipal law as 'expulsion'.[32] Furthermore, the combined effect of article 12(1), (2) and (4) and article 13 is such, according to General Comment 15, that an alien who is expelled must normally be allowed to leave for any country that accepts to take him or her, including his or her own country.[33] The Committee has also noted that national legal measures for the expulsion of aliens should be applied in good faith and in a manner that observes the various requirements of States under the Covenant, such as equality and non-discrimination before the law.[34] Article 13 should thus be read in conjunction with article 26 (discrimination), and articles 17 and 23 (interference with family).[35] Removal orders have often been challenged before the Human Rights Committee through allegations of violation of articles 13, 17, 23 and 26 combined.[36]

Aliens lawfully in the territory of a State party The starting point in the examination of this provision is to acknowledge that the rights contained within it are only applicable to aliens 'lawfully' in the territory of a State party. This means that illegal entrants, and aliens that have stayed longer than the law or their permit allows, are not afforded protection under article 13.[37] However, if the legality of

32 General Comment 15, above n 1, para 9.

33 General Comment 15, above n 1, para 9.

34 General Comment 15, above n 1, paras 9 and 10.

35 See Chapters 8 and 11.

36 See, for example: *Stewart v Canada*, above n 23; and *Truong v Canada*, Communication 743/1997, UN Doc CCPR/C/77/D/743/1997 (2003).

37 General Comment 15, above n 1, para 9.

an alien's entry or stay is in dispute, any decision on this point leading to his or her expulsion or deportation ought to be taken in accordance with article 13.[38]

Procedure versus substance It should also be clear from the wording of article 13 that the provision only regulates the procedure, and not the substantive grounds, for expulsion. Article 13 lays down a number of conditions that must be complied with when it expels an alien from its territory. The reference within article 13 of expulsion under a decision reached 'in accordance with the law' might be seen to imply a jurisdiction on the part of the Committee to consider the merits of each case. That position, however, was rejected in *Maroufidou v Sweden*, where the Committee said:[39]

> The Committee takes the view that the interpretation of domestic law is essentially a matter for the courts and authorities of the State party concerned. It is not within the powers or functions of the Committee to evaluate whether the competent authorities of the State party in question have interpreted and applied the domestic law correctly in the case before it under the Optional Protocol, unless it is established that they have not interpreted and applied it in good faith or that it is evident that there has been an abuse of power.

Having said this, a number of qualifications apply to the statement of the Committee. By only permitting expulsion orders carried out 'in pursuance of a decision reached in accordance with law', its purpose is clearly to prevent arbitrary expulsions. The Committee has accordingly taken the view that the procedural guarantees under article 13 should be understood as incorporating the notions of due process and fair trial, as reflected in article 14, including the right to submit reasons against removal, and to have such submissions reviewed by a competent authority, entailing a possibility to comment on the material presented to that authority.[40] Furthermore, it entitles each alien to a decision made on the basis of his or her own particular case and provides the right to have the decision reviewed by a competent authority or someone designated by it. Article 13 would therefore not be satisfied with laws or decisions providing for collective or mass expulsions.

The Committee has expressed a stronger position concerning appeal against expulsion and the entitlement to review such decisions. Here, it has commented that the right to have appeals and review considered by a competent authority may

---

38 Ibid.

39 *Maroufidou v Sweden*, Communication 58/1979, UN Doc CCPR/C/12/D/58/1979 (1981), para 10.1.

40 *General Comment 32: Article 14: Right to equality before courts and tribunals and to a fair trial*, UN Doc CCPR/C/GC/32 (2007), para 62. See, for example, *Ahani v Canada*, Communication 1051/2002, UN Doc CCPR/C/80/D/1051/2002 (2004), paras 10.8–10.9. On the right to a fair hearing, see Chapter 6.

only be departed from when 'compelling reasons of national security' so require.[41] The Committee has been less concerned with restrictions pertaining to the process of Ministerial decision-making, so long as proper avenues of review or appeal are retained.[42]

Extradition The case of *Ng v Canada*[43] involved the interesting question of whether article 13, or indeed the Covenant as a whole, applied to extradition procedures. Following an earlier decision on admissibility,[44] the majority of the Committee took the view that extradition was a matter outside the scope of application of the ICCPR. Dissenting, Francisco Urbina asserted that this was remiss, and even dangerous, as far as the full enjoyment of the rights set forth in the Covenant was concerned. Consistent with the Committee's consideration of the *travaux préparatoires* in *Kindler v Canada*, Committee member Urbina acknowledged that extradition did not fit within the legal situation defined in article 13. The essential difference lay, in his opinion, in the fact that article 13 refers exclusively to the expulsion of 'an alien lawfully in the territory of a State party'. Extradition is a kind of 'expulsion' that goes beyond what is contemplated in the rule. Firstly, extradition is a specific procedure, whereas the rule laid down in article 13 is of a general nature. Secondly, whereas expulsion constitutes a unilateral decision by a State (grounded on reasons that lie exclusively within the competence of that State), extradition constitutes an act based upon a request by another State. Thirdly, the rule in article 13 relates exclusively to aliens who are in the territory of a State party to the Covenant, whereas extradition may relate both to aliens and to nationals. Fourthly, the rule in article 13 relates to persons who are lawfully in the territory of a country. In the case of extradition, the individuals against whom the proceedings are initiated will not necessarily be lawfully within the jurisdiction of a country. Notwithstanding this analysis, the member did not see that this precluded consideration of extradition proceedings under other provisions of the Covenant:[45]

> Although extradition cannot be considered to be a kind of expulsion within the meaning of article 13 of the Covenant, this does not imply that it is excluded from the scope of the Covenant. Extradition must be strictly adapted in all cases to the rules laid down in the Covenant. Thus the extradition proceedings must follow the rules of due process as required by article 14 and, furthermore, their

41 General Comment 15, above n 1, para 10.

42 *Karker v France*, Communication 833/1998, UN Doc CCPR/C/70/D/833/1998 (2000), para 9.3.

43 *Ng v Canada*, Communication 469/1991, UN Doc CCPR/C/49/D/469/1991 (1994).

44 *Kindler v Canada*, Communication 470/1991, UN Doc CCPR/C/48/D/470/1991 (1993), paras 6.1–6.6.

45 At para 3 of his individual opinion.

> consequences must not entail a violation of any other provision. Therefore, a State cannot allege that extradition is not covered by the Covenant in order to evade the responsibility that would devolve upon it for the possible absence of protection of the possible victim in a foreign jurisdiction.

The Committee has subsequently determined that extradition does *not* fall outside the protection of the Covenant but that, to the contrary, several provisions (including articles 6, 7, 9 and 13) are necessarily applicable to extradition.[46]

Kidnapping The unlawful kidnapping and removal of the author by American authorities in Ecuador, with the assistance of Ecuadorian police, was the subject of consideration in *García v Ecuador*. While walking with his wife in the reception area of their hotel, the author was surrounded by ten armed men, reportedly Ecuadorian police officers acting on behalf of Interpol and the United States Drug Enforcement Agency. The author asked to consult with a lawyer or to speak with the Colombian Consul at Guayaquil, but his request was turned down. Instead, he was immediately made to board a plane bound for the United States. The author submitted that he never committed a drug-related offence, and argued that the United States authorities decided not to follow the formal extradition procedures under the United States-Ecuador Extradition Treaty, since the possibility of obtaining an extradition order by an Ecuadorian judge would have been remote. Ecuador did not seek to refute the author's allegations and conceded that his removal from Ecuadorian jurisdiction suffered from irregularities, resulting in a finding of a violation of article 13.[47]

Freedom of Expression, Thought, Conscience and Religion

The freedom of every person to exercise their own mind in the manner they choose and to express the resulting views and beliefs has been a stated flagship of Western democracies, but a feature of human rights that has caused much controversy and inconsistent application within all societies. Such freedom has the clear ability, in a number of ways more than other rights, to impact upon the natural tension between the interests of the individual and the society within which he or she lives. This is evident through the mix of rights and duties set out within articles 18 to 20 inclusive.

---

46 See, for example, *Everett v Spain*, Communication 961/2000, UN Doc CCPR/C/81/D/961/2000 (2004), para 6.4.

47 *García v Ecuador*, Communication 319/1988, UN Doc CCPR/C/43/D/319/1988 (1991), para 6.2.

Freedom of Thought, Conscience and Religion

Freedom of thought, conscience and religion, which includes the freedom to hold beliefs, is stated by the Human Rights Committee to be far-reaching and profound.[48] The overriding concern of article 18 is with the freedom of religion and potential impediments upon exercise of it. The balance of the article addresses the freedom of thought and conscience. The Committee has explained that article 18 does not permit any limitation whatsoever on freedom of thought and conscience or on the freedom to have or adopt a religion or belief of one's choice, whereas the right to *manifest* one's religion or beliefs may be subject to certain limitations under paragraph 3 (discussed below).[49] By combination of articles 18(2) and 17 (privacy), no one can be compelled to reveal his or her thoughts and beliefs. Article 18 of the ICCPR provides as follows:

> Article 18
> 1. Everyone shall have the right to freedom of thought, conscience and religion. This right shall include freedom to have or to adopt a religion or belief of his choice, and freedom, either individually or in community with others and in public or private, to manifest his religion or belief in worship, observance, practice and teaching.
> 2. No one shall be subject to coercion which would impair his freedom to have or to adopt a religion or belief of his choice.
> 3. Freedom to manifest one's religion or beliefs may be subject only to such limitations as are prescribed by law and are necessary to protect public safety, order, health, or morals or the fundamental rights and freedoms of others.
> 4. The States Parties to the present Covenant undertake to have respect for the liberty of parents and, when applicable, legal guardians to ensure the religious and moral education of their children in conformity with their own convictions.

The freedom of religion and belief has wide application. It protects theistic, non-theistic and atheistic beliefs, as well as the right not to profess any religion or belief.[50] Likewise, the terms 'religion' and 'belief' have been broadly construed so as not to limit themselves to traditional religions or to religions and beliefs with institutional characteristics or practices that are similar to traditional religions.[51]

---

48 *General Comment 22: The right to freedom of thought, conscience and religion (Art 18)*, UN Doc CCPR General Comment 22 (1993), para 1.

49 See *Malakhovsky and Pikul v Belarus*, Communication 1207/2003, UN Doc CCPR/C/84/D/1207/2003 (2005), para 7.2.

50 General Comment 22, above n 48, para 2.

51 Ibid.

That approach makes perfect sense, since it is often the newly established or minority religions and beliefs that are the subject of hostility on the part of the predominant religious or secular community.

Manifestation of religion or belief Article 18(1) includes the right to manifest one's religion or beliefs. This entails the right to do so through 'worship, observance, practice and teaching' and either 'individually or in community with others and in public or private', encompassing a broad range of acts.[52] The concept of worship extends to ritual and ceremonial acts giving direct expression to belief, as well as various practices integral to such acts, including the building of places of worship, the use of ritual formulae and objects, the display of symbols, and the observance of holidays and days of rest. The observance and practice of religion or belief may include not only ceremonial acts but also such customs as the observance of dietary regulations, the wearing of distinctive clothing or head coverings, participation in rituals associated with certain stages of life, and the use of a particular language customarily spoken by a group.[53] The practice and teaching of religion or belief includes acts integral to the conduct by religious groups of their basic affairs, such as the freedom to choose their religious leaders, priests and teachers, the freedom to establish seminaries or religious schools, and the freedom to prepare and distribute religious texts or publications.[54] The Committee has observed that, for numerous religions, it is a central tenet to spread knowledge, propagate their beliefs to others, and provide assistance to others.[55]

In *Boodoo v Trinidad and Tobago*, the author had been forbidden from wearing a beard and from worshipping at religious services, and his prayer books were taken from him. In finding a violation of article 18, the Committee reaffirmed that the freedom to manifest religion or belief in worship, observance, practice and teaching encompasses a broad range of acts and that the concept of worship extends to ritual and ceremonial acts giving expression to belief, as well as various practices integral to such acts.[56] While the Committee's decision in this case, and its General Comment 22, refer to article 18 as protecting acts which are *integral* to the religion, the examples it provides appear to be more inclusive than the approach taken by the European Court of Human Rights, namely that only those

52 Ibid, para 4.

53 On the wearing of the *hijab*, for example, see *Hudoyberganova v Uzbekistan*, Communication 931/2000, UN Doc CCPR/C/82/D/931/2000 (2004), para 6.2.

54 See, for example, *Malakhovsky and Pikul v Belarus*, above n 49, para 7.2.

55 *Sisters of the Holy Cross of the Third Order of Saint Francis in Menzingen of Sri Lanka v Sri Lanka*, Communication 1249/2004, UN Doc CCPR/C/85/D/1249/2004 (2005), para 7.2.

56 *Boodoo v Trinidad and Tobago*, Communication 721/1996, UN Doc CCPR/C/74/D/721/1996 (2002), para 6.6.

manifestations which form a *necessary* part of the religion or belief are protected under article 9 of the European Convention on Human Rights.[57]

In 1990, the Canadian government revised the Royal Canadian Mounted Police (RCMP) regulations allowing the Commissioner to 'exempt any member from wearing any item of the significant uniform … on the basis of the member's religious beliefs'. Subsequently, one Khalsa Sikh officer was authorized to substitute turbans for the traditional wide brimmed 'mountie' stetson and forage cap. It was claimed before the Human Rights Committee that the Commissioner was prohibited from allowing the wearing of religious symbols as part of the RCMP uniform. The authors, members of an organization whose goal was to maintain tradition within the RCMP, claimed violation of their rights under article 18 on the basis that the subject of their complaint introduced a denominational face to the most visible State agency of Canada. The Committee took the view that the authors had failed to show how the enjoyment of their rights under the Covenant was affected by allowing Khalsa Sikh officers to wear religious symbols.[58]

Also unsuccessful was a communication brought by members and plenipotentiaries of the 'Assembly of the Church of the Universe', whose beliefs and practices, according to the authors, necessarily involved the care, cultivation, possession, distribution, maintenance, integrity and worship of the 'Sacrament' of the Church, generally known under the designation cannabis sativa or marijuana. The worship and distribution of a narcotic drug was dismissed as being protected, the Committee making it clear that this could not conceivably be brought within the scope of article 18 of the Covenant.[59] The Committee readily dismissed a claim that article 18 protects the right to manifest one's conscience by refusing to pay taxes on grounds of conscientious objection, stating that this clearly fell outside the scope of protection of this article.[60]

Limitations Restrictions upon the manifestation of religion or belief are permitted under article 18(3). Limitations must be prescribed by law, and necessary to protect 'public safety, order, health, or morals or the fundamental rights and freedoms of others'. They must not be applied in an arbitrary manner, nor in a way that vitiates the rights within article 18(1). As it has for all limitations, the Committee

57 See, for example: *Arrowsmith v United Kingdom* (1978) European Commission No 7050/75; *Kalaç v Turkey* [1997] ECHR 37; and *Stedman v United Kingdom* [1997] ECHR 178.

58 *Riley et al v Canada*, Communication 1048/2002, UN Doc CCPR/C/74/D/1048/2002 (2002), para 4.2.

59 *M.A.B., W.A.T. and J.-A.Y.T. v Canada*, Communication 570/1993, UN Doc CCPR/C/50/D/570/1993 (1994), para 4.2. See also *Prince v South Africa*, Communication 1474/2006, UN Doc CCPR/C/91/D/1474/2006 (2007), para 7.2, concerning the use of cannabis use as an alleged manifestation of the Rastafari religion.

60 *J v K and CMG v K-S v The Netherlands*, Communication 483/1991, CCPR/C/45/D/483/1991 (1992), para 4.2.

has also stated that limitations under paragraph 3 must be rationally connected to the permitted objectives of the limitations and implemented in a proportionate manner.[61]

One of the purposes for which limitations may be placed upon the right to manifest one's religion or belief is for the protection of morals. In this regard, the Committee has noted that the concept of morals derives from many social, philosophical and religious traditions and that, consequently, limitations on the freedom to manifest a religion or belief for the purpose of protecting morals must be based on principles not deriving exclusively from a single tradition.[62] In the case of persons already subject to legitimate constraints, such as prisoners, the enjoyment of their rights to manifest their religion or belief must continue to the fullest extent compatible with the specific nature of the constraint.[63]

The Committee considered the question of preconditions to the registration of a religious association in *Malakhovsky and Pikul v Belarus*. The condition in question meant that a religious association's right to carry out its religious activities was predicated on it having the use of premises which satisfy public health and safety standards, including certain health and fire safety standards, and was found to be a limitation which was necessary for public safety, and proportionate to this need.[64]

Coercion Within the terms of article 18(2), the freedom to 'have or adopt' a religion or belief entails the right to retain one's religion or belief; the right to replace one's current religion or belief with another; or to adopt atheistic views.[65] Most significantly, it prohibits coercion that would impair the ability to have or adopt a religion or belief. This applies to all modes of coercion by the State, including the use or threat of physical force, or the use or threat of penal sanctions, to compel believers or non-believers to adhere to religious beliefs, or to recant their religion or belief, or to convert. Policies or practices having the same intention or effect are similarly inconsistent with article 18(2) including, for example, those restricting access to education, medical care, employment or the rights guaranteed by article 25 (electoral rights) and other provisions of the Covenant.[66] Application by Korea of an 'oath of law-abidance system' was found to have been applied in discriminatory fashion with a view to alter the political opinion of an inmate by offering inducements of preferential treatment within prison and improved possibilities of parole. The Committee considered that this violated both articles

61 General Comment 22, above n 48, para 8.

62 Ibid.

63 Ibid.

64 *Malakhovsky and Pikul v Belarus*, above n 49, para 7.4.

65 General Comment 22, above n 48, para 5.

66 Ibid.

18(1) and 19(1).[67] Coercive conduct on the part of an individual, rather than the State, would not amount to a violation of article 18 where the State is willing and able to protect the threatened person.[68]

Conscientious objectors The issue of conscientious objectors to military service has been dealt with in a number of communications before the Committee. In *LTK v Finland*, a Finnish citizen claimed to be a victim of a breach by Finland of articles 18 and 19 of the Covenant, claiming that his status as a conscientious objector to military service had not been recognized. The author informed the competent authorities that, due to serious moral considerations based on his ethical convictions, he was unable to perform military service, and offered to do some alternative form of service. The Military Service Examining Board decided that it had not been proved that serious moral considerations based on an ethical conviction prevented the author from performing armed or unarmed military service and ordered that he should perform armed service. Rejecting the author's claim, the Human Rights Committee observed that the ICCPR does not provide for the right to conscientious objection, and could not be construed as implying that right.[69] In its General Comment five years later, however, the Committee took a more liberal approach and summarized the position as follows:[70]

> Many individuals have claimed the right to refuse to perform military service (conscientious objection) on the basis that such right derives from their freedoms under article 18. In response to such claims, a growing number of States have in their laws exempted from compulsory military service citizens who genuinely hold religious or other beliefs that forbid the performance of military service and replaced it with alternative national service. The Covenant does not explicitly refer to a right to conscientious objection, *but the Committee believes that such a right can be derived from article 18, inasmuch as the obligation to use lethal force may seriously conflict with the freedom of conscience and the right to manifest one's religion or belief.* When this right is recognized by law or practice, there shall be no differentiation among conscientious objectors on the basis of the nature of their particular beliefs; likewise, there shall be no discrimination against conscientious objectors because they have failed to perform military service. [emphasis added]

67 *Kang v Republic of Korea*, Communication 878/1999, UN Doc CCPR/C/78/D/878/1999 (2003), para 7.2.

68 *Khan v Canada*, Communication 1302/2004, UN Doc CCPR/C/87/D/1302/2004 (2006), para 5.6.

69 *LTK v Finland*, Communication 185/1984, UN Doc CCPR/C/25/D/185/1984 (1985), para 5.2. For discussion on the content and effect of article 8(3)(c)(ii) of the Covenant, see Chapter 5.

70 General Comment 22, above n 48, para 11.

The rationale behind the Committee's apparent shift in position is not entirely clear, but it does reflect a pattern of constant jurisprudence since *LTK v Finland*. In *Brinkhof v The Netherlands*, for example, the author, a conscientious objector to both military service and substitute civilian service, did not report for his military service. He was arrested and brought to the military barracks, where he refused to obey orders on the basis of his pacifist convictions. He was subsequently found guilty of violating articles 23 and 114 of the Military Penal Code and article 27 of the Penal Code. The author alleged a violation of article 18, and also of article 26 (discrimination), on the grounds that, whereas conscientious objectors could be prosecuted under the Military Penal Code, Jehovah's Witnesses were exempt from such prosecution. The Committee took the view that the exemption of only one group of conscientious objectors (Jehovah's Witnesses) and the inapplicability of exemption for all others could not be considered reasonable. However, it also considered that the author had failed to show that his particular convictions as a pacifist were incompatible with the system of substitute service in the Netherlands or that the privileged treatment accorded to Jehovah's Witnesses adversely affected his own rights as a conscientious objector.[71] The decision appears to introduce the notion of potential incompatibility between an individual's beliefs and military service, rather than focusing on a specific implied right to conscientious objection.[72] It has likewise observed that it is in principle possible, and in practice common, to conceive alternatives to compulsory military service that do not erode the basis of the principle of universal conscription but render equivalent social good and make equivalent demands on the individual, eliminating unfair disparities between those engaged in compulsory military service and those in alternative service.[73]

Religious studies in schools The scope of article 18 is added to by paragraph 4, guaranteeing parents and guardians the right to determine the religious and moral education of their children, in conformity with their own convictions. A challenge to the ability of a State to include religious studies at school was made in *Hartikainen v Finland*. The author claimed that the effect of the School System Act of Finland was that, since the textbooks used for classes on the history of religion and ethics had been written by Christians, such classes were unavoidably religious in nature. The Committee did not consider, however, that instruction in the study of the history of religion and ethics was in itself incompatible with article 18(4), so long as this was given in a neutral and objective way.[74] In any event, paragraph 6 of the

71 *Brinkhof v The Netherlands*, Communication 402/1990, UN Doc CCPR/C/48/D/402/1990 (1993), para 9.3.

72 See also *Westerman v The Netherlands*, Communication 682/1996, UN Doc CCPR/C/67/D/682/1996 (1999), para 9.5.

73 See, for example, *Yoon and Choi v Republic of Korea*, Communications 1321/2004 and 1322/2004, UN Doc CCPR/C/88/D/1321-1322/2004 (2006), para 8.4.

74 *Hartikainen v Finland*, Communication 40/1978, UN Doc CCPR/C/12/D/40/1978 (1981), para 10.4.

School System Act expressly permitted any parents or guardians who did not wish their children to be given either religious instruction or instruction in the study of the history of religions and ethics to obtain exemption by arranging for them to receive comparable instruction outside of school.

At the same time, however, the Committee has said that education that includes instruction in a particular religion or belief is inconsistent with article 18(4), unless provision is made for non-discriminatory exemptions or alternatives that would accommodate the wishes of parents and guardians.[75] The plurality of acceptable arrangements in the relationship between State and religion also relates to education. In some countries, all forms of religious instruction or observance are prohibited in public schools, and religious education, protected under article 18(4), therefore takes place either outside school hours or in private schools. In some other countries there is religious education in the official or majority religion in public schools, with provision for full exemption for adherents of other religions and non-religious persons. In a third group of countries instruction in several or even all religions is offered, on the basis of demand, within the public system of education. A fourth arrangement is the inclusion in public school curricula of neutral and objective instruction in the general history of religions and ethics. All these arrangements allow for compliance with the Covenant.[76]

Divorce and custody In *LESK v The Netherlands*, the author submitted a communication alleging that her right to freedom of expression under article 19, as well as her right to freedom of conviction and religion under article 18, had been violated because the Netherlands courts held that her marriage had irrevocably broken down on account of the spouses' diverging convictions of life. The argument was dismissed as failing to substantiate any violation of article 18 or 19.[77]

PS v Denmark involved child custody issues. During divorce and custody proceedings between the author and his wife, a temporary agreement was concluded whereby the author's wife held custody of their son and the author had certain rights of access. However, after discovering that the author had converted to the faith of Jehovah's Witnesses, and that he had taken his son to a rally of Jehovah's Witnesses, authorities ordered that he had to refrain from teaching the faith to his son on the basis that Danish law provided the custodial parent with the ability to decide on the child's religious education. Following a complaint by the author, the Parliamentary Ombudsman accepted the position of the administrative authorities, although the authorities were requested to define the conditions more precisely. The author claimed that the Ombudsman's decision, in conjunction with the administrative decisions in his case, violated his rights under article 18

75 General Comment 22, above n 48, para 6.

76 See *Waldman v Canada*, Communication 694/1996, UN Doc CCPR/C/67/D/694/1996 (1999), individual opinion (concurring) of Martin Scheinin, para 2.

77 *LESK v The Netherlands*, Communication 381/1989, UN Doc CCPR/C/45/D/381/1989 (1992), para 5.3.

of the Covenant. The Committee dismissed the communication for failure to exhaust domestic remedies, although there was disagreement as to whether further remedies were in fact available.[78]

The Right to Hold Opinions

The right to hold opinions is guaranteed under article 19(1), without interference and without exception. It should be noted that the limiting provision in article 19(3) is expressed as applying only to paragraph 2 (freedom of expression).

Expression of political opinions In *Mpandajila v Zaire*, a group of parliamentarians in Zaire sent an open letter to the President of Zaire, which was subsequently held by the Central Committee of the Government to be improper in form and content. Along with various other consequences, their Party stripped them of their membership of parliament. The Committee found that, in violation of article 19(1), the parliamentarians had been punished solely because of their opinions.[79] The Committee has also been willing to find violation of article 19 where any form of reprisal is made upon those expressing protest against a government's policies.[80]

Dergachev v Belarus concerned a poster used during a picket organized by a member of Belarus People's Front, a political party in Belarus Republic. The poster carried an inscription stating 'Followers of the present regime! You have led the people to poverty for five years. Stop listening to lies. Join the struggle led by the Belarus People's Front for you.' The author was later convicted on the basis that the inscription amounted to a call for insubordination against the existing government and/or to the destruction of the constitutional order of the Byelorussian Republic. The author successfully argued that his rights under articles 19 had been violated by conviction for expressing his political opinion.[81] In *Jaona v Madagascar*, the author was a candidate in the 1982 presidential elections and, during his campaign, he denounced the allegedly corrupt policies of the Government. It was claimed that election fraud caused Jaona's defeat, resulting in him making a public denunciation of the alleged fraud and a call for new elections. Mr Jaona was arrested on the basis that demonstrations organized in his support

78 *PS v Denmark*, Communication 397/1990, UN Doc CCPR/C/45/D/397/1990 (1992), para 6. See also the individual opinion of Committee member Mr Bertil Wennergren.

79 *Mpandajila v Zaire*, above n 9, para 9. See also *Mpaka-Nsusu v Zaire*, above n 10, para 10.

80 See, for example, *Kalenga v Zambia*, above n 17, para 6.2.

81 *Dergachev v Belarus*, Communication 921/2000, UN Doc CCPR/C/74/D/921/2000/Rev.1 (2002), para 7.2. The individual opinion of Christine Chanet should be noted, in which the view was taken that the decision by the judge of 31 August 2000 ending the proceedings and finding for the party could not *a priori* be considered as not forming part of a decision falling within the context of domestic remedies which the applicant must have exhausted before submitting a communication to the Committee.

were endangering public order and security. The Committee considered that the facts disclosed violation of article 19(2).[82]

Membership in political parties Following several hours of ill-treatment, the author in *Motta v Uruguay* was interrogated for the purpose of obtaining an admission that he held an important position in the Communist Party and in order to induce him to identify fellow detainees as active members of the Communist Youth. He was subsequently committed to trial on charges of subversive association. In the absence of a response from Uruguay, the Committee considered those facts to establish a violation of article 19.[83] Various other similar allegations have been made against the State of Uruguay, with the Committee expressing concern about the position and often seeking clarification as to the scope and meaning of 'subversive activities' as a criminal offence under Uruguay's law.[84]

Other forms of opinion The Committee has expressed the view that disciplinary or other sanctions against a municipal official for writing a critical report to his or her employer, when the employer considered the language to be defamatory, could raise issues under article 19 of the Covenant. In that communication, however, because all disciplinary sanctions imposed as a consequence of the report in question were later quashed by the courts of the State party, the Committee considered that the author had no remaining claim under article 19.[85]

Freedom of Expression

Freedom of expression, together with freedom of assembly and association, is integral to human dignity and is also vital to the valid exercise of electoral rights and democratic participation guaranteed under article 25 (discussed below). Citizens, the Committee has recognized, take part in the conduct of public affairs by exerting influence through public debate and dialogue with their representatives or through their capacity to organize themselves.[86] The free communication of information and ideas about public and political issues between citizens, candidates and elected representatives is also essential through a free press and other media that are able to

---

82 *Jaona v Madagascar*, Communication 132/1982, UN Doc CCPR/C/24/D/132/1982 (1985), para 14. See also *Miha v Equatorial Guinea*, Communication 414/1990, UN Doc CCPR/C/51/D/414/1990 (1994), para 6.8.

83 *Motta v Uruguay*, Communication 11/1977, UN Doc CCPR/C/10/D/11/1977 (1980), para 17.

84 See, for example, *Carballal v Uruguay*, Communication 33/1978, UN Doc CCPR/C/12/D/33/1978 (1981), para 12.

85 *Strik v The Netherlands*, Communication 1001/2001, UN Doc CCPR/C/76/D/1001/2001 (2002).

86 *General Comment 25: The right to participate in public affairs, voting rights and the right of equal access to public service (Art 25)*, UN Doc CCPR General Comment 25 (1996), para 8.

comment on public issues without censorship or restraint.[87] It includes the ability of individuals openly to criticize or evaluate their governments without fear of interference or punishment.[88] Freedom to engage in political activity, individually or through political parties and other organizations, freedom to debate public affairs, to hold peaceful demonstrations and meetings, to criticize and oppose, to publish political material, to campaign for election and to advertise political ideas are seen as integral to this.

Modes of expression Expression of one's ideas includes various forms listed in article 19(2), including forms of art.[89] Although the freedom of expression includes a broad list of media, the Committee has determined that it does not amount to an unfettered right of any individual or group to hold press conferences, within the Parliamentary precincts for example, or to have such press conferences broadcast by others.[90] It has also expressed doubt as to whether a hunger strike could be understood as engaging article 19(2).[91] Expression through language was a matter considered in *Singer v Canada*, concerning the Charter of the French Language (Bill No 101), which the author claimed discriminated against him because it restricted the use of English for commercial purposes. In particular, section 58 prohibited the posting of commercial signs in English outside the author's store. The Committee concluded that although a State party is able to choose one or more official languages, it cannot exclude, outside the spheres of public life, the freedom to express oneself in a language of one's choice.[92]

Freedom of the press Due both to the fact that the Covenant was drafted at a time when mass media had not developed to the extent it has today, and that the ICCPR is concerned with individual rights, no mention is made of the freedom of the press within article 19. Indeed, communications brought by printing companies have been found inadmissible on the basis that article 1 of the Optional Protocol only gives individuals the ability to submit a communication to the Human Rights Committee.[93] The Committee has allowed, however, communications brought

87 Ibid, para 25.

88 See, for example: *de Morais v Angola*, above n 18, paras 6.7–6.8; *Madani v Algeria*, above n 5, para 8.8; and *Benhadj v Algeria*, Communication 1173/2003, UN Doc CCPR/C/90/D/1173/2003 (2007), para 8.10.

89 Forms of art have been treated as including paintings: see *Shin v Republic of Korea*, Communication 926/2000, UN Doc CCPR/C/80/D/926/2000 (2004), para 7.2.

90 *Zündel v Canada*, Communication 953/2000, UN Doc CCPR/C/78/D/953/2000 (2003), para 8.5.

91 *Baban v Australia*, Communication 1014/2001, UN Doc CCPR/C/78/D/1014/2001 (2003), para 6.7.

92 *Singer v Canada*, Communication 455/1991, UN Doc CCPR/C/51/D/455/1991 (1994), para 12.2.

93 *A Newspaper Publishing Company v Trinidad and Tobago*, Communication 360/1989, UN Doc CCPR/C/36/D/360/1989 (1989), para 3.2; and *A Publication and a*

before it by individual members of the press.[94] As to whether article 19(2) obliges States to guarantee freedom of the press, as a matter separate to whether or not such a freedom may be enforced under the Optional Protocol, three observations can be made in support of such an obligation. The first is that paragraph 2 includes not only freedom to impart information and ideas of all kinds, but also freedom to seek and receive them regardless of frontiers and in whatever form. The Committee has also commented upon the means of controlling mass media by States, thus implying that it considers that freedom of the press is engaged by article 19(2).[95] It has furthermore referred to the importance, in a democratic society, of the right to freedom of expression and of a free and uncensored press.[96]

Limitations Article 19 sets out the rights to hold opinions and to express oneself, subject to certain limitations as specified in paragraph 3. The exercise of the right to freedom of expression carries with it special duties and responsibilities and for this reason certain restrictions on the right are permitted which may relate either to the interests of other persons or to those of the community as a whole. Any restriction must cumulatively meet the following conditions: it must be provided for by law, it must address one of the aims enumerated in article 19, paragraph 3(a) and (b), and it must be necessary to achieve those legitimate purposes.[97] Any limit must also be proportional and not implemented in a manner that nullifies the substance of the right to expression.[98] The Committee has stated that the right to freedom of expression is of paramount importance in any democratic society, and that any restrictions on its exercise must therefore meet strict tests of justification.[99] Where a State seeks to justify limitations as falling within the ambit of article 19(3), the Committee will require the State party to specify the precise nature of the threat allegedly posed by a person's exercise of freedom of expression and how the limitation achieves dissipation of that threat.[100] A failure to explain the reasons for

---

Printing Company v Trinidad and Tobago, Communication 361/1989, UN Doc CCPR/C/36/D/361/1989 (1989), para 3.2.

94 *Kankanamge v Sri Lanka*, Communication 909/2000, UN Doc CCPR/C/81/D/909/2000 (2004), paras 9.3–9.4; and *Njaru v Cameroon*, Communication 1353/2005, UN Doc CCPR/C/89/D/1353/2005 (2007), para 6.4.

95 *General Comment 10: Freedom of expression (Art 19)*, UN Doc CCPR General Comment 10 (1983), para 2.

96 *De Morais v Angola*, above n 18, para 6.8.

97 See, for example: *Mukong v Cameroon*, Communication 458/1991, UN Doc CCPR/C/51/D/458/1991 (1994), para 9.7; and *Lovell v Australia*, Communication 920/2000, UN Doc CCPR/C/80/D/920/2000 (2004), para 9.3.

98 General Comment 10, above n 95, para 4.

99 See, for example, *Shchetko v Belarus*, Communication 1009/2001, UN Doc CCPR/C/87/D/1009/2001 (2006), para 7.3.

100 See, for example: *Pietraroia v Uruguay*, Communication 44/1979, UN Doc CCPR/C/12/D/44/1979 (1981), para 17; *Kim v Republic of Korea*, Communication 574/1994, UN Doc CCPR/C/64/D/574/1994 (1999), para 12.5; *Laptsevic v Belarus*, Communication

punishing a call to boycott a particular election, where voting was not compulsory, thus led to a finding of a violation of article 19(2).[101] Failure to justify the need for prior authorization of public meetings, during which material is disseminated or speeches made, has similarly resulted in adverse findings.[102]

The list of objectives, the pursuit of which might justify limitations upon the freedom of expression, is shorter than the equivalent list in article 10(2) of the European Convention on Human Rights, which also includes the protection of territorial integrity, preventing the disclosure of information received in confidence, or maintaining the authority and impartiality of the judiciary. Absence of reference to the authority and impartiality of the judiciary might suggest that restrictions by the judiciary upon the publication of certain information could not be justified under article 19(3). The Committee has concluded, however, that such restrictions are permissible if necessary to protect the interests of another, including the right to a fair hearing, or protecting public order.[103]

Limitation on the basis of national security was considered in *Park v Republic of Korea*. Korea stated that the restrictions in question were justified in order to protect national security and that they were provided for by law, under article 7 of the National Security Law. Despite the potentially sensitive nature of security issues, however, the Committee took the view that it must still determine whether any measures taken are in fact necessary for the purpose stated. On the facts of the communication, the State party invoked national security by reference to the general situation in the country and the threat posed by 'North Korean communists'. The Committee considered that the State had failed to specify the precise nature of the threat posed by the author's exercise of freedom of expression and therefore found that there was no basis upon which the restriction could be considered compatible with article 19(3).[104]

A more relaxed approach seems to have been taken in *Hertzberg v Finland*, concerning a decision of the Finnish Broadcasting Corporation that radio and television were not the appropriate forums to discuss issues related to homosexuality. The Committee placed emphasis upon the special duties that attach to the exercise of the rights provided for in article 19(2). In finding that there was no violation, and applying what it described as a 'margin of discretion', it seemed

780/1997, UN Doc CCPR/C/68/D/780/1997 (2000), para 8.5; and *Shchetko v Belarus*, ibid, paras 7.4–7.5.

101 *Svetik v Belarus*, Communication 927/2000, UN Doc CCPR/C/81/D/927/2000 (2004), paras 7.2–7.3.

102 See *Velichkin v Belarus*, Communication 1022/2001, UN Doc CCPR/C/85/D/1022/2001 (2005), paras 7.2–7.3; and *Coleman v Australia*, Communication 1157/2003, UN Doc CCPR/C/87/D/1157/2003 (2006), para 7.3.

103 *Lovell v Australia*, above n 97, para 9.4.

104 *Park v Republic of Korea*, Communication 628/1995, UN Doc CCPR/C/64/D/628/1995 (1998), para 10.3. See also *Shin v Republic of Korea*, above n 89, para 7.3.

to be influenced by the fact that the audience could not be controlled and that, in its view, harmful effects on minors could not be excluded.[105]

Restrictions upon attendance at Parliamentary proceedings was considered in *Gauthier v Canada*, concerning restrictions on the use of publicly funded media facilities. Access to the facilities was limited to members of the Canadian Press Gallery. The author had been denied full membership of the Canadian Press Gallery. As such, he was not allowed to gain access to the media facilities or to take notes of Parliamentary proceedings. The State party claimed that the author did not suffer any significant disadvantage because of technological advances that make information about Parliamentary proceedings readily available to the public, including reliance upon broadcasting services. In view of the importance of access to information about the democratic process, however, the Committee did not accept the State party's argument and was of the opinion that the author's exclusion constituted a restriction upon his right to seek and receive information. The question was then whether or not the restriction could be justified under article 19(3). The restriction was, arguably, imposed by law, in that the exclusion of persons from the precinct of Parliament or any part thereof, under the authority of the Speaker, followed from the law of Parliamentary privilege. It was argued that the restrictions were justified to achieve a balance between the right to freedom of expression and the need to ensure both the effective and dignified operation of Parliament and the safety and security of its members. In this respect, the Committee agreed that the protection of Parliamentary procedure could be seen as a legitimate goal of public order and an accreditation system could thus be a justified means of achieving that goal. Such an accreditation system must, however, be shown as necessary and proportionate to the goal in question and not arbitrary. Canada's defence failed here, the Committee taking the view that it was not a matter exclusively for the State to determine. The relevant criteria for the accreditation scheme should be specific, fair and reasonable, and their application should be transparent, whereas Canada had allowed a private organization (the Canadian Press Gallery) to control access to the Parliamentary press facilities, without intervention.[106]

The Committee considered, in *Jong-Cheol v Republic of Korea*, a law restricting the publication of opinion polls for a limited period in advance of an election, based on the desire to provide the electorate with a limited period of reflection, during which they are insulated from considerations extraneous to the issues under contest in the elections. It concluded that such a law does not necessarily fall outside the aims contemplated in article 19(3), so long as it is proportional in its application. The author's conviction for publication of opinion polls seven days

105 *Hertzberg v Finland*, Communication 61/1979, UN Doc CCPR/C/15/D/61/1979 (1982), paras 10.3–10.4. The individual opinion of Torkel Opsahl disagreed with that conclusion.

106 *Gauthier v Canada*, Communication 633/1995, UN Doc CCPR/C/65/D/633/1995 (1999), para 13.5.

prior to the election, and the sanction imposed, were considered to be proportionate and thus falling within article 19(3).[107]

The prohibitions against propaganda and certain forms of incitement Added to the permissible restrictions upon the freedom of expression under article 19(3), article 20 acts to prohibit certain forms of expression:

> Article 20
> 1. Any propaganda for war shall be prohibited by law.
> 2. Any advocacy of national, racial or religious hatred that constitutes incitement to discrimination, hostility or violence shall be prohibited by law.

These restrictions not only impact upon an individual's exercise of the right to express oneself, but also place a duty on States parties to adopt the necessary legislative measures prohibiting the actions referred to in article 20. In this respect, the Committee has expressed disappointment that State party periodic reports show that in some States such actions are neither prohibited by law nor are appropriate efforts intended or made to prohibit them.[108] For article 20 to become fully effective, the HRC saw a need for law making it clear that propaganda and prohibited advocacy are contrary to public policy, and providing for an appropriate sanction in the case of violation.[109]

The prohibition under paragraph 1 extends to all forms of propaganda threatening or resulting in an act of aggression or breach of the peace contrary to the Charter of the United Nations, while paragraph 2 is directed against any advocacy of national, racial or religious hatred that constitutes incitement to discrimination, hostility or violence, whether such propaganda or advocacy has aims which are internal or external to the State concerned. The Committee has recognized that article 20 does not prohibit advocacy of the sovereign right of self-defence or the right of peoples to self-determination and independence in accordance with the Charter of the United Nations.[110]

Faurisson v France involved a professor of literature at the Sorbonne University in Paris and the University of Lyon who was, in 1991, removed from his chair. Aware of the historical significance of the Holocaust, he had repeatedly sought proof of the methods of killings, in particular by gas asphyxiation, and expressed doubt as to the existence of gas chambers for extermination purposes at Auschwitz and in other Nazi concentration camps. The author's opinions had been rejected

---

107 *Jong-Cheol v Republic of Korea*, Communication 968/2001, UN Doc CCPR/C/84/D/968/2001 (2005), para 8.3.

108 *General Comment 11: Prohibition of propaganda for war and inciting national, racial or religious hatred (Art 20)*, UN Doc CCPR General Comment 11 (1983), para 1.

109 Ibid, para 2.

110 Ibid.

in numerous academic journals and ridiculed in the daily press. As a result of public discussion of his opinions and the polemics accompanying these debates, he contended that, since 1978, he became the target of death threats and that he was physically assaulted on eight occasions. He further contended that, although these attacks were brought to the attention of the competent judicial authorities, they were not seriously investigated and none of those responsible for the assaults had been arrested or prosecuted. France responded that it considered the author's 'activities', within the meaning of article 5 of the Covenant, as containing elements of racial discrimination, prohibited under the Covenant and other international human rights instruments.

The Committee took a sympathetic view and dismissed the application, although it based its views on article 19(3) (permitted limitation upon the freedom of expression), rather than the prohibition against the incitement of racial hatred within article 20(2). In its consideration of the communication, the Committee began by noting that the permitted restrictions on the freedom of expression under article 19(3) may relate to the interests of other persons, or to those of the community as a whole. Since the statements made by the author, read in their full context, were of a nature as to raise or strengthen anti-Semitic feelings, the restriction served to respect the right of the Jewish community to live free from fear of an atmosphere of anti-Semitism.[111] In discussing the direct application of article 20(2), Committee members Elizabeth Evatt and David Kretzmer took the position that in particular social and historical contexts, statements that do not meet the strict legal criteria of 'incitement' might nevertheless be shown to constitute part of a pattern of incitement against a given racial, religious or national group, or where those interested in spreading hostility and hatred adopt sophisticated forms of speech.[112] Rajsoomer Lallah added that article 20(2) primarily concerns itself with the particular expression that might be restricted, whereas article 19(3) focuses upon the adverse effect that any expression has.[113]

A more intricate approach was taken in *Ross v Canada*, concerning publications by the author of the communication which were submitted as falling within the scope of article 20(2) of the Covenant. It was pointed out that the Supreme Court of Canada had found that the publications denigrated the faith and beliefs of Jewish people, calling upon Christians not merely to question the validity of those beliefs but to hold those of the Jewish faith in contempt, and identifying Judaism as the enemy against which Christians should battle. The Committee considered that restrictions on the freedom of expression that might fall within the scope of article 20 must *also* be permissible under article 19(3). In applying article 19(3), said the Committee, the fact that a restriction is claimed to be required under article 20 will

111 *Faurisson v France*, Communication 550/1993, UN Doc CCPR/C/58/D/550/1993 (1996), para 9.6.

112 individual opinion of Elizabeth Evatt and David Kretzmer, para 4.

113 individual opinion of Rajsoomer Lallah, para 5.

be relevant.[114] In view of the findings of the Supreme Court of Canada as to the nature and effect of the author's public statements, the Committee concluded that the restrictions imposed on the author (the termination of his teaching position and placement in a non-teaching post) were for the purpose of protecting the rights or reputations of persons of Jewish faith and thus justifiable under article 19(3).[115]

Freedom of Assembly and Association

The Human Rights Committee has commented that the rights contained within articles 21 and 22 are integral to human dignity, and important to the exercise of electoral rights and democratic participation guaranteed under article 25:[116]

> Article 21
> The right of peaceful assembly shall be recognized. No restrictions may be placed on the exercise of this right other than those imposed in conformity with the law and which are necessary in a democratic society in the interests of national security or public safety, public order (ordre public), the protection of public health or morals or the protection of the rights and freedoms of others.
>
> Article 22
> 1. Everyone shall have the right to freedom of association with others, including the right to form and join trade unions for the protection of his interests.
> 2. No restrictions may be placed on the exercise of this right other than those which are prescribed by law and which are necessary in a democratic society in the interests of national security or public safety, public order (ordre public), the protection of public health or morals or the protection of the rights and freedoms of others. This article shall not prevent the imposition of lawful restrictions on members of the armed forces and of the police in their exercise of this right.
> 3. Nothing in this article shall authorize States Parties to the International Labour Organisation Convention of 1948 concerning Freedom of Association and Protection of the Right to Organize to take legislative measures which would prejudice, or to apply the law in such a manner as to prejudice, the guarantees provided for in that Convention.

114 *Ross v Canada*, Communication 736/1997, UN Doc CCPR/C/70/D/736/1997 (2000), para 10.6.

115 At paras 11.6 and 11.7.

116 General Comment 25, above n 86, para 26.

Association

Most communications concerning *political* association and assembly have been dealt with by the Committee as allegations of the violation of the right to freedom of thought and expression under article 19 of the Covenant. In a rare exception to this approach, violation of articles 22(1) and 19(1) and (2) was found in *Lopez v Uruguay*, in circumstances where the victim was subjected to various forms of harassment by authorities, ultimately leading to his arrest and detention, due to his active participation in trade union activities.[117]

In *Lee v Republic of Korea*, the Committee considered a conviction against the author by reason of his membership in the group Hanchongnyeon. Membership in the group had been prohibited, under article 7(1) of the National Security Law, on the basis that the group 'may' endanger the existence and security of the State or its democratic order. The Committee took the view that no evidence had been put before it to explain why prosecution for membership in such a group was necessary to avert a *real*, rather than possible, danger to national security.[118]

Registration of Associations

The right to freedom of association relates not only to the right to form an association, but also guarantees the right of such an association freely to carry out its activities. A requirement for registration of associations will not, by itself, violate the requirements of article 22. The examination of any such requirement will focus on the conditions imposed upon registration, and the consequences of this, as was the case in *Zvozskov v Belarus*. The Committee there found that, in the absence of any reasons linked to the objectives under article 22(2), it was a violation of article 22 for Belarus to require, as a condition for registration, that an association be restricted in its activities to the exclusive representation and defence of the rights of its own members.[119]

In *Korneenko v Belarus*, the Committee was concerned with the prohibition against unregistered associations and the ability of registered associations to be dissolved. Dissolution of the group Civil Initiatives was based, according to Belarus, on the improper use of equipment, received through foreign grants, for the production and conduct of 'propaganda' materials and activities; and deficiencies in the association's documentation. The Committee noted that the first basis was disputed and that Belarus had failed to establish how this was necessary in pursuit

117 *Lopez v Uruguay*, Communication 52/1979, UN Doc CCPR/C/13/D/52/1979 (1981), para 13.

118 *Lee v Republic of Korea*, Communication 1119/2002, UN Doc CCPR/C/84/D/1119/2002 (2005), para 7.3. See also *Belyatsky et al v Belarus*, Communication 1296/2004, UN Doc CCPR/C/90/D/1296/2004 (2007), para 7.3.

119 *Zvozskov et al v Belarus*, Communication 1039/2001, UN Doc CCPR/C/88/D/1039/2001 (2006), para 7.4.

of any of the article 22(2) objectives. As to the second basis, and taking into account the consequences of dissolution, it took the view that dissolution in response to deficient documentation was a disproportionate response by the State.[120]

Peaceful Assembly

Of import to the application of article 21 is the distinction to be made between the peaceful assembly of more than one person,[121] and non-peaceful demonstrations. This was an issue considered within *Kivenmaa v Finland.* On the occasion of a visit of a foreign head of State, and his meeting with the President of Finland, the author and about twenty-five members of her organization, amid a larger crowd, gathered across from the Presidential Palace where the leaders were meeting, distributed leaflets and raised a banner critical of the human rights record of the visiting head of State. The police immediately took the banner down and the author was charged with violating the Act on Public Meetings by holding a 'public meeting' without prior notification. The majority of the Committee found that a requirement to notify the police of an intended meeting in a public place six hours before its commencement might be compatible with the permitted limitations laid down in article 21 of the Covenant. In the circumstances of the specific case, however, it considered that the restriction was unreasonable, with none of those motives identified in article 21 applying.[122]

Strike Action

A question before the Committee in *JB and others v Canada* was whether the right to strike is guaranteed by article 22(1) of the Covenant. Since the right to strike is not *expressis verbis* included in article 22, the Committee took the view that it was required to interpret whether the right to freedom of association necessarily implied the right to strike, as contended by the authors of the communication. The authors argued that such a conclusion was supported by decisions of organs of the International Labour Organization (ILO) in interpreting the scope and the meaning of labour law treaties enacted under the auspices of ILO. The Human Rights Committee pointed out, however, that each international treaty, including the ICCPR, has a life of its own and must be interpreted in a fair and just manner by the body entrusted with the monitoring of its provisions.[123]

---

120 *Korneenko et al v Belarus*, Communication 1274/2004, UN Doc CCPR/C/88/D/1274/2004 (2006), paras 7.4–7.7.

121 See *Coleman v Australia*, Communication 1157/2003, UN Doc CCPR/C/87/D/1157/2003 (2006), para 6.4.

122 *Kivenmaa v Finland*, Communication 412/1990, UN Doc CCPR/C/50/D/412/1990 (1994), para 9.2.

123 *JB and others v Canada*, Communication 118/1982, UN Doc CCPR/C/28/D/118/1982 (1986), para 6.2.

In interpreting the scope of article 22, the Committee placed emphasis upon the ordinary meaning of each element of the article in its context and in the light of its object and purpose, consistent with article 31 of the Vienna Convention on the Law of Treaties (VCLT). The Committee also took into account the *travaux preparatoires* of the Covenant, a supplementary means of interpretation identified in article 32 of the VCLT. It noted that in the course of drafting the ICCPR and the Covenant on Economic, Social and Cultural Rights (ICESCR), the then Commission on Human Rights based its work on the Universal Declaration of Human Rights, which does not refer to the right to strike. The Commission adopted the text of a single 'draft covenant on human rights', comprising 73 articles, in 1951. Two of these draft articles are relevant: draft article 16 (freedom of association) and draft article 27 (a more specific provision concerning trade unions). During the 1952 session of the Commission, inclusion of an express right to strike was not proposed for draft article 16, but was proposed and rejected for draft article 27. The General Assembly ultimately decided to divide the single text into one on civil and political rights, and the other on economic, social and cultural rights. Draft article 16 (association) became article 22 of the ICCPR, while draft article 27 (trade unions) became article 8 of the ICESCR. The latter was amended five years later to include 'the right to strike, provided that it is exercised in conformity with the laws of the particular country', but no similar amendment was introduced or discussed with respect to article 22 of the ICCPR. Against that background, the Human Rights Committee found itself unable to deduce that the drafters intended article 22 to guarantee the right to strike.[124] The Committee went on to comment that this conclusion was corroborated by a comparative analysis of the ICCPR and the ICESCR. By expressly recognizing the right to strike in article 8(1)(d) of the ICESCR, in addition to the right of everyone to form and join trade unions for the promotion and protection of his economic and social interests in the preceding parts of article 8, the right to strike could not be considered an implicit component of the right to form and join trade unions.[125]

Recognition as a Person before the Law

Article 16 of the Covenant provides that every person 'shall have the right to recognition everywhere as a person before the law'. Alongside an allegation of discrimination, the authors in *Joslin v New Zealand* argued that article 16 was aimed at permitting persons to assert their essential dignity, through their recognition as proper subjects of law, both as individuals and as members of a couple. By preventing them, as a same-sex couple, from acquiring the legal attributes and advantages flowing from marriage, including advantages in the law of adoption, succession, matrimonial property, family protection and evidence,

124 Ibid, para 6.3.
125 Ibid, para 6.4.

the authors claimed that the Marriage Act deprived them of access to a significant institution through which individuals acquire and exercise legal personality. Given the existence of article 23(2) (the right to marriage), however, the Committee considered that any claim alleging violation of article 16 must be considered in the light of article 23. By application of the particular wording of article 23(2), the Committee concluded that the mere refusal to provide for marriage between homosexual couples was not a breach of the rights of the authors under articles 16, 17, 23 or 26 of the ICCPR.[126] It is unfortunate that the Committee did not give a more particular consideration of the authors' argument pertaining to article 16, although it should be noted that the views in *Joslin* are a typical example of most communications in which violation of article 16 is pleaded, but where the substance of the complaint is dealt with by the Committee within the context of other more explicit provisions.[127] It is common, also, that many claims invoking article 16 do so without presenting specific reasons as to why the right to recognition before the law has been violated.[128]

The author in *Werenbeck v Australia* claimed that his sentence of 13 years and four months' imprisonment contradicted the recognition of him as a person of equality before the law. He explained that, in 1991, the Court acquitted a Lebanese citizen, who was arrested at the airport with two kilograms of heroin concealed in a bag. The author contended that the circumstances in that case and his own were similar. The Committee took the view, however, that each criminal case must be examined on its own merits and that the acquittal of one accused and the conviction of another do not as such raise issues of recognition as a person before the law.[129]

A successful claim of violation of article 16 was made in *Kimouche v Algeria*, where the question before the Committee was whether and in what circumstances an enforced disappearance could constitute a refusal to recognize the victim as a person before the law. The Committee accepted that intentionally removing a person from the protection of the law for a prolonged period of time may constitute a refusal to recognize that person before the law if the victim was in the hands of the State authorities when last seen and, at the same time, if the efforts of his or her relatives to obtain access to potentially effective remedies have been

126 *Joslin v New Zealand*, Communication 902/1999, UN Doc CCPR/C/75/D/902/1999 (2002), para 8.2.

127 See also, by way of example: *HS v France*, Communication 184/1984, UN Doc CCPR/C/27/D/184/1984 (1986); *Avellanal v Peru*, Communication 202/1986, UN Doc CCPR/C/34/D/202/1986 (1988); *Polay v Peru*, Communication 577/1994, UN Doc CCPR/C/61/D/577/1994 (1998); and *Aber v Algeria*, Communication 1439/2005, UN Doc CCPR/C/90/D/1439/2005 (2007), para 7.9.

128 See, for example: *Tulyaganov v Uzbekistan*, Communication 1041/2001, UN Doc CCPR/C/90/D/1041/2001 (2007), para 7.5; *Chikunova v Uzbekistan*, Communication 1043/2002, UN Doc CCPR/C/89/D/1043/2002 (2007), para 6.3; and *Tcholatch v Canada*, Communication 1052/2002, UN Doc CCPR/C/89/D/1052/2002 (2007), para 3.7.

129 *Werenbeck v Australia*, Communication 579/1994, UN Doc CCPR/C/59/D/579/1994 (1997), para 9.9.

systematically impeded. In such situations, disappeared persons are in practice deprived of their capacity to exercise entitlements under law, including all of their other rights under the Covenant, and of access to any possible remedy as a direct consequence of the actions of the State, which the Committee concluded must be interpreted as a refusal to recognize such victims as persons before the law. It found, on the facts before it, that Algeria had violated article 16.[130]

Democracy

Article 25 of the Covenant recognizes and protects the right of every citizen to take part in the conduct of public affairs, the right to vote and to be elected, and the right to participate in the public administration of one's country. These are rights that go to the heart of democratic society and it appears that the drafters of article 25 may have taken the view that the enjoyment of human rights is dependent upon the existence of a democratic government based on the consent of the people. In part, this might be viewed as a troubling and slightly paternalistic approach: an approach that tends to undermine, rather than respect, the different bases of political governorship. For a document that repeatedly advocates tolerance, this is a slightly puzzling attitude. Having said this, it is plain that the Committee has taken a robust approach to the application of article 25. In its General Comment 25, it said:[131]

> Whatever form of constitution or government is in force, the Covenant requires States to adopt such legislative and other measures as may be necessary to ensure that citizens have an effective opportunity to enjoy the rights it protects.

It should be noted that, other than articles 13 and 25, the rights contained in the ICCPR are guaranteed to all persons within a State party's territory. In contrast, article 13 applies to aliens alone, concerning expulsion procedures, and article 25 only to citizens of the State. Within the latter category, it is clear that no distinctions are permitted between citizens in the enjoyment of these rights on the grounds of race, colour, sex, language, religion, political or other opinion, national or social origin, property, birth or other status. In *Aumeeruddy-Cziffra v Mauritius* for example, although no substantive application of article 25 was made, the Committee did observe that restrictions established by law in various areas may prevent the practical exercise of rights under article 25 if, for example, such interference with opportunity infringed the principle of sexual equality.[132]

---

130 *Kimouche v Algeria*, Communication 1328/2004, UN Doc CCPR/C/90/D/1328/2004 (2007), paras 7.8–7.9.

131 General Comment 25, above n 86, para 1.

132 *Aumeeruddy-Cziffra v Mauritius*, Communication 35/1978, UN Doc CCPR/C/12/D/35/1978 (1981), para 9.2(c)2.

Although the Committee has not addressed the issue within any communication, it has commented that distinctions between those who are entitled to citizenship by birth and those who acquire it by naturalization may raise questions of compatibility with article 25.[133]

Limitations

Although article 25 does not contain a specific limitations clause, as a number of other provisions within the Covenant do, it does say that the rights within it are to be enjoyed by every citizen 'without unreasonable restrictions'. No further guidance is provided within the text as to what might or might not constitute reasonable restrictions, although the Committee has commented:[134]

> Any conditions which apply to the exercise of the rights protected by article 25 should be based on objective and reasonable criteria. For example, it may be reasonable to require a higher age for election or appointment to particular offices than for exercising the right to vote, which should be available to every adult citizen. The exercise of these rights by citizens may not be suspended or excluded except on grounds which are established by law and which are objective and reasonable. For example, established mental incapacity may be a ground for denying a person the right to vote or to hold office.

Limiting electoral rights on the basis of criminal convictions was a justification claimed by Uruguay in *Touron v Uruguay*. The author's husband was convicted of subversive association and consequently barred from taking part in the conduct of public affairs and from being elected for a period of 15 years. The Committee noted that, under the legislation of many countries, criminal offenders might be deprived of certain political rights. It emphasized, however, that article 25 of the Covenant permits only reasonable restrictions and found that the 15-year ban was not reasonable.[135]

---

133 General Comment 25, above n 86, para 3.

134 Ibid, para 4. See also *Sohn v Republic of Korea*, Communication 518/1992, UN Doc CCPR/C/54/D/518/1992 (1995), para 10.4; *Crippa, Masson and Zimmermann v France*, Communications 993–5/2001, UN Doc CCPR/C/85/D/993-995/2001 (2005), para 6.13; and *Solís v Peru*, Communication 1016/2001, UN Doc CCPR/C/86/D/1016/2001 (2006), para 6.3.

135 *Touron v Uruguay*, Communication 32/1978, UN Doc CCPR/C/12/D/32/1978 (1981), para 11. See also *Altesor v Uruguay*, Communication 10/1977, UN Doc CCPR/C/15/D/10/1977 (1982), para 15; and *Silva v Uruguay*, Communication 34/1978, UN Doc CCPR/C/12/D/34/1978 (1981), para 9.

Participation in the Conduct of Public Affairs

The conduct of public affairs, participation in which is secured under article 25(a), is a broad concept which relates to the exercise of political power, in particular the exercise of legislative, executive and administrative powers. Article 25(a) provides citizens with the opportunity to take part in all aspects of public administration, as well as the formulation and implementation of policy at international, national, regional and local levels. The Human Rights Committee has commented that the constitution and other laws of member States should establish the allocation of powers and the means by which individual citizens may exercise their right to participate in the conduct of public affairs.[136]

The scope of the right under subparagraph (a) was considered in *Marshall v Canada*, where the Committee took the view that the right is to be interpreted in the framework of the legal and constitutional system of States parties, which provide for the modalities of such participation. The Committee expanded on this approach:[137]

> It must be beyond dispute that the conduct of public affairs in a democratic State is the task of representatives of the people, elected for that purpose, and public officials appointed in accordance with the law. Invariably, the conduct of public affairs affects the interest of large segments of the population or even the population as a whole, while in other instances it affects more directly the interest of more specific groups of society. Although prior consultations, such as public hearings or consultations with the most interested groups may often be envisaged by law or have evolved as public policy in the conduct of public affairs, article 25(a) of the Covenant cannot be understood as meaning that any directly affected group, large or small, has the unconditional right to choose the modalities of participation in the conduct of public affairs. That, in fact, would be an extrapolation of the right to direct participation by the citizens, far beyond the scope of article 25(a).

The authors in that communication had sought, unsuccessfully, to be invited to attend constitutional conferences as representatives of the Mikmaq people. Notwithstanding the right of every citizen to take part in the conduct of public affairs without discrimination and without unreasonable restrictions, the Committee concluded that Canada's failure to invite representatives of the Mikmaq tribal society to the constitutional conferences on aboriginal matters did not infringe the right under article 25(a) of the authors or other members of the Mikmaq tribal society.[138]

---

136 General Comment 25, above n 86, para 5.

137 *Marshall v Canada*, Communication 205/1986, UN Doc CCPR/C/43/D/205/1986 (1991), para 5.5.

138 Ibid, para 6.

Bwalya v Zambia concerned facts impacting upon both subparagraphs (a) and (b). The author ran for a parliamentary seat in the constituency of Chifubu, Zambia. He complained that the authorities prevented him from properly preparing his candidacy and from participating in the electoral campaign and that, in retaliation for the dissemination of his opinions and his activism, the authorities subjected him to threats and intimidation. In January 1986 he was dismissed from his employment. The Ndola City Council subsequently expelled him and his family from their home, while the payment of his father's pension was suspended indefinitely. The author claimed that, as a political activist and former prisoner of conscience, he was placed under strict surveillance by the authorities, and continued to be subjected to restrictions on his freedom of movement, including being denied a passport. The Committee was satisfied that violation of articles 12 (freedom of movement) and 19 (political expression) had occurred. As to the alleged violation of article 25 of the Covenant, the Committee accepted that the author had been prevented from participating in a general election campaign as well as from preparing his candidacy for the party. This was considered as amounting to an unreasonable restriction on the author's right to take part in the conduct of public affairs. The Committee expressed that restrictions on political activity outside the only recognized political party amounted to an unreasonable restriction upon the right to participate in the conduct of public affairs.[139]

Elections

The holding of elections is regulated by article 25(b). The provision addresses both the rights of voters and candidates, as well as the manner in which elections are to be conducted is order to secure 'the free expression of the will of the electors'.

The right to vote From a citizen's perspective, participation in the electoral process is guaranteed by the right to vote and to be elected, which must be established by domestic law.[140] The right to vote is not an absolute right and the Committee has taken the approach that limitation may be acceptable so long as no distinction is made between citizens on the grounds mentioned in article 2(1),[141] and that no unreasonable restrictions are imposed.[142] As already indicated, article 25 only permits objective and reasonable restrictions to be placed upon the rights within the text. It has been ruled that it is acceptable to set a minimum age limit

139 *Bwalya v Zambia*, Communication 314/1988, UN Doc CCPR/C/48/D/314/1988 (1993), para 6.6.

140 General Comment 25, above n 86, para 7.

141 Namely, without distinction such as race, colour, sex, language, religion, political or other opinion, national or social origin, property, birth or other status.

142 General Comment 25, above n 86, para 6. See, for example, *Debreczeny v The Netherlands*, Communication 500/1992, UN Doc CCPR/C/53/D/500/1992 (1995); and *Gorji-Dinka v Cameroon*, above n 5, para 5.6.

for the right to vote or hold office, but that it would be unreasonable to restrict the right to vote on the ground of physical disability or to impose literacy, educational or property requirements. The Committee has also commented that membership of political parties should not be a condition of eligibility to vote, nor a ground of disqualification.[143] If conviction for an offence is a basis for suspending the right to vote, the period of such suspension should be proportionate to the offence and the sentence. Persons who are deprived of liberty but who have not been convicted should not be excluded from exercising the right to vote (discussed further below).[144]

As with various other provisions in the Covenant, the right to vote imposes a positive duty upon the State to guarantee its enjoyment. The Committee has expanded upon this principle, saying:

> States must take effective measures to ensure that all persons entitled to vote are able to exercise that right. Where registration of voters is required, it should be facilitated and obstacles to such registration should not be imposed. If residence requirements apply to registration, they must be reasonable, and should not be imposed in such a way as to exclude the homeless from the right to vote. Any abusive interference with registration or voting as well as intimidation or coercion of voters should be prohibited by penal laws and those laws should be strictly enforced. Voter education and registration campaigns are necessary to ensure the effective exercise of article 25 rights by an informed community.

The Human Rights Committee has gone further to say that States parties must also take steps to overcome specific difficulties that citizens may face in the exercise of their voting rights, such as illiteracy, language barriers, poverty, or impediments to freedom of movement which prevent persons entitled to vote from exercising their rights effectively.[145] It has suggested, by way of example, that information and materials about voting should be available in minority languages and that methods such as photographs and symbols should be adopted to ensure that illiterate voters have adequate information on which to base their choice.

Prisoners' right to vote The coming into force of the ICCPR and its Optional Protocol has seen, in a number of instances, the introduction of amending legislation to provide the right to vote to those imprisoned within States parties. In Canada, for example, the National Assembly of Quebec adopted several amendments to the Quebec Election Act in order to bring the legislation into conformity with the provisions of article 25. The amendments established, inter alia, the right of every inmate to vote in general elections in Quebec and added special provisions relating to voting procedures for inmates. Article 64 of the Act provided in particular that

143 General Comment 25, above n 86, para 10.

144 Ibid, para 14.

145 Ibid, para 12.

'to allow inmates to exercise their right to vote, the Director General of Elections may make any agreement he considers expedient with the warden of any house of detention established under an Act of Parliament of Canada or of the Legislature'. This provision came into question in *CF v Canada*. In view of upcoming general provincial elections in Quebec, the Director General of Elections of Quebec, on 11 March 1981, concluded an agreement with representatives of the wardens of the provincial detention centre of Quebec concerning the voting of the detainees of provincial detention centres. To enable such voting to occur, a similar agreement was required between the Solicitor General of Canada, as head of the federal penitentiary system, and the appropriate provincial authorities. The Solicitor General of Canada determined, however, not to conclude such an administrative agreement, the effect of which precluded detainees in federal penitentiaries from voting in general provincial elections. He argued that that matter required further study.

Canada argued before the Committee that this decision did not constitute an unreasonable restriction upon prisoners' rights under article 25(b) because of the substantial administrative problems involved in enabling inmates in federal penitentiaries to vote in general elections; and for the reason that it was not unreasonable to withhold the right to vote in general elections from people who have engaged in criminal misconduct sufficiently serious to justify their detention in a federal penitentiary.[146] On procedural issues, the Committee determined that the latter communication was inadmissible for failure to pursue domestic remedies.[147] Canada subsequently advised the Committee, however, that pursuant to a decision of the Federal Court of Canada in December 1985 in the case *Levesque v Attorney-General of Canada*, the right of penitentiary prisoners in Quebec to vote in provincial elections was upheld and an order made requiring the Federal Minister of Justice and the Solicitor General to make the necessary arrangements to put this into effect.[148]

The right to vote for citizens abroad The question of whether such a right exists was raised in *Colchúin v Ireland*. The author, ordinarily resident in Australia, was unable to vote in elections for the Irish Parliament, for the Presidency and in referenda, by operation of the Electoral Act (Ireland). The Act limited registration as an elector to those ordinarily resident in an Irish constituency. The author argued that this was inconsistent with article 25 of the Covenant, which guarantees the right to vote to 'every citizen'. In contrast, Ireland argued that in order to qualify as a victim of a violation of article 25, an individual must be a citizen of the country, as well as being within its territory and subject to the jurisdiction of a State party. The communication was ultimately dismissed on the basis that

146 *CF v Canada*, Communication 113/1981, UN Doc CCPR/C/24/D/113/1981 (1985), para 8. See also *Gorji-Dinka v Cameroon*, above n 5, para 5.6.

147 Ibid, para 10.

148 *Levesque v Attorney-General of Canada* [1986] 2 FC 287.

the author was not a 'victim' as required under the Optional Protocol, since the author's communication challenged his inability to participate in certain elections in the abstract.[149] Regrettably, the Committee made no comment on the substance of either position expressed by the author or State.

The conduct of elections To ensure the accountability of representatives for the exercise of legislative and executive powers vested in them, elections are required to be genuine and periodic. Elections must be held at intervals that are not unduly long and which ensure that the authority of government continues to be based on 'the free expression of the will of electors' (as expressed within article 25(b)).[150] This means that elections must be conducted by universal and equal suffrage, and held by secret ballot. The Committee has said that an independent electoral authority to achieve the stated aims should supervise the conduct of elections and of candidacy to stand for elections.[151]

Because elections must be held by secret ballot, States are required to take measures to guarantee the requirement of the secrecy of the vote during elections, including absentee voting, where such a system exists. This implies that voters should be protected from any form of coercion or compulsion to disclose how they intend to vote or how they voted, and from any unlawful or arbitrary interference with the voting process. The security of ballot boxes must be guaranteed and votes should be counted, the Committee has said, in the presence of the candidates or their agents. There should be independent scrutiny of the voting and counting process and access to judicial review or other equivalent process so that electors have confidence in the security of the ballot and the counting of votes. Likewise, assistance provided to the disabled, blind or illiterate should be independent. Electors should be fully informed of these guarantees.[152] It would seem, from the wording of article 25(b), that there is no further prescription upon the voting and vote-counting procedures for elections. The issue of whether automated vote-counting was in breach of article 25(b) was raised in *Clippel v Belgium*. Belgium argued that the Covenant neither prescribed nor prohibited any specific voting system and the substance of the communication was ultimately unresolved since it was declared inadmissible through a failure by the author to exhaust local remedies.[153]

---

149 *Colchúin v Ireland*, Communication 1038/2001, UN Doc CCPR/C/77/D/1038/2001 (2003), para 6.3.

150 General Comment 25, above n 86, para 9.

151 Ibid, para 20; and *Sinitsin v Belarus*, Communication 1047/2002, UN Doc CCPR/C/88/D/1047/2002 (2006), para 7.3.

152 Ibid.

153 *Clippel v Belgium*, Communication 1082/2002, UN Doc CCPR/C/77/D/1082/2002 (2003), para 6.3.

Voters should be able to form opinions independently, free of violence or threat of violence, compulsion, inducement or manipulative interference of any kind.[154] The Committee has expressed that the principle of one person, one vote must apply to elections and that the vote of one elector should be equal to the vote of another. Also, the drawing of electoral boundaries and the method of allocating votes should not distort the distribution of voters or discriminate against any group and should not exclude or unreasonably restrict the right of citizens to choose their representatives freely.[155] The drawing up of electoral regions was considered in *Mátyus v Slovakia*, where the Committee said:[156]

> As regards the question whether article 25 of the Covenant was violated, the Committee notes that the Constitutional Court of the State party held that by drawing election districts for the same municipal council with substantial differences between the number of inhabitants per elected representative, despite the election law which required those voting districts to be proportional to the number of inhabitants, the equality of election rights required by the State party's constitution was violated. In the light of this pronouncement, based on a constitutional clause similar to the requirement of equality in article 25 of the Covenant, and in the absence of any reference by the State party to factors that might explain the differences in the number of inhabitants or registered voters per elected representative in different parts of Rožòava, the Committee is of the opinion that the State party violated the author's rights under article 25 of the Covenant.

Standing for office As for all other aspects of article 25, the right to stand for office may be the subject of reasonable limitations. The Committee has found that it is unreasonable to require candidates to be members of parties or specific parties. In contrast, it has said that requiring candidates to have a minimum number of supporters is not unreasonable, so long as this requirement is not so burdensome as to act as a barrier to candidacy.[157]

Proficiency in the official language of the State has been implicitly accepted as being a permissible condition. In *Ignatane v Latvia*, the author was a teacher in Riga. In 1993, she had appeared before a certification board (a panel of five experts) to take a Latvian language test and was subsequently awarded a language aptitude certificate stating that she had level 3 proficiency (the highest level). In 1997, she stood for local elections as a candidate of the Movement of Social Justice and Equal Rights in Latvia list. Prior to the elections, she was struck off the list by decision of the Riga Election Commission, on the basis of an opinion issued

154 General Comment 25, above n 86, para 19.

155 Ibid, para 21.

156 *Mátyus v Slovakia*, Communication 923/2000, UN Doc CCPR/C/75/D/923/2000 (2002), para 9.2.

157 General Comment 25, above n 86, para 17.

by the State Language Board that she did not have the required proficiency in the official language. The Committee placed emphasis on the fact that five experts had assessed the first examination, in 1993, whereas the 1997 review was conducted in an *ad hoc* manner and assessed by a single individual. The annulment of the author's candidacy was therefore not found to be based on objective criteria and thereby incompatible with the State party's obligations under article 25 of the Covenant.[158]

Conditions relating to nomination dates, fees or deposits should also be reasonable and not discriminatory. Where elective offices are seen as incompatible with tenure of specific positions, such as judicial, military or public service, measures to avoid any conflicts of interest should not unduly limit the right to stand for political office. Laws based on objective and reasonable criteria and incorporating fair procedures should establish any grounds for the removal of elected office holders.[159] Restrictions on the right to be elected to a municipal council were regulated, in *Debreczeny v The Netherlands*, by law and based on the electee's professional appointment by or subordination to the municipal authority. The Netherlands explained that these restrictions were invoked to guarantee the democratic decision-making process by avoiding conflicts of interest. In such circumstances, the Committee considered that the restrictions were reasonable and compatible with the purpose of the law. In the context of the communication before it, the Committee observed that the author was at the time of his election to the council of Dantumadeel serving as a police officer in the national police force, and was in that role accountable to the mayor of Dantumadeel. The Committee thus agreed that a conflict of interest could arise and that the application of the restrictions to the author did not constitute a violation of article 25 of the Covenant.[160]

Of significance, and going to the very substance of the right, candidacy may not be restricted on the basis of political opinion.[161] This must, of course, be tempered by the prohibition under article 5(1) from acting in a manner aimed at the destruction of any of the rights and freedoms recognized in the Covenant. Reasonable limitations on campaign expenditure may be justified where this is necessary to ensure that the free choice of voters is not undermined or the democratic process distorted by disproportionate expenditure on behalf of any candidate or party.[162]

---

158 *Ignatane v Latvia*, Communication 884/1999, UN Doc CCPR/C/72/D/884/1999 (2001), para 7.4.

159 General Comment 25, above n 86, para 16.

160 *Debreczeny v The Netherlands*, above n 142, para 9.3.

161 General Comment 25, above n 86, para 17. See, for example, *Gorji-Dinka v Cameroon*, above n 5, para 5.6.

162 General Comment 25, above n 86, para 19.

Access to Public Service

Every citizen has the right of access to public service within his or her country, without distinction and on general terms of equality. To ensure this, the criteria and processes for appointment, promotion, suspension and dismissal must be objective and reasonable. Affirmative measures may be taken in appropriate cases to ensure that there is equal access to public service for all citizens.[163] To ensure that the right is capable of being truly exercised, rather than being a right in name alone, persons holding public service positions must be free from political interference or pressures. It is of particular importance to ensure that persons do not suffer discrimination on any of the grounds set out in article 2(1).[164] *Mpandajila v Zaire* concerned a group of former parliamentarians in Zaire who, during 1982, were negotiating with representatives of the President of Zaire concerning the establishment of a new political party. Seven of them were arrested and subsequently all 12 were brought to trial before the State Security Court on charges of plotting to overthrow the regime and planning to establish a political party. The Committee did not give views on whether this constituted a violation of article 22, as claimed by the former parliamentarians, but did find violations of articles 19 (freedom of expression) and 25 (electoral rights).[165] In *Mpaka-Nsusu v Zaire*, the author presented his candidacy for the presidency of the Government Party and, at the same time, for the presidency of Zaire in conformity with existing Zairian law. The author was refused those requests and the Committee found this to be in violation of article 25 of the Covenant.[166]

Munoz v Peru concerned an administrative decision by which the author was suspended from police service on disciplinary grounds (for the alleged offence of insulting a superior) and later discharged from service. Although the majority of the Committee adopted views based upon a violation of article 14 (judicial process),[167] Committee member Bertil Wennergren took the view that the facts of the communication also disclosed a violation of article 25(c). He was of the view that the suspension and discharge from the Peruvian Guardia Civil were not founded upon objective and justifiable grounds. Whatever the ground may have been, whether, for instance, political or merely subjective, he considered it to be arbitrary. The Committee member said that 'to suspend and discharge someone arbitrarily, from public service and to refuse him reinstatement, just as arbitrarily, constitutes, in my opinion, a violation of his right, under article 25(c) of the Covenant, to have access on general terms of equality to public service'.[168]

163 See further Chapter 3.

164 General Comment 25, above n 86, para 23.

165 *Mpandajila v Zaire*, above n 9, para 9.

166 *Mpaka-Nsusu v Zaire*, above n 10, para 10.

167 *Munoz v Peru*, Communication 203/1986, UN Doc CCPR/C/34/D/203/1986 (1988), para 12.

168 Ibid, Appendix II, para 4.

Following an attempted *coup d'état* in Cameroon in 1984, the author in *Mazou v Cameroon*, who at that time was a second class magistrate, was arrested on suspicion of having sheltered his brother, who was wanted by the police for having taken part in the *coup*. The author was found guilty and sentenced by a military court to five years' imprisonment. While the author was detained, the President of Cameroon signed a decree removing the author from his post as Secretary-General in the Ministry of Education and Chairman of the Governing Council of the National Sports Office. The Decree gave no reasons for the action. Mr Mazou requested reinstatement following his release and, in 1997, obtained a ruling from the Supreme Court holding the 1984 decree illegal and annulled. Despite that decision, the Committee was concerned by the tardiness of the decision, made more than ten years after the author's removal from his post, and the fact that it was not followed by restoration of his career on reinstatement. This could not, the Committee found, be considered to be a satisfactory remedy within the meaning of articles 2 and 25 of the Covenant.[169]

Securing access to the public sector *Gedumbe v Democratic Republic of Congo* concerned a failure by the State to adequately secure the communicant's employment in the public service. In 1985 the author was appointed director of a Zairian consular school in Burundi. He was suspended in 1988 by Mboloko Ikolo, the then Zairian ambassador to Burundi. This was allegedly in response to a complaint by the author and by other staff members of the school to several administrative authorities of Zaire concerning the embezzlement by Mr Ikolo of the salaries for the personnel of the consular school. In September 1989 the Ministry of Primary and Secondary Education issued an order to reinstate the author in his post. Subsequently, however, Mr Ikolo informed the authorities in Zaire that the author was a member of a network of political opponents of the Zairian Government, and requested the authorities of Burundi to expel him. The author said that, for this reason, Mr Ikolo and his successor refused to reinstate him in his post or to pay his salary arrears. In the absence of a response by the State party, the Committee found that the facts showed that the decisions by the authorities in the author's favour had not been acted upon and could not be regarded as an effective remedy for violation of article 25(c), read in conjunction with article 2 of the Covenant.[170]

Interface with discrimination It is notable that a number of communications concerning violation of article 25(c) have come before the Committee in combination with allegations of discrimination under article 26. Such claims

169 *Mazou v Cameroon*, Communication 630/1995, UN Doc CCPR/C/72/D/630/1995 (2001), para 8.4.

170 *Gedumbe v Democratic Republic of Congo*, Communication 641/1995, UN Doc CCPR/C/75/D/641/1995 (2002), para 5.2. See also *Vargas-Machuca v Peru*, Communication 906/2000, UN Doc CCPR/C/75/D/906/2000 (2002), para 7.4.

have in general seen the Committee make its findings in reliance upon article 26, rather than article 25(c).[171] In *Costa v Uruguay*, the Committee was called upon to consider what might be described as 'affirmative action'. The author had submitted job applications to various governmental agencies, seeking employment in the public service. He was told that only former public employees who were dismissed as a result of the application of Institutional Act No 7 of June 1977, under the former military regime, were at that time being admitted to the public service. The author claimed that this created an inequality to public access, in violation of article 25(c). The Committee took a pragmatic approach. Taking into account the social and political situation in Uruguay during the years of military rule, in particular the dismissal of many public servants pursuant to Institutional Act No 7, the Committee considered that the new legislation, adopted and implemented by the new democratic Government of Uruguay, was a measure of redress. The Committee observed that Uruguayan public officials that had been dismissed on ideological, political or trade-union grounds (clearly victims of violations of article 25 in the Committee's view) and were thus entitled to have an effective remedy under article 2(3)(a) of the Covenant. Implementation of the new legislation should, in that context, be looked upon as such a remedy and could not be regarded as incompatible with the reference to 'general terms of equality' in article 25(c) of the Covenant.[172] The Committee accepted, in *Solís v Peru*, that age limits used for continued post occupancy was an objective distinguishing criterion and that its implementation in the context of a general plan for the restructuring of the civil service was not unreasonable.[173]

Other Considerations under Article 25

Self-determination The rights under article 25 are related to, but distinct from, the right of peoples to self-determination. By virtue of the rights covered by article 1(1), peoples have the right to freely determine their political status and to enjoy the right to choose the form of their constitution or government. Article 25 deals with the right of individuals to participate in those processes which constitute the conduct of public affairs. The Committee does not have the competence under the Optional Protocol to consider communications alleging violation of the right to self-determination protected in article 1 of the Covenant, as it is a group right

171 See, for example: *Danning v The Netherlands*, Communication 180/1984, UN Doc CCPR/C/29/D/180/1984 (1987); and *Gómez v Spain*, Communication 865/1999, UN Doc CCPR/C/73/D/865/1999 (2001), para 9.2. Compare with *Šmíde v Czech Republic*, Communication 1062/2002, UN Doc CCPR/C/87/D/1062/2002 (2006), para 11.5.

172 *Costa v Uruguay*, Communication 198/1985, UN Doc CCPR/C/30/D/198/1985 (1987), para 10. See also *Guido Jacobs v Belgium*, Communication 943/2000, UN Doc CCPR/C/81/D/943/2000 (2004), para 9.2–9.6.

173 *Solís v Peru*, above n 134, para 6.4.

rather than an individual one.[174] The Committee has taken the view, however, that it is able to consider article 1, where relevant, in determining whether rights protected in parts II and III of the Covenant have been violated. It has taken this approach in the interpretation of article 25 of the Covenant.

In *Gillot et al v France*, it was claimed that the criteria governing the right to vote in referenda had the effect of creating a restricted electorate and hence a differentiation between (a) persons deprived of the right to vote, including the author(s) in the ballot in question, and (b) persons permitted to exercise this right, owing to their sufficiently strong links with the territory whose institutional development was at issue. The Committee disagreed, but made the following observations relating to the issue of self-determination:[175]

> It [the Committee] therefore considers that the [election] criteria established are reasonable to the extent that they are applied strictly and solely to ballots held in the framework of a self-determination process. Such criteria, therefore, can be justified only in relation to article 1 of the Covenant, which the State party does. Without expressing a view on the definition of the concept of 'peoples' as referred to in article 1, the Committee considers that, in the present case, it would not be unreasonable to limit participation in local referendums to persons 'concerned' by the future of New Caledonia who have proven sufficiently strong ties to that territory. The Committee notes, in particular, the conclusions of the Senior Advocate-General of the Court of Cassation, to the effect that in every self-determination process limitations of the electorate are legitimized by the need to ensure a sufficient definition of identity. The Committee also takes into consideration the fact that the Noumea Accord and the Organic Law of 19 March 1999 recognize a New Caledonian citizenship (not excluding French citizenship but linked to it), reflecting the common destiny chosen and providing the basis for the restrictions on the electorate, in particular for the purpose of the final referendum.

'Political rights' The Committee has clearly expressed that access to public service on general terms of equality encompasses a duty, for the State, to ensure that there is no discrimination on the ground of political opinion or expression. This applies a fortiori to those who hold positions in the public service. The rights enshrined in article 25 should also be read to encompass the freedom to engage in political activity individually or through political parties, freedom to debate public affairs, to criticize the Government and to publish material with political content.[176]

In an early decision of the Committee, *Ambrosini v Uruguay*, a violation of article 25 was declared to exist 'because of unreasonable restrictions on his [the

---

174 See Chapter 2.

175 *Gillot et al v France*, Communication 932/2000, UN Doc CCPR/C/75/D/932/2000 (2002), para 13.16.

176 *Aduayom and others v Togo*, Communications 422–4/1990, UN Doc CCPR/C/57/D/422-424/1990 (1996), para 7.5.

author's] political rights'. Jose Massera, a professor of mathematics and former Deputy to the National Assembly, was arrested in October 1975 and had, at the time of the Committee's adoption of views, remained imprisoned since that date. It was found as a matter of fact that he was denied the remedy of *habeas corpus*. On 15 August 1976 he was tried on charges of 'subversive association' and remained in prison. As indicated, the Committee found the facts to establish a breach of article 25 of the Covenant.[177] Certainly, the conduct of the State interfered with the author's participation in political affairs as Deputy to the National Assembly. The views of the Committee were somewhat incomplete in their failure to mention, let alone consider, article 19 (freedom of expression).[178]

Clearer and more well-founded views have since been adopted, as in *Weisz v Uruguay*. Here, the author's brother also faced charges of subversive association under the Military Penal Code, with aggravating circumstances of conspiracy against the Constitution. The author asserted that his brother has been prosecuted solely for having contributed information on trade union activities to a newspaper opposed to the Government. He also alleged that to be tried on a charge of 'associacion para delinquir' amounted to prosecution for membership in a political party, with such membership having been perfectly lawful at the time when Weinberger was affiliated with it. As a result of conviction, Weinberger was barred from taking part in the conduct of public affairs and from being elected for 15 years. The Committee considered this to amount to a violation of both articles 19(2) and 25 of the Covenant.[179]

177 *Ambrosini v Uruguay*, Communication 5/1977, UN Doc CCPR/C/7/D/5/1977 (1979), para 10(ii).

178 See also *Silva v Uruguay*, above n 135, para 8.4.

179 *Weisz v Uruguay*, Communication 28/1978, UN Doc CCPR/C/11/D/28/1978 (1980), para 16. See also *Pietraroia v Uruguay*, above n 100, para 17.

Chapter 5
Security of the Person

Alex Conte

In considering the issue of security of the person, various rights and freedoms come to mind. This chapter focuses on those rights contained within articles 6 to 10 inclusive of the International Covenant on Civil and Political Rights: the right to life; freedom from torture or degrading treatment or punishment; freedom from medical treatment or experimentation without prior consent; the prohibition against slavery; and liberty rights.

Liberty and Security of the Person

The expression 'liberty and security of the person' is one found within article 9(1) of the ICCPR, although this chapter takes a broader approach to the phrase for the purpose of discussion. Consideration is given in this part of the chapter to the circumstances in which a person's liberty may be deprived (article 9(1)) and also to those issues which might be taken to be inherent to one's personal security: the prohibitions against slavery and servitude (article 8); the prohibition against medical and scientific experimentation (article 7); and personal security outside the context of formal arrest or detention (article 9(1) again).[1]

Deprivation of Liberty

Most of the provisions contained within article 9 of the Covenant are applicable only to persons against whom criminal charges are brought. It has been pointed out by the Committee, however, that paragraph 1 is applicable to all deprivations of liberty, whether in criminal cases or in other cases such as, for example, mental illness, vagrancy, drug addiction, educational purposes, immigration

1 The expression 'security of the person' might also be understood to encompass issues concerning privacy of the person: see Chapter 7.

control or the like.[2] A deprivation of liberty has been treated as including 'house arrest'.[3] Article 9(1) provides:

> 1. Everyone has the right to liberty and security of person. No one shall be subjected to arbitrary arrest or detention. No one shall be deprived of his liberty except on such grounds and in accordance with such procedure as are established by law.

This part of the chapter concerns itself with article 9(1) of the ICCPR: the right to liberty and the circumstances in which one's liberty might be deprived. On the latter question, the Committee has stated that any deprivation of a person's liberty must be subsequent to law, necessary, reasonable and absent arbitrariness.[4] The Committee has also repeated that every decision to keep a person in detention should be open to periodic review, in order to reassess the necessity of detention, and ensure that the detention does not continue beyond the period for which a State party can provide appropriate justification.[5]

As will be seen, a common justification relied upon by States in response to claims under article 9(1) has been the imposition of detention for security or 'preventive' reasons. On this issue, the Committee has said:[6]

> … if so-called preventive detention is used, for reasons of public security, it must be controlled by these same provisions, i.e. it must not be arbitrary, and must be based on grounds and procedures established by law (para 1), information of the reasons must be given (para 2) and court control of the detention must be available (para 4) as well as compensation in the case of a breach (para 5). And if, in addition, criminal charges are brought in such cases, the full protection of article 9 (2) and (3), as well as article 14, must also be granted.

Justifying the deprivation of liberty The deprivation of a person's liberty must be pursuant to the law, and strictly within the terms of the law including

2 *General Comment 8: Right to liberty and security of persons (Art 9)*, UN Doc CCPR General Comment 8 (1982), para 1. See further, for example: *Sultanova v Uzbekistan*, Communication 915/2000, UN Doc CCPR/C/86/D/915/2000 (2006), para 7.8; and *Shafiq v Australia*, Communication 1324/2004, UN Doc CCPR/C/88/D/1324/2004 (2006), para 7.2.

3 See: *Jaona v Madagascar*, Communication 132/1982, UN Doc CCPR/C/24/132/1982 (1985), paras 13–14; *Gorji-Dinka v Cameroon*, Communication 1134/2002, UN Doc CCPR/C/83/D/1134/2002 (2005), para 5.4; and *Abbassi v Algeria*, Communication 1172/2003, UN Doc CCPR/C/89/D/1172/2003 (2007), para 8.3.

4 See, for example *Gridin v Russian Federation*, Communication 770/1997, UN Doc CCPR/C/69/D/770/1997 (2000), para 8.1.

5 *Shafiq v Australia*, above n 2, para 7.2; *Ashurov v Tajikistan*, Communication 1348/2005, UN Doc CCPR/C/89/D/1348/2005 (2007), para 6.5.

6 General Comment 8, above n 2, para 4.

any requirement to obtain a warrant for arrest.[7] Arbitrary arrest and detention is specifically prohibited within the second sentence of article 9(1). Arbitrariness has been interpreted more broadly than conduct which is simply 'against the law', so as to include elements of unreasonableness. To be deemed arbitrary, the detention of a person must include elements of inappropriateness, injustice, lack of predictability and lack of due process of law.[8] Compliance with other rights within the Covenant in the determination of whether to detain will be essential to satisfy this.[9] The arrest of a person on false pretences, in *Mulezi v Democratic Republic of the Congo*, was found to violate article 9(1).[10]

In the context of security certificates issued against non-nationals who are, or might become, subject to expulsion proceedings the Committee commented as follows in *Ahani v Canada*:[11]

> … detention on the basis of a security certification by two Ministers on national security grounds does not result ipso facto in arbitrary detention, contrary to article 9, paragraph 1. However, given that an individual detained under a security certificate has neither been convicted of any crime nor sentenced to a term of imprisonment, an individual must have appropriate access, in terms of article 9, paragraph 4, to judicial review of the detention, that is to say, review of the substantive justification of detention, as well as sufficiently frequent review.

7 See, for example: *Wilson v Philippines*, Communication 868/1999, UN Doc CCPR/C/79/D/868/1999 (2003), para 7.5; *Sarma v Sri Lanka*, Communication 950/2000, UN Doc CCPR/C/78/D/950/2000 (2003), para 9.4; *de Gomez v Peru*, Communication 981/2001, UN Doc CCPR/C/78/D/981/2001 (2003), para 7.2; and *Rouse v Philippines*, Communication 1089/2002, UN Doc CCPR/C/84/D/1089/2002 (2005), para 7.7.

8 See: *de Guerrero v Colombia*, Communication 45/1979, UN Doc CCPR/C/15/D/45/1979 (1982); *Van Alphen v The Netherlands*, Communication 305/1988, UN Doc CCPR/C/39/D/305/1988 (1990); *Mukong v Cameroon*, Communication 458/1991, UN Doc CCPR/C/51/D/458/1991 (1994), para 9.8; *de Morais v Angola*, Communication 1128/2002, UN Doc CCPR/C/83/D/1128/2002 (2005), para 6.1; and *Gorji-Dinka v Cameroon*, above n 3, para 5.1.

9 See, for example, *Jaona v Madagascar*, Communication 132/1982, UN Doc CCPR/C/24/D/132/1982 (1985), where Monja Jaona was arrested in December 1982 and detained until August 1983 on account of his political opinions (in violation of both article 9(1) and 19).

10 *Mulezi v Democratic Republic of the Congo*, Communication 962/2001, UN Doc CCPR/C/81/D/962/2001 (2004), para 5.2. See also: *Busyo et al v Democratic Republic of the Congo*, Communication 933/2000, UN Doc CCPR/C/78/D/933/2000 (2003), para 5.3; *Más v Peru*, Communication 1058/2002, UN Doc CCPR/C/85/D/1058/2002 (2005), para 6.2; and *Fernando v Sri Lanka*, Communication 1189/2003, UN Doc CCPR/C/83/D/1189/2003 (2005), para 9.2.

11 *Ahani v Canada*, Communication 1051/2002, UN Doc CCPR/C/80/D/1051/2002 (2004), para 10.2.

As well as being lawful and lacking arbitrariness, any arrest or detention must be necessary and reasonable in all the circumstances.[12] This will be relevant not only to the decision to detain, but also as to the length of the deprivation of liberty. In *Spakmo v Norway*, the Committee considered that the author's arrest was reasonable and necessary in order to stop him from undertaking demolition work, which the police considered unlawful and a disturbance of the peace in the neighbourhood. The author's arrest of the next day was again a result of him refusing to follow the orders of the police. While accepting that the arrest may also have been reasonable and necessary, the Committee took the view that it was not, however, necessary to detain the author for eight hours in order to make him stop his activities. Due to the period of time involved, the Committee found that the author's detention to be unreasonable and thereby constituting a violation of article 9(1) of the Covenant.[13] Similarly, the continued detention of the author in *Baritussio v Uruguay*, after having served her prison sentence, was held to constitute a violation of article 9(1);[14] as was a detention without trial between the author's arrest in July 1979 and trial in January 1981, in *Mpaka-Nsusu v Zaire*.[15]

Detention pending removal Deprivation of liberty pending refugee and/or deportation status of aliens was a matter given considerable attention in *C v Australia*.[16] The author, who had close family ties in Australia but none in Iran, was lawfully in Australia for a period of six months in 1990 and left thereafter. He returned to Australia in July 1992 with a visitor's visa but no return air ticket, and was therefore detained in immigration detention, as a 'non-citizen' without an entry permit. He subsequently made an application for refugee status, on the basis of a well-founded fear of religious persecution in Iran as an Assyrian Christian. The application was refused by a delegate for the Minister of Immigration and Multicultural Affairs, and upheld by the Refugee Status Review Committee. The author appealed to the Federal Court and, meanwhile, applied to the Minister for Immigration for interim release from detention pending the decision of the Federal

12 *Van Alphen v The Netherlands*, above n 8. See also *Bousroual v Algeria*, Communication 992/2001, UN Doc CCPR/C/86/992/2001 (2006), para 9.5.

13 *Spakmo v Norway*, Communication 631/1995, UN Doc CCPR/C/67/D/631/1995 (1999), para 6.3. See also: *van Alphen v The Netherlands*, above n 8, para 5.8; *Chambala v Zambia*, Communication 856/1999, UN Doc CCPR/C/78/D/856/1999 (2003), paras 7.2–7.3; *D and E, and their two children v Australia*, Communication 1050/2002, UN Doc CCPR/C/87/D/1050/2002 (2006), para 7.2; *Bakhtiyari v Australia*, Communication 1069/2002, UN Doc CCPR/C/79/D/1069/2002 (2003), para 9.2; and *Abbassi v Algeria*, above n 3, para 8.4.

14 *Baritussio v Uruguay*, Communication 25/1978, UN Doc CCPR/C/16/D/25/1978 (1982), para 13.

15 *Mpaka-Nsusu v Zaire*, Communication 157/1983, UN Doc CCPR/C/27/D/157/1983 (1986), para 10.

16 *C v Australia*, Communication 900/1999, UN Doc CCPR/C/76/D/900/1999 (2002).

Court. This application was also rejected, the Minister observing that there was no power under section 89 of the Migration Act to release a person unless the person was removed from Australia or granted an entry permit. The Federal Court rejected the author's application for judicial review of the latter decision, confirming that no residual or discretionary power existed in the Migration Act, either expressly or by implication, enabling release of a person detained under the Act. The Full Court of the Federal Court later dismissed the author's further appeal, rejecting the argument that article 9(1) of the ICCPR favoured an interpretation of section 89 which would authorize only a minimum period of detention, and implied, where necessary, a power of release from custody pending the determination of an application for refugee status.

In August 1993, C was psychologically assessed, following some concern for his emotional and physical health following a lengthy incarceration. The author, who had attempted to commit suicide by electrocution, repeated his attempts to commit suicide and exhibited extreme scores on all the depression scales. He was assessed to be 'a serious danger to himself' and, in August 1994, was released from detention into his family's custody on the basis of special (mental) health needs. In December 1996, the author was interviewed by a delegate of the Minister with a view to possible deportation as a non-citizen. The author underwent a further psychiatric assessment, which found 'little doubt that there was a direct causal relationship between the offence for which he is currently incarcerated and the persecutory beliefs that he held on account of his [paranoid schizophrenic] illness'. It found, as a result of treatment, a decreasing risk of future acts based on his illness, but an ongoing need for careful psychiatric supervision. In January 1997, the author underwent a further psychiatric assessment resulting in similar conclusions. On 8 April 1997, the Minister ordered the author deported on this basis.

In his communication before the Committee it was argued that the facts described amounted to violations of article 9(1), freedom from arbitrary detention, and article 9(4), entitlement to take proceedings to determine the lawfulness of one's detention. As to the claims relating his detention (article 9(1)), the Committee recalled its jurisprudence in *A v Australia* that, in order to avoid a characterization of arbitrariness, detention should not continue beyond the period for which the State party can provide appropriate justification.[17] In the present case, the author's detention as a non-citizen without an entry permit continued, in mandatory terms, until he was removed or granted a permit. Australia advanced various reasons to justify the detention, linked to its immigration and border security policies.[18] The Committee did not consider that Australia had demonstrated a justification for the author's continued detention in the light of the passage of time and intervening circumstances. It took the view that Australia had failed to show that there were

17 *A v Australia*, Communication 560/1993, UN Doc CCPR/C/59/D/560/1993 (1997), para 9.4.

18 *C v Australia*, above n 16, paras 4.28–4.30.

not less invasive means of achieving the same ends by, for example, the imposition of reporting obligations, sureties or other conditions which would take account of the author's deteriorating condition. In these circumstances, whatever the reasons for the original detention, continuance of immigration detention for over two years without individual justification and without any chance of substantive judicial review was, in the Committees view, arbitrary and constituted a violation of article 9(1).[19]

Jalloh v The Netherlands also concerned the question of whether the author's detention was arbitrary, or necessary and proportionate. Considering the author's escape from an open facility at which he had been accommodated from the time of his arrival in the Netherlands as an illegal immigrant, the Committee here considered that it was not unreasonable to have detained him for a limited time until the administrative procedure relating to his case was completed. Once a reasonable prospect of expelling him no longer existed his detention was terminated. In those circumstances, the Committee found that the author's detention was not arbitrary and thus not in violation of article 9 of the Covenant.[20]

Detention pursuant to mental health legislation The main issue before the Committee in *A v New Zealand* was whether the author's detention under the Mental Health Act from 1984 to 1993 constituted a violation of the Covenant, in particular of article 9. The author's assessment under the Act followed threatening and aggressive behaviour on the author's part. The committal order was issued under, and in accordance with, the Mental Health Act, based on an opinion of three psychiatrists. A panel of psychiatrists continued to review the author's situation periodically. The Committee took the view, in those circumstances, that the deprivation of liberty was neither unlawful nor arbitrary, and thus not in violation of article 9(1) of the Covenant.[21]

Personal Security

Article 9(1) of the Covenant also protects the right to security of person outside the context of a formal deprivation of liberty.[22] The Committee has clarified that the

---

19 Ibid, para 8.2. See also: *Madafferi v Australia*, Communication 1011/2001, UN Doc CCPR/C/81/D/1011/2001 (2004), para 9.2; *Baban v Australia*, Communication 1014/2001, UN Doc CCPR/C/78/D/1014/2001 (2003), para 7.2; *Bakhtiyari v Australia*, above n 13, para 9.4; and *Shafiq v Australia*, above n 2, para 7.4.

20 *Jalloh v The* Netherlands, Communication 794/1998, UN Doc CCPR/C/74/D/794/1998 (2002), para 8.2.

21 *A v New Zealand*, Communication 754/1997, UN Doc CCPR/C/66/D/754/1997 (1999), para 7.2. Contrast with *Fijalkowska v Poland*, Communication 1061/2002, UN Doc CCPR/C/84/D/1061/2002 (2005), paras 8.2–8.3.

22 *Dias v Angola*, Communication 711/1996, UN Doc CCPR/C/68/D/711/1996 (2000), para 8.3.

interpretation of article 9 does not allow a State to ignore threats to the personal security of non-detained persons subject to its jurisdiction. In *Chongwe v Zambia*, persons acting in an official capacity within the Zambian police forces shot at the author, wounded him, and barely missed killing him. Zambia refused to carry out independent investigations. Internal investigations by the Zambian police had not, at the time of the hearing of the communication more than three years after the incident, been concluded or made public. No criminal proceedings had been initiated, and the author's claim for compensation appeared to have been rejected. In those circumstances, the Committee found that the author's right to security of person had been violated.[23]

Matters of personal security are also applicable in the context of slavery or servitude, or medical or scientific experimentation, considered next in this chapter.

Slavery and Servitude

The prohibitions against slavery and servitude, set out within article 8, have been very rarely invoked in communications before the Human Rights Committee. Article 8 provides that:

> 1. No one shall be held in slavery; slavery and the slave-trade in all their forms shall be prohibited.
> 2. No one shall be held in servitude.
> 3. (a) No one shall be required to perform forced or compulsory labour;
>   (b) Paragraph 3 (a) shall not be held to preclude, in countries where imprisonment with hard labour may be imposed as a punishment for a crime, the performance of hard labour in pursuance of a sentence to such punishment by a competent court;
>   (c) For the purpose of this paragraph the term 'forced or compulsory labour' shall not include:
>   (i) Any work or service, not referred to in subparagraph (b), normally required of a person who is under detention in consequence of a lawful order of a court, or of a person during conditional release from such detention;
>   (ii) Any service of a military character and, in countries where conscientious objection is recognized, any national service required by law of conscientious objectors;

23 *Chongwe v Zambia*, Communication 821/1998, UN Doc CCPR/C/70/D/821/1998 (2000), para 5.3. See also: *Páez v Colombia*, Communication 195/1985, UN Doc CCPR/C/39/D/195/1985 (1990), para 5.5; *Dias v Angola*, above n 22, para 8.3; *Sankara et al v Burkina Faso*, Communication 1159/2003, UN Doc CCPR/C/86/D/1159/2003 (2006), para 12.3; *Rajapakse v Sri Lanka*, Communication 1250/2004, UN Doc CCPR/C/87/D/1250/2004 (2006), para 9.6; and *Njaru v Cameroon*, Communication 1353/2005, UN Doc CCPR/C/89/D/1353/2005 (2007), para 6.3.

(iii) Any service exacted in cases of emergency or calamity threatening the life or well-being of the community;
(iv) Any work or service which forms part of normal civil obligations.

Where article 8 has been invoked, it has been mainly on the part of the respondent State, in answer to communications challenging compulsory military service. The author in *TWMB v The Netherlands*, for example, objected to the power of the State to require him to do military or substitute national service. The Committee observed that the Covenant did not preclude the institution of compulsory military service by States parties, and referred to article 8(3)(c)(ii), which expressly excludes service of a military character as falling within the definition of 'forced or compulsory labour'.[24] The Committee consequently concluded that the requirement to do military service, or for that matter substituted service, did not constitute a violation of articles 6 and 7 of the Covenant.[25] A similar claim was dismissed on the same grounds in *CBD v The Netherlands*.[26] On the specific issue of military service and the recognition by the Committee of a right of conscientious objection under article 18, see Chapter 4.

More direct reliance upon article 8 was made in *Faure v Australia*, concerning Australia's 'Work for Dole' programme, whereby persons wanting to receive unemployment benefits were required to perform labour. The Committee took the view that there was a violation of the ICCPR by reason of the fact that the programme raised an arguable claim of forced or compulsory labour under article 8(3) of the Covenant and, importantly, that there were no means by which a person could challenge the substance of the scheme and thereby have access to a potential remedy, as required by article 2 of the ICCPR.[27] On the substance of article 8(3), however, the Committee concluded as follows:[28]

> In the Committee's view, the term 'forced or compulsory labour' covers a range of conduct extending from, on the one hand, labour imposed on an individual by way of criminal sanction, notably in particularly coercive, exploitative or otherwise egregious conditions, through, on the other hand, to lesser forms of labour in circumstances where punishment as a comparable sanction is threatened if the labour directed is not performed. The Committee notes, moreover, that article 8, paragraph 3(c)(iv), of the Covenant exempts from the term 'forced or

24 See also the consideration of conscientious objection in Chapter 4.

25 *TWMB v The Netherlands*, Communication 403/1990, UN Doc CCPR/C/43/D/403/1990 (1991), para 6.5.

26 *CBD v The Netherlands*, Communication 394/1990, CCPR/C/45/D/394/1990 (1992), para 6.3. See also *JPK v The Netherlands*, Communication 401/1990, UN Doc CCPR/C/43/D/401/1990 (1991), para 6.5.

27 *Faure v Australia*, Communication 1036/2001, UN Doc CCPR/C/85/D/1036/2001 (2005), paras 7.2–7.4.

28 Ibid, para 7.5.

> compulsory labour' such work or service forming part of normal civil obligations. In the Committee's view, to so qualify as a normal civil obligation, the labour in question must, at a minimum, not be an exceptional measure; it must not possess a punitive purpose or effect; and it must be provided for by law in order to serve a legitimate purpose under the Covenant. In the light of these considerations, the Committee is of the view that the material before it, including the absence of a degrading or dehumanizing aspect of the specific labour performed, does not show that the labour in question comes within the scope of the proscriptions set out in article 8. It follows that no independent violation of article 8 of the Covenant has been made out.

Medical or Scientific Experimentation

Article 7 of the ICCPR is concerned with the prohibition against torture or cruel, inhuman or degrading treatment or punishment, a matter dealt with in more detail later in this chapter. As this affects the security of the *physical* person, the second sentence of article 7 particularizes the prohibition in the context of medical or scientific experimentation without the free consent of the person concerned. Special protection is necessary, the Committee has said, with regard to such experiments in the case of persons not capable of giving their consent.[29] Such persons should not be subjected to any medical or scientific experimentation that may be detrimental to their health.[30]

Rights of Persons Deprived of Liberty

Rights Activated by the Deprivation of Liberty

Once a person's liberty has been deprived, by whatever means that may be, paragraphs 2 to 5 of article 9 set out specific rights which are activated by simple virtue of the arrest or detention:

> 2. Anyone who is arrested shall be informed, at the time of arrest, of the reasons for his arrest and shall be promptly informed of any charges against him.
> 3. Anyone arrested or detained on a criminal charge shall be brought promptly before a judge or other officer authorized by law to exercise judicial power and shall be entitled to trial within a reasonable time or to release. It shall not be the general rule that persons awaiting trial shall be detained in custody,

29 *General Comment 7: Article 7*, UN Doc HRI\GEN\1\Rev.1 at 7 (1994), para 3. General Comment 7 was replaced by *General Comment 20: Prohibition of torture and cruel treatment or punishment (Art 7)*, UN Doc CCPR General Comment 20 (1992).

30 General Comment 20, ibid, para 7.

> but release may be subject to guarantees to appear for trial, at any other stage of the judicial proceedings, and, should occasion arise, for execution of the judgement.
> 4. Anyone who is deprived of his liberty by arrest or detention shall be entitled to take proceedings before a court, in order that court may decide without delay on the lawfulness of his detention and order his release if the detention is not lawful.
> 5. Anyone who has been the victim of unlawful arrest or detention shall have an enforceable right to compensation.

Information as to reasons for arrest Article 9(2) of the ICCPR provides anyone who is arrested has the right to be informed, at the time of arrest, of the reasons for the arrest, and to be promptly informed of any charges. One of the authors in *Domukovsky and others v Georgia*, Mr Tsiklauri, was arrested in August 1992 without a warrant and was not shown a warrant for his arrest until after he had been in detention for a year. As well as finding that there was an arbitrary and unreasonable arrest, the Committee expressed that this amounted to a violation of article 9(2).[31] By way of further example, the author in *ex-Philibert v Zaire* was arrested on 3 June 1967 by the Surete Nationale, deported to the island of Mbula-Mbemba in Lower Zaire, and then transferred to the prison Osio in Upper Zaire where he was detained until 30 August 1968 without ever being charged or informed of the reason for his detention.[32] The Committee observed, in *Ilombe and Shandwe v Democratic Republic of the Congo*, that it was not sufficient to simply inform the authors that they were being arrested for breach of State security, without any indication of the substance of the complaint against them.[33]

---

31 *Domukovsky and others v Georgia*, Communications 623–7/1995, UN Doc CCPR/C/62/D/623-627/1995 (1998), paras 18.2 and 18.4.

32 *Ex-Philibert v Zaire*, Communication 90/1981, UN Doc CCPR/C/OP/2 at 124 (1990). See also, by way of example: *De Bazzano v Uruguay*, Communication 5/1977, UN Doc CCPR/C/7/D/5/1977 (1979); *Mulezi v Democratic Republic of the Congo*, above n 10, para 5.2; *Rolando v Philippines*, Communication 1110/2002, UN Doc CCPR/C/82/D/1110/2002 (2004), para 5.5; *Khomidova v Tajikistan*, Communication 1117/2002, UN Doc CCPR/C/81/D/1117/2002 (2004), para 6.3; *El Hassy v The Libyan Arab Jamahiriya*, Communication 1422/2005, UN Doc CCPR/C/91/D/1422/2005 (2007), para 6.5; *Wilson v Philippines*, above n 7, para 7.5; *Roque v Peru*, Communication 1125/2002, UN Doc CCPR/C/85/D/1125/2002 (2005), para 7.2; *de Morais v Angola*, above n 8, para 6.2; and *Bee v Equatorial Guinea*, Communications 1152/2003 and 1190/2003, UN Doc CCPR/C/85/D/1152 & 1190/2003 (2005), para 6.2.

33 *Ilombe and Shandwe v Democratic Republic of the Congo*, Communication 1177/2003, UN Doc CCPR/C/86/D/1177/2003 (2006), para 6.2.

Bringing a detainee before a competent authority Article 9(3) requires that, in criminal cases, any person arrested or detained must be brought 'promptly' before a judge or other officer authorized by law to exercise judicial power. The Committee has expressed the view that the time between arrest or detention and being brought before such an officer or judge must not exceed a few days.[34] In *Kennedy v Trinidad and Tobago*, the author alleged violations of articles 9(2) and (3), because he was not charged until five days after his arrest, and not brought before a judge until six days after arrest. The Committee stated that, while the meaning of the term 'promptly' must be determined on a case-by-case basis, delays should not exceed a few days. In the current case, the Committee considered that the author had not been brought promptly before a judge, in violation of article 9(3).[35] A delay of three days between arrest and being brought before a judicial officer, in *Borisenko v Hungary*, was also seen as failing this requirement;[36] as were delays of four days in *Freemantle v Jamaica* and seven days in *Kurbanov v Tajikistan*.[37]

The question of what constitutes a 'competent authority' for the purpose of article 9(3) came before the Committee in *Kulomin v Hungary*. After his arrest in August 1988, the author's pre-trial detention was ordered and subsequently renewed on several occasions by the public prosecutor, until the author was brought before a judge in May 1989. The majority of the Committee considered that it was inherent to the proper exercise of judicial power that it be exercised by an authority which is independent, objective and impartial in relation to the issues dealt with, and that a public prosecutor did not fulfil that role. The Committee did not therefore regard the public prosecutor to be an 'officer authorized to exercise judicial power' within the meaning of article 9(3).[38] In a dissenting opinion, President Nisuke Ando took a different approach. Rather than excluding the competence of a public prosecutor

---

34 General Comment 8, above n 2, para 2.

35 *Kennedy v Trinidad and Tobago*, Communication 845/1998, UN Doc CCPR/C/74/D/845/1998 (2002), para 7.6.

36 *Borisenko v Hungary*, Communication 852/1999, UN Doc CCPR/C/76/D/852/1999 (2002), para 7.4.

37 *Freemantle v Jamaica*, Communication 625/1995, UN Doc CCPR/C/68/D/625/1995 (2000), para 7.4; and *Kurbanov v Tajikistan*, Communication 1096/2002, UN Doc CCPR/C/79/D/1096/2002 (2003), para 7.2. See also: *Bousroual v Algeria*, above n 12, para 9.6; *Boimurodov v Tajikistan*, Communication 1042/2001, UN Doc CCPR/C/85/D/1042/2001 (2005), para 7.4; *de Morais v Angola*, above n 8, para 6.4; *Ilombe and Shandwe v Democratic Republic of the Congo*, above n 33, para 6.3; and *Medjnoune v Algeria*, Communication 1297/2004, UN Doc CCPR/C/87/D/1297/2004 (2006), para 8.6–8.7.

38 *Kulomin v Hungary*, Communication 521/1992, UN Doc CCPR/C/56/D/521/1992 (1996). See also: *Saimijon and Bazarov v Uzbekistan*, Communication 959/2000, UN Doc CCPR/C/87/D/959/2000 (2006), para 8.2; *Sultanova v Uzbekistan*, above n 2, para 7.7; *Platonov v Russian Federation*, Communication 1218/2003, UN Doc CCPR/C/85/D/1218/2003 (2005), para 7.2; *Bandajevsky v Belarus*, Communication 1100/2002, UN Doc CCPR/C/86/D/1100/2002 (2006), para 10.3.

as having the competence to be a competent authority *per se*, he took a more detailed approach, explaining:

> Even in that type of system, a prosecutor's decision on the extension of the detention of a particular suspect in a given case may well be impartial and objectively justifiable. To deny such impartiality and objectivity, the Committee needs to clarify the detailed circumstances of the instant case on which it bases its finding, but such clarification is totally lacking in the Committee's Views.

In *Zheludkova v Ukraine*, the author claimed that her son had been held in custody for more than 50 days without being informed of the charges against him and that he was not brought before a competent judicial authority during this period. The Ukraine did not contest the failure to bring Mr Zheludkov promptly before a judge after his arrest, but stated that he had been placed in pre-trial detention by a decision of the procurator. It did not, however, provide information showing that the procurator had institutional objectivity and impartiality, and the Committee therefore concluded that the Ukraine had violated the author's rights under article 9(3).[39]

Another matter of concern to the Committee within paragraph 3 is the total length of detention pending trial. In certain categories of criminal cases in some countries this matter has caused some concern within the Committee, and members have questioned whether their practices have been in conformity with the entitlement to 'trial within a reasonable time or to release' under article 9(3). Pre-trial detention, the Committee has said, should be an exception and as short as possible, and that bail should instead be granted, except in situations where the likelihood exists that the accused would abscond or destroy evidence, influence witnesses, or flee from the jurisdiction of the State party.[40] The right under article 9(3) is one that must be dealt with in the presence of the person, rather than *ex parte*.[41]

---

39 *Zheludkova v Ukraine*, Communication 726/1996, UN Doc CCPR/C/76/D/726/1996 (2002), para 8.3. See, also: *Motta v Uruguay*, Communication 11/1977, UN Doc CCPR/C/10/D/11/1977(1980), para 16; *Wilson v Philippines*, above n 7, para 7.5; and *Bee v Equatorial Guinea*, above n 32, para 6.2.

40 General Comment 8, above n 2, para 3. See also, by way of example: *Walker and Richards v Jamaica*, Communication 639/1995, UN Doc CCPR/C/60/D/639/1995 (1997), para 8.2; *Taright et al v Algeria*, Communication 1085/2002, UN Doc CCPR/C/86/D/1085/2002 (2006), para 8.3; and *Siewpersaud et al v Trinidad and Tobago*, Communication 938/2000, UN Doc CCPR/C/81/D/938/2000 (2004), para 6.1.

41 See, for example, *Smirnova v Russian Federation*, Communication 712/1996, UN Doc CCPR/C/81/D/712/1996 (2004), para 10.1.

Habeas corpus Paragraph 4 of article 9 guarantees the right of every person deprived of liberty by arrest or detention to take proceedings before a court, in order to determine, without delay, the lawfulness of the detention and order the person's release if the detention is not lawful. This falls squarely within the traditional notion of *habeas corpus*, described in *Black's Law Dictionary* as 'a writ employed to bring a person before a court, most frequently to ensure that the party's imprisonment or detention is not illegal'.[42] Where a statutory scheme authorizing detention does not allow for appeal or review to a competent authority in substantive terms, and entailing the possibility of release, such a regime has been held to violate article 9(4).[43] Holding a person incommunicado has been seen as an effective bar against the ability to challenge the validity of one's arrest, and thus also in breach of article 9(4), as well as the article 9(3) right to be brought promptly before a competent authority.[44]

The author in *Valcada v Uruguay* was arrested in the streets of Montevideo by four police officers dressed in civilian clothing and taken to the headquarters of the Investigation and Intelligence Department. There he learned that he was accused of receiving the clandestine newspaper 'Carta', and was later transferred to the Central Prison where he remained for a further 50 days in solitary confinement. He was brought before a military court, where he was informed that, in the absence of any reasonable grounds for charging him with an offence, he could go free. At no time during the 50 days of his detention, was the author able to communicate with defence counsel, nor to have recourse to *habeas corpus*, because he was detained under the security measures. The Committee found violation of article 9(4) because, *habeas corpus* being unavailable in his case, the author was denied an effective remedy to challenge his arrest and detention.[45]

---

42 Bryan Garner (ed.), *Black's Law Dictionary* (7th edn, St. Paul, MN: West Publishing Co, 1999). The quoted definition is also sometimes termed *habeas corpus ad subjiciedum*. Black's continues, saying: 'In addition being used to test the legality of an arrest or commitment, the writ may be used to obtain review of (1) the regularity of extradition process, (2) the right to or amount of bail, or (3) the jurisdiction of a court that has imposed a criminal sentence.'

43 *C v Australia*, above n 16, para 8.3.

44 See, for example: *Muteba v Zaire*, Communication 124/1982, UN Doc CCPR/C/22/D/124/1982 (1984), para 12; *Bousroual v Algeria*, above n 12, paras 9.6–9.8; *El Alwani v The Libyan Arab Jamahiriya*, Communication 1295/2004, UN Doc CCPR/C/90/D/1295/2004 (2007), para 6.4; *de Morais v Angola*, above n 8, para 6.5; and *Aber v Algeria*, Communication 1439/2005, UN Doc CCPR/C/90/D/1439/2005 (2007), para 7.6.

45 *Valcada v Uruguay*, Communication 9/1977, UN Doc CCPR/C/8/D/9/1977 (1979), para 12. See also: *Barbato v Uruguay*, Communication 84/1981, UN Doc CCPR/C/17/D/84/1981 (1982), para 10(b); *de Bazzano v Uruguay*, above n 32, para 10; *Mulezi v Democratic Republic of the Congo*, above n 10, para 5.2; *Smirnova v Russian Federation*, above n 41, para 10.1; *Fijalkowska v Poland*, above n 21, para 8.4; *Abbassi v Algeria*, above n 3, para 8.5; *Benhadj v Algeria*, Communication 1173/2003, UN Doc CCPR/C/90/

Where a State party seeks to claim security measures as justifying denial of *habeas corpus*, the Committee has taken a restrictive approach. It has reflected upon the fact that the ICCPR, under article 4, does not allow national measures derogating from any of its provisions except in strictly defined circumstances. It will therefore require respondent governments to justify with precision such derogation.[46] By way of a corresponding burden upon those that claim violation of article 9(4), the Committee noted in *Stephens v Jamaica* that the author did not himself apply for *habeas corpus*. He could have, after being informed on 2 March 1983 that he was suspected of murder, requested a prompt decision on the lawfulness of his detention. There was no evidence before the Committee that he or his legal representative did do so and the Committee could not in those circumstances, it said, conclude that Stephens was denied the opportunity to have the lawfulness of his detention reviewed in court without delay.[47]

Preventive detention in the form of minimum non-parole periods was a matter considered by the Committee in *Rameka et al v New Zealand*. The authors argued that the minimum non-parole regime meant that there was insufficient regular review of their future 'dangerousness', and that they were thus effectively being sentenced for what they *might* do when released, rather than what they had done. The majority of the Committee (members Shearer, Wierusezewski and Ando dissenting) considered that a minimum-non parole period could be consistent with the ICCPR, but only if it was combined with a *finite* sentence of imprisonment of a length equal to or greater than the non-parole period.[48]

Treatment of Detainees

Article 10 of the ICCPR deals with the rights of those deprived of liberty as they affect the way in which such persons are treated while in detention: paragraph 1 is applicable to all persons deprived of their liberty; paragraph 2 deals with accused as distinct from convicted persons; and paragraph 3 with convicted persons only:

> Article 10
> 1. All persons deprived of their liberty shall be treated with humanity and with respect for the inherent dignity of the human person.

D/1173/2003 (2007), para 8.4; and *Ilombe and Shandwe v Democratic Republic of the Congo*, above n 33, para 6.4.

46 As in *Motta v Uruguay*, above n 39, para 15.

47 *Stephens v Jamaica*, Communication 373/1989, UN Doc CCPR/C/55/D/373/1989 (1995), para 9.7.

48 *Rameka et al v New Zealand*, Communication 1090/2002, UN Doc CCPR/C/79/D/1090/2002 (2003), para 7.2. See further Alex Conte, 'Human Rights, Non-Parole Periods and Preventive Detention' (2004) *New Zealand Law Journal* 202–5; and contrast with *Manuel v New Zealand*, Communication 1385/2005, UN Doc CCPR/C/91/D/1385/2005 (2007).

2. (a) Accused persons shall, save in exceptional circumstances, be segregated from convicted persons and shall be subject to separate treatment appropriate to their status as unconvicted persons;

(b) Accused juvenile persons shall be separated from adults and brought as speedily as possible for adjudication.

3. The penitentiary system shall comprise treatment of prisoners the essential aim of which shall be their reformation and social rehabilitation. Juvenile offenders shall be segregated from adults and be accorded treatment appropriate to their age and legal status.

Humanity and respect for human dignity The humane treatment and the respect for the dignity of all persons deprived of their liberty is a basic standard that, according to the Committee's General Comment 9, is of universal application and which cannot depend entirely on material resources. While the Committee was prepared to acknowledge that the conditions of detention may vary according to available resources, they said that this must always be such that persons are always treated with dignity and humanity and without discrimination.[49] Responsibility for the observance of this principle rests with the State as regards all institutions where persons are lawfully held against their will, not only in prisons but also, for example, in detention camps, hospitals (particularly psychiatric hospitals) or correctional institutions.[50]

Article 10(1) thus complements, for those deprived of liberty, the ban against torture or other cruel, inhuman or degrading treatment or punishment under article 7 of the Covenant. Not only must persons deprived of their liberty *not* be subjected to treatment that is contrary to article 7, including medical or scientific experimentation, but neither may they be subjected to any hardship or constraint other than that resulting from the deprivation of liberty itself.[51] Respect for the dignity of such persons must be guaranteed under the same conditions as for that of free persons.[52] Allowing visits, in particular by family members, is normally (according to the Committee) a measure that is required for reasons of humanity.[53] No penitentiary system should be retributory only, but should instead aim to achieve the reformation and social rehabilitation of the

49 *General Comment 9: Article 10*, UN Doc HRI\GEN\1\Rev.1 at 9 (1994), para 1. Note that General Comment 9 was replaced by *General Comment 21: Humane treatment of persons deprived of liberty (Art 10)*, UN Doc CCPR General Comment 21 (1992).

50 General Comment 21, ibid, para 2.

51 General Comment 21, ibid, para 3.

52 Ibid.

53 General Comment 9, above n 49, para 3.

prisoner.[54] The Committee recently described the standard of treatment required under article 10 as follows:[55]

> Inhuman treatment must attain a minimum level of severity to come within the scope of article 10 of the Covenant. The assessment of this minimum depends on all the circumstances of the case, such as the nature and context of the treatment, its duration, its physical or mental effects and, in some instances, the sex, age, state of health or other status of the victim.

Prison facilities A lack of sanitation, light, ventilation and bedding provided to those that are detained will be treated as a violation of article 10(1) of the Covenant.[56] Between the date of his arrest and the date of his trial the author in *Teesdale v Trinidad and Tobago* was remanded in custody at State prison, Port-of-Spain, for almost one and a half years. During that time he was in a twelve-by-eight-foot cell in which conditions were unsanitary: there was no sunlight or air; there was no bedding, and nowhere to wash; and the men had to urinate and defecate in the cell. After being sentenced to death, he was detained in a slightly smaller cell with a light bulb directly overhead, which was kept on day and night. The author claimed that he did not get any visitors and lacked privacy. When he wanted to consult with counsel, the author was handcuffed and placed in a three-by-three-foot box, during which at least two guards would stand directly behind the attorney. The author was denied an eye test until September 1996, even though his glasses did not fit since 1990. In the absence of any response from Trinidad and Tobago, the Committee found the allegations of the author to be proved and, consequently, that the circumstances disclosed a violation of article 10(1) of the Covenant.[57]

Further consideration was given to the nature of facilities in which prisoners are held in the case of *Wanza v Trinidad and Tobago*. Here the author was detained in a small cell with no window, but a ventilation hole of eighteen-by-eight inches instead; he was kept in this cell for 22 to 23 hours a day; and, on weekends and holidays, he was not allowed to leave the cell because of lack of prison staff. Such conditions were found to constitute a violation of article 10(1).[58]

In 1981, *Gustavo Bequio* was imprisoned and held in what was called 'La Isla', a prison wing of small cells without windows, where the artificial light was left on 24 hours a day and there was a cement bed and a hole in the floor for a toilet.

---

54 General Comment 21, above n 49, para 10.

55 *Brough v Australia*, Communication 1184/2003, UN Doc CCPR/C/86/D/1184/2003 (2006), para 9.2.

56 *Daley v Jamaica*, Communication 750/1997, UN Doc CCPR/C/63/D/750/1997 (1998), para 7.6.

57 *Teesdale v Trinidad and Tobago*, Communication 677/1996, UN Doc CCPR/C/74/D/677/1996 (2002), para 9.1.

58 *Wanza v Trinidad and Tobago*, Communication 683/1996, UN Doc CCPR/C/74/D/683/1996 (2002), para 9.2.

He was kept in solitary confinement there for more than one month. A finding of a violation of articles 7 and 10(1) was made.[59] Sharing a cell with mentally ill inmates and having close to his cell a large pipe carrying wastewater with foul odour, has likewise resulted in a finding by the Committee of violations of article 10(1).[60] Denial of recreational facilities, the occasional deprivation of food and failure to provide medical assistance when needed was found to be in breach of the Covenant in *Kalenga v Zambia*.[61]

Alarming allegations of the treatment of prisoners were made against Trinidad and Tobago in communication 684/1996, including overcrowding; no room for prisoners to lie down, let alone sleep; an absence of useful employment, education and recreational facilities; an average of 23 hours per day spent in cells, with 24-hour illumination in the cells; the one hour per day not spent in cells allowed prisoners to bathe, attend with visitors or exercise, with handcuffs on, in a small yard; prisoners were required to share a 'slop pail' (a bucket) as a toilet, emptied once each day; prisoners were permitted a maximum of two visits per week, each of 20 minutes duration; and writing facilities were severely limited.[62] Similar conditions were found to violate articles 7 and 10(1) in *McTaggart v Jamaica*, where overcrowding existed without the provision of any toilet facilities, not even a 'slop bucket'.[63] The author in *Lluberas v Uruguay* was kept in complete isolation for six months, also in violation of article 10(1).[64]

---

59 *Bequio v Uruguay*, Communication 88/1981, UN Doc CCPR/C/18/D/88/1981 (1983), para 12.

60 See *Bennett v Jamaica*, Communication 590/1994, UN Doc CCPR/C/65/D/590/1994 (1999), para 10.8.

61 *Kalenga v Zambia*, Communication 326/1988, UN Doc CCPR/C/48/D/326/1988 (1993), para 6.5.

62 *RS v Trinidad and Tobago*, Communication 684/1996, UN Doc CCPR/C/74/D/684/1996 (2002), as described within paras 2.7 and 2.8. See also: *Sextus v Trinidad and Tobago*, Communication 818/1998, UN Doc CCPR/C/72/D/818/1998 (2001); *Francis v Trinidad and Tobago*, Communication 899/1999, UN Doc CCPR/C/75/D/899/1999 (2002); and *Deidrick v Jamaica*, Communication 619/1995, UN Doc CCPR/C/62/D/619/1995 (1998).

63 *McTaggart v Jamaica*, Communication 748/1997, UN Doc CCPR/C/67/D/748/1997(1999), para 8.5. See also: *Howell v Jamaica*, Communication 798/1998, UN Doc CCPR/C/79/D/798/1998 (2003), para 6.2; *Siewpersaud et al v Trinidad and Tobago*, above n 40, para 6.3; *Saidova v Tajikistan*, Communication 964/2001, UN Doc CCPR/C/81/D/964/2001 (2004), para 6.4; *El Hassy v The Libyan Arab Jamahiriya*, above n 32, para 6.4; *Smirnova v Russian Federation*, above n 41, para 10.5; and *Cabal and Bertran v Australia*, Communication 1020/2001, UN Doc CCPR/C/78/D/1020/2001 (2003), para 8.3; *Bandajevsky v Belarus*, above n 38, para 10.5; *Gorji-Dinka v Cameroon*, above n 3, para 5.2; *Titiahonjo v Cameroon*, Communication 1186/2003, UN Doc CCPR/C/91/D/1186/2003 (2007), para 6.3; and *Aber v Algeria*, above n 44, para 7.7.

64 *Lluberas v Uruguay*, Communication 123/1982, UN Doc CCPR/C/21/D/123/1982 (1984), para 9.2.

Medical treatment Persons derived of liberty must be provided with medical treatment, where required. For several years, the author in *Simpson v Jamaica* had been experiencing an undiagnosed and untreated medical condition giving rise to symptoms of great pain and swelling in his testicle. He also complained of a back problem, from which he had suffered since childhood, and which made it difficult for him to sit upright for long periods of time. He had also developed eye problems because of the darkness in his cell. Although he was visited by a doctor in prison, the tablets he was prescribed did not provide any relief and he was refused specialist treatment. In the absence of any explanation from Jamaica, the Committee considered that lack of medical treatment amounted to a violation of his right to be treated with humanity and with respect for the inherent dignity of the human person.[65]

The author in *Zheludkova v Ukraine* claimed that her son has suffered serious injuries as a result of beatings received by him at the hands of police during his interrogation on a charge of rape. It was claimed, in particular, that he suffered severe damage to his left eye. The author supplied no medical evidence, saying that this was due to the fact that her son was given no access to his medical records. She did provide, however, a report by a doctor of the institution where her son was detained, which showed that he did complain to the doctor about the state of his eye; and put before the Committee an extensive series of medical records aimed at showing that he was in good health until 1992, prior to the alleged events. In the absence of contradictory evidence from the Ukraine, the Committee gave weight to the allegations and concluded that the consistent and unexplained denial of access to medical records was sufficient ground for finding a violation of article 10(1) of the Covenant.[66]

In *Lantsov v The Russian Federation*, the author alleged that her son had received medical care, after the deterioration of his health, only during the last few minutes of his life, and that prison authorities had refused such care during the preceding days so that this failure had itself caused his death. The State party, claiming that several inquiries were carried out into the causes of the death (acute pneumonia leading to cardiac insufficiency), responded that Mr Lantsov had not requested medical assistance. The Committee affirmed that it is incumbent on States to ensure the right to life of detainees, which was not dependent on detainees to request protection or assistance. By arresting and detaining individuals, the State

65 *Simpson v Jamaica*, Communication 695/1996, UN Doc CCPR/C/73/D/695/1996 (2001), para 7.2. See also: *Levy v Jamaica*, Communication 719/1996,UN Doc CCPR/C/64/D/719/1996 (1998), para 7.4; *Mulezi v Democratic Republic of the Congo*, above n 10, para 5.3; and *Saidova v Tajikistan*, above n 63, para 6.4; *Rouse v Philippines*, above n 7, para 7.8; and *Bandajevsky v Belarus*, above n 38, para 10.5.

66 *Zheludkova v Ukraine*, above n 39, para 8.4.

takes the responsibility to care for the life of those individuals. Lack of financial means cannot reduce this responsibility.[67]

Finally, it should be noted that the need to provide medical treatment, as an element of the humane treatment of detainees, is a subjective issue. Thus, in *Whyte v Jamaica*, the convict's allergy to paint fumes present during the refurbishment of death row entitled him to medical treatment, despite the fact that he was the only person suffering ill-effects from the fumes.[68]

Segregation Subparagraphs 2(a) and 2(b) of article 10 provide for the segregation of accused from convicted persons.[69] In the case of adults, this is to be the case, 'save in exceptional circumstances'. The segregation of accused persons from convicted ones is required in order to emphasize their status as unconvicted persons who are at the same time protected by the presumption of innocence set out in article 14(2).[70]

In the case of juvenile accused persons, deviation from the obligations under subparagraph 2(b) cannot be justified by any consideration whatsoever.[71] Juvenile offenders must be segregated from adults and be accorded treatment appropriate to their age and legal status. The Committee has given the examples, in that regard, of shorter working hours and greater contact with relatives, with the aim of furthering their reformation and rehabilitation. Article 10 does not indicate any limits of juvenile age. While the Committee has expressed the view that this is to be determined by each State party in the light of relevant social, cultural and other conditions, it has also said that article 6(5) of the ICCPR (prohibiting, *inter alia*, the imposition of any sentence of death for crimes committed by persons below 18 years of age) suggests that all persons under the age of 18 should be treated as juveniles, at least in matters relating to criminal justice.[72] Application of the United Nations Standard Minimum Rules for the Administration of Juvenile Justice, known as the Beijing Rules (1987), is also seen as required under article 10(2)(b).[73]

The author in *Thomas v Jamaica* was, at the age of 15, sentenced to be detained on murder convictions. He was kept among adult prisoners at St Catherine's Prison, the Committee thus finding that Jamaica had failed to discharge its obligations

67 *Lantsov v The Russian Federation*, Communication 763/1997, UN Doc CCPR/C/74/D/763/1997 (2002), para 9.2.

68 *Whyte v Jamaica*, Communication 732/1997, UN Doc CCPR/C/63/D/732/1997 (1998), para 9.4.

69 Emphasized in *McTaggart v Jamaica*, above n 63, para 8.8.

70 General Comment 9, above n 49, para 4. See, for example, *Gorji-Dinka v Cameroon*, above n 3, para 5.3.

71 General Comment 9, above n 49, para 2.

72 General Comment 21, above n 49, para 13.

73 Ibid.

under the Covenant, article 10 paragraphs 2 and 3.[74] It should be noted that, when considering the status of juveniles in detention, account should also be taken of article 14(4), requiring that criminal proceedings take into account the age of juvenile offenders and the aim of rehabilitation.[75]

Rehabilitation The prison system must treat prisoners with the essential aim of achieving their reformation and social rehabilitation. The author in *Jensen v Australia* claimed that the penitentiary system did not, in his case, have as its essential aim his social rehabilitation and reformation. A variety of programmes and mechanisms were in place, however, in Australia's prison system that were geared towards this end. The Committee considered that the author had failed to substantiate that the assessments of his reformative progress raised issues of compliance with the requirements of article 10(3).[76]

Torture; and Cruel, Inhuman or Degrading Treatment or Punishment

Article 7 prohibits torture as well as the cruel, inhuman or degrading treatment or punishment of any person. As a specific example of conduct falling within the prohibition, the second sentence of article 7 expressly guarantees freedom from medical or scientific experimentation, a matter already discussed in this chapter. The text of article 7 allows no limitation and, even in situations of public emergency such as are envisaged by article 4(1), this provision is non-derogable. It should be noted that no distinction is made in this status as between torture on the one hand, and cruel, inhuman or degrading treatment or punishment on the other:

> Article 7
> No one shall be subjected to torture or to cruel, inhuman or degrading treatment or punishment. In particular, no one shall be subjected without his free consent to medical or scientific experimentation.

It is the duty of the State, the Committee said in its General Comment 20, to afford everyone protection, through legislative and other measures as may be necessary, against the acts prohibited by article 7, whether inflicted by people acting in their official capacity, outside their official capacity, or in a private capacity.[77]

---

74 *Thomas v Jamaica*, Communication 800/1998, UN Doc CCPR/C/65/D/800/1998 (1999), para 6.5.

75 See further Chapter 6 herein.

76 *Jensen v Australia*, Communication 762/1997, UN Doc CCPR/C/71/D/762/1997 (2001), para 6.4.

77 General Comment 20, above n 29, para 2.

The Nature of the Article 7 Prohibition

As for many other rights within the Covenant, article 7 carries with it a positive duty to protect. It is not sufficient for the implementation of this article to prohibit such treatment or punishment or to make it a crime. Most States have penal provisions applicable to cases of torture or similar practices. Read together with article 2 of the Covenant, however, the Committee has made it clear that States must ensure an effective protection through some machinery of control.[78] Complaints about ill-treatment must be investigated effectively by competent authorities. Those found guilty must be held responsible, and the alleged victims must themselves have effective remedies at their disposal, including the right to obtain compensation. Among the safeguards which may make control effective are provisions against detention incommunicado; granting, without prejudice to the investigation, persons such as doctors, lawyers and family members access to the detainees; provisions requiring that detainees should be held in places that are publicly recognized and that their names and places of detention should be entered in a central register available to persons concerned, such as relatives; provisions making confessions or other evidence obtained through torture or other treatment contrary to article 7 inadmissible in court; and measures of training and instruction of law enforcement officials not to apply such treatment.[79]

Within the same context, the Committee has taken the view that amnesties for gross violations of human rights, through legislation such as the Law No 15,848 in *Rodriguez v Uruguay*, are incompatible with the obligations of the State party under the Covenant. The Committee noted in that communication, with 'deep concern', that the adoption of this law effectively excluded in a number of cases the possibility of investigation into past human rights abuses and thereby prevented the State from discharging its responsibility to provide effective remedies to the victims of those abuses. The Committee was also concerned that, in adopting this law, the State party contributed to an atmosphere of impunity which could undermine the democratic order and give rise to further grave human rights violations.[80]

What level of treatment qualifies? The Covenant does not contain any definition of the concepts covered by article 7, nor does it distinguish between them. However, the terms of article 7, prohibiting cruel, inhuman or degrading treatment, establish that the scope of protection required goes beyond 'torture' as

78 General Comment 7, above n 29, para 1.

79 As suggested by the Committee in its General Comment 7, above n 29, para 1.

80 See: *Rodriguez v Uruguay*, Communication 322/1988, UN Doc CCPR/C/51/D/322/1988 (1994); and the Comments of the Committee on Uruguay's third periodic report under article 40 of the Covenant, adopted on 8 April 1993 (CCPR/C/64/Add.4). See also *Blancov v Nicaragua*, Communication 328/1988, UN Doc CCPR/C/51/D/328/1988 (1994), para 10.6.

normally understood.[81] It may not be necessary to draw sharp distinctions between the various prohibited forms of treatment or punishment. Such distinctions will depend on the kind, purpose and severity of the particular treatment. In the view of the Committee the prohibition must extend to corporal punishment, including excessive chastisement as an educational or disciplinary measure.[82]

The beating of a prisoner by a prison warden clearly falls within the bounds of prohibited conduct under article 7, as does violence by other inmates where prison officers have acquiesced in the conduct.[83] In the execution of a search of a prisoner's cell, the author in *Reynolds v Jamaica* was beaten up by three men with guns and batons. Later, in the corridor, he was stripped of his clothes, beaten, stabbed and hit with a metal detector. A warder, in the author's presence, told the assisting soldiers to kill the author. The items the author had in his cell were destroyed, and his clothes and sleeping mat were drenched with water. The author was then locked away without receiving any medical treatment. He complained to the Parliamentary Ombudsman by letter of 9 July 1988, to which he received no reply. The Committee did not hesitate to find a violation of articles 7 and 10(1) of the Covenant.[84]

Solitary confinement may, depending upon the circumstances, and especially when the person is kept incommunicado or in prolonged solitary confinement, be contrary to either or both articles 7 and/or 10(1).[85] The holding of a person incommunicado will, in and of itself, be considered to be ill-treatment within the terms of article 10(1), and has also been treated as a violation of article 9 as a whole.[86] Complaints of 'food not fit for human consumption' and only having 'a piece of sponge and old newspapers' to sleep on, together with being treated with brutality by the warders whenever complaints were made, were the subject of

81 General Comment 20, above n 29, para 4.

82 General Comment 7, above n 29, para 2. See also the discussion below on corporal punishment.

83 On the latter point, see *Wilson v Philippines*, above n 7, para 7.3.

84 *Reynolds v Jamaica*, Communication 587/1994, UN Doc CCPR/C/59/D/587/1994 (1997), para 10.2. See also: *Gilboa v Uruguay*, Communication 147/1983, UN Doc CCPR/C/26/D/147/1983 (1985), para 13.2; *Henry v Trinidad and Tobago*, Communication 752/1997, UN Doc CCPR/C/64/D/752/1997 (1999), para 7.1; *Siragev v Uzbekistan*, Communication 907/2000, UN Doc CCPR/C/85/D/907/2000 (2005), para 6.2; and *Benhadj v Algeria*, above n 45, para 8.5.

85 General Comment 7, above n 29, para 2; and General Comment 20, above n 29, para 6. See, for example: *de Voituret v Uruguay*, Communication 109/1981, UN Doc CCPR/C/21/D/109/1981 (1984), para 13; *Kang v Republic of Korea*, Communication 878/1999, UN Doc CCPR/C/78/D/878/1999 (2003), para 7.3; and *Arutyunyan v Uzbekistan*, Communication 917/2000, UN Doc CCPR/C/80/D/917/2000 (2004), para 6.2.

86 See, for example: *Romero v Uruguay*, Communication 85/1981, UN Doc CCPR/C/21/D/85/1981 (1984), para 13; and *Alegre v Peru*, Communication 1126/2002, UN Doc CCPR/C/85/D/1126/2002 (2005), paras 7.3–7.4.

consideration in *Elahie v Trinidad and Tobago*.[87] Moreover, the Committee has considered article 7 to protect not only persons arrested or imprisoned, but also pupils and patients in educational and medical institutions.[88]

De Bazzano v Uruguay concerned various victims and breaches of numerous articles of the Covenant. Amongst those claims, the author said that her husband, Mr Ambrosini, was detained and subjected to various forms of torture such as 'planton' (being forced to remain standing for 14 hours at a time), electric shocks, and 'bastinado' (physical blows to the body). He was accused of complicity in 'subversive association' for having participated in a demonstration, and subsequently indicted on the basis of his identification by a single alleged witness who did not appear during the preliminary investigation in order to confirm his prior statement. After one year's detention, the judge granted him conditional release, but this decision could not be put into effect because, shortly before the decision, Ambrosini had been removed from the place of detention without the judge's knowledge and had been taken to a place unknown to the judge. The Committee considered that these facts disclosed violation of articles 7 and 10(1), because he was detained under conditions seriously detrimental to his health; article 9(1), because he was kept in custody in spite of a judicial order of release; articles 9(3) and 14(1), (2) and (3), because he was not brought to trial within a reasonable time and was tried in circumstances in which he was denied the requisite safeguards of fair trial; article 9(4), because he was denied any effective remedy to challenge his arrest and detention; and article 10(1), because he was held incommunicado for months and was denied the right to be visited by any family member.[89]

The author in *Morrison v Jamaica* complained that the block in which he was detained was searched on 5 March 1997. He was, at that time, ordered to come out of his cell and beaten and his possessions burned. He complained to the superintendent, but apparently nothing was done about it. The author also claimed that one warder took $1,600 away from him, and he was told it was confiscated. It was further submitted that the author was locked in his cell on 12 August 1997 without food or water for the whole day, and was threatened when he asked for some water. On the basis that the State party did not reply to these allegations, although it had an opportunity to do so, the Committee concluded that the author was subjected to treatment in violation of articles 7 and 10(1) of the Covenant.[90]

---

87 *Elahie v Trinidad and Tobago*, Communication 533/1993, UN Doc CCPR/C/60/D/533/1993 (1997), para 8.3.

88 General Comment 7, above n 29, para 2.

89 *De Bazzano v Uruguay*, above n 32, para 10(i). See also *Machado v Uruguay*, Communication 83/1981, UN Doc CCPR/C/20/D/83/1981 (1983).

90 *Morrison v Jamaica*, Communication 635/1995, UN Doc CCPR/C/63/D/635/1995 (1998), para 23.3. See also: *Walker and Richards v Jamaica*, above n 40, para 8.1; and *Kimouche v Algeria*, Communication 1328/2004, UN Doc CCPR/C/90/D/1328/2004 (2007), para 7.6.

While in pre-trial detention, the author in *Boodoo v Trinidad and Tobago* was found with a hand-made weapon in his cell. He claimed to have been steadily persecuted since that time, including being transferred from Carrera Prison to Port-of-Spain Prison for brief periods of incarceration. When at Port-of-Spain Prison, the author reported being left in a dimly-lit cell 24 hours a day and not let out for recreation or airing. Upon returning to Carrera Prison, the author would be forced to strip naked, and pull back the foreskin of his penis as well as being forced to pull his buttocks apart and squat three to four times in front of the prison guards. According to the author, no other prisoners were subjected to such humiliation. The Committee decided that, in the absence of an explanation from the State, such treatment amounted to a violation of article 7 of the Covenant.[91]

In *Tshishimbi v Zaire*, the author was abducted and, since that time and up to the Committee's meeting, had no contact with his family or with the outside world. The Committee considered that this constituted cruel and inhuman treatment, in violation of article 7 of the Covenant.[92]

Physical and emotional pressure together have been found to breach article 7, although there have been only rare findings that emotional or psychological suffering alone has amounted to torture. In *Mukong v Cameroon*, for example, the Human Rights Committee considered that, quite apart from poor conditions of detention, the author's detention incommunicado, coupled with threats of torture and death and intimidation, deprivation of food, and being kept locked in his cell for several days on end without the possibility of recreation culminated in a violation of the Covenant. In *Domukovsky and others v Georgia*, the combination of physical ill-treatment, along with 'moral pressure' and threats to family were found to amount to breaches of article 7.[93] Anguish and stress caused to a mother by the disappearance of her daughter and by the continuing uncertainty concerning her fate and whereabouts was seen as qualifying her as a victim of the violation of article 7 in *de Quinteros v Uruguay*. The author in that communication, said the Committee, had the right to know what had happened to her daughter.[94] Failure to allow a woman to proceed with her right under domestic law to a therapeutic pregnancy has been treated as amounting to both a breach of article 7, as well as 17 (private and family life).[95]

---

91 *Boodoo v Trinidad and Tobago*, Communication 721/1996, UN Doc CCPR/C/74/D/721/1996 (2002), para 6.5.

92 *Tshishimbi v Zaire*, Communication 542/1993, UN Doc CCPR/C/56/D/542/1993 (1996), para 5.5. See also: *El Alwani v The Libyan Arab Jamahiriya*, above n 44, para 6.5; *El Hassy v The Libyan Arab Jamahiriya*, above n 32, para 6.2; *Sarma v Sri Lanka*, above n 7, para 9.5; and *Aber v Algeria*, above n 44, para 7.3.

93 *Domukovsky and others v Georgia*, above n 31, para 18.6.

94 *De Quinteros v Uruguay*, Communication 107/1981, UN Doc CCPR/C/19/D/107/1981 (1983), para 14. See also: *El Alwani v The Libyan Arab Jamahiriya*, above n 44, para 6.6; and *Sarma v Sri Lanka*, above n 7, para 9.5.

95 *Huamán v Peru*, Communication 1153/2003, UN Doc CCPR/C/85/D/1153/2003 (2005), para 6.3. See further Chapter 7 herein.

In the absence of special circumstances, such as procedural delays imputable to the State party, the Committee has repeatedly affirmed that prolonged judicial proceedings do not *per se* constitute cruel, inhuman and degrading treatment.[96] The Committee was not sympathetic to a claim in *Obodzinsky v Canada* that the author's poor health meant that citizenship revocation proceedings against him amounted to a violation of article 7, in circumstances where those proceedings were provoked by serious allegations that the author participated in the gravest crimes.[97]

Evidence obtained as a result of ill-treatment It has been observed by the Human Rights Committee that methods violating the provisions of articles 7 and article 10(1) are often used in order to compel an accused to confess or testify, and there has been a growing tendency to resort to such methods in the investigation of terrorist incidents or during counter-terrorism intelligence operations more generally since the events of 11 September 2001.[98] The Committee has taken a firm position that no statements or confessions or other evidence obtained in violation of article 7 may be invoked as evidence in judicial proceedings, including during a state of emergency, except in the case of a statement or confession used as evidence that torture or other treatment prohibited by the article 7 has occurred.[99] This is consistent with the approach taken under article 15 of the Convention against Torture and Other Cruel, Inhuman or Degrading Treatment or Punishment, albeit that article 15 of that Convention only applies to evidence obtained as a result of 'torture'. The same distinction does not exist under the terms of article 7, nor within the applicable General Comments and views of the Human Rights

---

96 See, for example: *Barrett and Sutcliffe v Jamaica*, Communications 270/1988 and 271/1988, UN Doc CCPR/C/44/D/270&271/1988 (1992), para 8.4; *Martin v Jamaica*, Communication 317/1988, UN Doc CCPR/C/47/D/317/1988 (1993), para 12.2; *Stephens v Jamaica*, above n 47, paras 9.3–9.4; *Chaplin v Jamaica*, Communication 596/1994, UN Doc CCPR/C/55/D/596/1994 (1995), para 8.1; and *Obodzinsky v Canada*, Communication 1124/2002, UN Doc CCPR/C/89/D/1124/2002 (2007), para 9.2.

97 *Obodzinsky v Canada*, above n 96, para 9.2.

98 See, for example: *General Comment 32: Article 14: Right to equality before courts and tribunals and to a fair trial*, UN Doc CCPR/C/GC/32 (2007), para 41; and *Report of the Special Rapporteur on the promotion and protection of human rights and fundamental freedoms while countering terrorism, Martin Scheinin, Mission to the United States of America*, UN Doc A/HRC/6/17/Add.3, Chapter IV.

99 General Comment 20, above n 29, para 12. See also Chapter 4 herein and: *General Comment 29: States of Emergency (Article 4)*, UN Doc CCPR/C/21/Rev.1/Add.11 (2001), paras 7 and 15; General Comment 32, ibid, para 6; *Saimijon and Bazarov v Uzbekistan*, above n 38, para 8.3; *Tulyaganova v Uzbekistan*, Communication 1041/2001, UN Doc CCPR/C/90/D/1041/2001 (2007), para 8.2; *Khudayberganova v Uzbekistan*, Communication 1140/2002, UN Doc CCPR/C/90/D/1140/2002 (2007), para 8.2; and *Kurbonov v Tajikistan*, Communication 1208/2003, UN Doc CCPR/C/86/D/1208/2003 (2006), para 6.3.

Committee. The Committee has taken the view that the burden of proving that a confession was entirely voluntary should not rest on the accused.[100] As a follow-up issue, it has also taken the position that it is essential that complaints about torture and ill-treatment must be investigated promptly and impartially by competent authorities.[101]

In this regard, however, the Committee has also taken the view that it is in general for the courts of States parties, and not for the Committee, to evaluate the facts in a particular case (in much the same way as it has done in the application of article 14 of the ICCPR).[102] In *Sahadeo v Republic of Guyana*, for example, the Committee was faced with claims of torture that had also been alleged during the trial of the author in 1989 and again in his retrial in 1994. The notes of evidence of the retrial suggested that Mr Sahadeo had the opportunity to give evidence and that witnesses of his treatment during his detention by the police were cross-examined. The Committee took the view that the author did not show that the Courts' evaluation of the facts was manifestly arbitrary or amounted to a denial of justice. In the circumstances, it found that the facts before it did not sustain a finding of a violation of article 7.[103]

Evidence of ill-treatment in communications before the Committee The Human Rights Committee has taken a robust approach to the issue of evidence of the ill-treatment of authors in situations where the respondent State provides no rejoinder to allegations made. The circumstances surrounding Rafael Mojica's disappearance, in *Mojica v Trinidad and Tobago* for example, gave rise to the Committee's view of a strong inference that he had been tortured or subjected to

---

100 See, for example: *Baboeram-Adhin and others v Suriname*, Communication 146/1983, UN Doc CCPR/C/24/D/146/1983 (1985), para 14.2; *Quinteros v Uruguay*, Communication 107/1981, UN Doc CCPR/C/19/D/107/1981 (1983), para 11; *Bousroual v Algeria*, above n 12, para 9.4; *Singarasa v Sri Lanka*, Communication 1033/2001, UN Doc CCPR/C/81/D/1033/2001 (2004), para 7.4; *Benhadj v Algeria*, above n 45, para 8.3; *Medjnoune v Algeria*, above n 37, 8.3–8.4; *Kimouche v Algeria*, above n 90, para 7.4; and *Aber v Algeria*, above n 44, para 7.2.

101 See, for example: *Shukurova v Tajikistan*, Communication 1044/2002, UN Doc CCPR/C/86/D/1044/2002 (2006), para 8.2; *Tarasova v Uzbekistan*, Communication 1057/2002, UN Doc CCPR/C/88/D/1057/2002 (2006), para 7.1; *Kurbanov v Tajikistan*, above n 37, para 7.4; *Khomidova v Tajikistan*, above n 32, para 6.2; *Khudayberganova v Uzbekistan*, above n 99, para 8.2; *Sankara et al v Burkina Faso*, above n 23, para 12.2; and *Zheikov v Russian Federation*, Communication 889/1999, UN Doc CCPR/C/86/D/889/1999 (2006), para 7.2.

102 On the application of article 14, see Chapter 6 herein.

103 *Sahadeo v Republic of Guyana*, Communication 728/1996, UN Doc CCPR/C/73/D/728/1996 (2001), para 9.3. See also: *Yakupova v Uzbekistan*, Communication 1205/2003, UN Doc CCPR/C/92/D/1205/2003 (2008), para 7.2; and *PK v Canada*, Communication 1234/2003, UN Doc CCPR/C/89/D/1234/2003 (2007), para 7.3.

cruel and inhuman treatment. Nothing had been submitted to the Committee by the State party to dispel or counter this inference.[104]

Removal to a jurisdiction where there is a risk of ill-treatment If a State party removes a person who is within its territory and subject to its jurisdiction in such circumstances that, as a result, there is a real risk that his or her rights under the Covenant will be violated in another jurisdiction, that State party may itself be in violation of the Covenant. This principle is applicable to real risks of death (discussed below), as well as of torture, or cruel, inhuman or degrading treatment.[105] On the question of what amounts to a 'real risk', the Committee understood this to mean a 'necessary and foreseeable consequence', this being a requirement of the admissibility process to qualify a person as a 'victim' within the meaning of article 1 of the Optional Protocol.[106] The expulsion of the author from Sweden to Egypt, in *Alzery v Sweden*, required the Committee to determine whether this exposed the author to a real risk of torture or other ill-treatment in Egypt, in breach of the prohibition on refoulement contained in article 7 of the Covenant. In determining the risk of such treatment, the Committee considered all relevant elements, including the general situation of human rights in Egypt. The existence of diplomatic assurances, their content, and the existence and implementation of enforcement mechanisms were also taken into account. On the question of diplomatic assurances, the Committee concluded:[107]

> The Committee notes that the assurances procured contained no mechanism for monitoring of their enforcement. Nor were any arrangements made outside

---

104 *Mojica v Trinidad and Tobago*, Communication 449/1991, UN Doc CCPR/C/51/D/449/1991 (1994), para 5.7. See also, for example: *Mulezi v Democratic Republic of the Congo*, above n 10, para 5.1; *Saidova v Tajikistan*, above n 63, para 6.2; *Khalilov v Tajikistan*, Communication 973/2001, UN Doc CCPR/C/83/D/973/2001 (2005), para 7.2; *de Gomez v Peru*, above n 7, para 7.1; *Aliboev v Tajikistan*, Communication 985/2001, UN Doc CCPR/C/85/D/985/2001 (2005), para 6.2; *Chikunova v Uzbekistan*, Communication 1043/2002, UN Doc CCPR/C/89/D/1043/2002 (2007), para 7.2; *El Hassy v The Libyan Arab Jamahiriya*, above n 32, para 6.3; *Sultanova v Uzbekistan*, above n 2, para 7.2; *Más v Peru*, above n 10, para 6.1; *Alegre v Peru*, above n 86, para 7.2; *Bee v Equatorial Guinea*, above n 32, para 6.1; *Ashurov v Tajikistan*, above n 5, para 6.2; and *Njaru v Cameroon*, above n 23, para 6.1.

105 General Comment 20, above n 29, para 9. See also *Singh v Canada*, Communication 1315/2004, UN Doc CCPR/C/86/D/1315/2004 (2006), para 6.3.

106 *GT v Australia*, Communication 706/1996, UN Doc CCPR/C/61/D/706/1996 (1997), para 8.1. See further Chapter 2 herein, and also: *Wobbes et al v The Netherlands*, Communication 429/1990, UN Doc CCPR/C/47/D/429/1990 (1993); and *Lindon v Australia*, Communication 646/1995, UN Doc CCPR/C/64/D/646/1995 (1998). Contrast with *Esposito v Spain*, Communication 1359/2005, UN Doc CCPR/C/89/D/1359/2005 (2007), para 7.5.

107 *Alzery v Sweden*, Communication 1416/2005, UN Doc CCPR/C/88/D/1416/2005 (2006), para 11.5. Contrast with *Soto et al v Australia*, Communication 1429/2005, UN Doc CCPR/C/92/D/1429/2005 (2008), para 6.3.

> the text of the assurances themselves which would have provided for effective implementation. The visits by the State party's ambassador and staff commenced five weeks after the return, neglecting altogether a period of maximum exposure to risk of harm. The mechanics of the visits that did take place, moreover, failed to conform to key aspects of international good practice by not insisting on private access to the detainee and inclusion of appropriate medical and forensic expertise, even after substantial allegations of illtreatment emerged. In light of these factors, the State party has not shown that the diplomatic assurances procured were in fact sufficient in the present case to eliminate the risk of ill-treatment to a level consistent with the requirements of article 7 of the Covenant.

Punishments of a Cruel, Inhuman or Degrading Nature

Article 7 not only prohibits torture, and the cruel, inhuman or degrading treatment of persons, but also guarantees that no person will be made subject to cruel, inhuman or degrading punishment. Such claims often allege violation to both articles 7 and 10(1). The Committee has taken a mixed approach to such claims. In the majority, it has tended to make its determinations based upon article 10(1) and, upon such finding, commented that there is no need to then consider article 7. Alternatively, it has based its findings on both articles 7 and 10(1).

Imprisonment awaiting execution of death sentence The imposition of the death penalty is a matter affecting the right to life under article 6, discussed later in this chapter. The question of imprisonment whilst awaiting death sentence has also been drawn to the attention of the Human Rights Committee. In *Ashby v Trinidad and Tobago*, the author claimed to be the victim of a violation of article 7 and 10(1), on the grounds of his prolonged detention on death row for a period of 4 years, 11 months and 16 days. According to counsel, the length of the detention, during which Ashby lived in cramped conditions with poor sanitary and recreational facilities, amounted to cruel, inhuman and degrading treatment within the meaning of article 7. The Committee reaffirmed its constant jurisprudence that detention on death row for a specific period does not, by itself, violate article 7 of the Covenant in the absence of further compelling circumstances.[108] The Committee has explained its

108 *Ashby v Trinidad and Tobago*, Communication 580/1994, UN Doc CCPR/C/74/D/580/1994 (2002), para 10.6. The Committee concluded that article 7 had not been violated in that communication. See also *McIntosh v Jamaica*, Communication 640/1995, UN Doc CCPR/C/61/D/640/1995 (1998), para 6.2; *Teesdale v Trinidad and Tobago*, above n 57, para 9.2; *Johnson v Jamaica*, Communication 558/1993, UN Doc CCPR/C/59/D/558/1993 (1997), para 8.2 – 8.5; *Wanza v Trinidad and Tobago*, above n 58, para 9.3; *Bailey v Jamaica*, Communication 709/1996, UN Doc CCPR/C/66/D/709/1996 (1999), para 7.6; and *Persaud and Rampersaud v Guyana*, Communication 812/1998, UN Doc CCPR/C/86/D/812/1998 (2006), para 7.3.

position as follows, in *Levende v Trinidad and Tobago*:[109]

> [An] implication of making the time factor per se the determining one, i.e. the factor that turns detention on death row into a violation of the Covenant, is that it conveys a message to States parties retaining the death penalty that they should carry out a capital sentence as expeditiously as possible after it was imposed. This is not a message the Committee would wish to convey to States parties. Life on death row, harsh as it may be, is preferable to death.

The Committee has, however, been divided on this point. In the latter communication, Committee members Fausto Pocar, Prafullachandra Bhagwati, Christine Chanet, Pilar de Pombo and Julio Vallejo expressed the following dissenting opinion:

> The Committee reiterates in the present cases the views that prolonged detention on death row cannot per se constitute a violation of article 7 of the Covenant. This view reflects a lack of flexibility that would not allow the Committee to examine the circumstances of each case, in order to determine whether, in a given case, prolonged detention on death row constitutes cruel, inhuman or degrading treatment within the meaning of the above-mentioned provision. This approach leads the Committee to conclude, in the present cases, that detention on death row for almost sixteen/eighteen years after the exhaustion of local remedies does not allow a finding of violation of article 7. We cannot agree with this conclusion. Keeping a person detained on death row for so many years, after exhaustion of domestic remedies, and in the absence of any further explanation of the State party as to the reasons thereof, constitutes in itself cruel and inhuman treatment. It should have been for the State party to explain the reasons requiring or justifying such prolonged detention on death row; however, no justification was offered by the State party in the present cases.

A similar division of views was expressed in *Bickaroo v Trinidad and Tobago*.[110] In *Fancis v Jamaica*, the Committee commented:[111]

---

109 *Levende v Trinidad and Tobago*, Communication 554/1993, UN Doc CCPR/C/61/D/554/1993 (1998), para 5.5.

110 *Bickaroo v Trinidad and Tobago*, Communication 555/1993, UN Doc CCPR/C/61/D/555/1993 (1998).

111 *Fancis v Jamaica*, Communication 606/1994, UN Doc CCPR/C/54/D/606/1994 (1995), para 9.2. See also *Williams v Jamaica*, Communication 609/1995, UN Doc CCPR/C/61/D/609/1995 (1997), para 6.5, where the mental deterioration of the author while serving time on death row was also considered. For an earlier and detailed consideration of the issue of detention on death row, see *Johnson v Jamaica*, above n 108. The dissenting opinion of Fausto Pocar and Rajsoomer Lallah in *Thomas v Jamaica*, Communication 532/1993, UN Doc CCPR/C/61/D/532/1993 (1997), also warrant consideration.

> Whereas the psychological tension created by prolonged detention on death row may affect persons in different degrees, the evidence before the Committee in this case, including the author's confused and incoherent correspondence with the Committee, indicates that his mental health seriously deteriorated during incarceration on death row. Taking into consideration the author's description of the prison conditions, including his allegations about regular beatings inflicted upon him by warders, as well as the ridicule and strain to which he was subjected during the five days he spent in the death cell awaiting execution in February 1988, which the State party has not effectively contested, the Committee concludes that these circumstances reveal a violation of Jamaica's obligations under articles 7 and 10, paragraph 1, of the Covenant.

In *Pennant v Jamaica*, the Committee considered that, in the absence of a detailed explanation by the State party as to the reasons for the author's two weeks stay in a 'death cell' well in advance of any execution date, which Jamaica acknowledged might cause 'some anxiety', this could not be deemed to be compatible with the provisions of the Covenant, to be treated with humanity.[112] The Committee has also been sympathetic to claims where a lengthy detention on death row is such that the treatment in, as well as the conditions of, detention have exacerbated the person's mental conditions and have resulted in long-term psychological damage.[113]

Corporal punishment In May 1995, the author in *Higginson v Jamaica* was convicted of illegal possession of a firearm, rape and aggravated robbery and sentenced to respectively 5, 10 and 7 years imprisonment with hard labour (to run concurrently) and, in addition, to receive 6 strokes of the tamarind switch. One of the questions faced by the Human Rights Committee was whether the tamarind switch was a cruel or inhuman punishment. Irrespective of the nature of the crime that is to be punished, or the permissibility of corporal punishment under domestic law, the Committee reiterated its earlier findings that corporal punishment does constitute cruel, inhuman and degrading treatment or punishment contrary to article 7 of the Covenant. The Committee found that the imposition or execution of a sentence of whipping with the tamarind switch constituted such a violation.[114] Similarly, in *Sooklal v Trinidad*, the author was sentenced to 12 strokes of the birch. In determining whether this disclosed a violation of article 7, the Committee again

112 *Pennant v Jamaica*, Communication 647/1995, UN Doc CCPR/C/64/D/647/1995 (1998), para 8.6. See also: *Reece v Jamaica*, Communication 796/1998, UN Doc CCPR/C/78/D/796/1998 (2003), para 7.8; and *Howell v Jamaica*, above n 63, para 6.3.

113 See, for example, *Wilson v Philippines*, above n 7, para 7.4.

114 *Higginson v Jamaica*, Communication 792/1998, UN Doc CCPR/C/74/D/792/1998 (2002), para 4.6. See also *Pryce v Jamaica*, Communication 793/1998, UN Doc CCPR/C/80/D/793/1998 (2004), para 6.2.

recalled its earlier decisions that corporal punishment constitutes cruel, inhuman or degrading punishment contrary to article 7 of the Covenant.[115]

Mental health issues The continued detention of the author in *C v Australia*, when the State party was aware of the author's mental condition and failed to take the steps to ameliorate his mental deterioration was found to constitute a violation of the author's rights under article 7 of the Covenant.[116] The dissenting opinion of three members, however, was that such a conclusion would expand the scope of article 7. The circumstances of the case showed that the author was psychologically assessed and under permanent observation. The fact that the State party did not immediately order his release, but decided only on the basis of a psychiatric report to recommend release and external treatment could not be considered, in their view, to amount to a violation of article 7. The dissenting members considered that the majority had gone too far by arguing that the conflict between the author's continued detention and his sanity could only be solved by his release, and that the State party would otherwise be in violation of the said provision.

Within the same communication, it was argued that the author's deportation would also amount to a violation of article 7. The Committee attached weight to the fact that the author was originally granted refugee status on the basis of a well-founded fear of persecution as an Assyrian Christian, coupled with the likely consequences of a return of his mental illness. In circumstances where the State party had recognized a protection obligation towards the author, the Committee considered that deportation to a country where it was unlikely that he would receive the treatment necessary for the illness (caused, in whole or in part, by the State party's violation of the author's rights under article 9) would also amount to a violation of article 7 of the Covenant.[117]

The Right to Life

The right to life enunciated in article 6 has been described by the Human Rights Committee as 'the supreme right'. It is one from which no derogation is permitted, even in time of public emergency threatening the life of the nation (article 4).[118] Article 6 expresses the basic principle of the right to life, then moves to deal with the death penalty and genocide:

115 *Sooklal v Trinidad*, Communication 928/2000, UN Doc CCPR/C/73/D/928/2000 (2001), para 4.6. The Committee cited, by way of example, its decision in *Osbourne v Jamaica*, Communication 759/1997, UN Doc CCPR/C/68/D/759/1997 (2000).

116 *C v Australia*, above n 16, para 8.4.

117 Ibid, para 8.5. See, again, the dissention opinion of President Nisuke Ando, Eckart Klein and Maxwell Yalden.

118 *General Comment 6: Article 6*, UN Doc HRI\GEN\1\Rev.1 at 6 (1994), para 1.

Article 6
1. Every human being has the inherent right to life. This right shall be protected by law. No one shall be arbitrarily deprived of his life.
2. In countries which have not abolished the death penalty, sentence of death may be imposed only for the most serious crimes in accordance with the law in force at the time of the commission of the crime and not contrary to the provisions of the present Covenant and to the Convention on the Prevention and Punishment of the Crime of Genocide. This penalty can only be carried out pursuant to a final judgement rendered by a competent court.
3. When deprivation of life constitutes the crime of genocide, it is understood that nothing in this article shall authorize any State Party to the present Covenant to derogate in any way from any obligation assumed under the provisions of the Convention on the Prevention and Punishment of the Crime of Genocide.
4. Anyone sentenced to death shall have the right to seek pardon or commutation of the sentence. Amnesty, pardon or commutation of the sentence of death may be granted in all cases.
5. Sentence of death shall not be imposed for crimes committed by persons below eighteen years of age and shall not be carried out on pregnant women.
6. Nothing in this article shall be invoked to delay or to prevent the abolition of capital punishment by any State Party to the present Covenant.

The Inherent Right to Life

The expression 'inherent right to life' cannot properly be understood in a restrictive manner, and the protection of this right requires that States adopt positive measures, including taking all possible measures to reduce infant mortality and to increase life expectancy, especially in adopting measures to eliminate malnutrition and epidemics.[119]

Arbitrary deprivation of life The protection against arbitrary deprivation of life, explicitly required by the third sentence of article 6(1), is of paramount importance. States parties are required to take measures not only to prevent and punish deprivation of life by criminal acts, but also to prevent arbitrary killing by

---

119 General Comment 6, ibid, para 5. Compare this with the unsuccessful claim that the authors were deprived of a healthy environment in violation of article 6 in *Dahanayake and 41 other Sri Lankan citizens v Sri Lanka*, Communication 1331/2004, UN Doc CCPR/C/87/D/1331/2004 (2006), para 6.4.

their own security forces.[120] In the case of *Camargo v Colombia*, a judge of the 77th Military Criminal Court of Investigation, himself a member of the police, ordered a raid to be carried out at house No 136-67 Transversal 31 in Bogota. The raid was ordered in the belief that the former Ambassador of Colombia to France, who had been kidnapped some days earlier by a guerrilla organization, was being held prisoner in the house. In spite of the fact that the former Ambassador was not found, the police patrol decided to hide in the house to await the arrival of the suspected kidnappers. They were killed as they arrived. The Committee viewed the action of the police to be disproportionate to the requirements of law enforcement in the circumstances of the case and that the victims were arbitrarily deprived of life contrary to article 6(1) of the Covenant. Inasmuch as the police action was held out to be justifiable under Colombian law by Legislative Decree No 0070, the Committee considered that the law of Colombia did not adequately protect the right to life.[121]

A further clear instance of arbitrary deprivation of life was found in *Burrell v Jamaica*, where Mr Burrell died following the hostage taking of some warders at St Catherine prison's death row section. Mr Burrell was shot after the warders had been rescued and released, and thus the Committee declared that the need for force no longer existed. The Committee concluded that Jamaica had failed to take effective measures to protect Mr Burrell's life, in violation of article 6(1) of the Covenant.[122] The need for a State to undertake an independent investigation into the circumstances of the death of any person under its effective control has been part of the Committee's constant jurisprudence.[123]

The Committee has also found a violation of article 6 in circumstances where Cameroon had condoned life threatening conditions of detention at Bafoussam prison, especially the apparently unchecked propagation of life-threatening diseases, and had failed to allow a nurse access to the victim's cell when he was clearly severely ill.[124]

Protecting life in response to threats In *Vaca v Colombia*, where threats were made against the life of the author, the Committee considered that the State there had a duty to investigate the threats and provide protection to Mr Vaca. It is no excuse, it said, that the person against whom such threats are made is at liberty, that

120 General Comment 6, above n 118, para 3. See also: *Barbato v Uruguay*, above n 45, para 10(a); *Páez v Colombia*, above n 23; *Chongwe v Zambia*, above n 23, para 5.2; and *El Alwani v The Libyan Arab Jamahiriya*, above n 44, paras 6.7–6.8.

121 *Camargo v Colombia*, Communication 45/1979, UN Doc CCPR/C/15/D/45/1979 (1982), para 13.2.

122 *Burrell v Jamaica*, Communication 546/1993, UN Doc CCPR/C/57/D/546/1993 (1996), para 9.5.

123 See, for example: *Burrell v Jamaica*, ibid; and *Telitsina v Russian Federation*, Communication 888/1999, UN Doc CCPR/C/80/D/888/1999 (2004), para 7.7.

124 *Titiahonjo v Cameroon*, above n 63, para 6.2.

is, not detained or imprisoned.[125] In *Jayawardena v Sri Lanka*, a medical doctor and member of the United National Party in Sri Lanka was appointed Shadow Minister of Rehabilitation, Resettlement and Refugees. From 1998, Mrs Kumaratunga, the President of Sri Lanka, made public accusations that the author was involved with the Liberation Tigers of Tamil Elam, with such allegations receiving wide publicity by the government-controlled radio and television corporations. In March 2000, the Secretary General of Parliament requested the Ministry of Defence to provide the author with the same security afforded to the Members of Parliament in the North-East of the country, as his work was concentrated in those provinces. The author claimed, before the Committee, that Sri Lanka had, notwithstanding the provision of security, violated his rights by failing to investigate the complaints of death threats he had received. Sri Lanka contended, in response, that the author did not in fact receive any death threats and that no complaints or reports of such threats were made. It did not, however, provide specific arguments or materials to refute the author's detailed account of at least two complaints made by him to the police. In the circumstances, the Committee concluded that the failure to investigate the threats violated the author's right to security of person.[126]

Disappearance of persons It has been said by the Human Rights Committee that States parties should take specific and effective measures to prevent the disappearance of individuals, something which it described as having become all too frequent and leading too often to the arbitrary deprivation of life. The Committee has consequently recommended that States should establish effective facilities and procedures to thoroughly investigate cases of missing and disappeared persons in circumstances which may involve a violation of the right to life.[127] In *Coronel et al v Colombia*, the Special Investigations Unit of the State party's Attorney-General's office established that State officials were responsible for the victims' detention and disappearance. The Human Rights Division of the Attorney-General's Office later acknowledged that State security forces had detained and killed the victims. These admissions might be taken as signifying acceptance of responsibility for such conduct that might thereby avoid an adverse finding against Colombia. However, by failing to take measures against the persons responsible for the murder of the victims, the Committee concluded that Colombia has not respected or guaranteed the right to life of the victims, in violation of article 6(1) of the Covenant.[128]

Drawing from article 7(2)(i) of the Statute of the International Criminal Court, the Committee has defined enforced disappearance as the 'arrest, detention or

125 *Vaca v Colombia*, Communication 859/1999, UN Doc CCPR/C/74/D/859/1999 (2002), paras 7.2–7.3.

126 *Jayawardena v Sri Lanka*, Communication 916/2000, UN Doc CCPR/C/75/D/916/2000 (2002), para 7.3.

127 General Comment 6, above n 118, para 4.

128 *Coronel et al v Colombia*, Communication 778/1997, UN Doc CCPR/C/76/D/778/1997 (2002), para 9.3.

abduction of persons by, or with the authorization, support or acquiescence of, a State or a political organization, followed by a refusal to acknowledge that deprivation of freedom or to give information on the fate or whereabouts of those persons, with the intention of removing them from the protection of the law for a prolonged period of time'. Any act of such disappearance constitutes a violation of many of the rights enshrined in the Covenant, including the right to liberty and security of the person (article 9), the right not to be subjected to torture or to cruel, inhuman or degrading treatment or punishment (article 7), and the right of all persons deprived of their liberty to be treated with humanity and with respect for the inherent dignity of the human person (article 10). It also violates or constitutes, the Committee has said, a grave threat to the right to life (article 6).[129]

Compulsory military service Claims of violation of articles 6 and 7 of the Covenant, through a requirement to do military service, have been repeatedly rejected by the Committee as holding any substance.[130] Such claims have been declared inadmissible under article 3 of the Optional Protocol, and have instead been dealt with in the context of conscientious belief under article 18 of the ICCPR.[131]

Refugees One of the most significant grounds for claims of refugee status is the fear of persecution or the loss of life. Against that background, the author in *VMRB v Canada* expressed fear for his life should he be deported to El Salvador and sought to challenge the deportation order made against him on that account. The Committee expressed the view that it could not examine hypothetical violations of Covenant rights that might occur in the future. Furthermore, the Government of Canada stated that it would not extradite the author to El Salvador and gave him the opportunity to select a safe third country.[132] This position should be distinguished from that where a person is subject to return to a country where the death penalty is either being sought in respect of, or has been imposed against, the person.

129 *Bousroual v Algeria*, above n 12, para 9.2. See also: *El Alwani v The Libyan Arab Jamahiriya*, above n 44, para 6.2; *El Hassy v The Libyan Arab Jamahiriya*, above n 32, paras 6.6–6.7; *Sarma v Sri Lanka*, above n 7, para 9.3; and *Kimouche v Algeria*, above n 90, para 7.2.

130 See: *JPK v The Netherlands*, above n 26; *TWMB v The Netherlands*, above n 25; and *ARU v The Netherlands*, Communication 509/1992, UN Doc CCPR/C/49/D/509/1992 (1993).

131 See Chapter 4 herein.

132 *VMRB v Canada*, Communication 236/1987, UN Doc CCPR/C/33/D/236/1987 (1988), para 6.3.

The Death Penalty

The deprivation of life by the authorities of a State is a matter of the utmost gravity and, accordingly, the Committee has seen a need for a State's municipal law to strictly control and limit the circumstances in which a person may be deprived of life.[133] It should be noted, in this regard, that the abolition of the death penalty is a matter provided for under the Second Optional Protocol to the ICCPR.[134] No one within the jurisdiction of States parties to the Second Optional Protocol may be executed and States parties to it are required to take all necessary measures to abolish the death penalty within their jurisdiction.[135]

It follows from the wording of paragraphs 2, 4, 5 and 6 of article 6 that States are not obliged to abolish the death penalty, although the Committee has taken the view that the wording of those paragraphs strongly suggests that abolition is desirable.[136] States are, however, obliged to limit its use and, in particular, to abolish it for other than 'the most serious crimes' (article 6(2)). The expression 'most serious crimes' must, according to the Human Rights Committee, be read restrictively to mean that the death penalty should be a quite exceptional measure.[137] It also follows from the express terms of article 6 that it can only be imposed in accordance with the law in force at the time of the commission of the crime, and in a manner that is not contrary to the Covenant. This notion was expanded upon in *Mbenge v Zaire*, the Committee stating that article 6(2) requires that both the substantive and procedural law in the proceedings leading to the imposition of the death penalty must be in compliance with the domestic law of the State and with the provisions of the Covenant. Consequently, in that case, a failure by the State to afford the author appropriate rights in the determination of the charges against him (contrary to the requirements of article 14(3)) led to a finding that the death sentence pronounced against the author was contrary to the provisions of the Covenant, and therefore in violation of article 6(2).[138]

The procedural guarantees prescribed in the ICCPR must therefore be observed, including the right to a fair hearing by an independent tribunal, the presumption of innocence, the minimum guarantees for the defence, and the right to review by a higher tribunal. The failure of States to observe the requirements of article 14

133 General Comment 6, above n 118, para 3.

134 Second Optional Protocol to the International Covenant on Civil and Political Rights, aiming at the abolition of the death penalty, adopted and proclaimed by General Assembly Resolution 44/128 of 15 December 1989.

135 Article 1 of the Second Optional Protocol.

136 General Comment 6, above n 118, para 6.

137 General Comment 6, above n 118, para 7.

138 *Mbenge v Zaire*, Communication 16/1977, UN Doc CCPR/C/18/D/16/1977 (1983), para 17. See also *Henry v Jamaica*, Communication 230/1987, UN Doc CCPR/C/43/D/230/1987 (1991), para 8.5; *Morrison v Jamaica*, Communication 461/1991, UN Doc CCPR/C/56/D/461/1991 (1996), para 10.6; and *Daley v Jamaica*, above n 56, para 7.7.

(fair trial) has repeatedly resulted in a finding of a violation of article 6 of the Covenant.[139] These rights are applicable in addition to the particular right to seek pardon or commutation of the sentence.[140] The Committee has determined that violation of article 6 *juncto* article 14 may be remedied by a subsequent commutation of sentence.[141]

Moreover, when the death penalty is applied by a State party for the most serious crimes, it must not only be strictly limited in accordance with article 6 but it must be carried out in such a way as to cause the least possible physical and mental suffering, in accordance with article 7.[142]

Mandatory imposition of death penalty An issue that has come before the Committee various times is whether criminal code provisions that include the mandatory imposition of the death penalty, whether in general or in relation to specific offences, constitute an 'arbitrary deprivation of life', in violation of article 6(1). In the case of *Ibao v Philippines*, for example, the operation of article 48 of the Revised Penal Code meant that the author's commission of three murders and an attempted murder resulted in the death penalty being imposed automatically. The Committee held that this amounted to an arbitrary deprivation of life, because the death penalty was imposed without regard being able to be paid to the defendant's personal circumstances or the circumstances of the particular offence. The Committee further commented that this was part of the established jurisprudence of the Committee.[143] The President of the Committee, Nisuke Ando, and Committee member Ruth Wedgwood, disagreed, pointing out that the facts in the previous cases were different and that two dissenting opinions were appended to the views in Kennedy. It was also pointed out that the Committee's views in the earlier Thompson case were a departure from the then existing practice of the Committee, rather than part of a line of consistent jurisprudence. Prior to that decision, the Committee had dealt with many communications from persons sentenced to death under legislation that makes a death sentence for murder

---

139 See further Chapter 6 herein.

140 See, for example, *Mansaraj et al v Sierra Leone*, Communications 839–41/1998, UN Doc CCPR/C/72/D/839-841/1998 (2001), para 5.6; and *Domukovsky and others v Georgia*, above n 31, para 8.10.

141 *Aliev v Ukraine*, Communication 781/1997, UN Doc CCPR/C/78/D/781/1997 (2003), para 7.4; *Zhurin v Russian Federation*, Communication 851/1999, UN Doc CCPR/C/82/D/851/1999 (2004), para 6.6; *Boimurodov v Tajikistan*, above n 37, para 6.3; *Gougnina v Uzbekistan*, Communication 1141/2002, UN Doc CCPR/C/92/D/1141/2002 (2008), para 5.6; and *Kharkhal v Belarus*, Communication 1161/2003, UN Doc CCPR/C/91/D/1161/2003 (2007), para 6.3.

142 General Comment 20, above n 29, para 6.

143 *Ibao v Philippines*, Communication 1077/2002, UN Doc CCPR/C/77/D/1077/2002 (2003), para 8.3. See also *Thompson v St Vincent and the Grenadines*, Communication 806/1998, UN Doc CCPR/C/70/D/806/1998 (2000); and *Kennedy v Trinidad and Tobago*, above n 35.

mandatory. However, in none of those communications had the Committee stated that a mandatory sentence involved a violation of article 6 or any other provision of the Covenant. The dissenting opinions in Kennedy added that, in fulfilling its function under article 40 of the Covenant, the Committee has considered reports from States parties whose domestic legislation provides for mandatory imposition of the death sentence for murder, but the Committee has never stated in its Concluding Observations to those reports that a mandatory death sentence for murder was incompatible with the Covenant. Moreover, in its first General Comment on article 6, the Committee gave no indication that mandatory death sentences were incompatible with article 6. While the Committee is not bound by its previous jurisprudence, the President of the Committee nevertheless opined that, if it wished to change its jurisprudence, the Committee should explain its reasons for the change. Such an explanation was lacking in the Committee's views in the Thompson case, nor was it supplied in Ibao.

Under common law jurisdictions, courts are obliged to take into account factual and personal circumstances in sentencing to the death penalty in homicide cases. Courts there scrutinize factors such as self-defence, provocation by the victim, proportionality of the response by the accused, and the accused's state of mind. Likewise, in civil law jurisdictions, various aggravating or extenuating circumstances such as self-defence, necessity, distress and mental capacity of the accused need to be considered in reaching a criminal conviction and/or sentence in each case of homicide. Accordingly, President Ando concluded that these points must have been dealt with before the relevant courts of the Philippines rendered their decisions. Finally, he wondered if the majority views were justifiable only on the assumption that the death penalty is *per se* an arbitrary deprivation of life. Such an assumption, he said, would be contradictory to the structure of the Covenant, which admits the death penalty for the most serious crimes under paragraph 2. It would be equally contradictory to the fact that the Protocol aiming at the abolition of the death penalty is 'Optional'. Article 6(6) suggests that the abolition of the death penalty is desirable, but does not make abolition a legal obligation. While in certain regions of the globe most States have abolished the death penalty, it is also true that in the other regions of the globe most States have retained the death penalty. In the President's opinion, therefore, the Human Rights Committee, which is based on the global community of States, should take into account this situation when interpreting and applying any provisions of the ICCPR.

The President's dissent in *Ibao v The Philippines* is firm in its denunciation of the majority views and backed by earlier dissenting opinions and inconsistent jurisprudence. As pointed out, however, the Committee is not bound by its previous jurisprudence. While it is regrettable that the Committee's recent views do not explain the basis upon which its jurisprudence has shifted, it is notable that these decisions have been consistent (at least by the majority) since 1999.[144] The Committee was unanimous, in *Larrañaga v Philippines*, in its latest finding to this effect.[145]

Imposition of death penalty while review pending The Committee has been very critical where a person subject to a sentence of execution has been so executed, notwithstanding the State's knowledge of appeals and reviews lodged by the sentenced person. In *Ashby v Trinidad and Tobago*, Ashby's counsel argued that her client had been arbitrarily deprived of his life when the State party executed him in full knowledge of the fact that Mr Ashby was still seeking remedies before the Courts of Appeal, the Judicial Committee of the Privy Council and the Human Rights Committee. The Committee found that Trinidad had acted in breach of its obligations under the Covenant. Having regard to the fact that the representative of the Attorney-General informed the Privy Council that Ashby would not be executed until all possibilities of obtaining a stay of execution had been exhausted, the Committee criticized the execution of Mr Ashby's sentence notwithstanding that assurance and commented that this constituted a breach of the principle of good faith which governs all States in their discharge of obligations under international treaties, including the Covenant. The execution of Mr Ashby when the sentence was still under challenge constituted a violation of article 6, paragraphs 1 and 2, of the Covenant. The Committee went on to say:[146]

> … [a] State party commits a serious breach of its obligations under the Optional Protocol if it engages in any acts which have the effect of preventing or frustrating consideration by the Committee of a communication alleging any violation of the Covenant, or to render examination by the Committee moot and the expression of its Views nugatory and futile. The behaviour of the State party represents a shocking failure to demonstrate even the most elementary good faith required of a State party to the Covenant and of the Optional Protocol.

Removal of a person to a jurisdiction with the death penalty If a State party deports a person within its territory and subject to its jurisdiction in such circumstances that, as a result, there is a real risk that his or her rights under the Covenant will be violated in another jurisdiction, that State party may itself be in violation of the

144 For views of the Committee since *Ibao v The Philippines*, see: *Persaud and Rampersaud v Guyana*, above n 108, para 7.2; *Hussain and Singh v Guyana*, Communication 862/1999, UN Doc CCPR/C/85/D/862/1999 (2005), para 6.2; *Chan v Guyana*, Communication 913/2000, UN Doc CCPR/C/85/D/913/2000 (2006), para 6.5; *Rolando v Philippines*, above n 32, para 5.2; and *Rayos v Philippines*, Communication 1167/2003, UN Doc CCPR/C/81/D/1167/2003 (2004), para 7.2.

145 *Larrañaga v Philippines*, Communication 1421/2005, UN Doc CCPR/C/87/D/1421/2005 (2006), para 7.3.

146 *Ashby v Trinidad and Tobago*, above n 108, para 10.8. See also *Taylor v Jamaica*, Communication 707/1996, UN Doc CCPR/C/60/D/707/1996 (1997), para 8.5.

Covenant. As discussed above, this principle is applicable to real risks of death, as well as of torture, or cruel, inhuman or degrading treatment.[147] The issue in *GT v Australia* was whether, by deporting the author to Malaysia, Australia exposed him to such a risk. States parties to the Covenant must ensure that they carry out all their other legal commitments, whether under domestic law or under agreements with other States, in a manner consistent with the Covenant. Relevant in this case was Australia's obligation, under article 2(1) of the Covenant, to ensure to all individuals within its territory and subject to its jurisdiction the rights recognized in the Covenant. The Committee observed that article 6, paragraphs 1 and 2 read together, allows the imposition of the death penalty for the most serious crimes, but that the Second Optional Protocol, to which Australia was a party, provided that no one within the jurisdiction of a State party shall be executed and that the State party shall take all necessary measures to abolish the death penalty in its jurisdiction.

However, the Committee considered that the intent of the country to which a person is to be deported, ascertainable from the pattern of conduct shown by the country in similar cases, should be taken into account. The Australian Government was deporting GT from its territory because he had no entitlement to remain in Australia; Malaysia has not requested GT's return; and nothing in the information before the Committee pointed to any intention on the part of Malaysian authorities to prosecute GT. Australia had itself made investigations into the possibility of the imposition of the death sentence upon GT in Malaysia and had been informed that in similar cases to the author's no prosecution had occurred. In the circumstances, therefore, the Committee took the view that it could not be concluded that it was a foreseeable and necessary consequence of GT's deportation that he would be tried, convicted and sentenced to death. The Committee therefore concluded that Australia would not violate GT's rights under article 6 of the Covenant if the decision to deport him was implemented.[148]

The Human Rights Committee found, in the case of *Judge v Canada*, however, that Canada had violated article 6 of the ICCPR as it had abolished the death penalty but, despite this, had deported a person to the United States where he was under a sentence of death. Going further than it had in *GT v Australia*, the Committee emphasized that this conclusion applies in respect of a State that has abolished capital punishment, irrespective of whether it is a party to the Second Optional Protocol or not.[149]

---

147 General Comment 20, above n 29, para 9. See also *Singh v Canada*, above n 105, para 6.3.

148 At para 8.5. See also *Ng v Canada*, Communication 469/1991, UN Doc CCPR/C/49/D/469/1991 (1994); and *ARJ v Australia*, Communication 692/1996, UN Doc CCPR/C/60/D/692/1996 (1997), in which consideration was given to the authors' removal to the United States of America and Iran respectively.

149 *Judge v Canada*, Communication 829/1998, UN Doc CCPR/C/78/D/829/1998 (2002), para 10.9.

Minors and pregnant women Article 6(5) provides that a sentence of death cannot be imposed for crimes committed by persons below eighteen years of age, nor in respect of pregnant women. The Committee has observed that it is incumbent on member States to make enquiries if any doubt is raised as to whether the accused in a capital case falls within this category.[150]

A right to have family present? The Committee, in *Schedko v Belarus*, was faced with facts whereby the author, whose son was to be executed, was not informed of the date, nor the hour or place, of her son's execution, nor of the exact place of her son's subsequent burial. As a matter unchallenged by Belarus, the Committee took stock of the continued anguish and mental stress caused to the author, as the mother of a condemned prisoner, by the persisting uncertainty of the circumstances that led to his execution, as well as the location of his gravesite. The secrecy surrounding the date of execution and the place of burial, and the refusal to hand over the body for burial, had the effect in the Committee's view of intimidating or punishing families by intentionally leaving them in a state of uncertainty and mental distress. The Committee therefore considered that the authorities' failure to notify the author of the scheduled date for the execution of her son, and their subsequent persistent failure to notify her of the location of her son's grave, amounted to inhuman treatment of the author, in violation of article 7 of the Covenant.[151]

In *Rolando v Philippines*, the question before the Committee was whether the author would be given sufficient opportunity to bid farewell to his family in circumstances where he would not be notified of the date of his execution until dawn of the day in question, whereupon he would be executed within eight hours, alleged to be in violation of article 7. The Committee was unsympathetic, however, noting that the legislation would provide the author with at least one year and at most eighteen months, after the exhaustion of all available remedies, during which he could make arrangements to see members of his family prior to notification of the date of execution.[152]

Exercise of the prerogative of mercy The communication in *Kennedy v Trinidad and Tobago* involved, amongst other issues, a request by the author for a pardon. He was not informed about the status of deliberations on this request, and it was

150 See, for example, *Johnson v Jamaica*, Communication 592/1994, UN Doc CCPR/C/64/D/592/1994 (1998), para 10.3; and *Perkins v Jamaica*, Communication 733/1997, UN Doc CCPR/C/63/D/733/1997 (1998), para 11.6.

151 *Schedko v Belarus*, Communication 886/1999, UN Doc CCPR/C/77/D/886/1999 (2003), para 10.2. See also: *Staselovich v Belarus*, Communication 887/1999, UN Doc CCPR/C/77/D/887/1999 (2003); *Khalilov v Tajikistan*, above n 104, para 7.7; *Aliboev v Tajikistan*, above n 104, para 6.7; *Shukurova v Tajikistan*, above n 101, para 8.7; and *Sultanova v Uzbekistan*, above n 2, para 7.10.

152 *Rolando v Philippines*, above n 32, para 5.4. See also *Rayos v Philippines*, above n 144, para 7.1.

claimed that his right under article 6(4) was thereby violated. Counsel for the author contended that the exercise of the right to seek pardon or commutation of sentence should be governed by the procedural guarantees of article 14. The Committee observed, however, that the wording of article 6(4) did not prescribe a particular procedure for the manner in which the prerogative of mercy is to be exercised. Accordingly, it said, States parties retain discretion for spelling out the modalities of the exercise of the rights under article 6(4).[153] The Committee did not comment, however, on whether such modalities should be exercised in compliance with article 14.

The Use of Force between States, and the Question of Nuclear Weapons

In the context of inter-State conflicts throughout the twentieth century, and the use of force against Afghanistan and Iraq during these first few years of the twenty-first century, it is interesting to note General Comments pertaining to the use of force between States. The Committee has described war and other acts of mass violence as a scourge of humanity that takes the lives of thousands of innocent human beings every year. It emphasized the fact that, under the Charter of the United Nations, the threat or use of force by any State against another, except in exercise of the inherent right of self-defence, is prohibited. The Committee considered that States therefore have a 'supreme duty' to prevent wars, acts of genocide, and other acts of mass violence causing arbitrary loss of life.[154] Every effort they make to avert the danger of war, especially thermonuclear war, and to strengthen international peace and security would constitute the most important condition and guarantee for the safeguarding of the right to life. In this respect, the Committee noted a connection between article 6 and article 20 (prohibition against propaganda for war or incitement to violence).

Just two years after its General Comment 6 on article 6, the Committee issued a further Comment during its twenty-third session of 1984, this time addressing the specific issue of nuclear weapons and the right to life.[155] Remaining concerned by the toll of human life taken by conventional weapons in armed conflicts, the Committee noted that, during successive sessions of the General Assembly, representatives from all geographical regions had expressed their growing concern at the development and proliferation of increasingly awesome weapons of mass destruction, which not only threaten human life but also absorb resources that could otherwise be used for vital economic and social purposes, particularly for the benefit of developing countries, and thereby for promoting and securing the enjoyment of human rights for all. In its Comment, the Committee expressly associated itself with this concern:[156]

153 *Kennedy v Trinidad and Tobago*, above n 35, para 7.4.

154 General Comment 6, above n 118, para 2.

155 *General Comment 14: Nuclear weapons and the right to life (Art 6)*, UN Doc CCPR General Comment 14 (1984).

156 Ibid, paras 4–7.

> It is evident that the designing, testing, manufacture, possession and deployment of nuclear weapons are among the greatest threats to the right to life which confront mankind today. This threat is compounded by the danger that the actual use of such weapons may be brought about, not only in the event of war, but even through human or mechanical error or failure. Furthermore, the very existence and gravity of this threat generates a climate of suspicion and fear between States, which is in itself antagonistic to the promotion of universal respect for and observance of human rights and fundamental freedoms in accordance with the Charter of the United Nations and the International Covenants on Human Rights. The production, testing, possession, deployment and use of nuclear weapons should be prohibited and recognized as crimes against humanity. The Committee accordingly, in the interest of mankind, calls upon all States, whether Parties to the Covenant or not, to take urgent steps, unilaterally and by agreement, to rid the world of this menace.

The Committee's comment was relied upon in *WBE v The Netherlands* to claim that the State party's preparations for the deployment of cruise missiles in Woensdrecht and the presence in the Netherlands of other nuclear weapons violated the authors' rights under article 6 of the Covenant. While the Committee acknowledged its own comments, it noted that the procedure laid down in the Optional Protocol was not designed for conducting public debate over matters of public policy, such as support for disarmament and issues concerning nuclear and other weapons of mass destruction. The Netherlands put to the Committee that the communication was inadmissible as an *actio popularis*, although the Committee took the view that, provided each of the authors was a 'victim' within the meaning of article 1 of the Optional Protocol, nothing precluded large numbers of persons from bringing a case under the Optional Protocol. On the question of whether the authors were indeed victims, the Committee reiterated its procedural jurisprudence that an author must show either that an act or an omission of a State party has already adversely affected his or her enjoyment of a right under the ICCPR, or that such an effect is imminent, for example on the basis of existing law and/or judicial or administrative decision or practice. The issue in this case was whether the preparation for the deployment or the actual deployment of nuclear weapons presented the authors with an existing or imminent violation of their right to life, specific to each of them. The Committee found that the facts did not, at the relevant period of time and in the particular circumstances of the case, place the authors in the position to claim to be victims whose right to life was then violated or under imminent prospect of violation.[157]

157 *WBE v The Netherlands*, Communication 429/1990, UN Doc CCPR/C/47/D/429/1990 (1993), para 6.10. See also *Aalbersberg and 2,084 other Dutch citizens v Netherlands*, Communication 1440/2005, UN Doc CCPR/C/87/D/1440/2005 (2006).

Chapter 6
The Judicial Process

Alex Conte

This chapter examines the conduct of civil and criminal proceedings, including sentencing. Consideration will be given to article 14 (principles applying to the judicial process overall), article 15 (concerning retrospective penalties) and article 11 (prohibiting imprisonment for failure to perform a contract).The chapter first considers the elements of fair trial guaranteed under article 14(1), applicable to both criminal proceedings and suits at law. It then focuses upon the determination of criminal charges, including sentencing. The chapter concludes with consideration of rights of appeal, again as applicable to both civil and criminal proceedings.

Right to a Fair Hearing

Article 14 of the Covenant is of a complex nature. Its provisions are aimed at ensuring the proper administration of justice, and to this end uphold a series of individual rights such as equality before the courts and tribunals, and the right to a fair and public hearing by a competent, independent and impartial tribunal established by law. The various rights espoused apply not only to procedures for the determination of criminal charges against individuals, but also to procedures for the determination of their rights and obligations in a 'suit at law' (civil proceedings), and are applicable to all States parties, regardless of their legal traditions and their domestic law.[1] Having said this, there is a clear division between the treatment of civil and criminal proceedings within the article: paragraph 1 applies to both civil and criminal proceedings, while the balance of article 14 applies to criminal proceedings alone.[2]

---

1 *General Comment 32: Article 14: Right to equality before courts and tribunals and to a fair trial*, UN Doc CCPR/C/GC/32 (2007), para 4.

2 As emphasized in *Silva v Sweden*, Communication 748/1997, UN Doc CCPR/C/67/D/748/1997 (1999), para 4.9; and *Strik v The Netherlands*, Communication 1001/2001, UN Doc CCPR/C/76/D/1001/2001 (2002), para 7.3. See also *AJ & G v The Netherlands*, Communication 1142/2002, UN Doc CCPR/C/77/D/1142/2002 (2003), para 5.7, where the author's claim that he had been denied the right to benefit from lighter penalties prescribed by law, in violation of article 15, was dismissed because his claim related to proceedings concerning child custody.

The Human Rights Committee recently adopted General Comment 32, which stands as a substantial commentary on the application of article 14, replacing General Comment 13 of 1984 and reflecting upon a considerable body of jurisprudence that has come before the Committee.[3] Such is the complexity of article 14 that, despite its absence from the list of non-derogable rights in article 4(2), the Committee has treated the right to a fair trial as one which may not be subject to derogation where this would circumvent the protection of non-derogable rights.[4] General Comment 32 contains two examples of this. First, because article 6 of the Covenant is non-derogable in its entirety, any trial leading to the imposition of the death penalty, even during a state of emergency, must conform to the provisions of the Covenant including 'scrupulous respect' for all the requirements of article 14.[5] The second example given relates to the prohibition under article 7 against torture or cruel, inhuman or degrading treatment or punishment, which is non-derogable in its entirety. The Committee has said, in this regard, that no statements or confessions or, in principle, other evidence obtained in violation of article 7 may be invoked as evidence in any proceedings covered by article 14, including during a state of emergency, except in the case of a statement or confession used as evidence that torture or other treatment prohibited by the provision has occurred.[6] Even when

3 General Comment 32, above n 1, replacing *General Comment 13, Equality before the courts and the right to a fair and public hearing by an independent court established by law (Art. 14)*, UN Doc HRI/GEN/1/Rev.6 at 135 (2003).

4 General Comment 32, above n 1, para 6. See also *General Comment 29: States of Emergency (Article 4)*, UN Doc CCPR/C/21/Rev.1/Add.11 (2001), para 15.

5 General Comment 32, above n 1, para 59. See, further, Chapter 5. See also, for examples: *Siragev v Uzbekistan*, Communication 907/2000, UN Doc CCPR/C/85/D/907/2000 (2005), para 6.4; *Deolall v Guyana*, Communication 912/2000, UN Doc CCPR/C/82/D/912/2000 (2004), para 5.3; *Chan v Guyana*, Communication 913/2000, UN Doc CCPR/C/85/D/913/2000 (2006), para 5.4; *Ruzmetov v Uzbekistan*, Communication 915/2000, UN Doc CCPR/C/86/D/915/2000 (2006), para 7.6; *Bazarov v Uzbekistan*, Communication 959/2000, UN Doc CCPR/C/87/D/959/2000 (2006), para 8.4; *Shakurova v Tajikistan*, Communication 1044/2002, UN Doc CCPR/C/86/D/1044/2002 (2006), para 8.5; *Rayos v Philippines*, Communication 1167/2003, UN Doc CCPR/C/81/D/1167/2003 (2004), para 7.3; *Tulyaganova v Uzbekistan*, Communication 1041/2001, UN Doc CCPR/C/90/D/1041/2001 (2007), para 8.3; *Chikunova v Uzbekistan*, Communication 1043/2002, UN Doc CCPR/C/89/D/1043/2002 (2007), paras 7.4–7.6; *Tarasova v Uzbekistan*, Communication 1057/2002, UN Doc CCPR/C/88/D/1057/2002 (2006), para 7.3; and *Kurbanov v Tajikistan*, Communication 1096/2002, UN Doc CCPR/C/79/D/1096/2002 (2003), para 7.7.

6 General Comment 32, above n 1, para 6, and General Comment 29, above n 4, paras 7 and 15. See also the discussion below concerning the privilege against self-incrimination; and also the *Convention against Torture and Other Cruel, Inhuman or Degrading Treatment or Punishment*, article 15, which refers to the use of evidence against a person accused of torture.

derogation from article 14 is permissible, the HRC has explained that the extent of any such derogation is limited:[7]

> The Committee is of the opinion that the principles of legality and the rule of law require that fundamental requirements of fair trial must be respected during a state of emergency. Only a court of law may try and convict a person for a criminal offence. The presumption of innocence must be respected. In order to protect non-derogable rights, the right to take proceedings before a court to enable the court to decide without delay on the lawfulness of detention, must not be diminished by a State party's decision to derogate from the Covenant.

The Committee has also noted that although reservations to particular clauses of article 14 may be acceptable, a general reservation to the right to a fair trial would be incompatible with the object and purpose of the ICCPR.[8]

Article 14(1) is of general application to the administration of justice and sets out various requirements. All persons are to be equal before courts and tribunals. Any determination of such courts and tribunals must be through a fair and public hearing by a competent, independent and impartial tribunal established by law. The Committee has determined that neither article 14(1) nor any other aspect of the International Covent confers the right to trial by jury, but rather that the touchstone is that all judicial proceedings, with or without a jury, must comport with the guarantees of fair trial.[9]

> Article 14
>
> 1. All persons shall be equal before the courts and tribunals. In the determination of any criminal charge against him, or of his rights and obligations in a suit at law, everyone shall be entitled to a fair and public hearing by a competent, independent and impartial tribunal established by law. The press and the public may be excluded from all or part of a trial for reasons of morals, public order (ordre public) or national security in a democratic society, or when the interest of the private lives of the parties so requires, or to the extent strictly necessary in the opinion of the court in special circumstances where publicity would prejudice the interests of justice; but any judgement rendered in a criminal case or in a suit at law shall be made public except where the interest of juvenile

7 General Comment 29, above n 4, para 16.

8 General Comment 32, above n 1, para 5. See also *General Comment 24: General comment on issues relating to reservations made upon ratification or accession to the Covenant or the Optional Protocols thereto, or in relation to declarations under article 41 of the Covenant*, UN Doc CCPR/C/21/Rev.1/Add.6 (1994), para 8.

9 See, for example, *Kavanagh v Ireland*, Communication 819/1998, UN Doc CCPR/C/71/D/819/1998 (2001), para 10.1; and *Wilson v Australia*, Communication 1239/2004, UN Doc CCPR/C/80/D/1239/2004 (2004), para 4.4.

persons otherwise requires or the proceedings concern matrimonial disputes or the guardianship of children.

Criminal Proceedings versus Proceedings relating to Rights and Obligations in a Suit at Law

There is a distinction to be made between the treatment of civil and criminal proceedings under article 14, with paragraph 1 applying to both civil and criminal proceedings while the balance of article 14 applies to criminal proceedings alone. Criminal charges normally relate to acts declared to be punishable under domestic criminal law, although the Committee has expressed that the notion may also extend to acts that are criminal in nature and are accompanied by sanctions that, regardless of their qualification in domestic law, must be regarded as penal because of their purpose, character or severity.[10]

The concept of determination of rights and obligations 'in a suit at law' is more complex, as noted by the Human Rights Committee in its General Comment 32.[11] It is based on the nature of the right in question rather than on the status of one of the parties or the particular forum for the determination of rights and obligations.[12] Consideration to the expression 'suit at law' was had in *Mahuika v New Zealand*, where a broad interpretation of the term appears to have been adopted. The authors claimed that the Treaty of Waitangi (Fisheries Settlement) Act 1992 prevented them from bringing claims concerning the extent of their indigenous fisheries before the courts. The Committee observed:[13]

> … article 14(1) encompasses the right to access to court for the determination of rights and obligations in a suit at law. In certain circumstances the failure of a State party to establish a competent court to determine rights and obligations may amount to a violation of article 14(1). In the present case, the Act excludes the courts jurisdiction to inquire into the validity of claims by Maori in respect to commercial fishing, because the Act is intended to settle these claims. In any event, Maori recourse to the Courts to enforce claims regarding fisheries was limited even before the 1992 Act; Maori rights in commercial fisheries were enforceable in the Courts only to the extent that s 88(2) of the Fisheries Act expressly provided that nothing in the Act was to affect Maori fishing rights. The Committee considers that whether or not claims in respect of fishery interests could be considered to fall within the definition of a suit at law, the 1992 Act

10 *Perterer v Austria*, Communication 1015/2001, UN Doc CCPR/C/81/D/1015/2001 (2004), para 9.2.

11 General Comment 32, above n 1, para 16.

12 *YL v Canada*, Communication 112/1981, UN Doc CCPR/C/OP/1 at 28 (1984), paras 9.1–9.2.

13 *Mahuika et al v New Zealand*, Communication 547/1993, UN Doc CCPR/C/70/D/547/1993 (2000), para 9.11.

> has displaced the determination of Treaty claims in respect of fisheries by its specific provisions. Other aspects of the right to fisheries, though, still give the right to access to court, for instance in respect of the allocation of quota and of the regulations governing customary fishing rights. The authors have not substantiated the claim that the enactment of the new legislative framework has barred their access to court in any matter falling within the scope of article 14, paragraph 1.

It thus appears that a key consideration in the triggering of article 14(1) is whether the domestic law entrusts a judicial body with a judicial task, however that might arise.[14] Child custody and other family proceedings have been treated as falling within the meaning of a 'suit at law';[15] as have disciplinary proceedings against a civil servant;[16] the determination of social security benefits,[17] or the pension rights of soldiers;[18] procedures relating to the use of public land;[19] and privacy and property rights.[20] The Committee has concluded that suits at law do not include extradition, expulsion and deportation procedures,[21] although certain procedural guarantees may apply to such proceedings by application of article 13 of the Covenant (concerning expulsion of aliens).[22] It has also taken the view that an unsuccessful bid for appointment to a civil servant position, including appointment

14 General Comment 32, above n 1, para 7. See also *Kazantzis v Cyprus*, Communication 972/2001, UN Doc CCPR/C/78/D/972/2001 (2003), para 6.5, concerning determinations of a non-judicial body.

15 See, for example, *Fei v Colombia*, Communication 514/1992, UN Doc CCPR/C/53/D/514/1992 (1995).

16 *Casanovas v France*, Communication 441/1990, UN Doc CCPR/C/51/D/441/1990 (1994), para 5.2; *Perterer v Austria*, above n 10, para 9.2; and *Vargas v Peru*, Communication 906/2000, UN Doc CCPR/C/75/D/906/2000 (2002).

17 *Garcia Pons v Spain*, Communication 454/1991, UN Doc CCPR/C/55/D/454/1991 (1995), para 9.3.

18 *YL v Canada*, above n 12, para 9.3.

19 *Äärelä and Näkkäläjärvi v Finland*, Communication 779/1997, UN Doc CCPR/C/73/D/779/1997 (2001), paras 7.2–7.4.

20 *Deisl v Austria*, Communication 1060/2002, UN Doc CCPR/C/81/D/1060/2002 (2004), para 11.1.

21 *Zundel v Canada*, Communication 1341/2005, UN Doc CCPR/C/89/D/1341/2005 (2007), para 6.7–6.8; *Esposito v Spain*, Communication 1359/2005, UN Doc CCPR/C/89/D/1359/2005 (2007), para 7.6; *PK v Canada*, Communication 1234/2003, UN Doc CCPR/C/89/D/1234/2003 (2007), paras 7.4–7.5.

22 As noted by the Committee in its General Comment 32, above n 1, para 62. See further Chapter 4 herein; *Everett v Spain*, Communication 961/2000, UN Doc CCPR/C/81/D/961/2000 (2004), para 6.4; and *Ahani v Canada*, Communication 1051/2002, UN Doc CCPR/C/80/D/1051/2002 (2004), para 10.9.

to a judicial office, or for promotion or title, does not constitute determination of rights and obligations in a suit at law.[23]

It should be noted that there are discrepancies between the various language texts of the Covenant pertaining to the concept of a 'suit at law'. The matter was raised before the Committee in *YL v Canada*, where the majority took the view that, despite the fact that the *travaux préparatoires* did not resolve the apparent discrepancies, the concept was based on the nature of the right rather than on the status of one of the parties (whether governmental, parastatal or autonomous statutory entities), or on the particular forum in which individual legal systems may provide that the right in question is to be adjudicated upon (especially in common law systems where there is no inherent difference between public law and private law and where the courts normally exercise control over the proceedings either at first instance or on appeal specifically provided by statute or else by way of judicial review). Each communication, said the Committee, must be examined in the light of its particular features.[24]

Access to the Administration of Justice

Article 14 encompasses the right of access to the courts in the determination of criminal charges and rights and obligations in a suit at law, for the purpose of ensuring that no individual is deprived of his or her right to claim justice. The right of access to courts and tribunals is not limited to citizens of States parties, but must also be available to all individuals, regardless of nationality or statelessness, or whatever their status (whether asylum seekers, refugees, migrant workers, unaccompanied children or other persons who may find themselves in the territory or subject to the jurisdiction of a State party).[25] A situation in which an individual's attempts to access the competent courts or tribunals are systematically frustrated *de jure* or *de facto* runs counter to the guarantee of article 14(1).[26] Any distinctions regarding access to courts and tribunals are prohibited if they are not based on law and cannot be justified on objective and reasonable grounds. Thus, in *Ato del Avellanal v Peru*, article 168 of the Peruvian Civil Code was found to violate the ICCPR because it provided that, when a woman is married, only the husband was entitled to represent matrimonial property before

23 *Kolanowski v Poland*, Communication 837/1998, UN Doc CCPR/C/78/D/837/1998 (2003), para 6.4; *Dimitrov v Bulgaria*, Communication 1030/2001, UN Doc CCPR/C/85/D/1030/2001 (2005), para 8.3; *Karatsis v Cyprus*, Communication 1182/2003, UN Doc CCPR/C/84/D/1182/2003 (2005), para 6.4; and *Fernández v Spain*, Communication 1396/2005, UN Doc CCPR/C/85/D/1396/2005 (2005), para 6.3.

24 *YL v Canada*, above n 12, para 9.2. Contrast with *Kolanowski v Poland*, above n 23, para 6.4.

25 General Comment 32, above n 1, para 9.

26 *Oló Bahamonde v Equatorial Guinea*, Communication 468/1991, UN Doc CCPR/C/49/D/468/1991 (1993), para 9.4.

the Courts.[27] In *Weiss v Austria*, an author's inability to appeal an adverse judgment of the Upper Regional Court, in circumstances where the prosecutor could, was held by the Constitutional Court of Austria to be unconstitutional and also found by the Committee to be a violation of article 14(1).[28]

Provision of legal aid The Committee has noted within its jurisprudence that the Covenant does not contain an express obligation for States parties to provide legal aid to individuals in *all* cases, but only in the determination of a criminal charge where the interests of justice so require (article 14(3)(d)).[29] Having said this, it has also pointed out that parties have an obligation, under article 2(3) of the Covenant, to ensure that effective remedies are available in relation to claims of violations of Covenant rights. In *Kennedy v Trinidad and Tobago*, the Constitutional Court of that State was the body charged with this task. As such, the Committee considered that the denial of legal aid to a person presenting a claim to the Constitutional Court constituted a violation of article 14(1), in conjunction with article 2(3).[30] In its General Comment 32, the Committee has added that the availability or absence of legal assistance often determines whether or not a person can access proceedings or participate in them in a meaningful way, and thus encouraged States parties to provide free legal aid in suits at law for individuals who do not have sufficient means to pay for representation.[31]

In the case of criminal proceedings, legal aid is a matter that will affect the ability of a number of those facing criminal charges to adequately prepare a defence (see below).[32] The gravity of the offence will be important in determining whether counsel should be assigned in the interest of justice, as will the existence of some objective chance of success at the appeals stage.[33] The HRC has gone as far as asserting that there may be some situations where the State is obliged to

27 *Ato del Avellanal v Peru*, Communication 202/1986, UN Doc Supp 40 (A/44/40) at 196 (1988), para 10.2. This aspect of the communication was dealt with as a violation of articles 3 and 26 of the Covenant, relating to equality and non-discrimination.

28 *Weiss v Austria*, Communication 1086/2002, UN Doc CCPR/C/77/D/1086/2002 (2003), para 9.6.

29 See, for example, *JO, ZS, and SO v Belgium*, Communication 1417/2005, UN Doc CCPR/C/85/D/1417/2005 (2005), para 4.4.

30 *Kennedy v Trinidad and Tobago*, Communication 845/1998, UN Doc CCPR/C/74/D/845/1998 (2002), para 7.10. See also *Evans v Trinidad and Tobago*, Communication 908/2000, UN Doc CCPR/C/77/D/908/2000 (2003), para 6.6.

31 General Comment 32, above n 1, para 32.

32 See, for example, *Touron v Uruguay*, Communication 32/1978, UN Doc CCPR/C/OP/1 at 61 (1984), para 12.

33 *ZP v Canada*, Communication 341/1988, UN Doc CCPR/C/41/D/341/1988(1991), para 5.4; and *Lindon v Australia*, Communication 646/1995, UN Doc CCPR/C/64/D/646/1995 (1998), para 6.5.

provide legal aid, giving the example of where a person sentenced to death seeks a constitutional review of irregularities in his or her criminal trial.[34]

It should be noted that the Committee has displayed a reluctance to examine the manner in which a State party administers the provision of legal aid within its territory. Although it has acknowledged a responsibility upon States parties to provide effective legal aid representation, it said in *Ricketts v Jamaica* that it is not for the Committee to determine how this should be ensured, unless it is apparent that there has been a miscarriage of justice.[35] An instance in which it found such an apparent miscarriage of justice was in the case of *Teesdale v Trinidad and Tobago*, where counsel was not assigned until the day of the accused's trial.[36]

Fees and costs The Human Rights Committee noted, in *Lindon v Australia*, that if the administrative, prosecutorial or judicial authorities of a State party laid such a cost burden on an individual that their access to court would *de facto* be prevented, then this might give rise to issues under article 14(1).[37] It concluded, in *Äärelä and Näkkäläjärvi v Finland*, that the imposition by the Court of Appeal of a substantial costs award, without the discretion to consider its implications for the particular authors, or its effect on the access to court of other similarly situated claimants, constituted a violation of the authors' rights under article 14(1), in conjunction with article 2 of the Covenant.[38]

Equality before Courts and Tribunals

Equality and non-discrimination is a matter reaffirmed within the Covenant many times. In the context of the conduct of judicial proceedings and the guarantees

---

34 Ibid. See the approach of the Committee in such cases in: *Currie v Jamaica*, Communication 377/1989, UN Doc CCPR/C/50/D/377/1989 (1994), para 13.4; *Shaw v Jamaica*, Communication 704/1996, UN Doc CCPR/C/62/D/704/1996 (1998), para 7.6; *Taylor v Jamaica*, Communication 707/1996, UN Doc CCPR/C/60/D/707/1996 (1997), para 8.2; *Henry v Trinidad and Tobago*, Communication 752/1997, UN Doc CCPR/C/64/D/752/1997 (1999), para 7.6; and *Kennedy v Trinidad and Tobago*, above n 30, para 7.10.

35 *Ricketts v Jamaica*, Communication 667/1995, UN Doc CCPR/C/74/D/667/1995 (2002), para 7.3. See also *Burrell v Jamaica*, Communication 546/1993, UN Doc CCPR/C/53/D/546/1993 (1996); *Amore v Jamaica*, Communication 634/1995, UN Doc CCPR/C/65/D/634/1995 (1999); *Darwish v Austria*, Communication 679/1996, UN Doc CCPR/C/60/D/679/1996 (1997); and *Agudo v Spain*, Communication 864/1999, UN Doc CCPR/C/76/D/864/1999 (2002).

36 *Teesdale v Trinidad and Tobago*, Communication 677/1996, UN Doc CCPR/C/74/D/677/1996 (2002), para 9.5.

37 *Lindon v Australia*, above n 33, para 6.4. See also *Sankara et al v Burkina Faso*, Communication 1159/2003, UN Doc CCPR/C/86/D/1159/2003 (2006) concerning a failure on the part of a court registrar to advise the author of the requirement to deposit a security, resulting in a dismissal of the appeal by the court (para 12.5).

38 *Äärelä and Näkkäläjärvi v Finland*, above n 19, para 7.2.

under article 14(1), it calls for equality of arms, and ensuring that the parties to proceedings are treated without any discrimination.[39]

Equality of arms The Human Rights Committee has described equality of arms as requiring the enjoyment of the same procedural rights by all the parties unless distinctions are based on law and can be justified on objective and reasonable grounds, not entailing actual disadvantage or other unfairness to the defendant.[40] The Committee has been reluctant to find breach of this aspect of a fair hearing, so long as a person has been afforded an opportunity to be present, examine witnesses and be represented if that is the person's wish. In *Agudo v Spain*, for example, the author claimed that there was no verbatim record of the statements of witnesses, experts, parties and counsel but only a summary drawn up by the clerk of the court, so that the proceedings lacked essential guarantees. The Committee failed to see how those facts alone constituted a breach of article 14(1).[41]

In *Jansen-Gielen v The Netherlands*, however, the Committee found that there had been an inequality of arms. The Central Appeals Tribunal had refused to append a psychological report to the case file, which had been submitted by the author's counsel two days before the hearing. The Netherlands argued that the Court considered that admission of the report two days before the hearing would have unreasonably obstructed the other party in the conduct of the case. The applicable procedural law did not, however, provide for a time limit for the submission of documents. The Committee accordingly found that it was the duty of the Court of Appeal, which was not constrained by any prescribed time limit, to ensure that each party could challenge the documentary evidence which the other filed or wished to file and, if need be, to adjourn proceedings.[42] In *Dudko v Australia*, the author was not present in the High Court at the application for leave to appeal because she was in custody, although prosecutorial authorities were represented, since the practice in New South Wales was that people in custody did not appear in the High Court. Due to a lack of explanation by the State in support of this procedural inequality, the Committee failed to understand why an unrepresented defendant in detention should be treated more unfavourably than an unrepresented defendant *not* in detention, and therefore found this to be in violation of article 14(1).[43] The refusal of a trial judge to order an adjournment to allow the author in *Robinson v Jamaica* to have legal representation, when several adjournments had already been ordered when the

39 General Comment 32, above n 1, para 8.

40 General Comment 32, above n 1, para 13.

41 *Agudo v Spain*, above n 35, para 9.4.

42 *Jansen-Gielen v The Netherlands*, Communication 846/1999, UN Doc CCPR/C/71/D/846/1999 (2001), para 8.2. See also *Nazarov v Uzbekistan*, Communication 911/2000, UN Doc CCPR/C/81/D/911/2000 (2004), para 6.3.

43 *Dudko v Australia*, Communication 1347/2005, UN Doc CCPR/C/90/D/1347/2005 (2007), para 7.4.

prosecution's witnesses were unavailable or unready, was found to violate article 14(1) due to an inequality of arms between the parties.[44]

In *Chadee et al v Trinidad and Tobago*, certain legislative amendments during the course of a jury trial meant, in the dissenting opinion of Committee member Mr Scheinin, that the trial was not conducted fairly. The State party resorted, in 1996, to legislative measures that affected the trial in two important respects, namely by providing for an unlimited number of potential jurors, through an amendment to the Jury Act, and by allowing the use of the deposition of a deceased witness as evidence, through an Amendment to the Evidence Act. Both amendments were passed while the prosecution against the authors was awaiting trial, and both had been designed for their particular case. Although the prohibition against retroactive criminal legislation (article 15) does not as such apply to criminal *procedure*, Committee member Scheinin concluded that article 14(1) and (2) must be understood to limit the enactment of retroactive legislation even in the procedural field when such legislation is designed for a concrete case.[45] The majority of the Committee distanced itself from such an examination of the legislative changes made by Trinidad and Tobago:[46]

> … the Committee refers to its jurisprudence that it is for the courts of States parties, and not for the Committee, to review the application of domestic law, unless it is evident that the application was manifestly arbitrary or amounted to a denial of justice. This not being so in the instant case, the Committee finds that the facts before it do not reveal a breach of article 14 of the Covenant.

The Committee has commented that, in exceptional cases, the principle of equality of arms might also require that the free assistance of an interpreter be provided where a party could not otherwise participate in the proceedings on equal terms, or witnesses produced by it be examined.[47]

Equal treatment Whereas equality of arms pertains to the enjoyment of procedural rights as between parties to the same proceeding, equal treatment is broader in its application and engages the principles of equality before the law, and non-discrimination. In *González v Spain*, the author claimed that there was a violation of article 14(1), together with article 26 (equality and non-discrimination), of the Covenant by virtue of the fact that she was unable to appear before the Constitutional Court without being represented by a procurador (legal counsel accredited to the Constitutional Court). The author claimed that this resulted in an inequality before the law, since those with a law degree did not need to be represented, whereas those

---

44 *Robinson v Jamaica*, Communication 223/1987, UN Doc Supp 40 (A/44/40) at 241 (1989), para 10.4.

45 *Chadee et al v Trinidad and Tobago*, Communication 813/1998, UN Doc CCPR/C/63/D/813/1998 (1998), para 9 of his dissenting opinion.

46 At para 10.1.

47 General Comment 32, above n 1, para 13.

without a law degree were required to be represented by a procurador. Following its earlier decisions in such claims, the Committee accepted the position of the Constitutional Court, that the requirement for representation reflected the need for a person with legal training to assume responsibility for proceedings in connection with appeals to that court. The Committee did not accept, on the evidence before it, that this failed to be based upon objective and reasonable criteria.[48] The Committee has concluded, however, that the prosecution of one person and the failure to prosecute another does not, by itself, raise an issue of equality before the law, since each prosecutorial decision must be judged on its own merits.[49]

Competent, Independent and Impartial Tribunal Established by Law

Each expression in the guarantee to a fair hearing before a 'competent, independent and impartial tribunal established by law' carries with it special requirements. The final part of the expression naturally requires that the tribunal is one established under a prescription by law. Although not considered by the Human Rights Committee, the ordinary meaning of 'competence' calls for the appointment of suitably qualified and experienced persons to act as judicial officers. The Committee's jurisprudence has focused upon the objective (independence) and subjective (impartiality) aspects of the right, which are treated as absolute requirements not capable of limitation.[50]

A somewhat puzzling observation is made by the Human Rights Committee in its recent General Comment 32 concerning the degree of enjoyment of a fair hearing before a tribunal which is competent, independent, impartial and established by law. The Committee expressed that while all criminal determinations must be made pursuant to a tribunal bearing these characteristics (at all stages), whenever rights and obligations in a suit at law are determined reference to such a tribunal must be had 'at least at one stage of the proceedings'.[51] Reasons are not given for making such a distinction, nor are any views of the Committee relied on in support of it.

48 *González v Spain*, Communication 1005/2001, UN Doc CCPR/C/74/D/1005/2001 (2002), para 4.3.

49 See the Committee's decisions declaring inadmissible *Werenbeck v Australia*, Communication 579/1994, UN Doc CCPR/C/59/D/579/1994 (1997), para 9.9; and *Hoelen v The Netherlands*, Communication 873/1999, UN Doc CCPR/C/67/D/873/1999 (1999), para 4.2.

50 General Comment 32, above n 1, para 19. See also *Gonzalez del Rio v Peru*, Communication 263/1987, UN Doc CCPR/C/46/D/263/1987 (1992), para 5.2.

51 General Comment 32, above n 1, para 18.

Independence The requirements of independence are explained succinctly by the Human Rights Committee in its General Comment 32:[52]

> States should take specific measures guaranteeing the independence of the judiciary, protecting judges from any form of political influence in their decision-making through the constitution or adoption of laws establishing clear procedures and objective criteria for the appointment, remuneration, tenure, promotion, suspension and dismissal of the members of the judiciary and disciplinary sanctions taken against them. A situation where the functions and competencies of the judiciary and the executive are not clearly distinguishable or where the latter is able to control or direct the former is incompatible with the notion of an independent tribunal. It is necessary to protect judges against conflicts of interest and intimidation. In order to safeguard their independence, the status of judges, including their term of office, their independence, security, adequate remuneration, conditions of service, pensions and the age of retirement shall be adequately secured by law.

The Committee has taken the view that judges may only be dismissed on serious grounds of misconduct or incompetence, in accordance with fair procedures ensuring objectivity and impartiality set out in the constitution or the law. Thus, the dismissal by the executive of a judge before the expiry of the term for which he had been appointed, without specific reasons given and without effective judicial protection available to contest the dismissal, was found to be incompatible with his independence as a member of the judiciary.[53] Likewise, the dismissal by the executive of judges alleged to be corrupt, without following any of the procedures provided for by the law, was found to be in violation of article 14, paragraph 1.[54]

Impartiality The impartiality of a tribunal involves an assessment of a subjective nature, focusing upon the individual judges themselves, and comprising two aspects: (1) requiring that judicial officers must not harbour preconceptions about any matter put before them, nor act in ways that promote the interests of one of the parties over another; and (2) requiring that the tribunal must also appear, to a reasonable observer, to be impartial.[55]

Consideration was given to the first of these features in *Perera v Sri Lanka* concerning proceedings between the author and his former employer. The author

---

52 General Comment 32, above n 1, para 19. On the issue of the control or direction of a tribunal by the judiciary, see *Oló Bahamonde v Equatorial Guinea*, above n 26, para 9.4.

53 *Pastukhov v Belarus*, Communication 814/1998, UN Doc CCPR/C/78/D/814/1998 (2003), para 7.3.

54 *Mundyo Busyo et al v Democratic Republic of Congo*, Communication 933/2000, UN Doc CCPR/C/78/D/933/2000 (2003), para 5.2.

55 See, for example: *Karttunen v Finland*, Communication 387/1989, UN Doc CCPR/C/46/D/387/1989 (1992), para 7.2; and *Perterer v Austria*, above n 10, paras 10.2–10.4.

claimed that the encouragement by the Chief Justice that both parties reach an amicable settlement on the quantum of damages exceeded the bounds of a superior court's proper management of its judicial resources. The Committee noted that counsel did not explicitly contest the Court's framing of the disposition of the case, and that, in substance, the High Court's findings in the author's favour were almost entirely upheld at the appellate level. It was therefore concluded that the author's claim had been unsubstantiated, for the purposes of admissibility, and consequently inadmissible under article 2 of the Optional Protocol.[56]

Perhaps due to the subjective nature of issues pertaining to bias, the Committee has otherwise appeared reluctant to examine the exercise of judicial functions within the jurisdiction of member States. The Committee took the view in *Bullock v Trinidad and Tobago*, for example, that it is generally for the appellate courts of States parties, and not for the Committee, to review a trial judge's discretion concerning the admission of evidence unless it can be ascertained that the exercise of the discretion was manifestly arbitrary or amounted to a denial of justice.[57] It has also taken the consistent position that it is generally for the courts of member States, in the absence of a clear miscarriage of justice, to determine the interpretation of law[58] and to evaluate facts and evidence in a particular case, including identification evidence.[59]

---

56 *Perera v Sri Lanka*, Communication 1091/2002, UN Doc CCPR/C/78/D/1091/2002 (2003), para 6.3.

57 *Bullock v Trinidad and Tobago*, Communication 553/1993, UN Doc CCPR/C/54/D/553/1993 (1995), para 7.4. See also *Khomidova v Tajikistan*, Communication 1117/2002, UN Doc CCPR/C/81/D/1117/2002 (2004), para 6.5.

58 See, for example, *G v Canada*, Communication 934/2000, UN Doc CCPR/C/69/D/934/2000 (2000), para 4.3.

59 *Gordon v Jamaica*, Communication 237/1987, UN Doc CCPR/C/46/D/237/1987 (1992), para 6.4; *Griffiths v Jamaica*, Communication 274/1988, UN Doc CCPR/C/47/D/274/1988 (1993); *Reece v Jamaica*, Communication 796/1998, UN Doc CCPR/C/78/D/796/1998 (2003), para 7.3; *Romanov v Ukraine*, Communication 842/1998, UN Doc CCPR/C/79/D/842/1998 (2003), para 6.4; *Padilla v Philippines*, Communication 869/1999, UN Doc CCPR/C/70/D/869/1999 (2000), para 7.2; *Filipovich v Lithuania*, Communication 875/1999, UN Doc CCPR/C/78/D/875/1999 (2003), para 6.3; *van Marcke v Belgium*, Communication 904/2000, UN Doc CCPR/C/81/D/904/2000 (2004), para 8.2; *Svetik v Belarus*, Communication 927/2000, UN Doc CCPR/C/81/D/927/2000 (2004), para 6.3; *Ostroukhov v Russian Federation*, Communication 967/2001, UN Doc CCPR/C/83/D/967/2001 (2005), para 6.4; *Weerasinghe v Sri Lanka*, Communication 1031/2001, UN Doc CCPR/C/91/D/1031/2001 (2007), para 6.2; *Bator v Poland*, Communication 1037/2001, UN Doc CCPR/C/84/D/1037/2001 (2005), para 6.2; *Agabekova v Uzbekistan*, Communication 1071/2002, UN Doc CCPR/C/89/D/1071/2002 (2007), para 6.4; *Johnson v Spain*, Communication 1102/2002, UN Doc CCPR/C/86/D/1102/2002 (2006), para 6.4; *Saldarriaga v Colombia*, Communication 1120/2002, UN Doc CCPR/C/87/D/1120/2002 (2006), para 7.3; *Amador v Spain*, Communication 1181/2003, UN Doc CCPR/C/88/D/1181/2003 (2006), para 9.2; *Kharkhal v Belarus*, Communication 1161/2003, UN Doc CCPR/C/91/D/1161/2003 (2007), para 6.5;

Juries The requirements of independence and impartiality have been held to apply to juries as well as judges. Allegations of attempted jury tampering by the investigating officer were made in communication 240/1987, *Collins v Jamaica.* The Human Rights Committee commented that in a trial by jury the necessity to evaluate facts and evidence independently and impartially applied to the jury and that it was therefore important that all the jurors be placed in a position in which they could assess the facts and the evidence in an objective manner, so as to be able to return a just verdict. On the other hand, the Committee also observed that where alleged improprieties in the behaviour of jurors or attempts at jury tampering come to the knowledge of either of the parties, these alleged improprieties should have been challenged before the court by the defence.[60]

Military or special courts The Human Rights Committee has noted the existence in many countries of military or special courts, often convened to enable exceptional procedures to be applied that might not comply with normal standards of justice. While the Covenant does not prohibit such categories of courts, the Committee has emphasized that any hearing before such courts must be in full conformity with article 14(1).[61] Furthermore, the trying of civilians by such courts should take place under conditions which genuinely afford the full guarantees stipulated in the article and should be resorted to in very exceptional cases only, that is, limited to cases where resort to such trials is necessary and justified by objective and serious reasons and where, with regard to the specific class of individuals and offences

---

Riedl-Riedenstein et al v Germany, Communication 1188/2003, UN Doc CCPR/C/82/D/1188/2003 (2004), para 7.3; *Munuera and Mateo v Australia*, Communications 1329/2004 and 1330/2004, UN Doc CCPR/C/84/D/1329-1330/2004 (2005), para 6.4; *AK v Russian Federation*, Communication 1357/2005, UN Doc CCPR/C/83/D/1357/2005 (2005), para 4.3; *Gueorguiev v Spain*, Communication 1386/2005, UN Doc CCPR/C/90/D/1386/2005 (2007), para 6.4; *Alonso v Spain*, Communication 1391/2005, UN Doc CCPR/C/90/D/1391/2005 (2007), para 6.2; *Casado v Spain*, Communication 1399/2005, UN Doc CCPR/C/84/D/1399/2005 (2005), para 4.3; and *Rovira v Spain*, Communication 1444/2006, UN Doc CCPR/C/87/D/1444/2006 (2006), para 4.2. Compare with *Wright v Jamaica*, Communication 349/1988, UN Doc CCPR/C/45/D/349/1989 (1992), where Committee member Bertil Wennergren reviewed the directions of the trial judge and concluded that, in the particular circumstances of that case, the direction given by him to the jury prejudiced the fair and impartial conduct of the trial. Compare also with *Arutyuniantz v Uzbekistan*, Communication 971/2001, UN Doc CCPR/C/83/D/971/2001 (2005), paras 6.4–6.5; *Tcholatch v Canada*, Communication 1052/2002, UN Doc CCPR/C/89/D/1052/2002 (2007), para 8.13; *Ashurov v Tajikistan*, Communication 1348/2005, UN Doc CCPR/C/89/D/1348/2005 (2007), para 6.6; and *Stow v Portugal*, Communication 1496/2006, UN Doc CCPR/C/92/D/1496/2006 (2008), para 6.5.

60 *Collins v Jamaica*, Communication 240/1987, UN Doc CCPR/C/43/D/240/1987 (1991), para 8.4. See also *Mulai v Guyana*, Communication 811/1998, UN Doc CCPR/C/81/D/811/1998 (2004), paras 6.1–6.2.

61 General Comment 32, above n 1, para 22.

at issue, regular civilian courts are unable to undertake the trials.[62] In order to safeguard the rights of the accused under paragraphs 1 and 3 of article 14, judges in military or special courts should have authority to consider any allegations made of violations of the rights of the accused during any stage of the prosecution.[63]

Faceless judges The Committee has considered trial by 'faceless judges' on more than one occasion. The initial approach of the Human Rights Committee to such cases was to treat trials before faceless judges as automatically failing to guarantee the independence and impartiality of the judges.[64] In *Campos v Peru* and *Vivanco v Peru*, however, Committee member Ivan Shearer took the view that the Committee's views do not amount to condemnation of the practice of 'faceless justice' in itself, and in all circumstances. The practice of masking, or otherwise concealing, the identity of judges in special cases, practised in some countries by reason of serious threats to their security caused by terrorism or other forms of organized crime, may become a necessity for the protection of judges and of the administration of justice. When States parties to the Covenant are faced with such an extraordinary situation they should take the steps set out in article 4 of the Covenant to derogate from their obligations, in particular those arising from article 14, but only to the extent strictly required by the exigencies of the situation.[65] In the present case, however, Committee member Shearer noted that the State had presented no observations on the claims of the author based on any situation of emergency; nor had the State party made any declarations of derogation under article 4 of the Covenant.[66]

In *De Polay v Peru*, the Committee articulated the following view:[67]

> As to Mr. Polay Campos' trial and conviction on 3 April 1993 by a special tribunal of 'faceless judges', no information was made available by the State party, in

62 General Comment 32, above n 1, para 22. See also *Madani v Algeria*, Communication 1172/2003, UN Doc CCPR/C/89/D/1172/2003 (2007), para 8.7; *Kurbanov v Tajikistan*, above n 5, para 7.6; *Bee v Equatorial Guinea*, Communications 1152/2003 and 1190/2003, UN Doc CCPR/C/85/D/1152 & 1190/2003 (2005), para 6.3; and *Benhadj v Algeria*, Communication 1173/2003, UN Doc CCPR/C/90/D/1173/2003 (2007), para 8.8.

63 *General Comment 13: Equality before the courts and the right to a fair and public hearing by an independent court established by law (Art 14)*, UN Doc CCPR General Comment 13 (1984), para 15.

64 *Campos v Peru*, Communication 577/1994, UN Doc CCPR/C/61/D/577/1994 (1997); *Vivanco v Peru*, Communication 678/1996, UN Doc CCPR/C/74/D/678/1996 (2002), para 7.1. See also *Gomez v Peru*, Communication 981/2001, UN Doc CCPR/C/78/D/981/2001 (2003), para 7.3.

65 Concerning the process of derogations from Covenant rights, see Chapter 3.

66 See also *Arredondo v Peru*, Communication 688/1996, UN Doc CCPR/C/69/D/688/1996 (2000).

67 *De Polay v Peru*, Communication 575/1994, UN Doc CCPR/C/53/D/575/1994 (1995), para 8.8.

> spite of the Committee's request to this effect in the admissibility decision of 15 March 1996. As indicated by the Committee in its preliminary comments of 25 July 1996 on the Third Periodic Report of Peru and its Concluding Observations of 6 November 1996 … such trials by special tribunals composed of anonymous judges are incompatible with article 14 of the Covenant. It cannot be held against the author that she furnished little information about her husband's trial: in fact, the very nature of the system of trials by 'faceless judges' in a remote prison is predicated on the exclusion of the public from the proceedings. In this situation, the defendants do not know who the judges trying them are and unacceptable impediments are created to their preparation of their defence and communication with their lawyers. Moreover, this system fails to guarantee a cardinal aspect of a fair trial within the meaning of article 14 of the Covenant: that the tribunal must be, and be seen to be, independent and impartial. In a system of trial by 'faceless judges', neither the independence nor the impartiality of the judges is guaranteed, since the tribunal, being established ad hoc, may comprise serving members of the armed forces. In the Committee's opinion, such a system also fails to safeguard the presumption of innocence, which is guaranteed by article 14, paragraph 2. In the circumstances of the case, the Committee concludes that paragraphs 1, 2 and 3 (b) and (d) of article 14 of the Covenant were violated.

Thus, the complete circumstances in which trials by faceless judges are conducted must be taken into account. Having said so, the Committee's recent General Comment points to the practical reality that such courts often suffer from other irregularities and infers that it should therefore be vigilant when considering the independence and impartiality of such courts.[68] In *Más v Peru*, for example, the author's trial was conducted by a court comprising faceless judges, in a situation where he did not have an opportunity to question witnesses and his lawyer had received threats, resulting in a finding of a violation of article 14.[69]

Indigenous or religious tribunals The authors in *Hopu and Bessert v France* claimed that they were denied access to an independent and impartial tribunal. They claimed, in this respect, that the only tribunals with competence to adjudicate land disputes in French Polynesia were indigenous tribunals and that such tribunals ought to have been made available to them. The Committee was not sympathetic to the claim, without further details as to how independence and impartiality was obfuscated. It observed that the authors could have brought their case before a French tribunal, but that they deliberately chose not to do so, claiming that French

68 General Comment 32, above n 1, para 23.

69 *Más v Peru*, Communication 1058/2002, UN Doc CCPR/C/85/D/1058/2002 (2005), para 6.4. See also *Roque v Peru*, Communication 1125/2002, UN Doc CCPR/C/85/D/1125/2002 (2005), para 7.3; *Alegre v Peru*, Communication 1126/2002, UN Doc CCPR/C/85/D/1126/2002 (2005), para 7.5; and *Barney v Colombia*, Communication 1298/2004, UN Doc CCPR/C/87/D/1298/2004 (2006), para 7.2.

authorities should have kept indigenous tribunals in operation.[70] An apparently more generous approach is reflected within General Comment 32:

> Article 14 is also relevant where a State, in its legal order, recognizes courts based on customary law, or religious courts, to carry out or entrusts them with judicial tasks. It must be ensured that such courts cannot hand down binding judgments recognized by the State, unless the following requirements are met: proceedings before such courts are limited to minor civil and criminal matters, meet the basic requirements of fair trial and other relevant guarantees of the Covenant, and their judgments are validated by State courts in light of the guarantees set out in the Covenant and can be challenged by the parties concerned in a procedure meeting the requirements of article 14 of the Covenant. These principles are notwithstanding the general obligation of the State to protect the rights under the Covenant of any persons affected by the operation of customary and religious courts.

Fair and Public Hearing

The conduct of a public hearing is a qualified right subject to certain exceptions to be discussed. Fairness of proceedings, the Committee has explained, entails the absence of any direct or indirect influence, pressure or intimidation or intrusion from whatever side and for whatever motive. This is based upon the notion that parties should not be prejudiced or otherwise disadvantaged in being able to put their case to a tribunal. The impartiality and fair treatment of a case by the tribunal is also central. The HRC referred, in its General Comment, to jurisprudence of the Committee on the Elimination of all forms of Racial Discrimination in this regard, citing as an example of unfairness the situation where expressions of racist attitudes were made by a jury which appeared to be tolerated by the tribunal.[71]

The Committee's General Comment further notes that article 14 guarantees procedural equality and fairness only and cannot be interpreted as ensuring the absence of error on the part of the competent tribunal,[72] explaining that it is generally for domestic courts to review facts and evidence, unless it can be shown that such evaluation was clearly arbitrary or amounted to a manifest error or denial of justice, or that the court otherwise violated its obligation of independence and

70 *Hopu and Bessert v France*, Communication 549/1993, UN Doc CCPR/C/60/D/549/1993/Rev.1 (1997), para 10.2.

71 *Narrainen v Norway*, Committee on the Elimination of Racial Discrimination, Communication 3/1991, UN Doc CERD/C/44/D/3/1991 (1994), para 9.3.

72 *B.d.B et al v The Netherlands*, Communication 273/1988, UN Doc Supp 40 (A/44/40) at 286 (1989), para 6.3; and *Martínez Mercader et al v Spain*, Communication 1097/2002, UN Doc CCPR/C/84/D/1097/2002 (2005), para 6.3.

impartiality.[73] The existence of a 'fair' hearing is one which incorporates a number of further elements, including equality of arms between parties (considered above, in the context of equality before courts), attendance at hearings, the ability to hear from and examine witnesses, and the prompt disposal of proceedings.

Open justice Paragraph 1 guarantees the open administration of justice and only permits exclusion of the press and public during the course of proceedings for reasons of morals, public order or national security in a democratic society; when the interest of the private lives of the parties so requires; or to the extent strictly necessary in the opinion of the court in special circumstances where publicity would prejudice the interests of justice. Open administration is further guaranteed through the requirement that any judgment must be made public, unless the interest of juvenile persons otherwise requires, or the proceedings concern matrimonial disputes or the guardianship of children. To be public, hearings must be conducted openly, the result of which is to ensure the transparency of proceedings and provide an important safeguard for the interest of the individual and of society at large.[74]

Failure to conduct a public hearing, or to make the resulting judgment public, has generally resulted in an adverse finding under article 14(1).[75] In *Mahmoud v The Slovak Republic*, however, the Committee considered a situation where a court building was cleared due to a bomb scare, resulting in a claim by the author that because delivery of the formal judgment was not public, then his rights were violated. The author conceded that, at the time the judgment was delivered, the hearing of his appeal had already been completed and that the judgment was subsequently served on him personally. The Committee dismissed his communication.[76]

The right to public hearing applies to the conduct of a criminal trial before the finder of fact (whether a judge or jury). It does not apply, however, to pre-trial decisions made by prosecutors and public authorities.[77] The right to a public

---

73 *Riedl-Riedenstein et al v Germany*, above n 59, para 7.3; *Bondarenko v Belarus*, Communication 886/1999, UN Doc CCPR/C/77/D/886/1999 (2003), para 9.3; and *Arenz et al v Germany*, Communication 1138/2002, UN Doc CCPR/C/80/D/1138/2002 (2004), para 8.6.

74 General Comment 32, above n 1, para 28. See, for example, *Vastilskis v Uruguay*, Communication 80/1980, UN Doc Supp 40 (A/38/40) at 173 (1983).

75 See, for example, *Touron v Uruguay*, above n 32, para 12; and *Weisz v Uruguay*, Communication 28/1978, UN Doc CCPR/C/OP/1 at 57 (1984), para 16.

76 *Mahmoud v The Slovak Republic*, Communication 935/2000, UN Doc CCPR/C/72/D/935/2000 (2001), para 6.3.

77 See *Kavanagh v Ireland*, above n 9, para 10.4, where the Committee concluded that there was no violation of the right to a public hearing in circumstances where the author was not heard by the Department of Public Prosecutions on the decision to convene a Special Criminal Court.

hearing does not necessarily apply to all appellate proceedings, if these take place on the basis of written presentations.[78]

Attendance of parties at hearing According to the *travaux préparatoires* to the Covenant, the concept of a 'public hearing' must be read against the background that in the legal system of many countries, trials take place on the basis of written documentation, which is deemed not to place at risk the parties' procedural guarantees, as the content of all these documents can be made public. In the individual opinion of Committee member Bertil Wennergren, in *Karttunen v Finland*,[79] the requirement in article 14(1) must be applied in a flexible way and cannot prima facie be understood as requiring a public oral hearing. He further considered that this explained why, at a later stage of the *travaux préparatoires* on article 14(3)(d), the right to be tried in one's own presence before the court of first instance was specifically inserted in the context of criminal proceedings. He concluded that there can be no a priori assumption in favour of public oral hearings in review procedures.

The Committee has held that a trial *in absentia* can be compatible with article 14, but only when an accused was summoned in a timely manner and informed of the proceedings against him or her.[80] In *Maleki v Italy*, the State party did not deny that Mr Maleki was tried *in absentia*. However, it failed to show that the author was summoned in a timely manner and that he was informed of the proceedings against him, stating that it assumed that the author was informed by his counsel of the proceedings. The Committee considered this to be insufficient to discharge the burden placed on the State when seeking to justify trying an accused *in absentia*. It was incumbent on the court that tried the case, said the Committee, to verify that the author had been informed of the pending case before proceeding to hold the trial.[81] The Committee added that the violation of the author's right to be tried in his presence could have been remedied if he had been entitled to a retrial in his presence when he was apprehended in Italy.

The extent of the right to be present at the hearing of a suit at law is less clear. The Committee has commented that article 14(1) 'may' require that an individual be able to participate in person in civil proceedings. In such circumstances the State party is under an obligation to allow that individual to be present at the hearing, even if the person is a non-resident alien. In assessing whether the requirements of article 14(1) were met in *Said v Norway*, the Committee noted that the author's

---

78 *RM v Finland*, Communication 301/1988, UN Doc Supp 40 (A/44/40) at 300 (1989), para 6.4.

79 *Karttunen v Finland*, above n 55.

80 General Comment 13, above n 63, para 11. See also: *Mbenge v Zaire*, Communication 16/79, UN Doc Supp 40 (A/38/40) at 134 (1983); and *Benhadj v Algeria*, above n 62, para 8.9.

81 *Maleki v Italy*, Communication 699/1996, UN Doc CCPR/C/66/D/699/1996 (1999), para 9.4.

lawyer did not request a postponement of the hearing for the purpose of enabling the author to participate in person; nor did instructions to that effect appear in the signed authorization given to the lawyer by the author and subsequently presented by the lawyer to the judge at the hearing of a child custody case. In those circumstances, the Committee adopted the view that there was no violation by the State through any failure by the Oslo City Court to postpone the hearing, on its own initiative, until the author could be present in person.[82] Regrettably, the Committee went no further to clarify *when* civil proceedings 'may' require that an individual be able to participate in person in civil proceedings.

Audi alteram partem The principles of a fair hearing have been viewed as incorporating what some systems call the 'rules of natural justice', including the concept of *audi alteram partem*. The latter principles were found to be violated in *Hermoza v Peru*, where administrative authorities deprived the author of a hearing, those same authorities having made the decisions to suspend him and, later, to discharge him.[83]

Witnesses at trial The question of the right to call, and the availability of, witnesses at trial was considered in *McLawrence v Jamaica*, where the author claimed a violation of article 14(1) on the basis that a witness deemed to be crucial was unavailable at trial. The right to a fair trial does not encompass an absolute right to have a certain witness testify in court on trial, said the Committee. In the instant case, where repeated efforts had been made to secure the attendance of the witness in question, the Committee did not consider that a violation of article 14(1) had been established.[84] In *Dugin v Russian Federation*, however, the failure to allow a witness to be summoned for cross-examination was found to violate article 14, in circumstances where the Court gave very considerable weight to the witness's statement in its decision.[85]

Prompt disposal of proceedings In the context of the criminal process, the prompt disposal of proceedings is a specific requirement of article 14(3)(c) (the right to be tried without undue delay). Prompt disposal of civil proceedings is also required and has been treated as arising from the general provisions of paragraph 1. Following

---

82 *Said v Norway*, Communication 767/1997, UN Doc CCPR/C/68/D/767/1997 (2000), para 11.3.

83 *Hermoza v Peru*, Communication 203/1986, UN Doc Supp 40 (A/44/40) at 200 (1988), individual opinion of Committee members Joseph Cooray, Vojin Dimitrjevic and Rajsoomer Lallah.

84 *McLawrence v Jamaica*, Communication 702/1996, UN Doc CCPR/C/60/D/702/1996 (1997), para 5.8. See also *Peart v Jamaica*, Communications 464 and 482/1991, UN Doc CCPR/C/54/D/464/1991 (1995) and CCPR/C/54/D/482/1991 (1995).

85 *Dugin v Russian Federation*, Communication 815/1998, UN Doc CCPR/C/81/D/815/1998 (2004), para 6.3.

his illegal detention in 1979, for example, the author in *Mukunto v Zambia* filed a complaint for compensation before the Supreme Court in 1982 and 1985. By 1999, when the Human Rights Committee considered his complaint under article 14(1), his claim for compensation had still not been adjudicated upon. Neither of the author's claims under article 14 were refuted by Zambia, which instead put before the Committee reasons for the non-payment of compensation, including economic difficulties to provide adequate conditions to all detained persons. The Committee did not consider this to be a relevant response to the claim of violation of article 14(1) and found that the author's rights had not been respected.[86] A similar approach was taken by the Committee concerning delays in the disposal of slander proceedings in *Paraga v Croatia*, a five-year delay in criminal proceedings in *Muñoz v Spain*, a seven-year delay in the disposal of administrative review proceedings in *Hermoza v Peru*, and a 12-year delay after the original events in *Gomez v Peru*.[87] In contrast, the Committee has considered that a delay of a little over two years between complaint and judgment did not constitute a violation of article 14(1), in circumstances where the proceedings resulted in the author's reinstatement in his post.[88]

In the context of custody proceedings, or proceedings concerning access of a divorced parent to his or her children, the Human Rights Committee has similarly required that such issues be adjudicated expeditiously.[89] Where delays in proceedings are caused by a lack of resources or under-funding, the Committee has commented that, to the extent possible, supplementary budgetary resources should be allocated for the administration of justice.[90] Notably, and in combination with the right to effective remedies under article 2(3) of the Covenant, excessive delays on the part of administrative authorities in implementing judicial decisions has been treated as a violation of article 14(1).[91]

---

86 *Mukunto v Zambia*, Communication 768/1997, UN Doc CCPR/C/66/D/768/1997 (1999), para 6.4.

87 *Paraga v Croatia*, Communication 727/1996, UN Doc CCPR/C/71/D/727/1996 (2001), para 9.7; *Muñoz v Spain*, Communication 1006/2001, UN Doc CCPR/C/79/D/1006/2001 (2003), para 7.1; *Hermoza v Peru*, above n 83, para 11.3; and *Gomez v Peru*, above n 64, para 7.3. See also *Fei v Colombia*, above n 15, para 8.4; *Filipovich v Lithuania*, above n 59, para 7.1; *Perterer v Austria*, above n 10, para 10.7; *Pimentel et al v Philippines*, Communication 1320/2004, UN Doc CCPR/C/89/D/1320/2004 (2007), para 9.2; and *Lederbauer v Austria*, Communication 1454/2006, UN Doc CCPR/C/90/D/1454/2006 (2007), para 8.2.

88 *Casanovas v France*, above n 16, paras 7.3–7.4.

89 *Tcholatch v Canada*, above n 59, paras 8.9–8.11. See also *EB v New Zealand*, Communication 1368/2005, UN Doc CCPR/C/89/D/1368/2005 (2007), paras 9.2–9.4.

90 General Comment 32, above n 1, para 27.

91 *Czernin v Czech Republic*, Communication 823/1998, UN Doc CCPR/C/83/D/823/1998 (2005), para 7.5.

In the Committee's consideration of a series of procedural delays in *Deisl v Austria*,[92] it very usefully identified a number of relevant factors which should be taken into account in determining the reasonableness or otherwise of any delay in the disposal of proceedings: (a) the length of each individual stage of the proceeding; (b) the complexity of the issues being determined; (c) any detrimental effect cased by the delay upon the individual's legal position;[93] (d) the availability of remedies to accelerate the proceedings, and whether these were called upon; and (e) the outcome of any appellate proceedings.

Pre-trial publicity The impact of pre-trial publicity on the ability to conduct a fair hearing is primarily a question of fact which should be considered by the trial court and any appeals court. The provision of clear instructions to a jury to consider only the evidence presented at trial will prevent any violation of article 14 on this account.[94]

Criminal Proceedings

Before considering the rights relevant to the *determination* of criminal charges, one must first reflect upon those rights applicable throughout the criminal process: the presumption of innocence; the privilege against self-incrimination; the principle of *ne bis in idem*; and the special position of juvenile accused and convicts.

Presumption of Innocence

Applicable to all stages up to conviction, and to criminal proceedings only,[95] the presumption of innocence is guaranteed under paragraph 2 of article 14, stating: 'Everyone charged with a criminal offence shall have the right to be presumed innocent until proved guilty according to law.' Not only does this right impact upon investigation and prosecution, but it also demands that public authorities refrain from prejudging the outcome of a trial. In *Gridin v Russian Federation*, where public statements given wide media coverage were made by high-ranking law enforcement officials portraying the author as guilty, the Committee did not hesitate to find a violation of the presumption of innocence.[96] The HRC added in

92 *Deisl v Austria*, above n 20, paras 11.2–11.6.

93 This factor should be taken to include any detrimental impact on the ability of a person to defend him or herself: see *Kurbanov v Tajikistan*, above n 5, para 7.3.

94 *Dudko v Australia*, above n 43, para 6.3.

95 *Morael v France*, Communication 207/1986, UN Doc Supp 40 (A/44/40) at 210 (1989), para 9.5; and *Cabal and Bertran v Australia*, Communication 1020/2001, UN Doc CCPR/C/78/D/1020/2001 (2003), para 7.6.

96 *Gridin v Russian Federation*, Communication 770/1997, UN Doc CCPR/C/69/D/770/1997 (2000), para 8.3.

its General Comment that defendants should normally not be shackled or kept in cages during trials, or otherwise presented to the court in a manner indicating that they may be dangerous criminals.[97]

The Committee has considered that the denial of bail or the imposition of preventive detention does not, *a priori*, affect the right of persons to be presumed innocent.[98] Nevertheless, in *Cagas v Philippines*, the Committee took the view than an excessive period of preventive detention, exceeding nine years in that case, did affect the right to be presumed innocent and thereby constituted a violation of article 14(2).[99] During the conduct of a trial itself, the principle of presumption of innocence has been taken to mean that the burden of proof for any criminal charge is on the prosecution, and that an accused must have the benefit of the doubt. An accused's guilt cannot therefore be presumed until a charge has been proven beyond reasonable doubt. Although the Committee will not normally look to evaluate evidence,[100] it has been prepared to find a violation of the presumption of innocence where uncontested information before it leaves room for considerable doubt about guilt.[101]

It should be noted that conduct of the State inconsistent with the presumption of innocence can be remedied by the State through the judicial process. In *Vargas-Machuca v Peru*, for example, the author had been dismissed from service in the Peruvian National Police based upon assertions that the author claimed never existed. Ultimately, however, both the Trujillo Third Special Civil Court and the Trujillo First Civil Division found that the author had been unlawfully dismissed and reinstated him in his post. Consequently, the Committee took the position that there was no violation of due process within the meaning of article 14(1) of the Covenant. It also considered that the domestic courts had recognized the author's innocence and that there was consequently no violation of the right contained in article 14(2).[102]

Privilege against Self-Incrimination

Article 14(3)(g) sets out the privilege against self-incrimination, providing that an accused cannot be compelled to testify against him or herself, or to confess guilt.

---

97 General Comment 32, above n 1, para 30.

98 *Wairiki Rameka et al v New Zealand*, Communication 1090/2002, UN Doc CCPR/C/79/D/1090/2002 (2003), para 7.4.

99 *Cagas v Philippines*, Communication 788/1999, UN Doc CCPR/C/73/D/788/1997 (2001), para 7.2.

100 Above n 59.

101 *Ashurov v Tajikistan*, above n 59, para 6.7; and *Larrañaga v Philippines*, Communication 1421/2005, UN Doc CCPR/C/87/D/1421/2005 (2006), para 7.4.

102 *Vargas-Machuca v Peru*, Communication 906/2000, UN Doc CCPR/C/75/D/906/2000 (2002), para 7.3. Compare with *Arutyuniantz v Uzbekistan*, above n 59, para 6.4.

In considering this safeguard, the provisions of article 7 (torture and inhumane treatment) and article 10(1) (treatment with humanity) should be borne in mind. In order to compel the accused to confess or to testify, the Committee has observed that methods that violate these provisions are frequently used.[103] It is unacceptable to treat an accused person in a manner contrary to article 7 of the Covenant in order to extract a confession. In *Burgos v Uruguay*, for example, Lopez Burgos and several others were forced, under threats of death or serious injury, to sign false statements that were subsequently used in legal proceedings against them.[104] Similarly, in *Berry v Jamaica*, the author claimed that the investigating officer threatened to shoot him and forced him to sign a prepared statement, whereas the officer testified during the trial that the author had made his statement after police cautioning. In order to reconcile these different versions, the Committee took a robust approach and required written depositions made and used during the preliminary hearing to be made available. This appeared to be particularly relevant in the communication, against the background of repeated requests by the author's counsel to make the transcript of the author's preliminary hearing available to him, including the depositions of witnesses, and that finally, after several reminders, he was informed by the judicial authorities that they were unable to locate them. These allegations were not denied by the State party and the Committee therefore gave weight to the author's claims, finding a violation of article 14(3)(g), *juncto* article 7, of the Covenant.[105]

In contrast, the Committee took a reasonably restrictive view in a later communication, *López v Spain*. A request was made of the author in that case on the basis of article 72(3) of the Road Safety Act, which provides that: 'The owner of the vehicle, on being duly asked to do so, has the duty to identify the driver responsible for the offence; if he fails to fulfil this obligation promptly

---

103 General Comment 32, above n 1, para 41.

104 *Burgos v Uruguay*, Communication 52/1979, UN Doc CCPR/C/OP/1 at 88 (1984), para 13. See also *Izquierdo v Uruguay*, Communication 73/1981, UN Doc CCPR/C/OP/1 at 7 (1985), para 9.

105 *Berry v Jamaica*, Communication 330/1988, UN Doc CCPR/C/50/D/330/1988 (1994), para 11.7. See also *Estrella v Uruguay*, Communication 74/1980, UN Doc Supp 40 (A/38/40) at 150 (1983), para 10; *Linton v Jamaica*, Communication 255/1987, UN Doc CCPR/C/46/D/255/1987 (1992), para 5.5; *Deolall v Guyana*, above n 5, paras 5.1–5.2; *Ruzmetov v Uzbekistan*, above n 5, paras 7.2–7.3; *Bazarov v Uzbekistan*, above n 5, para 8.3; *Tulyaganova v Uzbekistan*, above n 5 para 8.2; *Boimurodov v Tajikistan*, Communication 1042/2001, UN Doc CCPR/C/85/D/1042/2001 (2005), para 7.2; *Chikunova v Uzbekistan*, above n 5, para 7.2; *Shakurova v Tajikistan*, above n 5, para 8.2; *Kouidis v Greece*, Communication 1070/2002, UN Doc CCPR/C/86/D/1070/2002 (2006), paras 7.5–7.6; *Kurbanov v Tajikistan*, above n 5, para 7.5; *Khomidova v Tajikistan*, above n 57, para 6.5; *Khudayberganov v Uzbekistan*, Communication 1140/2002, UN Doc CCPR/C/90/D/1140/2002 (2007), para 8.4; *Bee v Equatorial Guinea*, above n 62, para 6.3; *Kurbonov v Tajikistan*, Communication 1208/2003, UN Doc CCPR/C/86/D/1208/2003 (2006), paras 6.3–6.4; and *Ashurov v Tajikistan*, above n 59, para 6.3.

without justified cause, he shall be liable to a fine for having committed a serious misdemeanour.' Pursuant to this request, Mr López sent the traffic authorities a letter in which he stated that he was not the driver of the vehicle and did not know who had been driving it since he had lent it to several people during that period. He was fined 50,000 pesetas. The author claimed before the HRC that his rights to the presumption of innocence and the right not to testify against himself were violated, since he had to identify the owner of the vehicle. The Committee concluded that the author had been punished for non-cooperation with the authorities and not for a traffic offence. It took the view that a penalty for failure to cooperate with the authorities falls outside the scope of application of paragraphs 2 and 3(g).[106]

Double Jeopardy

The principle against double jeopardy, *ne bis in idem*, is to be found in the final paragraph of article 14:

> 7. No one shall be liable to be tried or punished again for an offence for which he has already been finally convicted or acquitted in accordance with the law and penal procedure of each country.

The Human Rights Committee has clarified, in its recent General Comment, that article 14(7) does not prohibit the resumption of a criminal trial justified by exceptional circumstances, such as the discovery of evidence which was not available or known at the time of the acquittal.[107] Nor, due to the particular wording of article 14(7), can the guarantee be relied upon in cases involving the national jurisdictions of two or more States. As it observed in *AP v Italy*, the provision only prohibits double jeopardy with regard to an offence adjudicated within a given, respondent, State.[108]

In considering State party reports under article 40 of the ICCPR, the Committee has observed that differing views have often been expressed as to the scope of paragraph 7. Some States have even felt the need to make reservations in relation to procedures for the resumption of criminal cases.[109] In response, the Committee stated in its earlier General Comment on article 14:[110]

> It seems to the Committee that most States parties make a clear distinction between a resumption of a trial justified by exceptional circumstances and a

106 *López v Spain*, Communication 777/1997, CCPR/C/67/D/777/1997 (1999), para 6.4.

107 General Comment 32, above n 1, para 56.

108 *AP v Italy*, Communication 204/1986, UN Doc Supp 40 (A/43/40) at 242 (1988), para 7.3. See also *ARJ v Australia*, Communication 692/1996, UN Doc CCPR/C/60/D/692/1996 (1997), para 6.4.

109 For example, Denmark, Finland, Iceland and the Netherlands.

110 General Comment 13, above n 63, para 19.

> re-trial prohibited pursuant to the principle of *ne bis in idem* as contained in paragraph 7. This understanding of the meaning of *ne bis in idem* may encourage States parties to reconsider their reservations to article 14, paragraph 7.

Juvenile Accused and Convicts

In the case of juvenile persons, criminal procedures must be such as will take account of their age and the desirability of promoting their rehabilitation. Implicit in this, juveniles are to enjoy at least the same guarantees and protection as accorded to adults under article 14.[111] Juvenile accused should also receive special protection, including the provision of appropriate assistance and, taking into account their age and situation, the assistance and presence of their legal guardians during questioning or trial.[112] Articles 10(2)(b) and 10(3) should also be remembered, concerning the segregation of juveniles in detention and the provision for appropriate rehabilitative sentences.[113] The Committee has added:[114]

> States should take measures to establish an appropriate juvenile criminal justice system, in order to ensure that juveniles are treated in a manner commensurate with their age. It is important to establish a minimum age below which children and juveniles shall not be put on trial for criminal offences; that age should take into account their physical and mental immaturity.

Determination of Criminal Charges

Article 14(3) contains various rights concerning the determination of any criminal charge, each to be discussed in turn (although note that the privilege against self incrimination, reflected within article 14(3)(g), is discussed above). What should be considered before examining each of the subparagraphs is the meaning of the expression 'determination of any criminal charge', an issue raised in *Levy v Jamaica*. In that case, the author was arrested and charged with murder. He was subsequently found guilty and sentenced to death by the Home Circuit Court in Kingston. On 13 June 1994, the Court of Appeal of Jamaica dismissed his appeal and reclassified the author's offence as 'capital murder' under Section 2 of the Offences Against the Person (Amendment) Act 1992. In this regard, the Act adopted a procedure to reclassify established murder convictions expeditiously by entrusting the initial review of each case to a single judge, enabling the judge to promptly give a decision in favour of a prisoner who, in the judge's opinion, had committed a non-capital offence, and thus removing rapidly any uncertainty

111 General Comment 32, above n 1, para 42.
112 General Comment 32, above n 1, para 30.
113 See Chapter 5.
114 General Comment 32, above n 1, para 43.

as to whether the prisoner was still at risk of being executed. If, on the other hand, the single judge found that the offence was of a capital nature, the convict was notified and was granted the right to appeal the decision to a three-judge panel, which would address the matter in a public hearing. It was claimed that this reclassification violated article 14, as a 'determination' conducted by one judge alone and without a public hearing. It was not disputed before the Committee, however, that adequate procedural safeguards applied in proceedings before a three-judge panel. The author's complaint was directed solely at the first stage of the reclassification procedure, that is, the single judge's handling of the matter, of which the author was not notified and in which there was no public hearing where the author could comment on the relevant issues or be represented. The Committee took the view that the reclassification of an offence for a convict already subject to a death sentence was not a determination of a criminal charge within the meaning of article 14 of the Covenant and, consequently, that the provisions in article 14(3) did not apply.[115] The Committee has also taken the view that article 14(3) is not activated by criminal investigations preceding the laying of charges,[116] nor by proceedings in respect of which a body only has the jurisdiction to determine whether an author should be *committed* to stand trial.[117]

The Right to be Informed of the Charge(s) Faced (Article 14(3)(a))

The right to be informed of the charge(s) faced requires that information be given 'in detail in a language which he understands of the nature and cause of the charge against him'. This can be met by stating the charge in a language understood by the accused (either orally or in writing), with the information indicating both the law and the alleged facts on which it is based.[118] Where the information is provided orally, it should be later confirmed in writing.[119] Provision of that advice 'promptly' requires it to be given as soon as a court or an authority of the prosecution decides to take procedural steps against a person suspected of a crime or publicly names the person as such. In *Williams v Jamaica*, the Committee said:[120]

---

115 *Levy v Jamaica*, Communication 719/1996, UN Doc CCPR/C/64/D/719/1996 (1998), para 7.1. See also *Williams v Jamaica*, Communication 720/1996, UN Doc CCPR/C/64/D/720/1996 (1998), para 7.1, concerning the same reclassification procedure.

116 *Khachatrian v Armenia*, Communication 1056/2002, UN Doc CCPR/C/85/D/1056/2002 (2005), para 6.4.

117 *De Lorenzo v Italy*, Communication 1419/2005, UN Doc CCPR/C/90/D/1419/2005 (2007), para 6.4.

118 General Comment 32, above n 1, para 31.

119 Ibid.

120 *Williams v Jamaica*, Communication 561/1993, UN Doc CCPR/C/59/D/561/1993 (1997), para 9.2. See also *Kelly v Jamaica*, Communication 253/1987, UN Doc CCPR/C/41/D/253/1987 (1991), para 5.8; *Smirnova v Russian Federation*, Communication 712/1996, UN Doc CCPR/C/81/D/712/1996 (2004), para 10.3; *Márques de Morais v Angola*, Communication 1128/2002, UN Doc CCPR/C/83/D/1128/2002 (2005), para 5.4;

> Article 14, paragraph 3(a), gives the right to everyone charged with a criminal offence to be informed 'promptly and in detail in a language which he understands of the nature and cause of the charge against him'. The author contends that he was detained for six weeks before he was charged with the offence for which he was later convicted. For the purposes of article 14, paragraph 3(a), detailed information about the charges against the accused must not be provided immediately upon arrest, but with the beginning of the preliminary investigation or the setting of some other hearing which gives rise to a clear official suspicion against the accused.

The interaction of article 14(3)(a) with article 9(3) (promptly bringing a detainee before a competent authority) was considered in *McLawrence v Jamaica*. So long as article 9(3) is complied with, said the Committee, the details of the nature and cause of the charge need not necessarily be provided to an accused person immediately upon arrest.[121] This particular decision appears flawed since there is no explanation as to *why* such an approach should be taken, the effect of which is to restrict the rights under article 14(3)(a), and it is furthermore inconsistent with the approach taken by the Committee in other communications concerning the right to prompt disclosure for the preparation of a defence case (discussed next).

Preparation of the Defence Case (Article 14(3)(b))

States parties to the International Covenant have an obligation to ensure that any person accused of a crime is able to exercise the right to a defence.[122] Article 14(3)(b) provides, in that regard, that an accused must have adequate time and facilities for the preparation of his or her defence, and to communicate with counsel of choosing.

Disclosure and adequate time to prepare Determination of what constitutes adequate time requires an assessment of the individual circumstances of each case,[123] but the Committee has taken the view that time and facilities must include access to documents and other evidence that the accused requires to prepare the defence case, as well as the opportunity to engage and communicate with counsel.[124] It is important that the defence has the opportunity to familiarize itself with the documentary evidence against an accused, by way of full and prompt

---

Bee v Equatorial Guinea, above n 62, para 6.3; and *Medjnoune v Algeria*, Communication 1297/2004, UN Doc CCPR/C/87/D/1297/2004 (2006), para 8.6.

121 *McLawrence v Jamaica*, above n 84, para 5.9.

122 As confirmed, for example, in *Gueorguiev v Spain*, above n 59, para 6.3.

123 See *Hibbert v Jamaica*, Communication 293/1988, UN Doc CCPR/C/45/D/293/1988 (1992), para 7.4; and *Williams v Jamaica*, above n 120, para 9.3.

124 General Comment 32, above n 1, para 34. See also *van Marcke v Belgium*, above n 59, para 8.3.

disclosure.[125] All materials that the prosecution plans to offer in court against the accused, or that are exculpatory, must be disclosed to the defence. Exculpatory material should be understood, the Committee has explained, as including not only material establishing innocence but also other evidence that could assist the defence, such as indications that a confession was not voluntary. In cases of a claim that evidence was obtained in violation of article 7 of the Covenant, information about the circumstances in which such evidence was obtained must be made available to allow an assessment of such a claim.[126] It is notable that the requirement to disclose materials has not been taken to entail the right of an accused who does not understand the language used in court to be furnished with translations of all relevant documents in a criminal investigation, provided that the relevant documents are made available to his or her counsel.[127] Nor does the right extend to the preparation of an appeal.[128]

In *Yassen and Thomas v Guyana*, the author Thomas had been tried and, in the process, appeared at a preliminary hearing. At that preliminary inquiry, the police produced a written statement, alleged to be a confession made by Mr Thomas, and recorded in a pocket book. This pocket book, along with the Suddie Police station diary for the relevant days, disappeared between the time of the preliminary hearing and trial. The station diary was kept in a storeroom under lock and key. The relevant documents were produced at the first trial but disappeared shortly thereafter. The authors complained that these documents may have contained exculpatory evidence and that their disappearance therefore prejudiced the preparation of the defence case. Guyana failed to address this allegation and the Committee therefore gave weight to the authors' allegations. It concluded that the failure to produce police documents at the last trial, which were produced at the first trial and which may have contained evidence in favour of the authors, constituted a violation of article 14, paragraph 3(b) and (e), since it may have impeded the authors in the preparation of their defence.[129]

Where, however, the affect of non-disclosure upon the preparation of the defence case can be remedied through a remand of proceedings, the Committee has taken the view that it is incumbent on counsel to seek an adjournment.[130] The HRC has added that there is an obligation to grant reasonable requests for

125 See, for example, *Peart v Jamaica*, above n 84, para 11.5; and *Bee v Equatorial Guinea*, above n 62, para 6.3.

126 General Comment 32, above n 1, para 33.

127 *Harward v Norway*, Communication 451/1991, UN Doc CCPR/C/51/D/451/1991 (1994), para 9.5.

128 *Perterer v Austria*, above n 10, para 10.6.

129 *Yassen and Thomas v Guyana*, Communication 676/1996, UN Doc CCPR/C/62/D/676/1996 (1998), para 7.10.

130 *Adams v Jamaica*, Communication 607/1994, UN Doc CCPR/C/58/D/607/1994 (1996), para 8.3; *Henry v Jamaica*, Communication 610/1995, UN Doc CCPR/C/64/D/610/1995 (1998), para 7.5; *Reece v Jamaica*, above n 59, para 7.2; and *Morais v Angola*, above n 120, para 5.6.

adjournment, particularly when an accused is charged with a serious criminal offence and additional time for preparation of the defence is needed.[131]

The question of summaries of information redacted for security concerns arose in *Ahani v Canada* in the case of a hearing concerning the reasonableness of a security certificate issued against the author. The Committee noted that the Court took steps to ensure that the author was aware of, and able to respond to, the case made against him and that he was also able to, and did, present his own case and cross-examine witnesses. In the circumstances of national security involved, the Committee was persuaded that this process was fair to the author and thus found no violation of article 14.[132]

Representation When an accused does not want to defend him or herself in person, recourse to a lawyer should be made available. Denying a person access to legal counsel has been concluded to amount to a failure to permit the adequate preparation of a defence case.[133] Denial of representation when requested during an interrogation also constitutes a violation of rights under article 14(3)(b).[134] Lawyers should be able to counsel and to represent their clients promptly, and in accordance with their established professional standards and judgement without any restrictions, influences, pressures or undue interference from any quarter. The conditions of detention must be such that counsel can take adequate instructions,[135] in conditions giving full respect for the confidentiality of communications between counsel and the accused.[136] It goes without saying that a person held incommunicado is, due to such status, unable to give instructions and prepare his or her defence.[137] On the question of the choice of counsel, and representation during the conduct of a trial, see the discussion below.

---

131 *Phillip v Trinidad and Tobago*, Communication 594/1992, UN Doc CCPR/C/64/D/594/1992 (1998), para 7.2; and *Chan v Guyana*, above n 5, para 6.3.

132 *Ahani v Canada*, above n 22, para 10.4.

133 See, for example, *Ramirez v Uruguay*, where the author was kept in detention, never provided with any legal assistance, and never tried as no charges were brought against him: Communication 4/1977, UN doc CCPR/C/10/D/4/1977 (1980), para 18. See also *Pietraroia v Uruguay*, Communication 6/1977, UN Doc CCPR/C/10/D/6/1977 (1980), para 16.

134 *Gridin v Russian Federation*, above n 96, para 8.5. See also *Penarrieta and others v Bolivia*, Communication 176/1984, UN Doc Supp 40 (A/43/40) at 199 (1988), para 16, where, during the initial 44 days of detention, the authors had no access to legal counsel.

135 *Caraballal v Uruguay*, Communication 33/1978, UN Doc CCPR/C/12/D/33/1978 (1981), para 13.

136 *Gridin v Russian Federation*, above n 96, para 8.5; *Siragev v Uzbekistan*, above n 5, para 6.3; and *Khomidova v Tajikistan*, above n 57, para 6.4.

137 See, for example, the comments of the Committee in *Caldas v Uruguay*, Communication 43/1979, UN Doc Supp 40 (A/38/40) at 192 (1983), para 14; and *Machado v Uruguay*, Communication 83/1981, UN Doc Supp 40 (A/39/40) at 148 (1984), paras 1.3 and 12.

Trial without Undue Delay (Article 14(3)(c))

An accused must be tried without undue delay. This relates not only to the time by which a trial should commence, but also the time by which it should end and judgment be rendered.[138] In cases involving serious charges such as homicide or murder, and where the accused is denied bail by the court, the Human Rights Committee has repeatedly said that an accused must be tried in as expeditious a manner as possible.[139] What constitutes 'reasonable time' is a matter of assessment in each particular case, taking into account factors such as the complexity of the case, the conduct of the accused, and the manner in which the matter was dealt with by the administrative and judicial authorities.[140] A lack of adequate budgetary appropriations for the administration of criminal justice will not justify unreasonable delays in the adjudication of criminal cases.[141]

A delay of 16 months, in the context of Communication 677/1996, was found to be unreasonable.[142] The trial transcript in that case showed that all evidence for the case of the prosecution had been gathered by 1 June 1988 and no further investigations were carried out, whereas the trial did not begin until 6 October 1989. It did not assist the State party's position that it gave no explanation for this delay. In *Boodoo v Trinidad and Tobago*, the Committee concluded that a period of 33 months between arrest and trial constituted undue delay and could not be deemed compatible with the provisions of article 9(3).[143] Likewise, the arrest in September 1985 and continued detention of the author in *Sahadeo v Guyana* until he was first convicted and sentenced to death in November 1989 (four years and two months after his arrest) was found to be in violation of article 9(3) of the

138 *Taright, Touadi, Remli and Yousfi v Algeria*, Communication 1085/2002, UN Doc CCPR/C/86/D/1085/2002 (2006), para 8.5; and *Rouse v Philippines*, Communication 1089/2002, UN Doc CCPR/C/84/D/1089/2002 (2005), para 7.4.

139 See, for example, *Barroso v Panama*, Communication 473/1991, UN Doc CCPR/C/54/D/473/1991 (1995), para 8.5; and *Francis v Trinidad and Tobago*, Communication 899/1999, UN Doc CCPR/C/75/D/899/1999 (2002), para 5.4.

140 See the examples that follow, and also: *Cagas v The Philippines*, above n 99, at para 7.4; *Kelly v Jamaica*, above n 120, para 5.11; *Johnson v Jamaica*, Communication 588/1994, UN Doc CCPR/C/56/D/588/1994 (1996); *Yasseen and Thomas v Guyana*, above n 129, para 7.11; *Sextus v Trinidad and Tobago*, Communication 818/1998, UN Doc CCPR/C/72/D/818/1998 (2001); *Hendricks v Guyana*, Communication 838/1998, UN Doc CCPR/C/76/D/838/1998 (2002), para 8.4; and *Siewpersaud, Sukhram, and Persaud v Trinidad and Tobago*, Communication 938/2000, UN Doc CCPR/C/81/D/938/2000 (2004), para 6.2.

141 See *Fillastre and others v Bolivia*, Communication 336/1988, UN Doc CCPR/C/43/D/336/1988 (1991), para 6.5.

142 *Teesdale v Trinidad and Tobago*, above n 36, para 9.3.

143 *Boodoo v Trinidad and Tobago*, Communication 721/1996, UN Doc CCPR/C/74/D/721/1996 (2002), para 6.2.

Covenant.[144] A period of 11 months between arrest and hearing was not found to constitute a violation of article 14(3)(c) in *Hussain v Mauritius*.[145]

All stages within the criminal process, according to the HRC, must take place without undue delay. For instance, the requirement to dispose of proceedings without undue delay has been found to apply equally to appeals against sentence and/or conviction.[146] A delay of almost five years between an author's conviction in February 1989 and the judgment of the Court of Appeal, dismissing his appeal, in January 1994, was found to be incompatible with the requirements of article 14(3)(c) *juncto* article 14(5) of the Covenant.[147] A delay in producing trial transcripts for the purpose of an appeal was considered incompatible with the right to be tried with undue delay.[148]

A question raised various times is whether the wording of subparagraph 3(c) places a duty upon member States to prosecute where an allegation of criminal conduct is made. To that question the Committee has repeatedly answered that the Covenant does not provide a right for individuals to require that the State criminally prosecute another person.[149] Notwithstanding that position, the Committee has said, in *Andreu v Colombia*, that States are under a duty to thoroughly investigate alleged violations of human rights and, in particular, forced disappearances of persons and violations of the right to life, and to prosecute criminally, try and punish those held responsible for such violations. This duty, it said, applies *a fortiori* in cases in which the perpetrators of such violations have been identified.[150]

Conduct of the Trial (Article 14(3)(d), (e) and (f))

Various requirements fall within the ambit of what might be termed the 'conduct of the trial', as set out within subparagraphs 3(d), 3(e) and 3(f) of article 14: an

144 *Sahadeo v Guyana*, Communication 728/1996, UN Doc CCPR/C/73/D/728/1996 (2001), para 9.2.

145 *Hussain v Mauritius*, Communication 980/2001, UN Doc CCPR/C/77/D/980/2001 (2002), para 6.5.

146 *Teesdale v Trinidad and Tobago*, above n 36, para 9.4.

147 *Wanza v Trinidad and Tobago*, Communication 683/1996, UN Doc CCPR/C/74/D/683/1996 (2002), para 9.4. See also the Committee's Views in *Lubuto v Zambia*, Communication 390/1990, UN Doc CCPR/C/55/D/390/1990 (1995); and *Sextus v Trinidad and Tobago*, above n 140.

148 *Pinkney v Canada*, Communication 27/1977, UN Doc CCPR/C/OP/1 at 95 (1985), para 35.

149 *HCMA v The Netherlands*, Communication 213/1986, UN Doc Supp 40 (A/44/40) at 267 (1989), para 11.6; *SE v Argentina*, Communication 275/1988, UN Doc CCPR/C/38/D/275/1988 (1990), para 5.5; *R.A., V.N. et al v Argentina*, Communications 343–5/1988, UN Doc CCPR/C/38/D/343-345/1988 (1990), para 5.5.

150 *Andreu v Colombia*, Communication 563/1993, UN Doc CCPR/C/55/D/563/1993 (1995), para 8.6.

accused must; (1) be tried in his or her presence;[151] (2) be able to defend him or herself in person or through legal counsel of own choosing; (3) be informed of the latter right, where he or she does not have legal assistance; (4) have legal assistance assigned, in any case where the interests of justice so require, and without payment in any case where the accused does not have sufficient means to pay for it; (5) be free to examine, or have examined, the witnesses against him or her; (6) be able to obtain the attendance and examination of witnesses on his or her behalf under the same conditions as witnesses against the accused; and (7) have the free assistance of an interpreter if the accused cannot understand or speak the language used in court. On the subject of legal aid, see the discussion above concerning preparation of the defence case.

The Committee has treated communications in this area with care, seeking to balance its role under the Optional Protocol with due deference to municipal judicial bodies. By way of general principle the Committee has taken the view that it is for domestic courts to ensure that the conduct of a case by a lawyer is not incompatible with the interests of justice.[152] This includes an unwillingness to hold member States accountable for alleged errors made by a defence lawyer, unless it was or should have been manifest to the judge that the lawyer's behaviour was incompatible with the interests of justice.[153]

Trial in one's presence Under article 14(1) everyone is entitled not only to a fair but also to a public hearing. Moreover, in the determination of criminal charges, the right to be tried in one's presence is expressly guaranteed under article 14(3)(d).[154] In a communication relying upon article 14(3)(d), the author in *Orejuela v Colombia* complained that the proceedings against him were conducted only in writing, excluding any hearing, either oral or public. The State party did not refute these allegations but merely indicated that the decisions were made public. The Committee observed that, in order to guarantee the rights of the defence enshrined in article 14(3) of the Covenant (in particular those contained in subparagraphs (d) and (e)), all criminal proceedings must provide the person charged with the criminal offence the right to an oral hearing, at which he or she may appear in person or be represented by counsel, and may bring evidence and examine witnesses. Concluding that the author did not have such a hearing during the proceedings that culminated in his conviction and sentencing, the Committee found that there was a violation of the right of the author to a fair trial in accordance with article 14 of

151 See, for example, *Weisz v Uruguay*, above n 75, para 16.

152 See, for example, *Campbell v Jamaica*, Communication 618/1995, UN Doc CCPR/C/64/D/618/1995 (1998), para 7.4.

153 Ibid, para 7.3.

154 See, for example, *Lumley v Jamaica*, Communication 662/1995, UN Doc CCPR/C/65/D/662/1995 (1999), para 7.4; and *Dudko v Australia*, above n 43, paras 7.3–7.4.

the Covenant.[155] As discussed above within the general provisions of article 14(1), it should be remembered that the Committee has held that a trial in absentia can be compatible with article 14 if the accused was summoned in a timely manner and informed of the proceedings against him or her.[156]

Representation at trial The accused or his lawyer must be allowed to act diligently and fearlessly in pursuing all available defences, and enjoy the ability to challenge the conduct of the case if they believe it to be unfair, unhindered by the court or relevant authorities.[157] The right to representation involves two types of advocacy: that by legal counsel of choosing; and self-representation. The right to represent oneself is clear from the wording of article 14(3)(d), although the Committee has commented that this right is not absolute, drawing from its views in *Correia de Matos v Portugal*:[158]

> The interests of justice may, in the case of a specific trial, require the assignment of a lawyer against the wishes of the accused, particularly in cases of persons substantially and persistently obstructing the proper conduct of trial, or facing a grave charge but being unable to act in their own interests, or where this is necessary to protect vulnerable witnesses from further distress or intimidation if they were to be questioned by the accused. However, any restriction of the wish of accused persons to defend themselves must have an objective and sufficiently serious purpose and not go beyond what is necessary to uphold the interests of justice. Therefore, domestic law should avoid any absolute bar against the right to defend oneself in criminal proceedings without the assistance of counsel.

The right to choose one's own counsel has also been treated as a limited one, qualified by situations where counsel is assigned under legal aid. In such circumstances, the Committee has found that an accused is not entitled to counsel of choice if he or she is being provided with a legal aid lawyer, and is otherwise unable to afford legal representation.[159] In contrast, however, a violation of the right to chose one's own counsel was found in *De Lopez v Uruguay*, where Lopez and several others

---

155 *Orejuela v Colombia*, Communication 848/1999, UN Doc CCPR/C/75/D/848/1999 (2002), para 7.3.

156 *Mbenge v Zaire*, above n 80; and *Maleki v Italy*, Communication 699/1996, UN Doc CCPR/C/66/D/699/1996 (1999), para 9.3.

157 *Arutyunyan v Uzbekistan*, Communication 917/2000, UN Doc CCPR/C/80/D/917/2000 (2004), para 6.3.

158 See General Comment 32, above n 1, para 37, and its corresponding views in *Correia de Matos v Portugal*, Communication 1123/2002, UN Doc CCPR/C/86/D/1123/2002 (2006), paras 7.4–7.5.

159 See, for example, *Teesdale v Trinidad and Tobago*, above n 36.

were forced under threats to refrain from seeking any legal counsel other than Colonel Mario Rodriguez in proceedings before a Military Tribunal.[160]

It is axiomatic, the Committee has said, that counsel be available at all stages of criminal proceedings, particularly in capital cases.[161] In *Brown v Jamaica*, for example, the Committee decided that a magistrate should not have proceeded with the deposition of witnesses during a preliminary hearing without allowing the author an opportunity to ensure the presence of his lawyer.[162] The Committee sees this as an obligation, imputable to the State, even where it is solely the fault of assigned counsel that he or she fails to attend a hearing.[163]

Having said this, the general position of the Committee has been that States parties cannot be held accountable for errors made by a defence lawyer, unless it was or should have been manifest to the judge that the lawyer's behaviour was incompatible with the interests of justice.[164] This will be the case, even where an accused is represented by inexperienced junior counsel who fails to follow instructions and makes mistakes in the presentation of the defence, as in *Whyte v Jamaica*.[165] In the case of counsel provided by the competent authorities, however, the Committee seems willing to impose a higher duty of care on the part of the presiding judge.[166]

Witnesses Article 14(3)(e) of the Covenant is designed to guarantee to the accused the same legal powers of compelling the attendance of witnesses, and of examining or cross-examining any witnesses, as are available to the prosecution.[167] It does

160 *Lopez v Uruguay*, Communication 52/1979, UN Doc CCPR/C/OP/1 at 88 (1984), para 13.

161 See *Robinson v Jamaica*, above n 44; *Wright and Harvey v Jamaica*, Communication 459/1991, UN Doc CCPR/C/55/D/459/1991 (1995); *LaVende v Trinidad and Tobago*, Communication 554/1993, UN Doc CCPR/C/61/D/554/1993 (1997), para 5.8; *Simpson v Jamaica*, Communication 695/1996, UN Doc CCPR/C/73/D/695/1996 (2001); *Levy v Jamaica*, above n 115; *Marshall v Jamaica*, Communication 730/1996, UN Doc CCPR/C/64/D/730/1996 (1998); *Aliev v Ukraine*, Communication 781/1997, UN Doc CCPR/C/78/D/781/1997 (2003), para 7.3; *Saidova v Tajikistan*, Communication 964/2001, UN Doc CCPR/C/81/D/964/2001 (2004), para 6.8; and *Aliboev v Tajikistan*, Communication 985/2001, UN Doc CCPR/C/85/D/985/2001 (2005), para 6.4.

162 *Brown v Jamaica*, Communication 775/1997, UN Doc CCPR/C/65/D/775/1997 (1999). See also *Hendricks v Guyana*, above n 140, para 8.4.

163 *Borisenko v Hungary*, Communication 852/1999, UN Doc CCPR/C/76/D/852/1999 (2002), para 7.5.

164 *Morais v Angola*, above n 120, para 5.4.

165 *Whyte v Jamaica*, Communication 732/1996, UN Doc CCPR/C/63/D/732/1997 (1998), para 9.2.

166 Contrast *HC v Jamaica*, Communication 383/1989, UN Doc CCPR/C/45/D/383/1989 (1992), para 6.3 (private counsel) with: *Kelly v Jamaica*, above n 120, para 9.5; *Brown v Jamaica*, above n 162, para 6.6; and *Hendricks v Guyana*, above n 140, para 6.4.

167 See, for example, *Khomidova v Tajikistan*, above n 57, para 6.5.

not, however, give rise to an absolute right to submit evidence at any time or in any manner.[168] It should also be noted that some legal systems exempt individuals from the obligation to testify against close relatives, the rationale being that an obligation to testify would be inhuman and thus unacceptable. Due to the lack of a generally recognized principle in this respect, however, the Committee has not given weight to the principle in ruling on claims before it under article 14(3)(e).[169]

Language If an accused cannot understand or speak the language used in court he or she is entitled to the assistance of an interpreter free of any charge. This right is independent of the outcome of the proceedings and applies to aliens as well as to nationals. It is of basic importance in cases in which ignorance of the language used by a court or difficulty in understanding may constitute an obstacle to the enjoyment of the rights of the defence. In *Domukovsky and others v Georgia*, Mr Domukovsky did not receive a copy of the indictment against him in his native Russian and was denied the services of an interpreter, whereas he was of Russian nationality, not Georgian. The State submitted that the court found that the author's knowledge of the Georgian language was excellent and that the author had made his statements in Georgian. The author's counsel submitted that he did his studies and research in Russian, but the Committee was unsatisfied that he did not have sufficient knowledge of Georgian. It therefore took the view that the information before it did not show that Mr Domukovsky's right under article 14(3)(f) had been violated.[170]

Should any issue arise during the course of a trial that an interpreter is, or is thought to be, incompetent, it is incumbent upon the defence to raise the issue during the course of the trial. In *Griffin v Spain*, for example, the author claimed that he had not received a fair trial because of the incompetence of the court interpreter and the judge's failure to intervene in this respect, and that he was convicted because of poor translation of a question, as a result of which his statement during the trial differed from his original statement to the examining magistrate. The Committee took the view that, because the author did not complain about the competence of the court interpreter to the judge (although he could have done so), it could not find a violation of article 14(3)(f) of the Covenant.[171]

The Committee has said, in jurisprudence that seems somewhat at odds with the latter cases and with the substance of article 14(3)(f), that this provision does not afford an accused with the ability to speak (presumably including the giving

168 *Johnson v Spain*, above n 59, para 6.5.

169 See the individual opinion of Committee member in *Campbell v Jamaica*, Communication 307/1988, UN Doc CCPR/C/47/D/307/1988 (1993).

170 *Domukovsky and others v Georgia*, Communications 623/1995, 624/1995, 626/1995, 627/1995, UN Docs CCPR/C/62/D/623/1995 (1998), CCPR/C/62/D/624/1995 (1998), CCPR/C/62/D/626/1995 (1998), and CCPR/C/62/D/627/1995 (1998), para 18.7.

171 *Griffin v Spain*, Communication 493/1992, UN Doc CCPR/C/53/D/493/1992 (1995), para 9.5.

of evidence) in the person's own tongue.[172] The author in *CLD v France* claimed to be a victim of violations of articles 14 and 26 of the Covenant because he was unable to give evidence in the language of his choice. The Committee took the view that article 14(1), *juncto* paragraph 3(f), does not imply that an accused be afforded an opportunity to express him of herself in the language which he normally speaks or in which he expresses himself with a maximum of ease.[173] In what must be seen as an unusual case, the Committee in *Singarasa v Sri Lanka* found a violation of article 14 in circumstances where the author's conviction relied solely on his confession where there was no interpreter provided during his interrogation. While noting that article 14(3)(f) provides for the right to an interpreter during a court hearing only, a right which was granted to the author, it was concluded that these circumstances denied a fair trial in accordance with article 14 as a whole.[174]

Sentencing

Retrospective Penalties

Article 15 of the International Covenant on Civil and Political Rights prohibits the application of retrospective penalties, while at the same time guaranteeing the retrospective benefit of *lighter* sentences:

> Article 15
> 1. No one shall be held guilty of any criminal offence on account of any act or omission which did not constitute a criminal offence, under national or international law, at the time when it was committed. Nor shall a heavier penalty be imposed than the one that was applicable at the time when the criminal offence was committed. If, subsequent to the commission of the offence, provision is made by law for the imposition of the lighter penalty, the offender shall benefit thereby.
> 2. Nothing in this article shall prejudice the trial and punishment of any person for any act or omission which, at the time when it was committed, was criminal according to the general principles of law recognized by the community of nations.

172 See *Guesdon v France*, Communication 219/1986, UN Doc CCPR/C/39/D/219/1986 (1990).

173 *CLD v France*, Communication 439/1990, UN Doc CCPR/C/43/D/439/1990 (1991), para 4.2.

174 *Singarasa v Sri Lanka*, Communication 1033/2001, UN Doc CCPR/C/81/D/1033/2001 (2004), para 7.2.

In considering whether article 15 is applicable, the Committee will limit itself to situations where an author's acts, at the material time of commission, constituted defined criminal offences under the criminal law of the State, or under international law.[175] After six months in administrative detention, the author in *Pietraroia v Uruguay* was charged under the Military Penal Code. The author claimed that the conduct in question was not illegal at the time when it had occurred.[176] In *Gombert v France*, a complaint of violation of article 15(1) of the Covenant was made, pertaining to changes in the law concerning maximum sentences. France argued that the author had not, however, received a sentence more severe than that which was applicable at the time of the crime to the acts constituting the offence for which the author was sentenced, and that he did not have a right to a lighter sentence under the transitional provisions of the new Criminal Code. The Committee therefore considered that the author had not substantiated his complaint for the purposes of admissibility under the Optional Protocol.[177] In *Filipovich v Lithuania*, the Committee similarly found no violation because the author's sentence was within the margin provided by the earlier law and the State party had referred to the existence of certain aggravating circumstances.[178]

An issue before the Committee in *Nicholas v Australia* was whether the lifting of a stay on the prosecution and the conviction of the author resulting from the admission of formerly inadmissible evidence amounted to a retroactive criminalization of conduct. In response, the Committee observed that article 15(1) is plain in its terms by prohibiting a finding of guilt on account of any act or omission which did not constitute a criminal offence at the time when it was committed. In the present case, the author was convicted of offences under section 233B of Australia's Customs Act, which had remained materially unchanged throughout the relevant period from the offending conduct through to the trial and conviction. Thus, the change in law affecting the admissibility of previously inadmissible evidence did not violate article 15(1) of the Covenant.[179]

175 *Baumgarten v Germany*, Communication 960/2000, UN Doc CCPR/C/78/D/960/2000 (2003), para 9.3.

176 *Pietraroia v Uruguay*, Communication 44/1979, UN Doc CCPR/C/12/D/44/1979 (1981), para 17. See also *Weisz v Uruguay*, above n 75, para 16.

177 *Gombert v France*, Communication 987/2001, UN Doc CCPR/C/77/D/987/2001 (2003), para 6.4.

178 *Filipovich v Lithuania*, above n 59, para 7.2. See also *Gomez v Peru*, above n 64, para 7.4; and *Gavrilin v Belarus*, Communication 1342/2005, UN Doc CCPR/C/89/D/1342/2005 (2007), para 8.3.

179 *Nicholas v Australia*, Communication 1080/2002, UN Doc CCPR/C/80/D/1080/2002 (2004), paras 7.3–7.7.

Failure to Fulfil Contractual Obligations

A further important limitation upon the sentencing process is to be found in article 11, which guarantees that no one is to be imprisoned merely on the ground of inability to fulfil a contractual obligation. This has been rarely invoked as a ground of complaint before the Human Rights Committee, and was unsuccessfully raised in *ARS v Canada*, where the author argued that legislation pertaining to parole agreements was contrary to article 11. The Committee considered that this claim was groundless since the choice offered to a prisoner to accept release under a system of mandatory supervision or to continue to serve his sentence did not result in a contractual obligation if the person concerned chooses release and signs the mandatory supervision certificate.[180] The Committee similarly found, in *Ràfols v Spain*, that a custodial sentence imposed on the author for failure to pay maintenance was inadmissible *ratione materiae* since the obligation arose not under a contract but instead pursuant to article 227 of the Spanish Criminal Code.[181]

Rights of Appeal from Criminal Convictions and/or Sentence

Everyone convicted of a crime has the right to have their conviction and/or sentence reviewed by a higher tribunal. Although neither paragraphs 1 nor 5 of article 14 oblige States to provide avenues for redress in respect of judgments relating to the determination of civil rights and obligations, the Human Rights Committee has taken the view that if a State party provides for such redress, the guarantees of a fair trial implicit in article 14 must be respected in that process also.[182] In the specific context of appeals against conviction or sentencing, the guarantee under paragraph 5 is not confined to the most serious offences.[183] The right is triggered not only following a conviction or sentence by a court of first instance, but also where a court of appeal imposes a conviction following acquittal by a lower court.[184]

---

180 *ARS v Canada*, Communication 91/1981, UN Doc CCPR/C/OP/1 at 29 (1984), para 7.

181 *Ràfols v Spain*, Communication 1333/2004, UN Doc CCPR/C/84/D/1333/2004 (2005), para 6.4.

182 *Puertas v Spain*, Communication 1183/2003, UN Doc CCPR/C/86/D/1183/2003 (2006), para 6.4; and *Linares v Spain*, Communication 1213/2003, UN Doc CCPR/C/89/D/1213/2003 (2007), para 6.5.

183 In making this observation, the Committee drew particular attention to the other language versions of the word 'crime' within the ICCPR ('infraction', 'delito' and 'prestuplenie'): General Comment 32, above n 1, para 45. See also *Conde v Spain*, Communication 1325/2004, UN Doc CCPR/C/88/D/1325/2004 (2006), para 7.2.

184 *Terrón v Spain*, Communication 1073/2002, UN Doc CCPR/C/82/D/1073/2002 (2004), para 7.4; *Gomariz Valera v Spain*, Communication 1095/2002, UN Doc CCPR/C/83/D/1095/2002 (2005), para 7.1; and *Moreno v Spain*, Communication 1381/2005, UN Doc CCPR/C/90/D/1381/2005 (2007), para 7.2.

Nature and Scope of Review

Of note, article 14(5) implies the right to a review of facts, as well as law, by a higher tribunal.[185] In circumstances where the law provides for judicial review without a hearing and on matters of law only, this kind of review falls short of the requirements of article 14(5).[186] In *Perera v Australia*, the Committee clarified that this does not mean that a court of appeal proceed to a factual retrial, but simply that a court be capable of conducting an evaluation of the evidence presented at the trial, as well as the procedural conduct of the trial.[187] Review of, or appeal against, both conviction and sentence must be available.[188]

Limitations on Rights of Appeal

The Committee has said that the expression 'according to law' in article 14(5) is not intended to leave the very existence of the right of review to the discretion of the member States, since the rights are those recognized by the Covenant, and not merely those recognized by domestic law. Rather, what is to be determined 'according to law' is the modalities by which the review by a higher tribunal are to be carried out.[189]

---

185 *Vásquez v Spain*, Communication 701/1996, UN Doc CCPR/C/69/D/701/1996 (2000); *Gelazauskas v Lithuania*, Communication 836/1998, UN Doc CCPR/C/77/D/836/1998 (2003), para 7.2; *Ratiani v Georgia*, Communication 975/2001, UN Doc CCPR/C/84/D/975/2001 (2005), paras 11.2–11.3; *Semey v Spain*, Communication 986/2001, UN Doc CCPR/C/78/D/986/2001 (2003), para 9.1; *Fernández v Spain*, Communication 1007/2001, UN Doc CCPR/C/78/D/1007/2001 (2003), paras 7–8; *Cabriada v Spain*, Communication 1101/2002, UN Doc CCPR/C/82/D/1101/2002 (2004), para 7.3; *Fernández v Czech Republic*, Communication 1104/2002, UN Doc CCPR/C/83/D/1104/2002 (2005), para 7.

186 *Domukovsky and others v Georgia*, above n 170, para 8.11; *Lumley v Jamaica*, above n 154, para 7.3; *Rogerson v Australia*, Communication 802/1998, UN Doc CCPR/C/74/D/802/1998 (2002), para 7.5; *Saidova v Tajikistan*, above n 161, para 6.5; *Khalilov v Tajikistan*, Communication 973/2001, UN Doc CCPR/C/83/D/973/2001 (2005), para 7.5; *Aliboev v Tajikistan*, above n 161, para 6.5; and *Bandajevsky v Belarus*, Communication 1100/2002, UN Doc CCPR/C/86/D/1100/2002 (2006), para 10.13.

187 *Perera v Australia*, Communication 536/1993, UN Doc CCPR/C/53/D/536/1993 (1995), para 6.4; *Juma v Australia*, Communication 984/2001, UN Doc CCPR/C/78/D/984/2001 (2003), para 7.5; and *Rolando v Philippines*, Communication 1110/2002, UN Doc CCPR/C/82/D/1110/2002 (2004), para 4.5.

188 *Gelazauskas v Lithuania*, above n 185, para 7.2; and *Bandajevsky v Belarus*, above n 186, para 10.13.

189 *Salgar de Montejo v Colombia*, Communication 64/1979, UN Doc CCPR/C/15/D/64/1979 (1982), para 10.4; *Gomaríz Valera v Spain*, above n 184, para 7.1; *Capellades v Spain*, Communication 1211/2003, UN Doc CCPR/C/87/D/1211/2003 (2006), para 7; *Sánchez and Clares v Spain*, Communication 1332/2004, UN Doc CCPR/C/88/D/1332/2004

The Committee has, in *Young v Jamaica*, dealt with the relevance of a verdict by jury for the Committee's own work. The Committee took the position that very limited possibilities to contest a verdict by jury in domestic appeal proceedings does not necessarily constitute a violation of article 14, provided that the trial itself was not unfair.[190] It further took the view, in *Rouse v Philippines*, that although article 14(5) does not require States parties to provide for several instances of appeal,[191] where the domestic law of a State does so, there must be effective access to each instance.[192]

Representation by Counsel on Appeal or Review

In *Teesdale v Trinidad and Tobago*, the author claimed that he was deprived of an effective appeal because he was represented by an attorney who never consulted with him and to whom the author could give no instructions. The Committee considered that, because appeals are argued on the basis of the record, it is for counsel to use his or her professional judgment in advancing the grounds for appeal, and in deciding whether to seek instructions from an appellant. A State party, it said, cannot be held responsible for the fact that legal aid counsel did not consult with the author.[193] The Committee has qualified this view, however. It has said that, particularly in a capital case, when counsel for the accused concedes that there is no merit in the appeal, the municipal court hearing the appeal should ascertain whether counsel has consulted with the accused and informed him accordingly.[194] The Committee has also taken the position that the requirements of fair trial and of representation require that the author be informed that his counsel does not intend to put arguments to the Court and that he have an opportunity to seek alternative representation if he chooses.[195] It has also decided that the withdrawal of an appeal without consultation would amount to a violation of article 14(3)(d) of the Covenant.[196]

(2006), para 7.2; and *Serena v Spain*, Communications 1351/2005 and 1352/2005, UN Doc CCPR/C/92/D/1351-1352/2005 (2008), para 9.3.

190 *Young v Jamaica*, Communication 615/1995, UN Doc CCPR/C/61/D/615/1995/Rev.1 (1997).

191 *Rouse v Philippines*, above n 138, para 7.6.

192 *Henry v Jamaica*, Communication 230/1987, UN Doc CCPR/C/43/D/230/1987 (1991), para 8.4.

193 *Teesdale v Trinidad and Tobago*, above n 36, para 9.7.

194 *Morrison v Jamaica*, Communication 461/1991, UN Doc CCPR/C/52/D/461/1991 (1994), para 10.5.

195 *Sooklal v Trinidad and Tobago*, Communication 928/2000, UN Doc CCPR/C/73/D/928/2000 (2001), para 4.10.

196 See, for example, *Collins v Jamaica*, Communication 356/1989, UN Doc CCPR/C/47/D/356/1989 (1993); *Steadman v Jamaica*, Communication 528/1993, UN Doc CCPR/C/59/D/528/1993 (1997); *Smith and Stewart v Jamaica*, Communication 668/1995, UN Doc CCPR/C/65/D/668/1995 (1999); *Morrison and Graham v Jamaica*, above n 194; *Morrison v Jamaica*, Communication 663/1995, UN Doc CCPR/C/64/D/663/1995 (1998); *McLeod v*

Effective Access to Appeal

In *Henry v Jamaica*, the Committee was required to consider whether the failure of the Court of Appeal of Jamaica to issue a written judgment violated the author's right to appeal against the court's decision. In doing so, it observed:[197]

> Article 14, paragraph 5, of the Covenant guarantees the right of convicted persons to have the conviction and sentence reviewed 'by a higher tribunal according to law'. In this context, the author has claimed that, because of the non-availability of the written judgment, he was denied the possibility of effectively appealing to the Judicial Committee of the Privy Council, which allegedly routinely dismisses petitions which are not accompanied by the written judgment of the lower court. In this connection, the Committee has examined the question whether article 14, paragraph 5, guarantees the right to a single appeal to a higher tribunal or whether it guarantees the possibility of further appeals when these are provided for by the law of the State concerned. The Committee observes that the Covenant does not require States parties to provide for several instances of appeal. However, the words 'according to law' in article 14, paragraph 5, are to be interpreted to mean that if domestic law provides for further instances of appeal, the convicted person must have effective access to each of them. Moreover, in order to enjoy the effective use of this right, the convicted person is entitled to have, within a reasonable time, access to written judgments, duly reasoned, for all instances of appeal.

The need to provide reasoned decisions for the purpose of compliance with article 14(5) was further emphasized in *Singh v Canada*.[198] Likewise, it may be important to ensure that evidential material is preserved for the purpose of review. This was a matter considered in *Robinson v Jamaica*, where the Committee recognized that, for the right to review of one's conviction to be effective, a State is under an obligation to preserve sufficient evidential material to allow for such a review. The Committee did qualify that position, however, by saying that article 14(5) will only be violated where such failure prejudices the convict's right to a review, that is, in situations where the evidence in question is indispensable to perform such a review.[199]

Jamaica, Communication 734/1997, UN Doc CCPR/C/62/D/734/1997 (1998); and *Jones v Jamaica*, Communication 585/1994, UN Doc CCPR/C/62/D/585/1994 (1998).

197 *Henry v Jamaica*, above n 192, para 8.4. See also *Simmonds v Jamaica*, Communication 338/1988, UN Doc CCPR/C/46/D/338/1988 (1992), para 8.4.

198 *Singh v Canada*, Communication 761/1997, UN Doc CCPR/C/60/D/761/1997 (1997), para 4.2. See also *Morrison v Jamaica*, above n 196, para 8.5; *Bailey v Jamaica*, Communication 709/1996, UN Doc CCPR/C/66/D/709/1996 (1999), para 7.2; and *Van Hulst v Netherlands*, Communication 903/1999, UN Doc CCPR/C/82/D/903/1999 (2004), para 6.4.

199 *Robinson v Jamaica*, Communication 731/1996, UN Doc CCPR/C/68/D/731/1996 (2000), para 10.7. See also *Lumley v Jamaica*, above n 154, para 7.5.

Implied Relinquishment

Any implied relinquishment of the right to appeal is not likely to be easily found. The Committee has nevertheless made such a finding in circumstances where a former judge with considerable experience insisted on being tried by the Supreme Court in Spain and, upon conviction, found himself without any higher level of judicial body capable of hearing an appeal. Because the author himself repeatedly insisted that he be tried directly by the Supreme Court, the Committee considered that the author had thereby renounced his right of appeal and that, in the circumstances, the allegation by the author constituted an abuse of the right to submit communications.[200]

Prompt Disposal of Appeal

The Committee's constant jurisprudence has provided that article 14(3)(c) and article 14(5) must be read together, so that the right to review of conviction and sentence must be made available and disposed of without delay.[201]

Appeals in Death Penalty Cases

The right of appeal in death penalty cases was a matter given consideration in the Committee's General Comment 32:[202]

> The right of appeal is of particular importance in death penalty cases. A denial of legal aid by the court reviewing the death sentence of an indigent convicted

200 *Esteville v Spain*, Communication 1004/2001, UN Doc CCPR/C/77/D/1004/2001 (2003), para 6.2.

201 See, for example, *Pratt and Morgan v Jamaica*, Communications 210/1986 and 225/1987, UN Doc Supp 40 (A/44/40) at 222 (1989), paras 13.3–13.5 ; *Henry v Jamaica*, above n 192; *Little v Jamaica*, Communication 283/1988, UN Doc CCPR/C/43/D/283/1988 (1991); *Francis v Jamaica*, Communication 320/1988, UN Doc CCPR/C/47/D/320/1988 (1993); *Champagnie and others v Jamaica*, Communication 445/1991, UN Doc CCPR/C/51/D/445/1991 (1994); *Bennett v Jamaica*, Communication 590/1994, UN Doc CCPR/C/65/D/590/1994 (1999), para 10.5; *Thomas v Jamaica*, Communication 614/1995, UN Doc CCPR/C/65/D/614/1995 (1999), para 9.5; *Brown and Parish v Jamaica*, Communication 665/1995, UN Doc CCPR/C/66/D/665/1995 (1999), para 9.5; *Daley v Jamaica*, Communication 750/1997, UN Doc CCPR/C/63/D/750/1997 (1998), para 7.4; *Sextus v Trinidad and Tobago*, above n 140, para 7.3; and *Kennedy v Trinidad and Tobago*, above n 30, para 7.5.

202 General Comment 32, above n 1, para 51. See also *LaVende v Trinidad and Tobago*, above n 161, para 5.8; *Smith and Stewart v Jamaica*, above n 196, para 7.3; *Gallimore v Jamaica*, Communication 680/1996, UN Doc CCPR/C/66/D/680/1996 (1999), para 7.4; *Daley v Jamaica*, ibid, para 7.5; and *Sooklal v Trinidad and Tobago*, above n 195, para 4.10.

person constitutes not only a violation of article 14, paragraph 3 (d), but at the same time also of article 14, paragraph 5, as in such cases the denial of legal aid for an appeal effectively precludes an effective review of the conviction and sentence by the higher instance court. The right to have one's conviction reviewed is also violated if defendants are not informed of the intention of their counsel not to put any arguments to the court, thereby depriving them of the opportunity to seek alternative representation, in order that their concerns may be ventilated at the appeal level.

Consequences upon Discovery of Miscarriage of Justice

Article 14, paragraph 6, provides for compensation according to law in certain cases of a miscarriage of justice as described therein:[203]

> 6. When a person has by a final decision been convicted of a criminal offence and when subsequently his conviction has been reversed or he has been pardoned on the ground that a new or newly discovered fact shows conclusively that there has been a miscarriage of justice, the person who has suffered punishment as a result of such conviction shall be compensated according to law, unless it is proved that the non-disclosure of the unknown fact in time is wholly or partly attributable to him.

Of interest is the fact that a number of States have made reservations to article 14(6), to the effect that 'compensation' within the terms of the paragraph may be by administrative procedures.[204] An issue that has arisen concerns the phrase 'when a person has by a *final decision* been convicted of a criminal offence'. This naturally affects the circumstances in which the Committee might require a State to provide compensation. There was an apparent division of opinion on what constitutes a 'final decision' in Communication 880/1999, *Irving v Australia*. The majority implied that a final decision is only made where there are no further available grounds of appeal from that decision:[205]

> As the decision of the Court of Appeal of Queensland was subject to appeal (albeit with leave) on the basis of the normal grounds for appeal, it would appear that until the decision of the High Court of Australia, the author's conviction may not have constituted a 'final decision' within the meaning of article 14,

203 See, generally: *Uebergang v Australia*, Communication 963/2001, UN Doc CCPR/C/71/D/963/2001 (2001), para 4.2; *Irving v Australia*, Communication 880/1999, UN Doc CCPR/C/74/D/880/1999 (2002), para 8.3; and *WJH v Netherlands*, Communication 408/1990, UN Doc CCPR/C/45/D/408/1990 (1992), para 6.3.

204 For example, Australia and Austria.

205 *Irving v Australia*, above n 203, para 8.4. See also *Anderson v Australia*, Communication 1367/2005, UN Doc CCPR/C/88/D/1367/2005 (2006), paras 7.4–7.5.

> paragraph 6. However, even if the decision of the Court of Appeal of Queensland were deemed to constitute the 'final decision' for the purposes of article 14, paragraph 6, the author's appeal to the High Court of Australia was accepted on the grounds that the original trial had been unfair and not that a new, or newly discovered fact, showed conclusively that there had been a miscarriage of justice.

In the opinion of two dissenting members, however, the word 'final' in article 14(6) does not mean that only a conviction that cannot be reversed is 'final'.[206] It was pointed out that, if that were the case, the reference to a final decision being 'reversed' within the wording of paragraph 6 would have no meaning. It was conceded, however, that due to differences between legal systems, there cannot be a single criterion of what a final conviction is. The Committee must make a case-by-case assessment of whether the conviction had become final. On the facts, the dissenting opinion was that the conviction of Mr Irving became 'final' when the ordinary period during which leave of appeal was to be sought expired, and, due to the denial of legal aid, Mr Irving was unable to apply for leave to appeal.

The same case also gave rise to debate about the consequences of new, or newly discovered, facts. The text of article 14(6) is unclear as to whether the words 'new or newly discovered fact' give rise only to a pardon or refer also to the case of reversal. The majority of the Committee adopted the view that the paragraph requires a new or newly established fact to justify both a reversal or pardon. The same dissenting members, relying on the Committee's earlier decision in *Muhonen v Finland*, took the position that, properly interpreted, this requirement applies only to pardons and not to reversals.[207]

---

206 Committee members Louis Henkin and Martin Scheinin.

207 *Muhonen v Finland*, Communication 89/1981, UN Doc Supp 40 (A/40/40) at 164 (1985).

Chapter 7
Privacy, Honour and Reputation

Alex Conte

A person's right to privacy is something that forms the foundation of, or at least part of the justification for, various rights espoused throughout human rights treaties and legislation.[1] The ICCPR guarantees privacy as a right in and of itself, the scope of which is detailed under article 17 of the Covenant as follows:

> Article 17
> 1. No one shall be subjected to arbitrary or unlawful interference with his privacy, family, home or correspondence, nor to unlawful attacks on his honour and reputation.
> 2. Everyone has the right to the protection of the law against such interference or attacks.

It will be seen that article 17 contains both a guarantee to individuals, under paragraph 1, and a duty upon States (to provide means by which those guarantees are protected), under paragraph 2. Article 17 affects personal privacy as well as that of the family and home. Within the realm of personal privacy, this chapter will consider privacy of the person and correspondence, and the right to be free from unlawful attacks on one's honour and reputation, as well as the issue of the collection of personal information. Consideration of the family and home will be had, although it should be noted that the rights of the family and child are considered in depth within Chapter 8.

---

1 Take, for example, the privilege against self-incrimination, the right to silence upon arrest, and the right to be free from unreasonable search and seizure. See further *Lovelace v Canada*, Communication 24/1977, UN Doc CCPR/C/13/D/24/1977 (1981), where the Committee took the view that article 27 of the ICCPR (minority rights, which formed the primary basis of the communication) must be construed and applied in light of other provisions within the Covenant, including the right to privacy.

Prohibition and Protection against Breaches of Privacy

Prohibition versus Protection

Article 17 provides that no person shall be subject to arbitrary or unlawful interference with their privacy. An issue that has come before the Human Rights Committee for consideration is whether the wording of article 17 carries a passive or positive duty for States parties. Does article 17 simply prohibit a State party from undertaking such arbitrary or unlawful interference or, in addition, does a State have a positive duty to prevent both private and public actors within its territory from interfering with the privacy of its citizens? If the latter duty is present, a subsidiary issue then becomes the extent to which a State must execute that duty and prohibit interference.

In its General Comment 16, the Human Rights Committee set out its view that the right to privacy must be guaranteed against all arbitrary or unlawful interferences and attacks, whether they emanate from State authorities or from natural or legal persons.[2] It further stated that States parties carry an obligation to adopt legislative and other measures to give effect to the prohibition against such interferences as well as for the protection of this right.[3] The Committee therefore took the view that article 17 carries both a prohibitive duty, not to inference, and a positive duty, to protect. The particular wording of article 17 supports this approach and is in fact divided into two parts, each reflecting the prohibitive and protective obligations. Article 17(1) prohibits interference and attacks by providing that no one shall be subjected to arbitrary or unlawful interference with his privacy, family, home or correspondence, nor to unlawful attacks on his honour and reputation. Article 17(2) requires States to protect those within its jurisdiction, by providing that everyone has the right to the protection of the law against such interference or attacks.

Naturally, the extent of a positive duty to protect against interference and attacks has its limitations. In *del Rio v Peru*, the Committee considered that the author's complaint of a libellous and defamatory campaign against him, allegedly constituting an unlawful attack against his honour and reputation, did not raise issues under article 17. On the basis of the information before the Committee, it considered that the articles published about the author's alleged involvement in fraudulent procurement policies in various local and national newspapers could not be attributed to the State party's authorities. It took the view that this would be so even if the newspapers were supportive of the government then in force.[4] In *LP v Czech Republic*, the author claimed that Czech authorities had refused to

2 *General Comment 16: The right to respect of privacy, family, home and correspondence, and protection of honour and reputation (Art 17)*, UN Doc CCPR General Comment 16 (1988), paras 1 and 9.

3 Ibid.

4 *Del Rio v Peru*, Communication 263/1987, UN Doc CCPR/C/46/D/263/1987 (1992).

act upon court decisions allowing him regular access to his son, thus violating his and his son's right to protection of their family life under article 17(1) and (2). The majority of the Committee took the view that article 17 generally includes effective protection to the right of a parent to regular contact with his or her minor children. While there may be exceptional circumstances in which denying contact is required in the interests of the child and cannot be deemed unlawful or arbitrary, in the present case the domestic courts of the Czech Republic had ruled that such contact should be maintained. Although the courts repeatedly fined the author's wife for failure to respect preliminary orders regulating access, these fines were neither fully enforced nor replaced with other measures aimed at ensuring the author's rights. The Committee therefore took the view that, here, the author's rights under article 17 of the Covenant did not receive effective protection.[5] While the majority took a firm view in support of a positive duty to protect article 17 rights, two Committee members considered that the State had done what it could.[6]

Limitations upon the Right to Privacy

A result of the fact that all persons live in a society is that the protection of privacy is necessarily relative.[7] In times of emergency, for example, article 4 of the ICCPR allows temporary derogation from the right to privacy for as long as the life of the nation concerned is threatened.[8] Furthermore, even outside the context of a state of emergency, the approach of the Committee is to treat article 17 as being capable of limitation, so long as such limits are directly linked to the interests of the society in question. Competent public authorities may only call for information relating to an individual's private life if knowledge of this information is essential to the interests of society, as understood under the Covenant.[9] Indeed, if one considers the wording of article 17(1), the prohibition against interference with one's privacy is limited to *arbitrary* or *unlawful* interference. These are cumulative factors, such that interference with privacy can be neither arbitrary nor unlawful.[10]

The term 'unlawful' is one that is easily determinable in any case. It means that no interference can take place except in cases envisaged by the domestic

5 *LP v Czech Republic*, Communication 946/2000, UN Doc CCPR/C/75/D/946/2000 (2002).

6 Committee members Nisuke Ando and Prafullachandra Bhagwati.

7 General Comment 16, above n 2, para 7.

8 Article 17 of the ICCPR is not listed within article 4(2) of the Covenant, which sets out the non-derogable rights. Any derogation must be within the terms of article 4(1) and (3): see *General Comment 29: States of Emergency (Article 4)*, UN Doc CCPR/C/21/Rev.1/Add.11 (2001); and Chapter 3 herein.

9 General Comment 16, above n 2, para 7.

10 See, for example, *García v Colombia*, Communication 687/1996, UN Doc CCPR/C/71/D/687/1996 (2001).

law of a State, as interpreted by national courts.[11] There are three points that arise from this. The first is that if a State wishes to authorize interference with the right to privacy, then it can only do so on the basis of law. For example, if a State wishes to permit the use of listening or tracking devices, it must do so through legal prescriptions such as legislation.[12] The second point is that any such prescription by law must itself comply with the provisions, aims and objectives of the ICCPR, a position stated by the Committee in General Comment 16.[13] The rationale is clear: by becoming a party to the Covenant, States have undertaken not to interfere unlawfully with the privacy rights of those within their territory and, in any event, to restrict interferences to those compatible with the Covenant as a whole. Finally, any legislation authorizing interference must specify in detail the precise circumstances in which interference is permitted and must designate an authority to determine, on case-by-case bases, such authorizations.[14] An example of the application of these points can be seen in *Aumeeruddy-Cziffra and Others v Mauritius*, which is discussed further below.[15]

Similar observations can be made about the prohibition against 'arbitrary' interference with the right to privacy. The ordinary meaning of the term implies an interference with privacy by random choice or on the basis of mere opinion or interference that is unrestrained or despotic.[16] In this regard, the HRC makes similar comments concerning law that authorizes interference, that is, that the expression 'arbitrary interference' can extend to interference provided for under the law. The concept of arbitrariness, said the Committee in General Comment 16, is intended to guarantee that even interference provided for by law should be in accordance with the provisions, aims and objectives of the Covenant and should be reasonable in the particular circumstances.[17] As to reasonableness, this implies that any interference with privacy must be proportionate to the end sought, and must be necessary in the circumstances of any given case.[18]

---

11 See: General Comment 16, above n 2, at para 3; and *Van Hulst v The Netherlands*, Communication 903/1999, UN Doc CCPR/C/82/D/903/1999 (2004), para 7.5.

12 For an analysis of what amounts to a 'prescription by law', see Chapter 3 herein.

13 General Comment 16, above n 2, para 3.

14 General Comment 16, above n 2, para 8.

15 *Aumeeruddy-Cziffra and Others v Mauritius*, Communication 35/1978, UN Doc CCPR/C/12/D/35/1978 (1981). See further 'Interference with Family or Home' within this chapter.

16 J.B. Sykes (ed.), *The Concise Oxford Dictionary* (7th edn, Oxford: Oxford University Press, 1984).

17 General Comment 16, above n 2, para 4.

18 See: *Toonen v Australia*, Communication 488/1992, UN Doc CCPR/C/50/D/488/1992 (1994), para 8.3; and *Van Hulst v The Netherlands*, above n 11, para 7.6.

Privacy of the Person

The first category of prohibited interference is that of 'his privacy', which has been regarded as protecting the privacy of the person. Privacy of the person in turn invokes various aspects of one's private life: from one's personal and sexual identity, to one's freedom from personal search or the collection of personal information.

Personal Identity

One's name The right to chose and change one's surname has been claimed to arise from the right to personal privacy as an important component affecting one's identity. In *Coeriel et al v The Netherlands*, the authors requested the Minister of Justice to have their surnames changed into Hindu names to enable them to study and practice the Hindu religion and to become Hindu priests which, they said, required them to adopt Hindu names. The Minister rejected the request, on the ground that their cases did not meet the requirements set out in the State's Guidelines for the Change of Surname. In response to the communication, the Netherlands argued that article 17(1) did not give rise to a right to change one's surname. The authors in turn responded that the rejection of their request to have their surnames changed deeply affected their private life, since it prevented them from practising as Hindu priests. The Committee observed:[19]

> … article 17 provides, inter alia, that no one shall be subjected to arbitrary or unlawful interference with his privacy, family, home or correspondence. The Committee considers that the notion of privacy refers to the sphere of a person's life in which he or she can freely express his or her identity, be it by entering into relationships with others or alone. The Committee is of the view that a person's surname constitutes an important component of one's identity and that the protection against arbitrary or unlawful interference with one's privacy includes the protection against arbitrary or unlawful interference with the right to choose and change one's own name. For instance, if a State were to compel all foreigners to change their surnames, this would constitute interference in contravention of article 17.

On the particular facts, the Committee was influenced by the fact that the Minister's refusal of the request to change the authors' surnames was expressed to be on the grounds that the authors had not shown that the changes sought were essential to pursue their studies, that the names had religious connotations and that they were not 'Dutch sounding'. It found that the grounds for so limiting the authors' rights under article 17 were unreasonable. A similar communication was

---

19 *Coeriel et al v The Netherlands*, Communication 453/1991, UN Doc CCPR/C/52/D/453/1991 (1994).

lodged against Namibia in *Müller and Engelhard v Namibia*, where the husband of a Namibian national was required to apply to change his surname under the Aliens Act, whereas the law allowed a wife to assume her husband's name without any formalities. Namibia contended that article 17 only protected the author from arbitrary (meaning unreasonable and purposelessly irrational) or unlawful interference with his privacy. Inasmuch as the author could change his surname upon application if he so wished, it submitted that the law was not unreasonable and did not violate the obligations under article 17(1). Ultimately, the Committee did not address the substance of the claim based on article 17, finding that the legislative provision was in violation of article 26 (non-discrimination) and that consideration of article 17 was therefore unnecessary.[20]

Sexuality Sexual identity has been treated by both the Human Rights Committee and the European Court of Human Rights as falling within the right to privacy. The criminalization of private conduct within same-sex relationships was challenged as an interference with personal privacy in *Toonen v Australia*. Toonen was an activist for the promotion of the rights of homosexuals in Tasmania, one of Australia's six constitutive States. He challenged two provisions of the Tasmanian Criminal Code, which included the criminalization of all forms of sexual contact between consenting adult homosexual men in private. He submitted that the provisions were in breach of article 17(1) in that: their enforcement resulted in a violation of the right to privacy, since they enabled the police to enter a household on the mere suspicion that two consenting adult homosexual men may be committing a sexual act; and they distinguished between individuals in the exercise of their right to privacy on the basis of sexual activity, sexual orientation and sexual identity.

The Committee noted that it was undisputed that adult consensual sexual activity in private is covered by the concept of 'privacy', and that Toonen was therefore actually and currently affected by the continued existence of Tasmanian law. The Committee considered that the relevant provisions 'interfered' with the author's privacy, even if the provisions had not been enforced for a decade. It noted, in that context, that a policy not to initiate criminal proceedings did not amount to a guarantee that no action would be brought in the future and that the continued existence of the provisions therefore continuously and directly interfered with privacy. The Committee then turned to the submission of Tasmanian authorities: that the laws were justified on public health and moral grounds, as they were intended in part to prevent the spread of HIV/AIDS in Tasmania; and that, in the absence of specific limitation clauses in article 17, moral issues must be deemed a matter for domestic decision.[21] The Committee did not agree:[22]

---

20 *Müller and Engelhard v Namibia*, Communication 919/2000, UN Doc CCPR/C/74/D/919/2000 (2002).

21 *Toonen v Australia*, above n 18, para 6.5. It should be noted that the Federal Government of Australia did not agree with that submission.

22 Ibid, para 8.6.

> The Committee cannot accept either that for the purposes of article 17 of the Covenant, moral issues are exclusively a matter of domestic concern, as this would open the door to withdrawing from the Committee's scrutiny a potentially large number of statutes interfering with privacy. It further notes that with the exception of Tasmania, all laws criminalizing homosexuality have been repealed throughout Australia and that, even in Tasmania, it is apparent that there is no consensus as to whether Sections 122 and 123 should not also be repealed. Considering further that these provisions are not currently enforced, which implies that they are not deemed essential to the protection of morals in Tasmania, the Committee concludes that the provisions do not meet the 'reasonableness' test in the circumstances of the case, and that they arbitrarily interfere with Mr. Toonen's right under article 17, paragraph 1.

Interference with Privacy of the Person

Collection of personal information Where necessary for the performance of the lawful activities of a State, public authorities may request such information from persons as may be necessary and proportionate to discharge those functions. Thus, in *Ngambi v France*, the Committee noted that inquiries conducted by French authorities concerning status and family relations, following a request for a visa for family reunification, amounted to a necessary interference upon private and family life.[23]

Within the ambit of protecting against breaches of privacy, States parties are required to regulate, by law, the collection and holding of personal information by public authorities and private individuals or bodies, whether on computers, data banks or by other means.[24] Effective protection is said to include measures to ensure that personal information does not reach the hands of unauthorized persons, and to ensure that personal information may never be used for purposes incompatible with the ICCPR.[25] Protection necessarily requires the individual to have the ability to ascertain whether, and if so what, personal data is stored about him or her and for what purpose, with a right to request rectification or elimination of information that the individual believes is incorrect.[26]

Interference through judicial proceedings Inconvenience caused in one's private life through judicial proceedings has not been accepted as constituting a breach of article 17. In *Fei v Colombia*, the Committee took the view that even serious inconvenience caused by judicial proceedings to which the author

23 *Ngambi v France*, Communication 1179/2003, UN Doc CCPR/C/81/D/1179/2003 (2004), para 6.5.

24 General Comment 16, above n 2, para 10.

25 Ibid.

26 Ibid.

of a communication is a party cannot be qualified as 'arbitrary' or 'unlawful' interference with that individual's privacy.[27]

Dwarf tossing as an aspect of private life In *Wackenheim v France*, the author (who suffered from dwarfism) began in July 1991 to appear in 'dwarf tossing' events organized by a company called Société Fun-Productions. Wearing protective gear, he would allow himself to be thrown short distances onto an air bed by clients of the establishment staging the event (a discotheque). By an order dated 25 October 1991, the Mayor of Morsang-sur-Orge banned a dwarf tossing event scheduled to take place in the local discotheque. The French Ministry of the Interior later issued a circular on the policing of public events, in particular dwarf tossing, which instructed prefects to use their policing powers to instruct mayors to keep a close eye on spectacles staged in their communes. The circular said that dwarf tossing should be banned on the basis of, among other things, article 3 of the European Convention for the Protection of Human Rights and Fundamental Freedoms (prohibiting inhuman or degrading treatment). The author affirmed that banning him from working had an adverse effect on his life and represented an affront to his dignity. He claimed to be the victim of various violations of his rights by France, including respect for his private life. France argued that the contested ban entailed no violation of article 17(1) of the Covenant. To begin with, France argued, allowing oneself to be 'tossed' in public for a living did not belong within the orbit of private and family life. Nor was it clear whether or how this activity extended beyond the realm of private life. France asserted that dwarf tossing was a public practice and that it could not therefore be protected on the strength of arguments deriving from the respect for private life. Even if the notion of private life could be broadly interpreted to include the possibility of being 'tossed' for a living, France argued that the limitation imposed upon this was not contrary to article 17, that is, the limitation was neither unlawful nor arbitrary. That limit, it was submitted, was justified by considerations deriving from the respect due to the dignity of the human person and was rooted in a fundamental principle, thus constituting neither an illegal nor an arbitrary encroachment upon the right to respect for private and family life.[28] The Committee concluded:[29]

> … the State party has demonstrated, in the present case, that the ban on dwarf tossing as practised by the author did not constitute an abusive measure but was necessary in order to protect public order, which brings into play considerations of human dignity that are compatible with the objectives of the Covenant. The

27 *Fei v Colombia*, Communication 514/1992, UN Doc CCPR/C/53/D/514/1992 (1995).

28 *Wackenheim v France*, Communication 854/1999, UN Doc CCPR/C/75/D/854/1999 (2002), para 4.2.

29 Ibid, para 7.4.

Committee accordingly concludes that the differentiation between the author and the persons to whom the ban ordered by the State party does not apply was based on objective and reasonable grounds.

Physical Interference with the Person

Search and arrest Privacy of the person has arisen as an issue in the context of search and seizure, and the conditions of arrest and detention.[30] Within the context of search and seizure, the Committee has commented that where a person is being subjected to a body search, such search should be carried out in a manner that is consistent with the dignity of the person who is being searched, including a requirement that persons of the same sex conduct any examination.[31] A further example of the interrelationship of the right to privacy with others in the ICCPR relates to a spouse's communication in *Caldas v Uruguay*, alleging that her husband had been illegally arrested and held incommunicado. Although the Committee's decision in that case was based upon articles 9, 10 and 14, and the principle of *habeas corpus*, it appeared to agree with the author's position that such issues involved the right to be free from interference of the person.[32]

Torture Privacy of the person has also been a relevant factor in communications concerning allegations of torture[33] and, in extreme cases, allegations of the killing of victims.[34] In such instances, views of the Committee have generally recognized the relevance of article 17 but relied, in decision-making, upon articles 6, 7, 9 and 10 (the right to life, the prohibition against torture, and rights to liberty and security of the person and humane treatment of those held in detention).[35] Consider also *Penarrieta and Other v Bolivia*, discussed below, where the ill-treatment of

30 On the conditions of arrest or detention, see Chapter 5.

31 General Comment 16, above n 2, para 8.

32 *Caldas v Uruguay*, Communication 43/1979, UN Doc CCPR/C/19/D/43/1979 (1983), para 2.4. Similar approaches were taken in *Barbato v Uruguay*, Communication 84/1981, UN Doc CCPR/C/17/D/84/1981 (1982); *Mangana ex-Philibert v Zaire*, Communication 90/1988, UN Doc CCPR/C/37/D/90/1988 (1989); *Alemeida v Uruguay*, Communication 107/1981, UN Doc CCPR/C/19/D/107/1981 (1983); *Bleier v Uruguay*, Communication 30/1978, UN Doc CCPR/C/15/D/30/1978 (1982); and *Carballal v Uruguay*, communication 33/1978, UN Doc CCPR/C/12/D/33/1978 (1981).

33 See *Caldas v Uruguay*, ibid; *Scarrone v Uruguay*, Communication 103/1981, UN Doc CCPR/C/20/D/103/1981 (1983); *Alemeida v Uruguay*, ibid; *Acosta v Uruguay*, Communication 110/1981, UN Doc CCPR/C/21/D/110/1981 (1984); *Gilboa v Uruguay*, Communication 147/1983, UN Doc CCPR/C/26/D/147/1983 (1985); and *Rubio v Colombia*, Communication 161/1983, UN Doc CCPR/C/31/D/161/1983 (1987).

34 For example, see *Baboeram and Others v Suriname*, Communications 146/1983, and 148/1983 to 154/1983, UN Doc CCPR/C/OP/2 at 5 (1990).

35 See further Chapter 5.

the authors' relatives was claimed to violate the freedom from attack upon one's honour and reputation.[36]

Mental health committals Communication 754/1997, *A v New Zealand*, involved an application under the Mental Health Act for a reception order to be made in respect of the author. The author was, pursuant to an order of the District Court, detained for observation at Carrington Hospital. Hospital staff examined him and concluded that he was not suffering from a committable mental disorder and he was consequently released, and the application for a reception order dismissed. The author alleged violation of article 17 because he was forced to answer questions by doctors and judges as a result of the committal. The Committee found the allegation to be unsubstantiated. Regrettably, it did not set out its reasoning on this finding, instead focusing on views regarding allegations made of breaches of other articles within the Covenant.[37]

Interference with Correspondence

Compliance with article 17 requires that the integrity and confidentiality of correspondence must be guaranteed *de jure* and *de facto*. The Committee succinctly explained this in General Comment 16 when it said:[38]

> Correspondence should be delivered to the addressee without interception and without being opened or otherwise read. Surveillance, whether electronic or otherwise, interceptions of telephonic, telegraphic and other forms of communication, wire-tapping and recording of conversations should be prohibited.

In *JRT and the WG Party v Canada*, the Human Rights Committee was presented with an allegation concerning the prohibition by Canadian authorities of use by the alleged victims of the Canadian mail. The prohibitory order was made under section 7 of the Post Office Act 1965 and was said by Canada to give effect to the obligation upon States to prohibit national, ethnic or religious hatred (article 20 of the Covenant). The Committee accepted that the broad scope of the order, extending to all mail whether sent or received, raised a question of compatibility with articles 17 and 19 (freedom of expression). It ultimately ruled the communication to be

36 *Penarrieta and Other v Bolivia*, Communication 176/1984, UN Doc CCPR/C/31/D/176/1984 (1987). See further 'Other Forms of Attack on Honour and Reputation' within this chapter.

37 *A v New Zealand*, Communication 754/1997, UN Doc CCPR/C/66/D/754/1997 (1999).

38 General Comment 16, above n 2, para 8.

inadmissible, however, since the author had failed to challenge the validity of the order before competent Canadian courts.[39]

Protection against interference with a person's correspondence extends to measures of control and censorship over prisoners' correspondence. In *Estrella v Uruguay*, it was accepted that such measures were normal, but that the protection afforded by article 17(1) required any such measures to be subject to satisfactory legal safeguards against arbitrary application. The degree of restriction must be consistent with the standard of humane treatment of detained persons required by article 10(1) of the Covenant. In particular, the Committee held that prisoners should be allowed, under supervision if necessary, to communicate with their family and reputable friends at regular intervals by correspondence, as well as receiving visits.[40] The Committee found that censorship and restrictions at Libertad prison in Uruguay were incompatible with article 17. Such restrictions were through punishments imposed on the victim by way of bans on receiving correspondence, including a seven-month period without mail; the forbidding of correspondence to lawyers and international organizations; the arbitrary deletion of sentences from correspondence by prison officials; and the refusal to dispatch letters.

Amongst various other claims in *Boodoo v Trinidad and Tobago*, the author asserted that his attempts to make a claim to the Committee about his treatment at Carrera Convict Prison were being frustrated by prison officials. In particular, he complained of threats from wardens, interference with his mail, and difficulties experienced by him in receiving information from, or forwarding information to, the United Nations. The State party did not provide an explanation in response to these matters and the Committee thus concluded that Boodoo's rights under article 17 had been violated. The Committee considered that the author was entitled to compensation, and that the State was under an obligation to ensure that similar violations did not occur in the future.[41] A number of similar claims involving interference with correspondence of prisoners and remand detainees have been made, where a lack of evidence existed to substantiate the claims, but where the Committee nevertheless reiterated its earlier findings that interference of this kind is not permissible under the Covenant.[42]

---

39 *JRT and the WG Party v Canada*, Communication 104/1981, UN Doc CCPR/C/18/D/104/1981 (1983), para 8(c).

40 *Estrella v Uruguay*, Communication 74/1980, UN Doc CCPR/C/18/D/74/1980 (1983), para 9.2. In saying this, the Committee referred to its earlier views in *Antonaccio v Uruguay*, Communication 63/1979, UN Doc CCPR/C/14/D/63/1979 (1981).

41 *Boodoo v Trinidad and Tobago*, Communication 721/1996, UN Doc CCPR/C/74/D/721/1996 (2002), paras 6.7 and 8. See also *Berry v Jamaica*, Communication 330/1988, UN Doc CCPR/C/50/D/330/1988 (1994).

42 See, for example, *Blancov v Nicaragua*, Communication 328/1988, UN Doc CCPR/C/51/D/328/1988 (1994); and *Tomlin v Jamaica*, Communication 589/1994, UN Doc CCPR/C/57/D/589/1994 (1996).

In the context of the surveillance of telephone conversations, the Committee dealt in *Van Hulst v The Netherlands* with the interception and recording of the author's telephone calls with his lawyer. While acknowledging the importance of protecting the confidentiality of communications, in particular those relating to the lawyer–client relationship, the Committee also acknowledged the need for States to take effective measures for the prevention and investigation of criminal offences. The Committee concluded that the interference was proportionate and necessary to achieve the legitimate purpose of combating crime, and therefore reasonable in the particular circumstances of the case, and that there was accordingly no violation of article 17 of the Covenant.[43]

Unlawful Attacks upon Honour and Reputation

At paragraph 11 of General Comment 16, the Human Rights Committee stated:

> Article 17 affords protection to personal honour and reputation and States are under an obligation to provide adequate legislation to that end. Provision must also be made for everyone effectively to be able to protect himself against any unlawful attacks that do occur and to have an effective remedy against those responsible. States parties should indicate in their reports to what extent the honour or reputation of individuals is protected by law and how this protection is achieved according to their legal system.

Attacks through Legal Proceedings

The Human Rights Committee has taken a restrictive approach in the application of article 17(1) where claims have been made of interference with honour and reputation through judicial process. In particular, the Committee has been careful to ensure that claims within this category have exhausted all domestic remedies.[44] In *Morael v France*, the author unsuccessfully claimed that he was denied the right to a fair hearing and that this amounted to an attack on his honour and reputation through tarnishing his reputation as a company officer.[45]

Rogerson v Australia concerned allegations of attacks upon the author's honour and reputation both through the manner in which judicial proceedings were conducted by the presiding judge, and also through what were claimed to be quasi-judicial proceedings by the Legal Society of the Northern Territory. With regard

---

43 *Van Hulst v The Netherlands*, above n 11, para 7.10.

44 See, for example, *PS v Denmark*, Communication 397/1990, UN Doc CCPR/C/45/D/397/1990 (1992), where the communication was found to be inadmissible for failure to exhaust all available domestic remedies.

45 *Morael v France*, Communication 207/1986, UN Doc CCPR/C/36/D/207/1986 (1989), para 2.4.

to the judicial proceedings, the author was brought before the Northern Territory Supreme Court on contempt of court charges. The author contended that he was brought before the judge with less than one-hour's notice, unrepresented, and that the judge adopted an inquisitorial approach and assumed the role of prosecutor. With regard to the procedure before the Law Society of the Northern Territory, Australia submitted that the author had given no grounds for bias of any particular member of the Law Society Council, but only made a sweeping and unfounded generalization. It further said that the author failed to address how the withdrawal of his practising certificate by the Council constituted an unlawful attack on honour and reputation within the terms of article 17(1). The Committee found that the author had indeed failed to substantiate that the remarks by the judge and the Law Society procedure against him constituted an arbitrary or unlawful attack on his honour and reputation.[46]

Likewise, in *HS v France*, the alleged victim claimed that he had been subjected to attacks on his honour and reputation in the process of legal proceedings to resolve issues of his nationality. France submitted that the legal proceedings before the Tribunal de Grande Instance of Bobigny, the purpose of which was to resolve the complex legal problem of his nationality, was at the author's request and did not support any assertion of an attack on his honour and reputation. In implicitly accepting the latter position, the communication was ruled inadmissible *ratione materiae* by the Committee.[47]

The author in *RM v Finland* claimed that the courts did not fairly evaluate the evidence presented by the prosecutor in criminal proceedings against him, and that they were unduly influenced by the media. Finland argued that serious offences, in particular offences in which several people, drugs and large sums of money are involved, are frequently closely followed by the press and that press coverage in itself cannot be held to be a violation of the right to privacy. Without further evidence, the Committee dismissed the communication.[48]

Attacks through Accusations of Wrongdoing

Police disciplinary practices were the subject of scrutiny in *Vargas-Machuca v Peru*. The author was a commander in the Peruvian National Police and Chief of the Police Drug Squad in the town of Trujillo. On 2 October 1991, Mr Arévalo, who had been arrested for international drug trafficking, died at the San Andrés police station (although, according to the author, the deceased was in the custody and charge of officials of the Preventive Police and not of the Drug Investigation

---

46 *Rogerson v Australia*, Communication 802/1998, UN Doc CCPR/C/74/D/802/1998 (2002), para 7.7.

47 *HS v France*, Communication 184/1984, UN Doc CCPR/C/27/D/184/1984 (1986), para 8.5.

48 *RM v Finland*, Communication 301/1988, UN Doc CCPR/C/35/D/301/1988 (1989).

Department). Following that death, the author was accused of violating Police Disciplinary Regulations and an administrative decision relieved him of his duties. He was at the same time taken to Lima, where he was forced to attend a press conference. The author asserted that no charges were ever brought against him, in either the ordinary or the military courts, for criminal negligence or liability in the course of his duties, or for any other criminal offence arising from the death of Mr Arévalo. He therefore maintained that article 17 of the Covenant was violated insofar as the accusation made against him affected his reputation, honour and image in his performance of his duties as a police officer. In a somewhat narrow approach, the Committee found that there was no violation of article 17, having regard to the fact that the domestic courts recognized the author's innocence.[49]

Other Forms of Attack on Honour and Reputation

Few other communications have relied on this protection, except in an indirect way. A claim concerning a State official's adulterous relations with the author's wife was not found to constitute a violation of article 17.[50] In *Penarrieta and Other v Bolivia*, the right to freedom from attack upon one's honour and reputation was claimed alongside other more serious allegations. The victims were alleged to have been illegally arrested, held incommunicado, and subjected to torture, which was said to amount to a severe attack on their privacy, honour and reputation. In expressing its views, the Committee did not reflect upon the relevance or otherwise of article 17 but relied, instead, upon articles 7 and 9 of the Covenant (prohibition against torture and rights to liberty and security of the person).[51]

The conduct of tax inspectors was at issue in *IP v Finland*. The author referred to the disclosure of sensitive information about the payment of his taxes to third parties. He claimed that this information was false, and that tax officials had not given him an opportunity to correct the information given, nor correct it themselves. Amongst a number of responses by Finland, the Committee found the communication inadmissible on the basis that the disclosure of the information was based on lawful regulations and necessary to determine the taxation of certain companies. The Committee observed that article 17 protects everyone from arbitrary or unlawful interference with his or her privacy, whereas this instance amounted to lawful and rational conduct.[52]

---

49 *Vargas-Machuca v Peru*, Communication 906/2000, UN Doc CCPR/C/75/D/906/2000 (2002), para 7.3.

50 *Gedumbe v Democratic Republic of Congo*, Communication 641/1995, UN Doc CCPR/C/75/D/641/1995 (2002), para 3.2.

51 *Penarrieta and Other v Bolivia*, above n 36. This communication is considered in more detailed within Chapters 5 and 6.

52 *IP v Finland*, Communication 450/1991, UN Doc CCPR/C/48/D/450/1991 (1993), para 6.3.

Interference with Family or Home

Freedom from arbitrary or unlawful interference with one's family and home is one further aspect of article 17. The question of interference with family life is addressed within Chapter 8 herein, in combination with articles 23 and 24 of the Covenant. While the question of interference with the home raises different issues to those of the family, brief mention is also made in this part of the chapter to cases where family law proceedings have been claimed to interfere with article 17.

Family Law Proceedings

When concerned with claims of interference with family through custody and other means of family law proceedings, the Committee has taken a cautious approach and required clear evidence of interference before finding any violation under article 17(1). In *Krausser v Austria*, the author claimed that judicial proceedings, through which a County Court granted custody over his daughter to his wife, were in violation of article 17 because reports by a social worker and police had been taken into account by the Court. Those reports, asserted the author, were unreliable and had been produced without his participation. The Committee agrees with Austria's submission that this failed to disclose any arbitrary or unlawful attacks on the author's honour and reputation.[53] In *AJ v The Netherlands*, the author claimed that he and his children had been subjected to mental torture and cruel, inhuman and degrading treatment, as a result of an order withdrawing his custody rights, refusing him to meet and talk to his children, and censoring his mail over a period of approximately three years. The communication was dismissed on the basis that he had failed to substantiate, for purposes of admissibility, why the loss of parental rights, in the circumstances, would amount to violations of article 17.[54]

Likewise, in *Van Puyvelde v France*, the author claimed violation of article 17 during the process of family court proceedings. Mr Van Puyvelde claimed to be the victim of a plot against him and oppression by lawyers and the French judicial system, asserting that the French courts had sided with his wife and tried to ruin him by insisting that he should pay maintenance to her. The Committee considered that the author has not substantiated his allegations for the purposes of admissibility under article 2 of the Optional Protocol.[55] The Committee concluded, in contrast, that a unilateral decision to terminate child access, without a judge

53 *Krausser v Austria*, Communication 890/1999, UN Doc CCPR/C/76/D/890/1999 (2002), para 4.11.

54 *AJ v The Netherlands*, Communication 1142/2002, UN Doc CCPR/C/77/D/1142/2002 (2003), para 5.5. See also: *EB v New Zealand*, Communication 1368/2005, UN Doc CCPR/C/89/D/1368/2005 (2007), para 9.5; and *Winkler v Austria*, Communication 1468/2006, UN Doc CCPR/C/90/D/1468/2006 (2007), para 6.5.

55 *Van Puyvelde v France*, Communication 1049/2002, UN Doc CCPR/C/77/D/1049/2002 (2003), para 6.2. See further: *Laing v Australia*, Communication 901/1999,

having reassessed the situation or the author having been given the opportunity to present a defence, constituted arbitrary interference with the author and her daughter's family in *Tcholatch v Canada*.[56]

The Committee had to deal, in *Madafferi v Australia*, with deportation proceedings and the impact which removal may have upon the family life of the person being removed and other members of the family. It observed that in cases where one part of a family must leave the territory of a State party while the other part would be entitled to remain, the relevant criteria for assessing whether or not the specific interference with family life can be objectively justified must be considered, on the one hand, in light of the significance of the State party's reasons for the removal of the person concerned and, on the other, the degree of hardship the family and its members would encounter as a consequence of such removal. The Committee noted the considerable hardship that would be imposed on the family, which had been in existence for 14 years, by reason of Mr Madaferri's removal if the family remained in Australia. In the alternative, if Mrs Madafferi and her children were to decide to emigrate to Italy in order to avoid separation of the family, they would not only have to live in a country they did not know and whose language the children (two of whom were already 13 and 11 years old) did not speak, but would also have to take care, in an environment alien to them, of a husband and father whose mental health had been seriously troubled, in part by acts that could be ascribed to Australia. In these very specific circumstances, the Committee considered that interfering with the family life of the individuals concerned would be unreasonable and, as such, arbitrary under article 17.[57]

The Committee, in *Huamán v Peru*, was called upon to deal with the issue of abortion and its relation to the right to private life under article 17. A public-sector hospital doctor had diagnosed anencephaly in the author's foetus, and advised her that she has the option of terminating the pregnancy in accordance with domestic legislation allowing abortions in cases of risk to the life of the mother. The author elected to terminate her pregnancy, but the hospital director refused termination. In the absence of information provided by Peru, and in the circumstances of the case, the Committee took the view that the omission on the part of the State in not

---

UN Doc CCPR/C/81/D/901/1999 (2004); and *Martínez v Spain*, Communication 1092/2002, UN Doc CCPR/C/83/D/1092/2002 (2005), para 6.6.

56 *Tcholatch v Canada*, Communication 1052/2002, UN Doc CCPR/C/89/D/1052/2002 (2007), para 8.6.

57 *Madafferi v Australia*, Communication 1011/2001, UN Doc CCPR/C/81/D/1011/2001 (2004), para 9.8. See also: *Bakhtiyari v Australia*, Communication 1069/2002, UN Doc CCPR/C/79/D/1069/2002 (2003), para 9.6; and *Faris v Libyan Arab Jamahiriya*, Communication 1143/2002, UN Doc CCPR/C/90/D/1143/2002 (2007), para 6.3. Compare with *Byahuranga v Denmark*, Communication 1222/2003, UN Doc CCPR/C/82/D/1222/2003 (2004), para 11.9.

enabling the author to benefit from a therapeutic abortion was not justified and was thus arbitrary, so as to amount to a violation of articles 7 and 17.[58]

Interference with the Home

Within the framework of article 17, 'home' is understood to indicate the place where a person resides. It has also been taken to include the place where a person carries out his or her usual occupation, which might be outside the ordinary meaning of the term 'home' but is nevertheless consistent with the objective of protecting the places in which a person is habitually present. It was argued by the author in *Stewart v Canada* that the term 'home' should be interpreted even more broadly, to encompass the entire community of which an individual is a part. The author claimed, in this sense, that his 'home' was Canada and that it was therefore an interference with his home for Canadian authorities to deport him. The Committee did not address that submission, although it did discuss the definition of the term 'his own country' under article 12.[59]

Search of a person's home should be restricted to a search for necessary evidence and should not be allowed to amount to harassment.[60] *Coronel et al v Colombia* involved allegations of breaches of article 17(1), through interference with personal privacy, the family and home. Between 12 and 14 January 1993, troops of the Motilones Anti-Guerrilla Battalion, attached to the Colombian National Army, conducted a military operation in the indigenous community of San José del Tarra, making incursions into a number of neighbouring settlements and villages. During these operations, soldiers raided several houses and arrested a number of people, including the alleged victims. It was asserted that both the raids and the arrests were carried out illegally, since the soldiers did not have the judicial warrants required by Colombian law to conduct searches or make arrests. The authors alleged a violation of article 17 of the Covenant, inasmuch as the victims' right to privacy and freedom from interference in family life and privacy of the home were violated when they were arrested in their homes. The Committee noted that Colombia had not provided any explanation to justify the action described and found that there had been a violation of article 17(1).[61]

A raid on the family house of Rojas García was considered by the Committee in *García v Colombia*. The raid was carried out by hooded men entering through the roof at 2:00 in the morning. Colombia submitted that the raid was carried out

58 *Huamán v Peru*, Communication 1153/2003, UN Doc CCPR/C/85/D/1153/2003 (2005), para 6.4.

59 *Stewart v Canada*, Communication 538/1993, UN Doc CCPR/C/58/D/538/1993 (1996), para 3.3. On the meaning of the expression 'his own country' (as used in article 12) see Chapter 4.

60 General Comment 16, above n 2, para 8.

61 *Coronel et al v Colombia*, Communication 778/1997, UN Doc CCPR/C/76/D/778/1997(2002), para 9.7.

in accordance with article 343 of the Colombian Code of Criminal Procedure. The Committee refused to enter into the question of the legality of the raid, instead emphasizing that article 17 of the Covenant requires any interference to be lawful, as well as not arbitrary. The Committee considered that the concept of arbitrariness in article 17 is intended to guarantee that even interference provided for by law should be in accordance with the provisions, aims and objectives of the Covenant and should be, in any event, reasonable in the particular circumstances. It found that the raid was not reasonable and that Colombia was thus obliged to provide García and his family with an effective remedy, including reparation.[62]

62 *García v Colombia*, Communication 687/1996, UN Doc CCPR/C/71/D/687/1996 (2001).

Chapter 8
Rights of the Family and Children

Richard Burchill

Articles 17, 23 and 24 protect the different rights related to the family and children. They are all stand-alone rights, but at the same time they are closely inter-related and very often dealt with together.[1] The protection of the family and marriage under article 23 is the only right in the Covenant protecting a status acquired under private law.[2] The rights related to family protection directly impact upon an emotional and often controversial area of domestic law. Perhaps due to this the Committee tends to give a significant degree of latitude to State actions in this area. The extent to which the Committee will give wide discretion to States is clear from the decision in *Hendriks v The Netherlands* where the Committee deferred to the actions and decisions taken by the national courts even though it was recognized that the handling of the situation by the State was not necessarily in conformity with the Covenant.[3] While the Committee has tended to exercise extreme caution concerning the extent to which it will intervene in family issues, more recent decisions have shown a tendency toward more active intervention in matters concerning family rights based on ensuring States meet their obligations under the Covenant.

Positive and Negative Obligations

The articles of the Covenant dealing with the family and children impose a range of negative and positive obligations upon the State.[4] Article 17 is clearly worded in negative terms requiring non-interference with the family. Articles 23 and 24 are positive in nature calling for necessary actions to ensure the protection of the family unit and the protection of children due to their status as minors. The obligation upon the State not to interfere with family life requires that any

1 *General Comment 19: Protection of the family, the right to marriage and equality of the spouses*, UN Doc HRI/GEN/1/Rev 6 at 149 (2003), para 1.

2 Manfred Nowak, *UN Covenant on Civil and Political Rights* (2nd revised edn, Kehl, Germany: NP Engel, 2005) p 514.

3 *Hendriks v The Netherlands*, Communication 201/1985, UN Doc CCPR/C/33/D/201/1985 (1988), para 10.4.

4 *General Comment 3: Article 2 Implementation at the national level*, UN Doc HRI/GEN/1/Rev.6 at 125 (2003), para 1.

interference can only occur 'on the basis of law, which itself must comply with the provisions, aims and objectives of the Covenant'.[5] Even if the interference is based on law it cannot be arbitrary and 'should be in accordance with the provisions, aims and objectives of the Covenant and should be, in any event, reasonable in the particular circumstances'.[6] States are under an obligation to protect the family from any interference 'whether they emanate from State authorities or from natural or legal persons'.[7] It is recognized by the Committee that the obligations upon the State in this regard 'may vary from country to country and depend on different social, economic, political and cultural conditions and traditions'.[8]

To ensure the effective protection of family rights, States are under an obligation to adopt legislative and other measures to ensure the rights in the Covenant are real and effective. This includes measures that ensure respect not only from the State but also from other social institutions, including private parties, concerned with family rights.[9] Article 24 calls for 'special measures' to protect children which are over and above the obligations in set out in article 2.[10] The positive obligations upon the State to ensure children are given the protection due to their status as minors is comprehensive, so there is an obligation upon the State to ensure this right regardless of who is directly involved when child rights are at stake, be it State, family or private bodies concerned with child care.[11] The positive measures to protect family rights frequently involve socio-economic measures such as benefits or allowances. These measures are inherent in the effective protection of family rights, as Nowak explains:[12]

> [t]he state is obligated to contribute to the maintenance of familial relations and to alleviate the negative effects of their dissolution. In the broadest sense, protection of the family covers a number of other measures provided for in most states, such as financial assistance, protection of mothers, tax privileges, relief in setting up a household, etc.

---

5 *General Comment 16: The right to respect of privacy, family, home and correspondence, and protection of honour and reputation*, UN Doc HRI/GEN/1/Rev.6 at 142 (2003), para 3.

6 General Comment 16, above n 5, para 4.

7 General Comment 16, above n 5, para 1.

8 *Aumeeruddy-Cziffra et al v Mauritius*, Communication 35/1978, UN Doc CCPR/C/OP/1 at 67 (1985), para 9.2(b)2(ii)1.

9 General Comment 19, above n 1, para 3; *General Comment 17: Rights of the child*, UN Doc HRI/GEN/1/Rev.6 at 144 (2003), para 1.

10 General Comment 17, ibid, para 1. The Committee has noted that 'The reports submitted by States parties often seem to underestimate this obligation …'.

11 *Huamán v Peru*, Communication 1153/2003, UN Doc CCPR/C/85/D/1153/2003 (2005).

12 Nowak, above n 2, pp 519–20.

The result is that in some circumstances the protection of family rights will be economically relative.[13] In *Oulajin and Kaiss v The Netherlands* the applicants were challenging Dutch child benefit regulations which are only applicable to foster children if the foster children are brought up and maintained as if they were the foster parents' own children. The applicants were claiming discriminatory treatment in the denial of child benefit for their foster children were living in Morocco and the State had argued the children were not being brought up as if they were the applicants' own. In these circumstances the Committee held that there was no obligation to provide benefits on the basis that limitations in the granting of benefits is inevitable and legitimate distinctions could be made.[14] In a separate concurring opinion it was further explained that the request of the applicants that the State provide child benefit for foster children living abroad was out of proportion with the aims of the rights concerned and while the States may choose to extend benefits to a wide range of dependants they are not required to do so.[15] Other challenges to the benefit system in the Netherlands have also failed, with the Committee deciding that various distinctions in the granting of welfare benefits based on the existence of different forms of family life are not contrary to the Covenant.[16] However, in circumstances where the child is somehow discriminated against in the distribution of benefits and the discrimination cannot be objectively justified, this will be contrary to a State's Covenant obligations towards the child.[17]

Definition of the Family Unit

Article 17 uses the term 'the family', without defining it and article 23 establishes the family unit as the 'natural and fundamental group unit of society', again without definition. The terms family and family unit are used interchangeably and carry the same meaning. The concept of the family unit is not static, as its definition will be reflective of the nature and changes that occur in society and will be given a broad interpretation in order to reflect differing views that exist in

13 Sarah Joseph, Jenny Schultz and Melissa Castan, *The International Covenant on Civil and Political Rights: Cases, Materials and Commentary* (2nd edn, Oxford: Oxford University Press, 2004), p 586.

14 *Oulajin and Kaiss v The Netherlands*, Communication 406 and 426/1990, UN Doc CCPR/C/46/D/406/1990 and 426/1990 at 117 (1992), paras 7.4–7.5.

15 Ibid, separate opinion of Kurt Herndl, Rein Müllerson, Birame N'Diaye and Waleed Sadi.

16 See *Danning v The Netherlands*, Communication 180/84; UN Doc CCPR/C/OP/2 at 205 (1990); *Sprenger v The Netherlands*, Communication 395/50, UN Doc CCPR/C/44/D/395/1990 (1992); *Hoofdman v The Netherlands*, Communication 602/1994, UN Doc CCPR/C/64/D/602/1994 (1998).

17 *Derksen v Netherlands*, Communication 976/2001, UN Doc CCPR/C/80/D/976/2001 (2004), para 9.3.

various social contexts.[18] The understanding of what constitutes a family ranges from monogamous marriages and the traditional nuclear family to polygamous marriages and extended family units. The Committee recognizes that the legal definition of what constitutes a family or family unit will vary, making it impossible to establish a standard definition of general applicability.[19]

Even though the Committee does not subscribe to any particular definition of the family it has explained that the common residence of husband and wife 'has to be considered as the normal behaviour of the family'.[20] Furthermore, '[t]he idea of the family must necessarily embrace relations between parents and child.'[21] And even if the parents divorce, family life is understood to continue between parent and child if the child and the separated parent maintain their close relations. However, it is necessary for close relationships to exist in order to be afforded the protection under the Covenant. In *AS v Canada* the applicants argued that the refusal of the Canadian authorities to allow the applicants' relatives to join them violated their rights under articles 17 and 23. The application failed at the admissibility stage as the Committee held no rights in the Covenant were at issue since 'except for a brief period of 2 years some 17 years ago, A. S. and her adopted daughter have not lived together as a family'.[22] The same opinion was expressed in *Oulajin and Kaiss v The Netherlands* where the children lived in Morocco and the foster parents were in the Netherlands. In these decisions it was not an issue of understanding the particular social and cultural values of those involved but the fact that the parents and the children had no close relationships.[23]

In determining the existence of a family unit, due consideration is given to the particular circumstances involved and will involve looking at, *inter alia*, blood ties, legal relations (marriage, adoption), life together, economic ties or other forms of intensive regular relationships. The Committee has stated:[24]

---

18 General Comment 16, above n 5, para 5; General Comment 19, above n 1, para 2; *Ngambi v France*, Communication 1179/2003, UN Doc CCPR/C/81/D/1179/2003 (2004), para 6.4.

19 *Aumeeruddy-Cziffra et al v Mauritius*, above n 8, para 9.2(b) 2(ii) 1.

20 Ibid, para 9.2 (b) 2 (i) 2.

21 *Hendriks v The Netherlands*, above n 3, para 10.3.

22 *AS v Canada*, Communication 68/1980, UN Doc CCPR/C/OP/1 at 27 (1985), para 8.2.b.

23 In *Oulajin and Kaiss v The Netherlands*, above n 14, it was argued that the Committee did not understand the cultural norms involved and that the distinctions drawn discriminated against migrant workers who are often separated from their families. All of these arguments failed. It appears that separation of the family members is not an automatic bar to the existence of family but there must be evidence of efforts to maintain close, personal relations, see *Byahuranga v Denmark*, Communication 1222/2003, UN Doc CCPR/C/82/D/1222/2003 (2004), para 11.6.

24 *Ngambi v France*, above n 18, para 6.4.

> the term 'family', for purposes of the Covenant, must be understood broadly as to include all those comprising a family as understood in the society concerned. The protection of such family is not necessarily obviated, in any particular case, by the absence of formal marriage bonds, especially where there is a local practice of customary or common law marriage. Nor is the right to protection of family life necessarily displaced by geographical separation, infidelity, or the absence of conjugal relations. However, there must first be a family bond to protect.

It is the final point which weighs heavily in any consideration of the existence of family life. In *Balaguer Santacana v Spain* the applicant had entered into a sporadic extra-marital affair and the Committee felt that the 'unstable relationship' which existed could not be considered as family life since the basic aspects of close relationships, economic ties, and so on did not exist.[25] The Committee has further explained, '[w]here there are biological ties, there is a strong presumption that a "family" exists and only in exceptional circumstances will such relationship not be protected by article 17.'[26] The existence of family relations have to be real and current and not only future possibilities, as determined in *Aumeeruddy-Cziffra et al v Mauritius* where the Committee held that women who were engaged and not married were not 'victims' as their family rights under article 17 and/or 23 were not in question at that time.[27]

Even when close family relationships exist, the extent and nature of the relationships will influence whether or not the family unit is able to claim protection from the Covenant. In *Stewart v Canada* and *Canepa v Canada* the applicants faced removal from Canada for criminal convictions. In both cases they had been living in Canada for a significant period of time as had most of their immediate family. In both applications claims under articles 17 and 23 failed on the basis that the applicants did not have effective links to their family in Canada which in turn would make their removal disproportionate. In *Canepa* the Committee pointed out that the applicant had family in Italy, his country of nationality, which was a contributing justification for his removal from Canada.[28] In *Stewart* the matter was less clear as Stewart had been legally residing in Canada for over 20 years, he had been married and divorced, there were two children from this marriage, and his mother and one brother also resided in Canada. The Committee

25 *Balaguer Santacana v Spain*, Communication 417/1990, UN Doc CCPR/C/51/D/417/1990 (1994), para 10.2.

26 *Tcholatch v Canada*, Communication 1052/2002, UN Doc CCPR/C/89/D/1052/2002 (2007), para 8.2.

27 *Aumeeruddy-Cziffra et al v Mauritius*, above n 8, para 9.2 (a); *Ngambi v France*, above n 18, where the claim for the existence of family life was rejected as it was based on falsified documents, para 6.4.

28 *Canepa v Canada*, Communication 558/1993, UN Doc CCPR/C/59/D/558/1993 (1997), para 11.5.

held that his removal would not impact his family life in Canada, as he would be able to communicate with his relations and visit them if he wished.[29] In *Sahid v New Zealand* the applicant argued that he, one of his four daughters and her youngest son constituted a family unit deserving of protection. The applicant was attempting to challenge a removal order issued by New Zealand. Even though it was claimed by the applicant that he was a primary caregiver to his grandson in New Zealand and that his extended family is culturally important, the Committee did not feel that the three individuals concerned constituted a family unit amenable to protection under article 23.[30]

In determining the existence of a family unit the Committee has been presented with a number of claims based on cultural practices and beliefs that call for the recognition of the extended family. In *Sahid*, as well as in *X v Australia*,[31] cultural arguments as to the nature of the family unit did not influence the Committee's decisions and the focus was on the existence of close, personal relations between the individuals concerned. Cultural considerations for the definition of the family unit were a prominent issue in *Hopu and Bessert v France*. This application concerned a decision to build a hotel complex on a site that was claimed by the applicants to be an ancestral burial site. The applicants argued that the building of the hotel and destruction of the burial site would violate their rights under articles 17 and 23(1) on the basis that members of their family were buried on the site and the destruction of the burial ground would be an interference with the family. France challenged this on the basis that the authors had not demonstrated that the remains in the burial ground were members of their family, forensic tests had only demonstrated that the remains pre-dated the arrival of Europeans to Polynesia. The Committee explained that the term family:[32]

> … has to be given a broad interpretation so as to include all those comprising the family as understood in the society in question. It follows that cultural traditions should be taken into account when defining the term 'family' in a specific situation.

The Committee then noted that the burial grounds and the remains were an essential part of the identities of the applicants and therefore played an important part in

29 *Stewart v Canada*, Communication 538/1993, UN Doc CCPR/C/58/D/538/1993 (1996), para 12.10.

30 *Sahid v New Zealand*, Communication 893/1999, UN Doc CCPR/C/77/D/893/1999 (2003), para 8.2.

31 *X v Australia*, Communication 557/1993, UN Doc CCPR/C/57/D/557/1993 (1996).

32 *Hopu and Bessert v France*, Communication 549/1993, UN Doc CCPR/C/60/D/549/1993/Rev.1. (1997). para 10.3.

their family life. Even though the applicants could not demonstrate any direct link to the individual remains in the burial ground the Committee felt:[33]

> the authors' failure to establish a direct kinship link cannot be held against them in the circumstances of the communication, where the burial grounds in question pre-date the arrival of European settlers and are recognized as including the forbears of the present Polynesian inhabitants of Tahiti.

A strong dissenting opinion issued by three members of the Committee felt that articles 17 and 23 were not applicable to this application since it could be proven that any direct family ties with the deceased in the burial grounds existed. The dissent explained:[34]

> the term 'family', when applied to the local population in French Polynesia, might well include relatives, who would not be included in a family, as this term is understood in other societies, ... However, even when the term 'family' is extended, it does have a discrete meaning. It does not include all members of one's ethnic or cultural group. Nor does it necessarily include all one's ancestors, going back to time immemorial.

The dissent felt that a general claim was not sufficient and the applicants would need to demonstrate a direct familial link 'even on the assumption that the notion of family is different from notions that prevail in other societies'.[35] The dissent went on to explain that the Committee's decision reveals that family rights were not at stake, but rather based on cultural rights and therefore the majority's views should have reflected this instead of the construction given to the term 'family' taking it beyond its ordinary and generally accepted meaning. But as discussed in Chapter 10 France's reservation to the Covenant concerning minority rights barred any consideration of this aspect of the application making it necessary for the Committee to take the view it did on the existence of family life.

The existence or not of a family unit is obviously a crucial first step to considering the obligations upon States under articles 17, 23 and, if relevant, 24. Even though the definition of the family unit can extend beyond biological and legal relationships depending upon the close relationships involved, marriage does appear to have a particular status when it comes to defining a family unit, in the absence of any particular cultural beliefs. In *Aumeeruddy-Cziffra et al v Mauritius* the individuals who were engaged to be married were not considered victims, meaning they had not yet formed a family unit with their partners. The same approach appears in the various challenges to the Dutch benefits system where

33 Ibid.

34 Ibid, dissenting opinion of David Kretzmer and Thomas Buergenthal, co-signed by Nisuke Ando and Lord Colville, *Hopu* para 4.

35 Ibid.

individuals who were cohabiting or had close physical and economic relationships short of marriage were not entitled to the same rights to family welfare benefits as married couples. The decisions by the Committee in these applications demonstrate the economically relative nature of the obligations regarding family rights and the high level of discretion given to the State. The Committee is obviously sensitive to the varying definitions of the family that exist. It has tended to fluctuate between a rather narrow interpretation of what constitutes a family unit[36] and the use of rather broad interpretations in an instrumental way in pursuit of particular outcomes.[37]

Non-Interference and Protection of the Family Unit

In assessing whether or not the actions or omissions by a State are contrary to the provisions of the Covenant, the Committee's main concern is whether or not the actions or omissions of the State have been arbitrary and the extent to which the aims and objectives of the Covenant have been respected, which includes making an assessment of what may be in the best interest of any child that may be involved.[38] The interference with family life need not actually occur but if there is the strong possibility that family life may be arbitrarily interfered with then this will run contrary to the obligations under the Covenant. In *Aumeeruddy-Cziffra et al v Mauritius* Mauritian immigration law was being challenged on the basis that foreign wives of Mauritian citizens were automatically granted a right of residence, but the foreign husbands of Mauritian women had to apply for it, with no guarantee that they would be granted permanent residency. The Committee explained:[39]

> not only the future possibility of deportation, but the existing precarious residence situation of foreign husbands in Mauritius represents, an interference by the authorities of the State party with the family life of the Mauritian wives and their husbands.

Even though none of the applicants had actually been deported the threat of such action which would obviously impact upon family life was enough to constitute arbitrary interference.

36 See *Aumeeruddy-Cziffra et al v Mauritius*, above n 8, para 9.2; *Hendriks v The Netherlands*, above n 3, para 10.3. In *Winata v Australia*, Communication 930/2000, UN Doc CCPR/C/72/D/930/2000 (2001) the Committee confined its consideration of the family to the nuclear family of parents and one child without investigating the existence of any extended family relations in Indonesia, the parents' country of nationality.

37 As demonstrated *Hopu and Bessert v France*, above n 32.

38 *Tcholatch v Canada*, above n 26, para 8.3.

39 *Aumeeruddy-Cziffra et al v Mauritius*, above n 8, para 9.2 (b) 2 (i) 3.

This may be contrasted with the Committee's views in *Laing v Australia* where the applicant and her two children had been living in Australia for eight years following the mother's divorce from her former spouse who lived in the USA. The custody of the oldest child was subject to proceedings in the USA under the Hague Convention on the Civil Aspects of Child Abduction. Australia was attempting to remove the child to the USA in compliance with the Hague Convention order. The family initially went into hiding and then pursued various appeals before the Australian courts challenging the removal order. The applicant argued that enforcement of the order would impair the enjoyment of family life for herself and her two children and that the removal of the oldest daughter to the USA would be contrary to the rights of the child under article 24. The Committee took the view that the applicant would need to participate in the court proceedings in the USA before there could be any determination as to how family life or the children would be affected.[40] The Committee viewed the Hague Convention proceedings as something which was in the best interest of the child despite the circumstances of the application. It appears that a custody order giving the father sole custody over the oldest daughter had already been approved and evidence was submitted supporting the contention that the daughter did not wish to return to the USA. The Committee held that the Hague Convention does not exclude the applicability of the Covenant but it is clear that it was not prepared to question the proceedings under that regime in any way. Two members of the Committee dissented claiming that since a significant period of time had passed since the oldest child had left the USA, it was necessary to examine the impact any actions in pursuit of the proceedings in the USA would have upon family life and the child.[41] It is clear the Committee was not prepared to question the Hague Convention regime even when Australia's actions under that treaty were clearly responsible for creating circumstances that could be considered to be contrary to the object and purpose of the Covenant.[42] At the same time if the Committee took the view that the child could not be removed from Australia because of Covenant obligations, this would result in a potential clash between the legal regimes.

---

40 *Laing v Australia*, Communication 901/1999, UN Doc CCPR/C/81/D/901/1999 (2004) paras 7.4–7.5.

41 Ibid, dissenting opinion from Mr Prafullachandra Natwarlal Bhagwati and Mr Walter Kälin. The Committee has consistently held that proceedings involving custody or family related matters cannot be unduly delayed due to the impact this has on family life. See also *Tcholatch v Canada*, above n 26, para 8.9; *LP v Czech Republic*, Communication 946/2000 UN Doc CCPR/C/75/D/946/2000 (2002) para 7.4. Given the considerable passage of time involved in the Laing application its reasoning is confusing when read next to the Committee's views in the latter two applications.

42 Admittedly Australia was in a very difficult position as it was attempting to adhere to its other obligations under international law. But there is the view that considerations of human rights must inform other international legal obligations, something the Committee failed to act upon in this application.

In applications involving removal or deportation the Committee has consistently held that the decision to remove an individual will involve articles 17 and 23 when family relations exist, and article 24 if children are involved. The decision to deport an individual who has family relations in the removing State is an obvious interference with family life.[43] The question then becomes whether or not the removal order is an arbitrary interference. In removal cases the Committee looks at any criminal record that may exist for the individual being deported, the domestic proceedings involving the removal, the direct impact any removal will have on family life being enjoyed in the applicant territory, the ability for family life to be enjoyed elsewhere and the impact of a removal upon any children directly concerned. The Committee has decided in three deportation cases involving Canada that the criminal record of the individual concerned, the lack of effective family relations in Canada and the belief that family relations could be maintained by other means justified the removal orders. In *Stewart v Canada* a deportation order was served to Stewart for his removal to the United Kingdom due to his extensive criminal record. Much of the argument in *Stewart* focused on article 12 claims, but interference with family life was obviously a major issue as all of Stewart's family, with the exception of one brother, lived in Canada and this included two children from a failed marriage. The Committee explained that the decision to deport Stewart was not an arbitrary interference as the decision was taken in pursuit of 'a legitimate State interest' and due consideration had been given to the impact upon family life.[44] The Committee appeared to agree with the government's submissions that 'the nature and quality' of Stewart's family relationships 'could be adequately maintained through correspondence, telephone calls and visits to Canada'.[45]

In *Canepa v Canada* a removal was ordered issued for Canepa to be returned to Italy, his country of nationality, again based on an extensive criminal record. Canepa had lived in Canada with his immediate family for over 20 years since he was five years old. The Committee felt that the absence of children or a spouse in Canada, the existence of extended family in Italy and no evidence that his immediate family in Canada would provide any support for overcoming his drug addiction or criminal tendencies meant that the removal decision could not be considered arbitrary.[46] Finally, in *Truong v Canada* the applicant had come to Canada after fleeing Vietnam in the late 1970s and was given permanent residency and declared a 'stateless' person. The author had been convicted of a number of criminal offences over the years and Canada ordered his removal to Vietnam and was in discussions with that government for his return. The applicant had three sisters, and their respective families, in Canada, but his wife, mother and two brothers lived in Vietnam. The Committee held that Truong had spent less time in

43 *Sahid v New Zealand*, above n 30, para 7.4.

44 *Stewart v Canada*, above n 29, para 12.10.

45 Ibid, para 9.4.

46 *Canepa v Canada*, above n 28, para 11.5.

Canada than Stewart, had less family living in Canada than Stewart and given that he had family in Vietnam, no 'arguable issues' concerning family life arose.[47]

Removal was also at issue in *GT v Australia* where it was argued that the deportation of T following a conviction for drug smuggling would be an arbitrary interference with the family life he had established in Australia following his conviction. T had been convicted in 1992 and married an Australian national in 1996, becoming the stepfather of her sons. Despite the fact that the removal of T would impact upon the existence of a family life, the majority of the Committee held that the author had failed to sufficiently substantiate claims under articles 17 and 23 for the application to be declared admissible.[48] In a separate dissenting opinion it was explained that the application did raise significant issues under articles 17 and 23(1) and that it was important to consider the State's failure[49]

> … to address the issue of whether the reasons justifying the deportation of a person who has fully served his criminal sentence and who has already been able to re-establish his family life are weighty enough to legitimize the adverse consequences for the family life of the person and his closest ones.

Even though the applicant was married and was the legal father to two children it is difficult to understand how the Committee decided the claims under article 17 and 23 were unsubstantiated as the removal would obviously interfere with family life. The Committee may have been influenced by the nature of the crime (drug smuggling), feeling that in the circumstances the individual concerned did not deserve the full protection of the Covenant. But it is more likely the Committee felt that since the family relations had been entered into after the convictions the individuals concerned knew that the applicant's status was precarious as there was a strong likelihood of deportation, therefore there was no guarantee they would be able to rely upon the full protection of the Covenant.

Where stable family relations have existed for a considerable period of time and when the removal of an individual would have a serious impact upon these relations continuing, the justifications for removal need to be considerable. The application of *Madafferi v Australia* involved an individual of Italian citizenship who had travelled to Australia in 1989 as a visitor, overstayed his visa and then married an Australian citizen with whom he had four children; and his extended family are also resident in Australia. Prior to leaving Italy, Madafferi had served a two-year prison term and while he was living in Australia he was the subject of trials *in absentia* that were carried out in Italy and sentences were handed down of which he was not aware; Italy never requested his extradition as a result of

47 *Truong v Canada*, Communication 743/1997, UN Doc CCPR/C/77/D/743/1997 (2003), para 7.4.

48 *GT v Australia*, Communication 706/1996, UN Doc CCPR/C/61/D/706/1996 (1997), para 7.4.

49 Ibid, dissenting opinion of Martin Scheinin.

these sentences. When Madafferi attempted to normalize his status in Australia he was denied a visa on account of his 'bad character'. Australia argued the removal would not be an interference with the family as his family would be able to go to Italy with him, where, in the view of the State, they would be able to integrate, or they could chose to remain in Australia.[50] Similar arguments were put forth in response to allegations under articles 23 and 24. The Committee rejected these views, explaining:[51]

> … that a decision by the State party to deport the father of a family with four minor children and to compel the family to choose whether they should accompany him or stay in the State party is to be considered 'interference' with the family, at least in circumstances where, as here, substantial changes to long-settled family life would follow in either case.

The Committee went on to say that Australia's assessment of Madafferi as a bad character, which was the main justification for his removal, was not appropriate in the circumstances as the events in question had taken place 20 years prior and other outstanding criminal sentences had been removed. The Committee also pointed out that his removal would bring considerable hardship to his wife and children as any move to Italy would be difficult as it would be 'an environment alien to them'. But in *Byahuranga v Denmark* where similar circumstances existed, the Committee's decision went the other way on procedural grounds as the applicant's family was not part of the application. The Committee recognized that for the family the circumstances would be the same as set out in *Madafferi* but since the application was only in the name of the individual being removed the Committee held the justification for the removal was reasonable and did not take into consideration the impact the removal would have on the family unit.[52]

These applications demonstrate how the Committee has engaged in a balancing exercise between the ability of the State to determine who may enter and reside in its territory and the right of an individual to remain in a territory where they are not a citizen but where they have either lived for a considerable period of time or have family present. In *Canepa* and *Truong* the presence of family in the country of nationality was a major consideration for the Committee, even though it can be rightly said that the Committee's attitude in *Canepa* was 'judgmental and insensitive'.[53] Such an accusation can be levelled more strongly in the case of Stewart who had his entire family, except one brother, living in Canada. The Committee held in *Canepa* that the family that was present in Canada could not help him overcome his criminal problems. But in *Stewart* the Committee failed to

---

50 *Madafferi v Australia*, Communication 1011/2001, UN Doc CCPR/C/81/D/1011/2001 (2004) para 4.17.

51 Ibid, para 9.8.

52 *Byahuranga v Denmark*, above n 23, paras 11.8–11.9.

53 Joseph et al, above n 13, p 596.

give consideration to the fact that much of the author's criminal record was due to his drug and alcohol dependence and that he was receiving treatment, something which his family could have provided support for. The decision in *Madafferi* demonstrates more careful consideration by the Committee as account was taken of a whole range of factors related to the applicant and his family members, including his health and the ability of other family members to integrate into another society.[54] However, the Committee's views in *Byahuranga* lead back to claims about insensitivity. While it is important for the Committee to maintain procedural strictness, it has constantly held that family issues require a broad and expansive interpretation, something lacking in its consideration of that application.

The Committee took a seemingly activist approach in *Winata v Australia* where it was held that the enforcement of immigration laws concerning illegal immigrants could be considered arbitrary without due consideration given to the impact the removal would have on the child. Frederick Winata and So Lan Li had entered Australia legally but had overstayed their visas and subsequently had a child, Barry. When Barry was ten years old he was able to claim Australian citizenship by virtue of his birth in the territory, and on the next day Winata and Li claimed asylum on the basis they faced persecution in Indonesia, their country of nationality. Australia stressed that Winata and Li were in the territory illegally, that the Covenant does not protect any right to remain in a State or to establish a family there in circumstances where they have stayed unlawfully and that Winata and Li were aware of the consequences faced for overstaying their visas. Australia argued that their removal could not be considered arbitrary as it was duly enforcing its immigration laws and the applicants were given full due process in their appeals against the removal decision. Australia further contended the family could remain together in Indonesia, or if Barry remained in Australia the parents would be able to visit and keep in contact with him, maintaining the family relationship in a situation analogous with many who have children in boarding schools.

The Committee recognized that a State party is able to control entry and exit into its own territory and may require the departure of individuals who have remained unlawfully. The Committee also pointed out that even if a child has been born in a State party and received citizenship from that State, the removal of the parents would not necessarily be an arbitrary interference. However, the Committee stressed that States do not have an unlimited discretion in removal cases and based on the particular circumstances of this application, the actions of the State party could be deemed arbitrary. Therefore the Committee held that Australia had 'to demonstrate additional factors justifying the removal of both parents that go beyond a simple enforcement of its immigration law in order to avoid a characterisation of arbitrariness'.[55]

---

54 In *Madafferi v Australia*, above n 50, Ruth Wedgewood provided a dissenting view explaining 'The human sympathy that may be felt for a visa applicant and his family does not create a license to disregard reasonable criteria for the grant or denial of visas.'

55 *Winata v Australia*, above n 36, para 7.3.

Four members of the Committee dissented[56] with the majority's views on the basis that the Committee had come to a conclusion based on emotions and doubted whether the decision of Australia to remove the parents constitutes interference with family life and certainly do not feel the decision was arbitrary. They point out that the separation of the family is not inevitable and that the Committee's opinion relies on 'substantial changes' to the family life and not interference as required by article 17. The dissenters concluded that since there is no obstacle to keeping the family together somewhere else, the decision of Australia cannot be construed as interference with the family life. The dissenters recognized that there may be cases where a decision of the State to remove a family member would be arbitrary interference with family life since the removal would be disproportionate to the aims being pursued. However, in the circumstances of the present application they disagreed with the Committee that the State must demonstrate additional factors to avoid having its actions being considered arbitrary.

The Committee's decision in *Winata* is obviously narrow in its application but does leave open the extent to which family considerations have to be taken into account when applying immigration laws. The Committee took the view in *Rajan and Rajan v New Zealand* that since the State has taken into consideration applicable international obligations relevant to family life and the children, the removal of the parents would not be contrary to the Covenant.[57] In this application the parents were being removed for immigration violations and had children who possessed New Zealand citizenship and had spent a significant amount of their early life in New Zealand, but the authors had failed to substantiate how their removal would result in a violation of the Covenant.

In *Sahid v New Zealand* the applicant was not given permission to remain in New Zealand but argued that his removal would be an arbitrary interference with the family life which existed between himself, his daughter and his grandson, as he claimed to be the primary caregiver for the grandson. The Committee decided that his removal would not be an arbitrary interference as the child would have his mother and a father to look after him and the grandfather could remain in contact through other means, so the family life of the child would not be severely disrupted. In *Toala et al v New Zealand* the applicants were illegally present in New Zealand and the subject of removal orders, at the same time some of their children were legally resident in New Zealand. The claims of arbitrary interference with family life were declared inadmissible for non-exhaustion of local remedies in relation to articles 17 and 23. However, in a separate opinion[58] the circumstances of Mr and

56 Ibid, dissenting opinion of Prafullachandra Natwarlal Bhagwati, Tawfik Khalil, David Kretzmer and Max Yalden.

57 *Rajan and Rajan v New Zealand*, Communication 820/1998, UN Doc CCPR/C/78/D/820/1998 (2003), para 7.3.

58 *Toala et al v New Zealand*, Communication 675/1995, UN Doc CCPR/C/70/D/675/1995 (20000), dissenting opinion of Abdelfattah Amor, Prafullachandra Bhagwati, Pilar de Pombo and Hipólito Yrigoyen.

Mrs Toala, who were ill, were considered as they had no children in Western Samoa with the children in New Zealand being the only care providers. The separate opinion felt that the authors had developed effective family ties during their time in New Zealand and the majority did not adequately consider this. Therefore it was felt that the removal was disproportionate since the most effective family ties for the applicants were in New Zealand.

It is important that the various administrative procedures of the State properly take into account the impact actions and decisions may have on the family life of the individuals concerned. In two decisions involving Colombia, *José Antonio Coronel et al v Colombia* and *Rafael Armando Rojas García v Colombia* armed government troops carried out operations which involved entering houses with force along with physical and verbal abuse to the occupants. In both applications the Committee felt that actions by the State had a significant impact upon the family life of those concerned and that the State had not provided adequate explanations for the conduct of the raids.[59] In *Hopu and Bessert v France* the authors claimed that the construction of a hotel complex on an ancient burial site would destroy their ancestral burial grounds and would arbitrarily interfere with family life. The Committee decided that in the specific circumstances the burial grounds constituted an essential element of identity and family life and that France needed to properly consider the importance of the burial grounds for the applicants when it allowed for the development.[60]

Ensuring proper procedures are in place and that adequate consideration has been given to the particulars of family life avoid findings of arbitrary interference. In *Margaret Buckley v New Zealand* the author's six children (aged at the time between 8 and 1 year of age) were removed from her care in 1994 allegedly because of her inability to look after them adequately. New Zealand demonstrated that the decisions were carried out appropriately with all due consideration given to the impact upon family life and the interests of the children. The Committee noted that 'extensive procedures' were followed and that the case was under regular review, therefore the State's actions could not be considered contrary to the Covenant.[61] This was not the case in *de Gallicchio v Argentina*, where the parents had disappeared when the child was nine months old and the domestic investigations found nothing. The author subsequently located the child when she

59 In *Coronel v Colombia*, Communication 778/1997, UN Doc CCPR/C/76/D/778/1997 (2002) the operation was deemed illegal since the soldiers did not have the proper judicial warrants as prescribed by Colombian law, para 9.7. In *García v Colombia*, Communication 687/1996, UN Doc CCPR/C/71/D/687/1996 (2001) the raid upon the house was carried out with the appropriate legal process but the raid apparently occurred on the wrong house. The Committee held that the Government could not provide an adequate explanation for the conduct and therefore a violation did occur, para 10.3.

60 *Hopu and Bessert v France*, above n 32, para 10.3.

61 *Buckley v New Zealand*, Communication 858/1999, UN Doc CCPR/C/70/D/858/1999 (2000), paras 9.1–9.2; *Rajan and Rajan v New Zealand*, above n 57.

was seven years old and it was proven that they were in fact related. The domestic proceedings that followed in order to reinstate Ximena Vicario's true identity were unduly protected, taking ten years. The Committee felt that the situation as a whole, which was marked by administrative failings, was clearly an arbitrary and unlawful interference with family life and adequate consideration was not given to the interests of the child.[62] A similar conclusion was reached in *Tcholatch v Canada* where the domestic authorities had removed a child from her mother due to various assessments involving the mother's capacity to care for the child. Even though the State party followed all the necessary procedures, the Committee held that adequate consideration was not given to the Covenant obligations concerning family life. It explained:[63]

> Given the need to ensure family bonds, it is essential that any proceedings which have an impact on the family unit deal with the question of whether the family bonds should be broken, keeping in mind the best interests of the child and of the parents.

The Committee has been presented with applications involving immigration proceedings for parents that include detention in an immigration centre. The applicants have argued that accompanying children should not be detained along with the parent(s). The implications of these arguments are apparent for if the child was not also within the detention facility the parent(s) could argue that their continued detention is an interference with family life as they should be reunited with the children. In applications involving Australia the Committee has held that 'in the light of the State party's explanation of the efforts undertaken to provide children with appropriate educational, recreational and other programs, including outside the facility', keeping both the parent(s) and children in the facility was not contrary to the Covenant.[64] In these circumstances much will depend on the nature of family life, the particulars of the family unit and whether or not other means were available to the State to achieve a similar outcome.[65] The key feature is the extent to which the State has considered the impact their

62 *De Gallicchio v Argentina*, Communication 400/1990, UN Doc CCPR/C/53/D/400/1990 (1995), para 10.4.

63 *Tcholatch v Canada*, above n 26, para 8.8.

64 *Baban v Australia*, Communication 1014/2001, UN Doc CCPR/C/78/D/1014/2001 (2003), para 6.8; *D and E, and their two children v Australia*, Communication 1050/2002, UN Doc CCPR/C/87/D/1050/2002 (2006), para 6.4.

65 See *Bakhtiyari and Bakhtiyari v Australia*, Communication 1069/2002, UN Doc CCPR/C/79/D/1069/2002 (2003) where the length of detention, the age of the children and the potential for alternative arrangements resulted in the State's actions being contrary to the Covenant, paras 9.3 and 9.6–9.7.

actions have upon family life which includes considering other alternatives to detention in an immigration facility.[66]

Right to Marry and to Found a Family

Article 23(2) covers the rights of a man and woman to marry and found a family and paragraph 3 stipulates that marriage will be freely entered into. The right to marriage is not absolute and compatible restrictions to prohibit bigamy and incest are allowed. As a generalization, restrictions upon this right are to be narrow and in pursuit of a legitimate purpose; but see below on the discussion of same-sex marriages. The Committee has explained that requiring a marriage which has been conducted according to religious rights, to be conducted, registered or affirmed through civil law is in pursuit of a legitimate purpose.[67] There is no specific marriageable age in the Covenant but individuals do need to be old enough to give their free and full personal consent to marriage.[68] According to General Comment 19: 'The right to found a family implies, in principle, the possibility to procreate and live together.'[69] The right to found a family is not dependent upon the right to marry being exercised first and article 23(2) covers all acts that are intended to found a family.[70] In the current interpretation of the provisions it appears same-sex couples or single individuals do not have the right to found a family under article 23(2) since the provision clearly states the right applies to men and women. It does apply to situations where married or mixed-sex couples are unable to procreate naturally placing an obligation upon the State not only to prevent restrictions on natural means of reproduction but also to ensure measures exist that allow for a family to develop through other means.[71] Once a family has developed, regardless of its origins, the right to respect for family life is covered by articles 17 and 23 (1).

The language of article 23 in stating that the provisions protecting marriage and the right to found a family only apply to men and women has been upheld by the Committee in the one application it has considered under article 23(2), *Joslin et al v New Zealand*. Here two lesbian couples challenged the New Zealand law stipulating that marriage can only occur between a man and a woman. Before the Committee it was argued that the refusal to allow same-sex couples to marry resulted in a number of violations of the Covenant including article 17.

66 It must be noted that in applications concerning detention in immigration facilities the Committee will consider the impact the detention has on family life but this occurs in the context of article 9 with family circumstances being one of the factors involved, see *D and E, and their two children v Australia*, above n 64, para 7.2.

67 General Comment 19, above n 1, para 4.

68 Ibid, para 4.

69 Ibid, para 5.

70 Nowak, above n 2, p 532.

71 Nowak, above n 2, p 533.

This allegation was based on the refusal of the State to recognize their marriage being contrary to the positive obligations upon the State to protect family life and to respect their sexual identity. The applicants claimed that the interference with family life was arbitrary and discriminatory as it only applies to same-sex marriages and was without justification, being based on the prejudicial attitudes of society. The interference in relation to article 17 also raised issues under article 23 where the family is seen as 'the natural and fundamental group unit of society and is entitled to protection by society and the State', and the applicants claimed that the refusal of the State to allow them to marry was contrary to the obligations under this right. The applicants asserted that the language of article 23(2) has to be read in line with article 2(1) which says that the rights in the Covenant are to be exercised without any distinction, thereby negating the specific wording of article 23(2) which confines marriage to an act between a man and a woman. The Committee's decision was brief and to the point:[72]

> The Committee notes that article 23, paragraph 2, of the Covenant expressly addressed the right to marry. Given the existence of a specific provision in the Covenant on the right to marriage, any claim that this right has been violated must be considered in light of this provision. Article 23, paragraph 2, of the Covenant is the only substantive provision in the Covenant which defines a right by using the term 'men and women', rather than 'every human being', 'everyone', and 'all persons'. Use of the term 'men and women', rather than the general terms used elsewhere in Part III of the Covenant, has been consistently and uniformly understood as indicating that the treaty obligations of the States parties stemming from article 23, paragraph 2, of the Covenant is to recognize as marriage only the union between a man and a woman wishing to marry each other.

Based on this the Committee found that 'the mere refusal' to recognize same-sex marriages did not give rise to any violation of the Covenant. Two Committee members did provide a separate concurring opinion where they explained that the denial of marriage for same-sex couples did not entail a violation of human dignity in the same way that child marriages or forced marriages would.[73]

Recent developments have made the Committee's views expressed in *Joslin* appear outdated, demonstrating the dynamic nature of family law. A major factor in the Committee's reasoning was that, at the time, only one State party to the Covenant, the Netherlands, allowed for same-sex marriage which supported the assertion that article 23 only applies to a marriage involving a man and a women. This is no longer the case as other State parties have either legalized or provided

72 *Joslin et al v New Zealand*, Communication 902/1999, UN Doc CCPR/C/75/D/902/1999 (2002), para 8.2.

73 Ibid, separate opinion of Rajsoomer Lallah and Martin Scheinin.

some form of recognition for same-sex marriages.[74] Furthermore the European Court of Human Rights has decided that the explicit wording of the ECHR where it also states that marriage is between a man and a woman is outdated and needs to be interpreted in light of developments in society.[75]

In *Joslin* the Committee gave the impression that marriage was only an inconsequential status. However, the institution of marriage does create a different status for individuals in comparison to cohabitation or any civil arrangement short of marriage. This in turn impacts upon the ability of individuals to receive the protection afforded by the Covenant. In the Dutch social security cases, the Committee drew a distinction between married and unmarried couples and the consequences following on from this status:[76]

> The Committee observes, in this connection, that the decision to enter into a legal status by marriage, which provides, in Netherlands law, both for certain benefits and for certain duties and responsibilities, lies entirely with the cohabiting persons. By choosing not to enter into marriage, Mr. Danning and his cohabitant have not, in law, assumed the full extent of the duties and responsibilities incumbent on married couples.

In *Balaguer Santacana v Spain* where the author had an irregular relationship with a woman and they had conceived a child, the Committee held that since the couple had not married, and therefore legally established their relationship, they could not claim protection under article 23.[77] The Committee's decision in *Joslin* did not appropriately consider the full extent the refusal of the right to marriage has upon the applicants. The Committee's opinion that the legal act of marriage was somehow inconsequential goes against the importance it has given to marriage in other circumstances.

Equality of Spouses

Article 23 (4) requires States to 'take appropriate steps to ensure equality of rights and responsibilities of spouses as to marriage, during marriage and at its dissolution'. Equality of spouses is one of the more contentious areas of family law and this

74 At the time of writing same-sex marriages have been legalized in Canada, Spain, Belgium, the Netherlands, Norway and South Africa. A number of the federal states of the United States have also legalized same-sex marriages in their jurisdiction. The recognition of civil partnerships exists in approximately fifteen States parties to the Covenant.

75 *I v United Kingdom* [2002] ECHR 592 and *Christine Goodwin v United Kingdom* [2002] ECHR 588.

76 *Danning v The Netherlands*, above n 16, para 14.

77 *Balaguer Santacana v Spain*, above n 25, para 10.4.

provision was heavily disputed during the Covenant's drafting.[78] The Committee has explained that article 23(4) does not exist in isolation and needs to be read in conjunction with the obligation in article 23(1) to protect the family and the second branch of article 23(4) ensuring provisions are made for the protection of children.[79]

Equality between spouses 'extends to all matters arising from their relationship, such as choice of residence, running of the household, education of the children and administration of assets'.[80] The equality provisions also apply during and after the dissolution of a marriage and any discriminatory treatment 'in regard to the grounds and procedures for separation or divorce, child custody, maintenance or alimony, visiting rights or the loss or recovery of parental authority must be prohibited ...'.[81] Article 23(4) does not necessarily create a justiciable right for individuals as it is more focused upon the obligation upon the State to progressively eliminate and obstacles to equality with regard to marriage.[82] The progressive nature of realizing equality differs from the other equality provisions of the Covenant. In *Hendriks*, where the divorced parents were disputing custody rights, the Committee agreed that the applicant's right to equality was not being recognized but did not make a favourable finding for the applicant on the basis that the Dutch government was considering the necessary reforms in order to bring the national laws in line with the Covenant. However this raises problems with the object and purpose of the Covenant as article 26 creates immediate obligations for the elimination of discrimination based on sex or other status. Further General Comment 19 does not make any reference to progressive realization of equality between spouses making the exact status of the obligations upon States in this area unclear.

In *Joslin et al v New Zealand* the applicants argued that the general non-discrimination provisions in the Covenant should be paramount to any particular discrimination which may be allowed under specific articles. New Zealand argued the exact opposite pointing out that particular forms of discriminatory treatment are possible under certain articles and the general provisions cannot trump these, as they were included in the Covenant for a reason. The Committee did not address this point in its views in *Joslin*, but in *Aumeeruddy-Cziffra et al v Mauritius* the Committee did explain that:[83]

> the principle of equal treatment of the sexes applies by virtue of articles 2 (1), 3 and 26, of which the latter is also relevant because it refers particularly to the 'equal protection of the law'. Where the Covenant requires a substantial

78 Nowak, above n 2, pp 535–6.

79 *Hendriks v The Netherlands*, above n 3, para 10.3.

80 General Comment 19, above n 1, para 8.

81 General Comment 19, above n 1, para 9.

82 Nowak, above n 2, pp 536–7.

83 *Aumeeruddy-Cziffra et al v Mauritius*, above n 8, para 9.2 (b) 2 (ii) 2.

> protection as in article 23, it follows from those provisions that such protection must be equal, that is to say not discriminatory, for example on the basis of sex.

The majority of claims involving the equality of spouses under article 23(4) involve custody disputes in the wake of the dissolution of marriage. As demonstrated in *Balaguer Santacana v Spain* article 23(4) only applies when the couple is, or has been, legally married. In *Hendriks v The Netherlands* the applicant and his wife had divorced and custody of their two-year-old son was given to the mother. The family had been living in Germany but after the divorce the mother moved to the Netherlands and denied access to the father. The father had made applications for access to the Dutch courts but these failed due to the lack of co-operation by the mother. The Committee explained that article 23 is to apply in full and:[84]

> … barring exceptional circumstances, that these criteria should include the maintenance of personal relations and direct and regular contact between the child and both parents. The unilateral opposition of one of the parents, cannot, in the opinion of the Committee, be considered an exceptional circumstance.

Even though the Committee held there was an equal right to access it found no violation in this application but did call on the Netherlands to review its relevant legislation.[85] In separate opinions it was explained that even though the Dutch courts may have been right in not enforcing Mr Hendriks' access rights on the basis that it was in the best interest of the child, it was felt 'that this approach does not sustain the family rights to which Mr. Hendriks and his son were entitled under article 23 of the Covenant.'[86]

In *Fei v Colombia* the applicant left her husband and the custody of two children was given to the father, with generous visiting rights for the applicant. On one occasion when the children were visiting the mother agents for the father allegedly kidnapped them. From this point the father refused to co-operate in any matters relating to visitation. The mother tried various legal channels in Colombia and at the same time the father instituted proceedings for a change in the custody/visitation conditions. Throughout the proceedings there were a range of procedural irregularities such as changing the dates of the hearings, the applicant was not always given a defence lawyer and a Prosecutor General who was responsible for the case had claimed close personal relations with the father. In the final decision of the domestic court comments were made about the author's irresponsibility in relation to her children, she was ordered to stop pursuing a book about the events related to the case and she was granted only brief visits with her children which were monitored and/or obstructed. The Committee recalled its statement

---

84 *Hendriks v The Netherlands*, above n 3, para 10.4.

85 Ibid, para 11.

86 Ibid, separate opinion of Vojin Dimitrijevic, Omar El Shafei, Rosalyn Higgins and Adam Zielinski, para 4.

in *Hendriks* that article 23(4) does ensure equal access of parents to the children after dissolution and the refusal of one parent to co-operate is not an exceptional circumstance to deny this equality. In these circumstances, given the violations of the fair trial provisions of the Covenant, the Committee found there was also a violation of the equality provisions of article 23(4).[87] The Committee explained that it did not find the father's refusal to allow the applicant access was in the best interest of the children which was a factor in *Hendriks*. The Committee explained 'it appears that the author's ex-husband sought to stifle, by all means at his disposal, the author's access to the girls, or to alienate them from her. The severe restrictions imposed by Mrs. Fei's ex-husband on Mrs. Fei's rare meetings with her daughters support this conclusion.'[88] The essential distinction between *Fei* and *Hendriks* is the nature of the domestic proceedings that in *Fei* were obviously unfair. In Hendriks the Committee deferred to the domestic proceedings that were found to be fair and did not find any violation of article 23.[89]

The importance of equality between spouses in administrative matters extends beyond custody cases. In *LESK v The Netherlands* the applicant claimed that the conjugal residence was sold without her knowledge or consent. The Committee found the application inadmissible as it was based on a right to property which is not covered by the Covenant but also noted that the domestic proceedings concerning the ownership of the conjugal residence were not arbitrary so the Committee would not review the merits involved.[90] In *Müller and Engelhard v Namibia* the husband wanted to take on the wife's name after marriage. Under Namibian domestic law a women can take on the husband's name after marriage automatically but the wife's name can only be taken after specific guidelines and administrative procedures are followed. The State argued that this requirement was not discriminatory as it only entailed different procedures based on traditional practices. The Committee disagreed and explained that even if long-held traditions determined differential treatment, this could not be used as a justification to act contrary to the principle of equality between men and women.[91] The Committee's findings in this application were based on article 26 and not 23(4), but the importance given to equality between men and women in the face of long-standing traditions will have equal importance in the equality between spouses under article 23(4).

87 *Fei v Colombia*, Communication 514/1992, UN Doc CCPR/C/53/D/514/1992 (1995), paras 8.4 and 8.7.

88 Ibid, para 8.10.

89 Also see *Said v Norway*, Communication 767/1997, UN Doc CCPR/C/68/D/767/1997 (2000) where the author was involved in hearings relating to his expulsion, custody and access to his children but again there was no question of a violation of a fair trial so no further issues arose regarding article 23.

90 *LESK v The Netherlands*, Communication 381/1989, UN Doc CCPR/C/45/D/381/1989 (1992), para 5.4.

91 *Müller and Engelhard v Namibia* Communication 919/2000, UN Doc CCPR/C/74/D/919/2000 (2002) para 6.8.

Rights of Children

The rights of children receive explicit mention in article 24 of the Covenant. Paragraph 1 of article 24 provides that every child, without discrimination, has the right 'to such measures of protection as are required by his status as a minor'. Paragraph 2 states all children will be registered after birth and shall have a name and paragraph 3 protects the right of every child to acquire nationality. The rights of children in the family context are also covered by article 23(4) where in the event of dissolution of marriage the interests of the child are to be protected.[92] The rights of children are directly linked to the protection of the family unit in articles 17 and 23 as explained in *Hendriks v The Netherlands*:[93]

> The idea of the family must necessarily embrace relations between parents and child. Although divorce legally ends a marriage, it cannot dissolve the bond uniting father – or mother – and child ~ this bond does not depend on the continuation of the parents' marriage. It would seem that the priority given to the child's interests is compatible with this rule.

The inclusion of a specific article concerning the rights of children may give the impression that children are not entitled to the remaining rights in the Covenant, but this is certainly not the case.

Article 2(1) establishes that the rights in the Covenant are applicable to all individuals, which includes children. In General Comment 17 the Committee has explained 'the rights provided for in article 24 are not the only ones that the Covenant recognizes for children and that, as individuals, children benefit from all of the civil rights enunciated in the Covenant.'[94] At the same time, '[i]n enunciating a right, some provisions of the Covenant expressly indicate to States measures to be adopted with a view to affording minors greater protection than adults.'[95] The responsibility for ensuring the rights of the child lies with the States, family and society. The Committee has explained:[96]

> [a]lthough the Covenant does not indicate how such responsibility is to be apportioned, it is primarily incumbent on the family, which is interpreted broadly to include all persons composing it in the society of the State party concerned, and particularly on the parents, to create conditions to promote the harmonious

---

92 The Committee decision in *Balaguer Santacana v Spain*, above n 25 explains the limits to this provision: 'If paragraph 4 is placed into the overall context of article 23, it becomes clear that the protection of the second sentence refers only to children of the *marriage* which is being dissolved', para 10.4.

93 *Hendriks v The Netherlands*, above n 3, para 10.3.

94 General Comment 17, above n 9, para 2.

95 Ibid, para 2.

96 Ibid, para 6.

> development of the child's personality and his enjoyment of the rights recognized in the Covenant. However, since it is quite common for the father and mother to be gainfully employed outside the home, reports by States parties should indicate how society, social institutions and the State are discharging their responsibility to assist the family in ensuring the protection of the child. Moreover, in cases where the parents and the family seriously fail in their duties, ill-treat or neglect the child, the State should intervene to restrict parental authority and the child may be separated from his family when circumstances so require.

There is no definition of a child or an age limit for minor status included in article 24. General Comment 17 explains:[97]

> the Covenant does not indicate the age at which he attains his majority. This is to be determined by each State party in the light of the relevant social and cultural conditions. … However, the Committee notes that the age for the above purposes should not be set unreasonably low and that in any case a State party cannot absolve itself from its obligations under the Covenant regarding persons under the age of 18, notwithstanding that they have reached the age of majority under domestic law.

In situations where the applicant is clearly no longer a child the Committee will not entertain considerations under article 24.[98]

One of the primary issues in applications to the Committee involving children is the ability of an adult to make an application on behalf of the child. In *PS v Denmark* the government challenged the ability of the father to submit an application on behalf of his child on the basis the father did not have custodial rights over the child, which under Danish law meant he would be unable to take action on his behalf. The Committee stated that standing under the Optional Protocol can work independently of national law and that what must be considered are the circumstances facing the child.[99] The Committee has further explained:[100]

> that children must generally rely on other persons to present their claims and represent their interests, and may not be of an age or capacity to authorise any steps to be taken on their behalf. A restrictive approach should thus be avoided.

97 Ibid, para 4.

98 *Fatima Benali v Netherlands*, Communication 1272/2004, UN Doc CCPR/C/81/D/1272/2004 (2004), para 6.2.

99 *PS v Denmark*, Communication 397/1990, UN Doc CCPR/C/45/D/397/1990 at 22 (1992), para 5.2.

100 *Humanitarian Law Center v Serbia*, Communication 1355/2005, UN Doc CCPR/C/89/D/1355/2005 (2007), para 6.4.

The Committee will not always require explicit authorization from the child and will accept that a parent, either custodial or non-custodial, can bring an application on behalf of a child provided it can be substantiated by the parent or representative that the application is in the best interests of the child.[101]

In this respect the age of the child concerned, the capacity of the child, and the impact of the alleged violations upon the child will be major considerations. In *Rogl v Germany* the father applied to the Committee claiming that his ex-wife's actions, who had custody of their 15-year-old daughter, to change the daughter's surname would be a violation of his rights and his daughter's rights. The Committee held the application inadmissible based on the circumstances of the application whereby the author's arguments did not substantiate his daughter would suffer adverse effects to be considered a violation and 'there is no indication that the daughter supports any inference that her rights have been violated.'[102] In *Sahid v New Zealand* the author submitted the communication on behalf of himself, his daughter and her child, his grandson. The Committee denied the right of the applicant to submit a communication on behalf of his daughter as she was a fully consenting adult. The author had claimed in the communication that he was the primary caregiver for his grandson but the Committee held that in the absence of express assent from the child's mother, the applicant could not make a claim on his behalf.[103] In *Laing v Australia*, Martin Scheinin provided a separate concurring opinion explaining it would[104]

> ... be best if the Committee could receive either a letter of authorization or another expression of the child's opinion whenever a child has reached an age where his or her opinion can be taken into account.

It appears the Committee may become more rigid on this point[105] but the particular circumstances of an application will continue to determine whether or not a parent can bring an application on behalf of a child.[106] In situations involving an application brought on behalf of a child by a third party, if explicit authorization from the child is not forthcoming, the applicant needs to show it somehow has a 'sufficiently close relationship with the child to justify it acting without such authorisation'.[107]

---

101 See *Laing v Australia*, above n 40, para 7.3.

102 *Rogl v Germany*, Communication 808/1998, UN Doc CCPR/C/70/D/808/1998 (2000), para 9.8.

103 *Sahid v New Zealand*, above n 30, para 7.2.

104 *Laing v Australia*, above n 40, individual opinion by Martin Scheinin.

105 Something the Committee appears to be moving towards, see *Burgess v Australia*, Communication 1012/2001, UN Doc CCPR/C/85/D/1012/2001 (2005), para 6.3.

106 *Tcholatch v Canada*, above n 26, para 7.4.

107 *Humanitarian Law Center v Serbia*, above n 100, para 6.7.

Due to the special status of the child the State must ensure that appropriate protection and consideration is afforded to all children regardless of who is responsible for making the primary decisions about a child's circumstances.[108] Judicial proceedings affecting children and the family cannot be unduly delayed. In *Balaguer Santacana v Spain* the Committee recognized that much of the delay relating to a final decision on custody rights was attributable to the father, but still held that the lack of any judicial decision after several years of proceedings in custody rights and access to children constituted an unreasonable delay for which the State was responsible.[109] The Committee also requires that the necessary actions of the State need to be commensurate with the circumstances involved, with circumstances of a more extreme nature calling for a higher level of action for ensuring children received an appropriate level of treatment.[110]

Special protection for the child does not extend to all circumstances and depends on a range of factors involved, including the way in which administrative procedures are carried out. In *F v Australia* the son of F, was excluded from school because of behavioural problems and it was alleged that the procedures that the child had to go through in order to be readmitted to school were discriminatory and unreasonable. The Committee held that the domestic procedures were sufficient and the application was declared inadmissible.[111] In *Jalloh v The Netherlands* the applicant, who was suspected to be a minor, though this could not be confirmed, was detained as part of the immigration process. It was claimed that this detention was contrary to article 24. The Committee disagreed based on the circumstances whereby 'there were doubts as to the author's identity, where he had attempted to evade expulsion before, where there were reasonable prospects for expulsion, and where an identity investigation was still ongoing'.[112]

Ensuring due consideration is given to the circumstances faced by the child was the main point in *Winata v Australia*. Australia tried to argue that the removal of the parents would not have a detrimental impact upon the child as he would be free to go with them, or to visit them, a situation analogous to where children attend boarding school. The Committee disagreed and held that the removal of the parents would not be consistent with Australia's obligations under article 24 and in its remedy called on the State to appropriately consider the impact the removal order would have on the rights of the child. The Committee's view was based on the fact that the child in question had been born and spent his whole life in Australia, and even though he was described as 'multicultural' the Committee

108 *Huamán v Peru*, above n 11.

109 *Balaguer Santacana v Spain*, above n 25, para 9.2; *Tcholatch v Canada*, above n 26, para 8.11.

110 *Coronel et al v Colombia*, above n 59, para 9.7.

111 *F v Australia*, Communication 832/1998, UN Doc CCPR/C/72/D/832/1998 (2001), para 6.2.

112 *Jalloh v The Netherlands*, Communication 794/1998, UN Doc CCPR/C/74/D/794/1998 (2002), para 8.3.

felt that he would be unable to live in Indonesia with his parents if they were removed.[113] The dissent felt that the claim under article 24 was not substantiated on the basis that:[114]

> Many families the world over move from one country to another, even when their children are of school age and are happily integrated in school in one country. Are States parties required to take measures to protect children against such action by their parents? It seems to us that a vague value judgment that a child might be better off if some action were avoided does not provide sufficient grounds to substantiate a claim that a State party has failed to provide that child with the necessary measures of protection required under article 24.

While the Committee's reasoning in *Winata* is far from clear it is based on the belief that a 13/14-year-old child is not of an adaptable age and could not be expected to follow the parents to a foreign country.[115] At the same time a child of that age is not economically independent and could not live adequately without the parents. In this respect, the Committee demonstrated a willingness to be more interventionist in determining the obligations upon the State to protect family rights due to the particular circumstances involving the child. But this intervention will be much less where the child is able to lead a more independent and self-sufficient life.

Conclusions

The protection of family rights poses a particular problem for the Committee due to their emotive and often controversial nature. The discussion above shows that the Committee is easily susceptible to criticisms for doing too little or for going too far in its protection of family rights. Given the fact that each individual application will depend heavily upon the particular circumstances involved it is unrealistic to expect a generally coherent and consistent approach. The only consistent factor in the Committee's reasoning in this area is the desire to ensure the overall aims and objectives of the Covenant are met.

---

113 *Winata v Australia*, above n 36, para 7.3.

114 Ibid, dissenting opinion of Prafullachandra Bhagwati, Ahmed Khalil, David Kretzmer and Max Yalden, para 2.

115 Similar views have been expressed in *Byahuranga v Denmark*, above n 23, para 11.8; *Madafferi v Australia*, above n 50, para 9.8.

Chapter 9
Self-Determination

Richard Burchill

Self-determination has an extensive presence in international law and relations in the post-Second World War period appearing in the UN Charter, the 1960 Declaration on Decolonisation,[1] the 1970 Declaration on Principles of International law Concerning Friendly Relations[2] and as common article 1 in both UN Covenants. The right to self-determination has 'particular importance' for the protection of human rights 'because its realisation is an essential condition for the effective guarantee and observance of individual human rights and for the promotion and strengthening of those rights'.[3] The inclusion of self-determination in the Covenant was an important development moving self-determination from primarily a political principle to a justiciable right within a treaty regime. However, even though article 1 may be justiciable within the Covenant regime, the procedural requirements of the Optional Protocol have prevented any extensive discussion as to the meaning and scope of self-determination. This is unfortunate given the significant role it has in the Covenant and more widely in international law.

The three paragraphs of article 1 set out the different perspectives of self-determination. Paragraph 1 covers what is normally considered political self-determination where all peoples have the right to 'determine their political status and freely pursue their economic, social and cultural development'. Paragraph 2 concerns economic self-determination where a peoples may dispose of their natural wealth and resources for their own ends. Paragraph 3 establishes a solidarity position on self-determination as all State parties to the Covenant are to promote and respect the exercise of the right to self-determination.

The Committee has discussed issues concerning article 1 in the State reporting procedure, but by way of jurisprudence the Committee has said little. However, discussions relating to self-determination in article 1 are not wholly absent in the Committee's jurisprudence as it has been an important element of the Committee's treatment of other rights, in particular article 25 on participation rights and article 27 on minority rights.

---

1 GA Res 1514 (XV) (14 December 1960), GAOR 15th Sess, Supp 16, p 66.

2 GA Res 2625 (XXV) (24 October 1979), GAOR 25th Sess, Supp 28, p 121.

3 *General Comment 12: The Right to Self-Determination of Peoples (Art 1)*, UN Doc CCPR General Comment 12 (1984), para 1.

The Position of Self-Determination in the Covenant

During the drafting of the two UN Covenants common article 1 was purposely left vague for 'it was thought that any numeration of the components of the right of self-determination was likely to be incomplete. A statement of the right in an abstract form … was thought to be more preferable.'[4] The Committee has maintained this line through its General Comment 12 on article 1 which does not provide further specifics as to the meaning of the right, primarily repeating the language of the Covenant text. At the same time, in General Comment 12 the Committee clearly recognizes the importance of self-determination:

> The right of self-determination is of particular importance because its realization is an essential condition for the effective guarantee and observance of individual human rights and for the promotion and strengthening of those rights. It is for that reason that States set forth the right of self-determination in a provision of positive law in both Covenants and placed this provision as article 1 apart from and before all of the other rights in the two Covenants.[5]

The idea that article 1 is separate from all other rights in the Covenant has been confirmed in the Committee's views under the OP. At the same time the close relation self-determination has with the exercise of other rights has also been recognized.

The recognition of the importance of self-determination as a basis for all other rights has been due to the Committee's support for an interdependence approach when dealing with individual communications. As with all treaties, the rights in the Covenant can be read in two ways; through the distinction approach or the interdependence approach.[6] The former approach would view the rights in the Covenant as separate, exclusive in nature and to be dealt with accordingly. The latter approach involves viewing the individual provisions of the Covenant 'as being informed and enriched by every other provision' in the treaty.[7] Following the interdependence approach, article 1 is important as the basis for the exercise of all other rights and in particular it has an important role in article 25 rights to participation and article 27 minority rights. The rights contained in article 25 are described as being 'related to, but distinct from' article 1 as article 1 concerns the right of people to choose their own form of government and article 25 concerns

4 Marc Bossuyt, *Guide to the 'Travaux preparatoires' of the International Covenant on Civil and Political Rights* (Dordrecht: Nijhoff, 1987) p 34.

5 General Comment 12, above n 3, para 1.

6 See Martin Scheinin, 'The Right to Self-determination under the Covenant on Civil and Political Rights' in Pekka Aikio and Martin Scheinin (eds), *Operationalizing the Right of Indigenous Peoples to Self-Determination* (Turku/Abo: Institute for Human Rights, Abo Akademi University, 2000) 179, pp 181–6.

7 Ibid, p 181.

the ability of individuals to participate in the public affairs of government.[8] The HRC has held that the realization of article 1 depends upon the participation of all citizens in public life which in turn means that article 25 rights must be ensured and guaranteed.[9]

A close relationship also exists between articles 1 and 27 and the Committee has noted that there is a good deal of confusion in grouping the two together.[10] The main distinction for the Committee is that article 27 applies to individuals belonging to minorities and article 1 applies to the collective entity as a people. At the same time article 27 concerns the ability of individuals, as part of a minority group, to enjoy a particular culture, which includes a collective element.[11] The enjoyment of a particular culture by a collective may involve the use of territory and resources, something clearly related to the scope of article 1, paragraph 2. The Committee has recognized this in its General Comment on the Rights of Minorities:

> With regard to the exercise of the cultural rights protected under article 27, the Committee observes that culture manifests itself in many forms, including a particular way of life associated with the use of land resources, especially in the case of indigenous peoples. That right may include such traditional activities as fishing or hunting and the right to live in reserves protected by law. The enjoyment of those rights may require positive legal measures of protection and measures to ensure the effective participation of members of minority communities in decisions which affect them.[12]

The practical manifestation of a peoples pursuing their culture will often involve the disposal of natural wealth and resources, along with measures necessary for maintaining subsistence. The distinction between a group exercising their rights of self-determination and individuals, in community with other members of their group, pursuing particular culture-related rights is extremely nebulous.

---

8 *General Comment 25: The right to participate in public affairs, voting rights and the right of equal access to public service (Art 25)*, UN Doc CCPR/C/21/Rev.1/Add.7 (1996), para 2.

9 Report of the HRC, GAOR 45th Sess, Supp 40, *Comments on Cameroon*, p 102, para 4.

10 *General Comment 23: The rights of minorities (Art 27)*, UN Doc CCPR/C/21/Rev.1/Add.5 (1984), para 2.

11 General Comment 23, ibid, para 3.2.

12 General Comment 23, above n 10, para 7.

Procedural Limitations upon Article 1

As discussed in Chapter 2 the application procedures under the OP apply to individuals and as article 1 is a right of peoples it is not amenable to the OP procedures.[13] The Committee was first presented with an application alleging a violation of article 1 in *AD (Mikmaq Tribal Society) v Canada*. Canada's response to the application was that it was inadmissible since A.D. could not claim to be an individual victim in accordance with the OP. The Committee's main concern was whether or not A.D. was the legitimate authority for representing the Mikmaq people. The Committee found the application inadmissible, saying:[14]

> The Human Rights Committee observes that the author has not proven that he is authorized to act as a representative on behalf of the Mikmaq tribal society. In addition, the author has failed to advance any pertinent facts supporting his claim that he is personally a victim of a violation of any rights contained in the Covenant.

The Committee's views on admissibility in this early communication raised a number of questions. The author had not individually been a victim of a violation precluding any standing he may have had under the OP. However, the Committee's views left it open for claims concerning violations of article 1 to be brought if there was proper representation and the victim test was met. That is, the author as an individual, and in community with others who constitute a peoples, claims to be a victim of a violation of article 1 would appear to meet the criteria of article 1 of the OP. In *AD* Committee member Roger Errera felt the Committee failed to consider the question of admissibility properly. He explained that it was necessary to consider whether or not article 1 of the Covenant constituted one 'of the rights set forth in the Covenant' in accordance with the terms of article 1 of the OP; if article 1 of the Covenant does meet this criteria than it would be necessary to determine if individuals could claim a violation has occurred. He felt that these were 'fundamental' issues for dealing with article 1 of the Covenant and the Committee had failed to consider them.

The Committee was soon given the opportunity to address Errera's concerns. In *Lubicon Lake Band v Canada*, Canada explained:[15]

---

13 Even though the 'constant jurisprudence' of the Committee holds that article 1 is not justiciable under article of the OP and individuals cannot bring an application for a violation of article 1, this appears to run contrary to the views of some Committee members during the drafting of General Comment 12, see Dominic McGoldrick, *The Human Rights Committee: Its Role in the Development of the ICCPR* (Oxford: Clarendon Press, 1991) p 255.

14 *AD (Mikmaq Tribal Society) v Canada*, Communication 78/1980, UN Doc CCPR/C/22/D/78/1980 (1984), para 8.2.

15 *Lubicon Lake Band v Canada*, Communication 167/1984, UN Doc Supp 40 (A/45/40) at 1 (1990), paras 6.1 and 6.3.

> … communications under the Optional Protocol can only be made by individuals and must relate to the breach of a right conferred on individuals. The present communication, the State party argues, relates to a collective right and the author therefore lacks standing to bring a communication pursuant to articles 1 and 2 of the Optional Protocol.

In response the Committee provided a much clearer explanation as to the admissibility of applications involving article 1:[16]

> The Optional Protocol provides a procedure under which individuals can claim that their individual rights have been violated. These rights are set out in part III of the Covenant, articles 6 to 27, inclusive. There is, however, no objection to a group of individuals, who claim to be similarly affected, collectively to submit a communication about alleged breaches of their rights.

The Committee's designation of the rights in part III of the Covenant as being the only one amenable to the OP differs from the terms of article 1 of the OP, which states individuals may submit applications concerning violations of 'any of the rights set forth in the Covenant'. But as the Committee explained in *Kitok v Sweden* article 1 differs fundamentally from the rights in part III of the Covenant:[17]

> … the Committee observed that the author, an individual could not claim to be the victim of a violation of the right of self-determination enshrined in article 1 of the Covenant. Whereas the Optional Protocol provides a recourse procedure for individuals claiming that their rights have been violated, article 1 of the Covenant deals with rights conferred upon peoples, as such.

This has now become the Committee's 'constant jurisprudence' in dealing with allegations of a violation of article 1.[18]

The Committee's position on admissibility does not prevent the Committee from considering any claim where article 1 issues are at stake in connection with

16 Ibid, para 32.1.

17 *Kitok v Sweden*, Communication 197/1985, UN Doc CCPR/C/33/D/197/1985 (1988), para 6.3.

18 *RL et al v Canada*, Communication 358/1989, UN Doc CCPR/C/43/D/358/1989 (1990), para 6.2; *Jouni Länsman et al v Finland*, Communication 1023/2001, UN Doc CCPR/C/83/D/1023/2001 (2005), para 6.1; *Shota Ratiani v Georgia*, Communication 975/2001, UN Doc CCPR/C/84/D/975/2001 (2005), para 10.3, where the Committee refers to 'past jurisprudence' on article 1, stating the applicant's claims under article 1 were not justiciable under the OP, but did not refer to any past decisions.

any of the rights in articles 6 to 27. The Committee has set out its position in the following terms:[19]

> With regard to the issue of the authors' standing, the Committee reaffirms that the Covenant recognizes and protects in most resolute terms a people's right to self-determination as an essential condition for the effective guarantee of observance of individual human rights and for the promotion and strengthening of those rights. However, the Committee reiterates that the authors cannot claim under the Optional Protocol to be victims of a violation of the right of self-determination enshrined in article 1 of the Covenant.

The Committee's statement demonstrates the dilemma it faces under the OP in relation to article 1. If self-determination is such an important right it is difficult to reconcile its absence from a complaint procedure under an international human rights instrument in which it is explicitly included. By recognizing article 1 'as an essential condition' the Committee is able to justify its inclusion, when applicable, in its consideration of applications under the OP.

In *Apirana Mahuika et al v New Zealand* the Committee declared the application admissible with regard to article 1 in relation to article 27, explaining that only an investigation into the merits would determine the extent to which article 1 was applicable to the article 27 issues.[20] New Zealand responded:[21]

> … it would be most concerned if the Committee were to depart from the position which has been accepted by States parties to the Covenant and by the Committee itself that the Committee has no jurisdiction to consider claims regarding the rights contained in article 1. Those rights have long been recognised as collective rights. Therefore, they fall outside the Committee's mandate to consider complaints by individuals, and it is not within the ambit of the Optional Protocol procedures.

In response, the Committee referred to its previous jurisprudence about the inadmissibility of complaints under article 1, adding 'the provisions of article 1 may be relevant in the interpretation of other rights protected by the Covenant, in particular article 27'.[22] In this respect the Committee is utilizing the interdependence approach for in many situations the rights of minorities will be directly related to self-determination issues. The interdependence approach has also been utilized

19 *EP et al v Colombia*, Communication 318/1988, UN Doc CCPR/C/39/D/318/1988 (1990), para 8.2.

20 Also see *Diergaardt v Namibia*, Communication 760/1997, UN Doc CCPR/C/69/D/760/1997 (2000).

21 *Apirana Mahuika et al v New Zealand*, Communication 547/1993, UN Doc CCPR/C/70/D/547/1993 (2000), para 7.6.

22 Ibid, para 9.2.

in linking article 1 with article 25, as demonstrated in *Diergaardt v Namibia* and *Gillot et al v France*. In both applications the Committee held that participation in public affairs and the process of self-determination were closely related, making it necessary to consider article 1 alongside article 25.

If the Committee maintained a strict distinction approach under the OP then article 1 would never be considered purely on procedural grounds. However, through the interdependence approach the Committee is able to undertake considerations of article 1 in coming to its views in relation to other rights in the Covenant, especially articles 25 and 27. In this respect the Committee has worked within the limitations of the OP to ensure that article 1, containing the basis for the exercise of all other rights, is applicable in certain circumstances.

Considerations of Self-Determination

The Committee's tendency to the interdependence approach is evident in communications where article 1 was the primary issue put forth by the applicants; even though the Committee declared the application inadmissible in this regard, an extensive discussion of the merits relating to self-determination has taken place. As the Committee explained in *Apirana Mahuika et al v New Zealand*, only an examination of the merits will reveal the extent to which article 1 is applicable. In doing so the Committee's view on a number of aspects of self-determination has been revealed, primarily with regard to issues of participation of peoples in matters impacting upon their livelihood and with regard to cultural practices.

The Committee's first consideration of article 1 came in *AD (Mikmaq Tribal Society) v Canada* where the applicant claimed that the Canadian government never legally obtained sovereignty over the Mikmaq nation and subsequently had deprived the alleged victims of their means of subsistence by enacting and enforcing laws and policies that had a detrimental impact upon the Mikmaq society. In the application the authors stated that the objective of the complaint was to obtain recognition of the Mikmaq nation as a State and clearly stated the application had nothing to do with article 27, as it was a claim of a 'peoples' and not a minority group.[23] Obviously such an objective had no chance of succeeding before the Committee as the claim engaged issues much wider than the Covenant. As discussed above the Committee found the application inadmissible. The Mikmaq situation was put before the Committee again in *Marshall v Canada*. This time the basis of the application was the right to participate under article 25. The applicants claimed that their exclusion from constitutional conventions on aboriginal affairs was a violation of article 25 and a denial of self-determination. In response to the article 25 claims the Committee's view had significant relevance for the process of internal self-determination. The Committee explained: '[i]t is for

23 *AD (Mikmaq Tribal Society) v Canada*, above n 14, paras 2.2–3.

the legal and constitutional system of the State party to provide for the modalities of [participation].' Furthermore:[24]

> … the conduct of public affairs affects the interest of large segments of the population or even the population as a whole, while in other instances it affects more directly the interest of more specific groups of society. … the Covenant cannot be understood as meaning that any directly affected group, large or small, has the unconditional right to choose the modalities of participation in the conduct of public affairs.

The application failed on the article 25 claims and the Committee's statements appear to leave a significant amount of discretion to States for determining how peoples are able to engage in the practice of internal self-determination by being able to participate in matters particular to their situation.

The issue of participation of peoples was a concern in *Apirana Mahuika et al v New Zealand* concerning a settlement related to fishing rights of the Maori people. In this situation the State had left it up to the Maori groups to organize discussion and debate on the proposed settlement and also for determining the means by which approval or rejection of the final settlement were voiced. The final agreement received widespread approval from the Maori and involved a large commercial settlement that brought benefits to the Maori people as whole. The applicants, however, argued that not all of the sub tribes approved of the settlement and that in their case it deprived them of the right to exploit their own resources as allowed in article 1. The Committee rejected the claim and an important factor in its views was that New Zealand had engaged in a process of broad consultation of those directly concerned with the settlement and even though not all individuals of the minority group were satisfied the group as a whole would benefit.[25]

Participation was also central to the application of *Diergaardt v Namibia*, concerning the Rehoboth Baster Community who are descendants of indigenous Khoi and Afrikaans settlers living in Namibia since 1872. During this time, they have developed their own laws and procedures for the selection of leaders and for the rights and duties of their citizens. The basis for the application was that with the creation of Namibia the Rehoboth Baster community lost its previous semi-independent status that had been recognized in law and that regional administrative organization in Namibia split the community over two different regions preventing the effective participation in public life for the community as whole. The Committee held that the Rehoboth Baster community could not be considered as a minority group but also explained that article 25 does not protect collective participation rights, only individual rights to participation. Therefore, so long as all individuals had equal access to public participation then no violation

24 *Marshall v Canada*, Communication 205/1986, UN Doc CCPR/C/43/D/205/1986 (1991), paras 5.4–5.5.

25 *Apirana Mahuika et al v New Zealand*, above n 21, paras 9.6 and 9.8.

exists.[26] In a separate opinion Martin Scheinin provided an important contribution to the process of self-determination explaining:

> … there are situations where article 25 calls for special arrangements for rights of participation to be enjoyed by members of minorities and, in particular, indigenous peoples. When such a situation arises, it is not sufficient under article 25 to afford individual members of such communities the individual right to vote in general elections. Some forms of local, regional or cultural autonomy may be called for in order to comply with the requirement of effective rights of participation.

Despite this statement, he also felt that in this application there was no violation of article 25 giving the opinion that the Rehoboth Baster community was not an indigenous or wholly distinctive group. His views make clear that in certain circumstances special arrangements must be in place allowing a people to be able to engage in self-determination.[27] This view runs contrary to the Committee's position in *Marshall* were it was held that not all distinct groups have a right to participate in matters concerning their general situation.

Sheinin's comments about the need for special arrangements arose in the interesting situation presented in *Marie-Hélène Gillot et al v France*. Here the applicants had been excluded from participating in referenda in New Caledonia relating to its future status, as they had not met the necessary residency requirements as set out in the domestic law for the holding of the referenda. The object of the domestic legislation was to ensure that only those individuals who had direct and constant links with the territory would be allowed to participate. The applicants were able to participate in all other elections held in the territory but they argued that the agreements on the referenda where drawn up exclusively between two particular groups resident in the territory which had the purpose of excluding all others. France argued that the various restrictions were legitimate as the referenda concerned the process of self-determination for New Caledonia and therefore participation in the referenda may be limited to individuals who have a direct concern with the territory as determined by particular characteristics.[28] The Committee stated that any consideration of article 25 had to involve considerations of article 1, since the restrictions upon participation in the referenda was based on ensuring the effective process of self-determination. In this regard the Committee considered that it would not be unreasonable to limit participation in a local referendum which was

---

26 *Diergaardt v Namibia*, above n 20, para 10.8.

27 Support for recognizing particular rights for distinct groups comes from the Committee's recognition of the internal aspect of self-determination. In General Comment 12, above n 3, it calls on States parties to: 'describe the constitutional and political processes which in practice allow the exercise of [article 1]'.

28 *Marie-Hélène Gillot et al v France*, Communication 932/2000, UN Doc CCPR/C/75/D/932/2000 (2002), para 8.3.

inherently tied to the exercise of self-determination. The Committee agreed with the local court's views that the restrictions in this circumstance were necessary 'to ensure a sufficient definition of identity'.[29] The Committee went on to explain that even though the applicants were able to participate in other elections concerning New Caledonia, their exclusion from the self-determination referenda was within the acceptable bounds of proportionality considerations and reasonable within the terms of the Covenant.[30]

The other major link with article 1 is article 27 and the right of individuals belonging to a minority to enjoy their culture. The primary link with article 1 comes with situations where the cultural life of a minority depends upon their link with the land they live on and its resources, bringing paragraph 2 of article 1 into consideration as to whether or not they are able to dispose freely of their natural wealth and resources. This was the issue in *Lubicon Lake Band v Canada* where the Canadian Government had allowed for the expropriation of lands within the Band's territory for the benefit of private corporate interests. It was argued that the development was destroying the environment and undermining the Band's economic base, depriving its means to subsist. The Committee itself reformulated the application from purely an article 1 application to entail article 27 and found a violation of the latter article. The Committee did not provide any extensive explanation of the factors influencing its decision but clearly the inability of the Lubicon Lake Band to enjoy its resources as part of its cultural existence, and by association part of their self-determination, was an important factor.

The application of *Apirana Mahuika et al v New Zealand* concerned both articles 25 and 27 in relation to article 1. The authors claimed that the fisheries settlement between the Maori and New Zealand wrongly confiscated their fishing resources and denied them the right to pursue their economic, social and cultural development freely. The authors further explained that self-determination is only effective when people have access to and control over their resources. In its consideration of the application the Committee took into account the impact the settlement had on the ability of the whole group to dispose freely of their natural wealth and resources as an integral part of the cultural life of the Maori as a whole. The Committee considered the long-term sustainability of the resources directly linked to the cultural and economic existence of the Maori and felt this should override the particular desire of individuals of the group to exercise their rights over the natural resources to their own choosing.

Following the Committee's close examination of the connection between culture and the land in *Lubicon Lake Band* and *Apirana Mahuika* the application of *Diergaardt v Namibia* was bound to fail on this point. The applicants claimed that their cultural life was violated because of the expropriation of their lands where they had been herding cattle for over 100 years. The Committee explained:[31]

29 Ibid, para 13.16.

30 Ibid, paras 13.17–13.18.

31 *Diergaardt v Namibia*, above n 20, para 10.6.

> Although the link of the Rehoboth community to the lands in question dates back some 125 years, it is not the result of a relationship that would have given rise to a distinctive culture. Furthermore, although the Rehoboth community bears distinctive properties as to the historical forms of self-government, the authors have failed to demonstrate how these factors would be based on their way of raising cattle.

As explained above the Committee held that the Rehoboth Baster community did not constitute a minority group or a peoples, so any chance of their article 1 rights being considered failed.[32]

Conclusions

The Committee's treatment of article 1 under the OP has come under heavy criticism. It has been expressed that the Committee's jurisprudence has been 'brief and disappointing' and that it should 'issue more significant contributions to the law surrounding this most controversial of rights'.[33] The Committee has chosen to stick by its 'constant jurisprudence' excluding article 1 of the Covenant from the OP procedure on the basis that it only applies to collective entities and the OP is only available to individuals. In doing so, it is argued that the Committee overlooks 'the reality that individuals can suffer owing to a breach of a right to self-determination of a people of which they are a member'.[34] If we take the view that individuals, as members of particular peoples, can be susceptible to violations directed at the group as a whole, then the Committee should be able to examine substantive issues under article 1.[35] The distinction between collective rights and individuals' rights is not as clear cut as the Committee appears to treat it, and it should be possible for collective entities to enforce relevant rights under the Covenant through the OP.[36] Furthermore the Committee has consistently held that

---

32 Elizabeth Evatt and Cecilia Medina Quiroga provided a concurring opinion on this point stating that the application only concerned economic issues and did not raise issues of cultural protection as the only cultural aspect claimed by the applicants was the grazing of cattle and they could not: 'show that they enjoy a distinct culture which is intimately bound up with or dependent on the use of these particular lands'.

33 Sarah Joseph, Jenny Schultz and Melissa Castan, *The International Covenant on Civil and Political Rights: Cases, Materials and Commentary* (2nd edn, Oxford: Oxford University Press, 2004) p 153.

34 Robert McCorquodale, 'The Right to Self-Determination' in David Harris and Sarah Joseph (eds), *The International Covenant on Civil and Political Rights and United Kingdom Law* (Oxford: Clarendon Press, 1995) p 92, n 4.

35 In particular, Scheinin feels there is room for a more intensive interdependence approach with articles 1 and 25, above n 6, p 187.

36 Manfred Nowak, *UN Covenant on Civil and Political Rights* (2nd revised edn, Kehl, Germany: NP Engel, 2005) pp 14–15.

determining whether or not an entity is a peoples is beyond them. The opinions expressed in *Diergaardt v Namibia* demonstrate that the Committee can make this determination for here it was held that there was nothing particular about the Baster community and their use of the land – in short they are not a peoples with a particular culture.[37] The Committee is in a unique position in this regard, being able to define this central issue to self-determination, and if it is able to determine a group or community is not a people then it should be able to make a determination as to whether or not they are a peoples for the purpose of article 1. It has been suggested that the Committee should exert itself more in relation to its ability in this area in order to help avoid 'explosive self-determination claims arising'.[38]

The minimal treatment of article 1 through the OP does not mean it has been completely excluded from any enforcement procedures under the Covenant as it is an important element of the reporting procedure and is susceptible to the inter-State completing procedures under article 41.[39] The reluctance of States to provide substantial information concerning article 1 in the reporting procedures, the never used inter-State complaint procedure and reluctance of the Committee to raise article 1 issues must be viewed in the context within which self-determination is part of international law and relations. Even though self-determination is an essential right for the exercise of all other rights or even a norm possessing *jus cogens* status, it is also a site of extreme controversy as it is too commonly seen as a threat to the territorial integrity of States or an issue at the core of a State's sovereign existence. Under these circumstances the Committee has had to take a cautious approach to self-determination under the Covenant. The political realities on the ground will influence the extent to which the Committee will take a more or less rigorous approach in investigating issues of self-determination.[40]

The Committee's limited treatment of article 1 has helped to develop our understanding of self-determination. In particular the Committee has advanced the particular importance to be given to the importance of cultural links with how groups exercise rights over their land. Along with this the importance of economic sustainability and the process of consultation are important elements in the ongoing process of self-determination.[41] Despite the dynamics of self-determination it appears unlikely that the Committee will further address aspects of article 1 as

37 In this particular application the Committee was able to hold that the Rehoboth Baster Community was neither a minority nor a people and one has to ask whether or not the Committee was influenced by the heritage of the Rehoboth Baster community being a white race, and connected with the former apartheid regime of South Africa.

38 McGoldrick, above n 13, p 250.

39 See Scheinin, above n 6, p 180; and McGoldrick, above n 13, pp 249–54.

40 See Scheinin, above n 6, pp 187–92. Scheinin notes that when the political sensitivities of a self-determination issue are great then the Committee will be cautious, but if the self-determination issue is subject to domestic discussions or less politically sensitive then a more rigorous approach will occur. See also McGoldrick, above n 13, pp 256–8.

41 Scheinin, above n 6, pp 193–9; and McCorquodale, above n 34, pp 118–19.

both applicants and the Committee have demonstrated a tendency to concentrate on related rights that are more amenable to the OP procedures than attempting to forward an article 1 claim in an individual communication.[42]

42 In the time that has passed since the first edition of this book there is a noticeable absence of article 1 of the Covenant in applications to the Committee. Instead attention is focused on claims concerning individuals involving democratic participation or minority rights.

Chapter 10
Minority Rights

Richard Burchill

Article 27 provides protection for individuals belonging to ethnic, religious or linguistic minorities. The article protects the right of individuals belonging to one of these designated groups to enjoy their own culture, profess and practice their own religion and use their own language. As such article 27 is included in Part 2 of the Covenant making it justiciable under the OP even though, as will be seen below, there exists a strong collective element to both the nature and realization of the protection provided by article 27. The inclusion of article 27 does not mean this is the only, or the primary means for rights protection for individuals belonging to minorities. The Committee has explained the scope of article 27 is 'distinct from, and additional to, all the other rights which, as individuals in common with everyone else, they are already entitled to enjoy under the Covenant'.[1]

The Nature of Article 27 Obligations

Article 27 is directed at 'ensuring the survival and continued development of the cultural, religious and social identity of the minorities concerned' based on the belief that ensuring that full range of rights applicable to those belonging to minorities will work to enrich society as a whole.[2] While this is a laudable aim, minority protection is a very contentious area of international law and relations, with the result that article 27 was 'formulated in an extremely cautious, vague, manner'.[3] In the General Comment on article 27 the Committee explains that States sometimes confuse their obligations under that article with their obligations under articles 2(1) and 26. Article 2(1) obliges States to ensure the enjoyment of the rights in the Covenant and article 26 guarantees the rights in the Covenant without discrimination and ensures equality before the law along with equal protection from the law. States believe that by ensuring equality among all individuals there

1 *General Comment 23: The rights of minorities (Art 27)*, UN Doc CCPR/C/21/Rev.1/Add.5 (1994), para 1.

2 Ibid, para 9.

3 Manfred Nowak, *UN Covenant on Civil and Political Rights* (2nd revised edn, Kehl, Germany: NP Engel, 2005) p 640.

is no need for any further action with regard to article 27. As a response the Committee explains:[4]

> The Covenant also distinguishes the rights protected under article 27 from the guarantees under articles 2.1 and 26. The entitlement, under article 2.1, to enjoy the rights under the Covenant without discrimination applies to all individuals within the territory or under the jurisdiction of the State whether or not those persons belong to a minority. In addition, there is a distinct right provided under article 26 for equality before the law, equal protection of the law, and non-discrimination in respect of rights granted and obligations imposed by the States. It governs the exercise of all rights, whether protected under the Covenant or not, which the State party confers by law on individuals within its territory or under its jurisdiction, irrespective of whether they belong to the minorities specified in article 27 or not.

The distinct place for article 27 is important for the Committee also makes the point that 'States parties who claim that they do not discriminate on grounds of ethnicity, language or religion, wrongly contend, on that basis alone, that they have no minorities'.[5]

A significant issue concerning the obligations under article 27 and their consideration under the OP relates to a reservation lodged by France. Article 2 of the French Constitution reads:

> France is a Republic, indivisible, secular, democratic and social. It shall ensure the equality of all citizens before the law, without distinction of origin, race or religion. It shall respect all beliefs.

On the basis of this provision France has declared 'that article 27 is not applicable so far as the Republic is concerned'.[6] A number of applications concerning article 27 have been brought to the Committee but have been declared to be inadmissible due to the position set out by France.[7] However, it has been argued that France's

---

4 General Comment 23, above n 1, para 4.

5 Ibid.

6 Text of reservation provided in *Multilateral Treaties Deposited with the Secretary-General*, UN Doc ST/LEG/SER.C/19, vol 1, p 177. Germany lodged a response to this reservation stating that due to the importance of article 27 it understands the reservation to mean that article 27 is fully protected in French law, ibid, at p 213, n 15.

7 *TK v France*, Communication 220/1987, UN Doc CCPR/C/37/D/220/1987 (1989); *HK v France*, Communication 222/1987, UN Doc CCPR/C/37/D/222/1987 (1989); *SG v France*, Communication 347/1988, UN Doc CCPR/C/43/D/347/1988 (1991); *RLM v France*, Communication 363/1989, UN Doc CCPR/C/44/D/363/1989 (1992); *CLD v France*, Communication 439/1990, UN Doc CCPR/C/43/D/439/1990 (1991); *Hopu and Bessert v France*, Communication 549/1993, UN Doc CCPR/C/60/D/549/1993/Rev.1 (1997).

statement on the applicability of article 27 is only a declaration of understanding and not a full-fledged reservation, meaning the Committee can examine the merits of article 27 applications. The Committee has held that it does not matter whether the statement by France is called a reservation or declaration as it is[8]

> … the effect the statement purports to have that determines its nature. If the statement displays a clear intent on the part of the State party to exclude or modify the legal effect of a specific provision of a treaty, it must be regarded as a binding reservation, even if the statement is phrased as a declaration.

Under the reporting procedures the Committee has expressed disagreement with France's position on article 27.[9] Also, Rosalyn Higgins, when a member of the Committee, expressed a significant opinion as to the full impact of France's position,[10] explaining that France's statement means that, in the opinion of the French government, no minorities exist in France, hence there is no need for article 27. She pointed out the Committee has not agreed with this sort of position in relation to France and other States and that even though a State is committed to full equality this does not mean there is no need for article 27. Therefore since France's position does not accord with the position of the Committee on the meaning and scope of article 27, the statement cannot act as a reservation. In *Hopu and Bessert v France* five individual members of the Committee challenged France's reservation arguing that it only applies to the territory of metropolitan France and is not 'of relevance in relation to overseas territories under French sovereignty'.[11] They explained that article 74 of the French Constitution deals with special legislative measures for overseas territories due to the geographic, social and economic particularities of these territories. As a distinction is made in the constitution as to the applicability of legislation then it follows that distinctions can be made as to the reach of the Covenant. France's reservation to article 27 is clearly controversial due to its exclusive nature in eliminating completely the application of article 27 under the OP and the fact that it clearly runs contrary to the object and purpose of the Covenant's protection of minority rights. However, the Committee has accepted this position affirming the legitimacy of the reservation for the purposes of the OP.

The extent of article 27 obligations goes beyond citizens or permanent residents of a State extending to all individuals belonging to a minority group in a particular State party. The Committee explains that article 2(1) requires States

8 See *TK v France*, ibid, para 8.6.

9 Human Rights Committee, *Concluding comments on France*, UN Doc CCPR/C/79/Add.80 (1997).

10 *TK v France*, above n 7 and *HK v France*, above n 7, individual opinion of Rosalyn Higgins.

11 *Hopu and Bessert v France*, above n 7, individual opinions of Committee members Elizabeth Evatt, Cecilia Quiroga, Fausto Pocar, Martin Scheinin and Maxwell Yalden.

to ensure the enjoyment of rights in the Covenant to all *individuals* in its territory and this has ramifications for article 27. If a minority group is present in a State and an individual belonging to that group is present in the territory, even if they are migrant workers or visitors, they can expect the full protection of article 27.[12]

Article 27 does not create more rights for individuals belonging to minorities; instead the issue is more of implementation and effective protection which often situates article 27 in a close relation with other rights in the Covenant. The Committee explained in *Lovelace v Canada* that '[a]rticle 27 must be construed and applied in the light of the other provisions [of the Covenant]'.[13] It is important to note that the exercise of the rights in article 27 cannot be inconsistent with the rest of the Covenant, so minority rights will not always trump other considerations.[14]

The protection afforded to minorities under article 27 only applies to existing situations having a direct impact upon the individuals of a minority group. In *O. Sara et al v Finland* the applicants contended that logging activity within a designated wilderness area impacted upon their right to enjoy their culture and also contended that plans by the State for future logging outside of the wilderness area was a threat to their culture. The Committee distinguished between the two areas and declared any claims relating to logging in the future was inadmissible.[15] In *Ilmari Länsman et al v Finland* the Committee gave a clear warning that the State must consider how future economic activities impact upon the minority group's ability to enjoy its culture and certain actions may be a violation if actually carried out.[16] But the extent to which the State needs to consider the impact of future actions remains unclear following the Committee's conclusions in *Jouni and Eino Länsman et al v Finland* where it was contended that the State had engaged in the activities the Committee cautioned against in *Ilmari Länsman et al v Finland*. The Committee explained:

> In weighing the effects of logging, or indeed any other measures taken by a State party which has an impact on a minority's culture, the Committee notes that the infringement of a minority's right to enjoy their own culture, as provided for in article 27, may result from the combined effects of a series of actions or measures taken by a State party over a period of time and in more than one area of the State occupied by that minority. Thus, the Committee must consider the overall effects of such measures on the ability of the minority concerned to continue to enjoy their culture. In the present case, and taking into account the

12 General Comment 23, above n 1, para 5.2.

13 *Lovelace v Canada*, Communication 24/1977, UN Doc CCPR/C/13/D/24/1977 (1981), para 16.

14 General Comment 23, above n 1, para 8.

15 *Sara et al v Finland*, Communication 431/1990, UN Doc CCPR/C/50/D/431/1990 (1994), para 5.3.

16 *Ilmari Länsman et al v Finland*, Communication 511/1992, UN Doc CCPR/C/52/D/511/1992 (1994), para 9.8.

> specific elements brought to its attention, it must consider the effects of these measures not at one particular point in time – either immediately before or after the measures are carried out – but the effects of past, present and planned future logging on the authors' ability to enjoy their culture in community with other members of their group.[17]

The Committee concluded that the effect of the logging carried out was not 'shown to be serious enough as to amount to a denial of the authors' right to enjoy their own culture in community with other members of their group under article 27 of the Covenant'.[18]

Individuals and Collectives

Article 27 addresses persons belonging to minorities and these persons shall not be denied the exercise of rights, either individually or in community with others, related to their minority status. The Committee recognizes that 'the right to enjoy one's own culture in community with the other members of the group cannot be determined in abstract but has to be placed in context',[19] which requires any consideration of article 27 to include both individual and collective interests. As an individual belonging to a minority will only enjoy a particular minority's culture, language or religion in community with other members of the minority, the collective aspects of a minority situation have to be taken into consideration. A further indicator of the collective nature of article 27 can be seen in how the applications to the Committee are presented. In *Lubicon Lake Band v Canada* the application was brought by the leader of the Band claiming violations of his rights and the rights of all other members of the Band. The Committee held the application admissible and considered it on the merits with regard to article 27. In considering the merits the Committee was required to look at the ability of the group as a whole to enjoy their culture. Of course it is possible to view the Committee's consideration as an assessment of the impact the alleged violations had upon the applicant as well as upon each and every individual of the Band. More realistically it was clear the Committee assessed the ability of the Band, as a group, to enjoy the rights protected by the Covenant.

In *Howard v Canada* the State party disputed the application at the admissibility stage on the basis that it was a collective complaint not an individual application. The State's argument was that the issues raised in the application applied to all members of the first nations groups in the State making it a collective complaint. The Committee rejected the State's argument on the basis that the application

---

17 *Jouni and Eino Länsman et al v Finland*, Communication 1023/2001, UN Doc CCPR/C/83/D/1023/2001 (2005), para 102.

18 Ibid, para 10.3.

19 *Kitok v Sweden*, Communication 197/1985, UN Doc CCPR/C/33/D/197/1985 (1988), para 9.3; and *Ilmari Länsman et al v Finland*, above n 16, para 9.3.

raised issues concerning the applicant's 'ability to exercise, individually and in community with other members of his aboriginal community, his aboriginal fishing rights which are an integral part of his culture'.[20] The Committee maintained a focus on the individual even though it was well aware that the implications of any decision would impact the wider collective group.

The Committee has explained that even though the rights in article 27 are individual rights, they do depend on the ability of the minority group as a whole being able to maintain its culture, language or religion.[21] This has a number of ramifications as the Committee must take into consideration a variety of factors when determining compliance with article 27 obligations. In *Lovelace v Canada* the Committee recognized that the domestic legislation in question did have merits with regard to protecting indigenous groups as a whole. However, the Committee explained that such efforts must have a reasonable and objective justification that aims to ensure the continued viability and welfare for the whole minority community. In *Lovelace* the substantial negative impact the domestic law had upon the individual could not be justified as a necessary measure for the viability of the group as a whole.[22] In *Kitok v Sweden* the applicant was, as a result of domestic legislation, denied certain rights relating to the use of the land that were connected with being part of the Sami community. Membership into the Sami community with its attendant rights was limited by law in order to preserve the natural resources and ensure economic viability for the whole group. The Committee felt in the circumstances that the applicant's rights were not substantially impacted and the legislation was reasonably justified for protection of the wider Sami community. A similar set of circumstances existed in *Apirana Mahuika et al v New Zealand* where the authors claimed that the fisheries settlement between New Zealand and the Maori as a whole was contrary to their particular rights under article 27. The Committee, relying on its decision in *Kitok*, expressed concern that the settlement had created divisions within the minority group but decided that the agreement met the requirements of article 27 as it benefited the substantial majority of the minority group.[23]

The protection of minority rights must also take into account society as a whole. The disputed fisheries settlement in *Apirana Mahuika et al v New Zealand* was also placed in the context of the economic consequences it had for all of New Zealand. The application of *Gillot et al v France* did not invoke article 27 but it concerned individuals living in New Caledonia who argued that their exclusion from a referendum concerning the island's status violated their rights under the Covenant. The individual applicants were in a minority as they were not born

20 *Howard v Canada*, Communication 879/1999, UN Doc CCPR/C/84/D/879/1999 (2005), para 8.6.

21 General Comment 23, above n 1, para 6.2.

22 *Lovelace v Canada*, above n 13, para 17.

23 *Apirana Mahuika et al v New Zealand*, Communication 547/1993, UN Doc CCPR/C/70/D/547/1993 (2000), para 9.8.

in New Caledonia and had not lived in the territory for a significant period of time. France argued, and the Committee agreed, that the referendum concerned the process of New Caledonia's self-determination and only those individuals with a substantial connection to the territory should be allowed to vote, even if it meant marginalizing a particular minority. The Committee considered it more important for the long-term residents of New Caledonia, who were a minority overall in relation to the population of France, to be entitled to special means of protection and that minorities in New Caledonia could not make substantial claims for the protection of their particular rights.[24]

Positive and Negative Obligations

Article 27 is couched in purely negative terms – individuals 'shall not be denied' – but this does not mean that the extent of obligations under article 27 simply suggest non-interference by the State. Article 27 is there to ensure individuals are fully able to enjoy the rights protected and to ensure the ongoing viability of the minority group which may require positive State action. The Committee explains:[25]

> Although the rights protected under article 27 are individual rights, they depend in turn on the ability of the minority group to maintain its culture, language or religion. Accordingly, positive measures by States may also be necessary to protect the identity of a minority and the rights of its members to enjoy and develop their culture and language and to practise their religion, in community with the other members of the group. In this connection, it has to be observed that such positive measures must respect the provisions of articles 2.1 and 26 of the Covenant both as regards the treatment between different minorities and the treatment between the persons belonging to them and the remaining part of the population. However, as long as those measures are aimed at correcting conditions which prevent or impair the enjoyment of the rights guaranteed under article 27, they may constitute a legitimate differentiation under the Covenant, provided that they are based on reasonable and objective criteria.

The positive obligations upon States in ensuring article 27 rights are not denied extends to ensuring private parties do not hinder or prevent the enjoyment of rights related to minority culture, religion or language.[26] In *Lubicon Lake Band v Canada* the government had granted exploitation rights to private companies making the government responsible for the negative economic impact upon the minority group. Significantly the positive obligation upon States even extends to disputes

24 *Gillot et al v France*, Communication 932/2000, UN Doc CCPR/C/75/D/932/2000 (2002), paras 13.7–13.8.

25 General comment 23, above n 1, para 6.2.

26 Ibid, para 6.1.

within the minority groups, as demonstrated in *Kitok v Sweden*. The government of Sweden explained that the dispute in question was between Kitok and the Sami community, but the Committee pointed out that even though the direct dispute was between the individual and the wider group, the basis for the dispute could be found in domestic legislation for which the State party is responsible.

The positive obligations upon States under article 27 include whatever is necessary to address the 'practical burdens applicable to minority groups' which impede the exercise of their rights.[27] At the same time the Committee has not accepted claims from applicants requiring States parties to take positive actions where it was held that the rights in question could still be exercised, albeit in an abbreviated form. In *Howard v Canada* the applicant argued the State party had an obligation to provide positive measures allowing him to exercise his aboriginal fishing rights. The fishing rights of the first nations groups had been limited by a prior treaty and the author was able to exercise his aboriginal rights on specified reserve lands without any fishing permit. Furthermore he was able to obtain a fishing permit allowing him to fish on other parts of the territory outside the reserve lands. The author argued that the circumstances felt short of the State's positive obligations under the Covenant as he asserted he should be able to fish on all traditional aboriginal lands as a matter of right; fishing under a permit was merely a privilege in the view of the applicant as it failed to take into account the concepts of aboriginal territory'.[28]

The Committee explained that it was necessary to determine if the regulation of fishing deprived the author of his ability to exercise, either individually or in community with others, his aboriginal fishing rights which were protected under article 27. In making assessments of this nature the Committee is of the view that various minority activities may be regulated by the State so long as they do not amount to a *de facto* denial of the right in question.[29] The Committee noted in this application that the applicant was able to engage in a wide range of fishing activities and therefore the need to fish under a permit in certain circumstances was not a denial of his rights under article 27.[30]

---

27 Sarah Joseph, Jenny Schultz and Melissa Castan, *The International Covenant on Civil and Political Rights: Cases, Materials and Commentary* (2nd edn, Oxford: Oxford University Press, 2004), p 792. In *Waldman v Canada*, Communication 694/1996, UN Doc CCPR/C/67/D/694/1996 (1999) the government argued 'The article only protects against State actions of a negative character: individuals "shall not be denied the right" … Although under article 27 a State party may be required to take certain positive actions, in the light of the intention of the drafters positive actions should be required only in rare circumstances': para 4.6.1.

28 *Howard v Canada*, above n 20, para 10.9.

29 *Ilmari Länsman et al v Finland*, above n 16, para, 9.4; *Jouni Länsman et al v Finland*, Communication 671/1995, UN Doc CCPR/C/58/D/671/1995 (1996), para 10.3.

30 *Howard v Canada*, above n 20, para 12.7. Also see *Kitok v Sweden*, above n 19, para 9.8.

Defining and Identifying a Minority

Nowhere does the Covenant provide a definition for what constitutes a minority group and this is in line with other international instruments dealing with the protection of rights for minorities. There are various proposals as to how to define a minority with the easiest and most influential being a numerical determination. Numerical determinations alone are not always adequate and further factors are to be considered, such as, the position of the group in the wider society, the existence of distinct ethnic, religious or linguistic characteristics, a sense of solidarity among its members, and some indication of relative stability of the group in the territory.[31] These factors do not create a specific test and some may be more relevant than others depending upon the particular circumstances involved. Minorities, for the purposes of article 27, differs from the term peoples used in article 1, even though the two can overlap in particular circumstances as a minority group may constitute a people, but not all peoples necessarily constitute a minority group for the purposes of article 27.[32]

The Committee has not accepted that States alone may make authoritative determinations as to whether or not a minority group exists and the Committee has also rejected the ability of minority groups themselves to make conclusive determinations as to membership.[33] However, France's reservation to article 27, which the Committee has respected, states that minorities do not exist in France. The failure of the Committee to consider article 27 claims concerning France demonstrates that a State can make conclusive determinations as to the existence of minority groups.[34]

In *Lovelace v Canada*, the applicant, Sandra Lovelace, had married a non-Indian and under the domestic law at the time this meant that she lost her status as an Indian. This loss of status had serious ramifications as she was no longer able to reside on the reservation, no longer had access to various support programmes and, perhaps most important, she experienced 'the loss of the cultural benefits of living in an Indian community, the emotional ties to home, family, friends and

---

31 Nowak, above n 3, p 643–5.

32 The distinction between a minority and a people can be a question of the group's aims and objectives as article 1 provides for the right to self-determination for a people, which is often conceived of as statehood or forms of self-government. Minority protection in article 27 may also include considerations of self-government but not to the same level as article 1 self-determination may provide for, see *AD (Mikmaq Tribal Society) v Canada* Communication 78/1980, UN Doc CCPR/C/22/D/78/1980 (1984) where the applicant rejected 'categorically' the application of article 27.

33 See *Lovelace v Canada*, above n 13; *Kitok v Sweden*, above n 19.

34 The legal argument of France's reservation would be that it prevents the application of article 27 and does not take any position as to the existence of minority groups, but this overlooks the reality of the situation and how the Committee has dealt with it under the OP.

neighbours, and the loss of identity'.[35] The Committee found in favour of the applicant on the basis that even though the domestic law stated she was no longer part of the minority group, the applicant still believed herself to be an Indian and wished to continue with that culture. The Committee stated that 'persons who are born and brought up on a reserve, who have kept ties with their community and wish to maintain these ties must normally be considered as belonging to that minority within the meaning of the Covenant'.[36]

The dispute in *Kitok v Sweden* involved domestic legislation which established the terms of membership for belonging to a Sami community. The Sami community itself was involved in determining who was a member of the community. Kitok, who was of Sami origin, had maintained close links with the Sami community and still engaged in reindeer husbandry, was denied membership to the community and the rights that came with it. The reason for his rejection was due to his engaging in other economic activities which, according to the domestic legislation, prevented him from full membership to the community. The Committee expressed concerns over the legislation and its implementation for it ignored 'objective ethnic criteria in determining membership of a minority'.[37]

Whether or not an individual belongs to a minority will depend upon the composition of the minority group and involve a combination of objective and subjective criteria in relation to the individual involved. Religious minorities are fairly easy to determine as individuals have either chosen to belong or not and belonging will be manifested by participation in religious activities. Linguistic minorities will depend on whether or not the individual truly speaks the language as part of their existence and primarily in private relations. Ethnic minorities can depend on objective characteristics but there will also be subjective considerations by the individual.[38] Determining the existence of a minority group does not depend solely upon the citizens of a State, as immigrants, visitors, aliens, non-nationals and so on may be included. This does not mean that a large group of individuals temporarily existing in a State can claim minority status with full protection of article 27. There is the necessity of some degree of stability in the minority group as well as some form of historical development in the State in question as a distinctive group with some sense of solidarity among the individual members.[39]

When determining the existence of a minority for the purposes of the Covenant it is the entire State territory that will be looked at in assessing the situation. If a group of individuals constitute a minority in a sub-State unit but are part of the

35 *Lovelace v Canada*, above n 13, para 9.9.

36 Ibid, para 14.

37 *Kitok v Sweden*, above n 19, para 9.6.

38 Nowak, above n 3, p 653.

39 Nowak, above n 3, pp 646–8. In *Bernard Ominayak et al (Lubicon Lake Band) v Canada*, Communication 167/1984, UN Doc CCPR/C38/D/167/1984 (1990) the Committee's facts point out the existence of the Band and its activities 'since time immemorial'.

State's majority group, then article 27 will not apply. In *Ballantyne et al v Canada* the applicants were claiming a violation of their right to use English, a minority language in the province of Quebec, but the majority in Canada as a whole, in certain circumstances. The Committee decided:[40]

> … the minorities referred to in article 27 are minorities within such a State, and not minorities within any province. A group may constitute a majority in a province but still be a minority in a State and thus be entitled to the benefits of article 27. English speaking citizens of Canada cannot be considered a linguistic minority. The authors therefore have no claim under article 27 of the Covenant.

The majority's approach on this point was considered too narrow a view by some members of the Committee which may result in situations where:[41]

> … a State party would have no obligation under the Covenant to ensure that a minority in an autonomous province had the protection of article 27 where it was not clear that the group in question was a minority in the State considered as a whole entity.

Indigenous Groups

Indigenous groups are an interesting area as most are minorities in the State where they live and at the same time constitute a people as well. Nowak explains that during the drafting of article 27 it was felt that indigenous groups should be excluded from the idea of minority on the basis that 'the cultures of such peoples were at such a primitive level that they were not in need of specific protection'.[42] Luckily this has not been the practice under the Covenant and the majority of applications based on article 27 have come from indigenous groups demonstrating the clear applicability of the provision to their circumstances. The Committee has given great consideration to the details involved with applications concerning indigenous groups and the final views reflect the importance given to ensuring that both individuals and the group as whole are able to maintain their chosen existence and be able to co-exist with the rest of the population. General Comment 23 makes specific mention to indigenous groups in relation to the use of territory and culture[43] but does not highlight any particular distinction between indigenous groups and other categories of minorities (such as national, ethnic, religious, linguistic) with regard to approaches to the protection of rights relevant

---

40 *Ballantyne et al v Canada*, Communications 359/1989 and 385/1989, UN Doc CCPR/C/47/D/385/1989 (1993), para 11.2.

41 Individual opinion of Elizabeth Evatt, co-signed by Nisuke Ando, Marco Tulio, Bruni Celli and Vojin Dimitrijevic.

42 Nowak, above n 3, pp 650–52.

43 General Comment 23, above n 1, paras 3.2 and 7.

or applicable to the particular groups. Often the nature of the claim involving individuals from indigenous groups differs substantially from claims from individuals from minority groups, in terms of both the articulation of the rights involved and the potential remedies and strategies available for upholding and protecting the rights in question.[44] However, the Committee does not appear to make any strict distinctions between indigenous and minority when dealing with applications under article 27.[45]

Areas of Substantive Protection

Culture

The enjoyment of cultural life is given a broad understanding encompassing a range of activities, such as customs, morals, traditions, rituals, housing, diet, the creation of art objects, the development of music, the creation of cultural organizations, publication of literature and education.[46] There does not appear to be any need to designate any specific practice as 'culture' in order to invoke article 27 as a general claim of a denial of cultural life can be made. In *Lovelace v Canada*, the domestic law which defined Indian status prevented the applicant from being a full-fledged member of the tribe. This meant that Lovelace was not allowed to live on the reserve of her tribe resulting in a general denial 'of the cultural benefits of living in an Indian community, the emotional ties to home, family, friends and neighbours, and the loss of identity'.[47] The Committee held that a similar possibility to enjoy her culture as an Indian did not exist outside the reserve, so the domestic law preventing her from living on the reserve ran contrary to the protection afforded by article 27. The Committee appeared to place significant weight on the fact that the applicant had divorced her non-Indian husband and therefore wanted to *return* to her culture. A similar set of facts existed in *LSN v Canada* but the applicant was still married to a non-Indian and was claiming the right to live on the reservation and, with reference to the Committee's views in *Lovelace*, being able to enjoy her culture fully. The application was withdrawn in light of Canada's response to the Committee's views in *Lovelace* but it would have been interesting to see how the Committee dealt with this important difference and how the link between the individual and a particular culture would have been conceptualized

44 For a full discussion of this point and UN practice see Will Kymlicka, 'The Internationalization of Minority Rights' (2007) 6 *International Journal of Constitutional Law* 1–32.

45 See for example *Jouni and Eino Länsman et al v Finland*, above n 17, where the Sami are categorized as a 'minority group', but are also considered to be an indigenous peoples: paras 7.2 and 10.1.

46 Nowak, above n 3, p 658.

47 *Lovelace v Canada*, above n 13, para 13.1.

in the circumstances. In *Howard v Canada* the applicant claimed that his inability to fish on lands outside the reserve was a denial of his cultural practice. But the Committee held that because the applicant was able to fish as part of his cultural practices both within the reserve as a matter of right and outside the reserve lands by obtaining a fishing permit, he was still able to exercise his cultural rights to a sufficient degree.[48]

The idea of culture is not static or frozen in time and the extent to which the enjoyment of culture is protected under article 27 will depend upon the circumstances particular to the individual making an application and the nature of the group. In *O. Sara et al v Finland* the applicants claimed that their particular practices of reindeer husbandry differed from how husbandry practices had developed amongst other Sami. The government argued that the domestic legislation in question had the purpose of protecting traditional cultural practices but in a way which accounts for recent developments in the cultural practice and the economic position of the minority group. The application was declared inadmissible but the facts presented by the Committee did distinguish between different forms of cultural practice.[49] A similar issue existed in *Apirana Mahuika et al v New Zealand* where the Maori as a whole negotiated a fisheries settlement but the individual applicants argued it was contrary to their traditional fishing practices. The Committee rejected their claims in this regard on the basis that Maori cultural practices overall were adequately protected. In *Ilmari Länsman et al v Finland,* another application involving different practices of reindeer husbandry, the Committee explained:[50]

> … article 27 does not only protect *traditional* means of livelihood of national minorities, as indicated in the State party's submission. Therefore, that the authors may have adapted their methods of reindeer herding over the years and practice it with the help of modern technology does not prevent them from invoking article 27 of the Covenant.

The Committee has not only taken a broad definition of culture but in *Hopu and Bessert v France* the Committee undertook a rather creative approach to the protection of culture through a strong interdependence approach between culture and other rights in the Covenant. Here the applicants were native Polynesians in Tahiti who argued that the decision to build a hotel complex upon an area of land containing an ancient burial site was a violation of articles 17 and 23 on the protection of family rights, as well as a violation of article 27. Consideration of the application by the Committee was heavily influenced by France's reservation concerning article 27 which prevented the Committee from entertaining any complaints under that article. The Committee agreed with the applicants that 'the construction of the hotel complex on the contested site would destroy their

48 *Howard v Canada,* above n 20, paras 12.7–12.8.

49 *Sara et al v Finland,* above n 15, para 7.4.

50 *Ilmari Länsman et al v Finland,* above n 16, para 9.3 (emphasis in original).

ancestral burial grounds, which represent an important place in their history, culture and life' on the basis that 'cultural traditions should be taken into account when defining the term "family" in a specific situation'.[51] The facts of the application and the Committee's final views clearly dealt with those cultural issues involving the applicants that concerned the place of the extended family in their cultural life. A dissenting view felt that the Committee had gone too far in its understanding of family life. It was felt that even in a situation concerning the cultural beliefs of a minority the idea of family cannot 'include all members of one's ethnic or cultural group. Nor does it necessarily include all one's ancestors, going back to time immemorial.'[52] The Committee was obviously placed in a difficult situation: the application clearly involved cultural protection for minorities, but the Committee was barred from considering this directly due to the procedural constraints presented by France's position on article 27. The Committee's views on the application are significant for demonstrating the broad understanding given to culture, even if the Committee can be criticized for extending the understanding of what constitutes family life under the Covenant to a potentially impractical degree.

Not all matters central to the cultural beliefs of a minority group will be protected by article 27. The application of *X v Australia* involved custody and property disputes between an Aboriginal individual and his wife who was of European descent.[53] The applicant argued that there existed strong cultural differences in the understanding of family life between Aboriginals and those of European descent and that the domestic courts did not take these into account. The Committee did not entertain these arguments and the application was declared inadmissible. In *José Vincent et al v Colombia* members of an indigenous community disappeared and the application claimed the authorities did not properly investigate the matter due to the fact that the individuals involved were from an indigenous community. The Committee felt that these claims were not substantiated as it was not demonstrated how the State had violated the cultural rights of the applicants.[54]

Economic Resources

The Committee has faced a number of applications where there is a direct link between the enjoyment of culture and the economic exploitation of natural resources. General Comment 23 recognizes this link, explaining:[55]

51 *Hopu and Bessert v France*, above n 7, para 10.3.

52 Individual opinion of David Kretzmer and Thomas Buergenthal, co-signed by Nisuke Ando and Lord Colville, para 4.

53 *X v Australia*, Communication 557/1993, UN Doc CCPR/C/57/D/557/1993 (1996).

54 *José Vincent et al v Colombia*, Communication 612/1995, UN Doc CCPR/C/60/D/612/1995 (1997), para 5.3.

55 General Comment 23, above n 1, para 7.

> With regard to the exercise of the cultural rights protected under article 27, the Committee observes that culture manifests itself in many forms, including a particular way of life associated with the use of land resources, especially in the case of indigenous peoples. That right may include such traditional activities as fishing or hunting and the right to live in reserves protected by law.

This was the Committee's position in *Lubicon Lake Band v Canada* stating article 27 includes 'the right of persons, in community with others, to engage in economic and social activities which are part of the culture of the community to which they belong'.[56] However, General Comment 23 also makes clear that the enjoyment of rights under article 27 'does not prejudice the sovereignty and territorial integrity of a State party'.[57] A balance is to be struck between the needs of the minority group to exercise their rights involving the exploitation of natural resources and the needs of the State as a whole. The Committee pointed out in *Lovelace v Canada* that it is legitimate for governments to define certain categories of persons who are entitled to live on certain parts of the territory as a means to protect and preserve resources.[58] In applications before the Committee involving the use of natural resources by minority groups the Committee's concern has been with the long-term economic viability of the minority group, ensuring the cultural practices may be maintained, and the economic consequences action has for the State as a whole. These considerations are broadly understood and will be influenced by the various circumstances involved. The Committee's views show that minority groups cannot demand absolute protection for their economic resources and how they are exploited.

In *Lubicon Lake Band v Canada* the application concerned the decision to allow private companies to exploit the natural resources on the Band's territory. The application alleged this amounted to a violation of article 1 as it prevented the Band from freely disposing of its resources. The Committee decided that article 1 could not be invoked but relying upon the same facts transformed the application into an article 27 claim as the facts displayed that the economic activities in question impacted upon the right to the enjoyment of culture.[59] In particular it was noted that the exploitation of the Band's territory had led to the loss of 'its economic base and the breakdown of its social institutions' leading to widespread negative effects.[60] The application detailed the various claims and counterclaims concerning the Canadian government's response to the exploitation of the tribal land where the government was offering land transfers to the Band, money for community development and federal support for development in order to allow the Band to establish a viable economy on the new land and to allow for the pursuit of

56 *Lubicon Lake Band v Canada*, above n 39, para 32.2.

57 General Comment 23, above n 1, para 3.2.

58 *Lovelace v Canada*, above n 13, para 15.

59 *Lubicon Lake Band v Canada*, above n 39, para 13.4.

60 Ibid, para 23.2.

traditional practices. Canada conceded 'that the Lubicon Lake Band has suffered a historical inequity and that they are entitled to a reserve and related entitlements'.[61] The Committee took this into account and felt that the recent actions by the State constituted a violation of article 27. The Committee also accepted that the government's proposed remedies were acceptable as they appeared to provide for the long-term enjoyment of culture in relation to economic resources for the Band, even though they did fully meet all of the Band's demands.

In *Kitok v Sweden* the issue before the Committee was the ability of the applicant to exercise his rights regarding reindeer husbandry in the face of domestic legislation which had excluded him from his membership in the Sami village. The legislation reduced the number of individuals involved in reindeer husbandry as its purpose was to ensure that reindeer husbandry remained economically viable, was sustainable in the long-term, and contributed to improved conditions for the Sami involved in this practice. Kitok had been denied membership into the Sami village as he had engaged in other economic practices. This meant he was not entitled to certain land and water rights but he was able to maintain his status as a reindeer owner in the Sami society. The Government argued this meant he was still able to enjoy his culture, even though not in the same way as other members of the Sami community were able to. The Committee's views first set out that:[62]

> ... [t]he regulation of an economic activity is normally a matter for the State alone. However, where that activity is an essential element in the culture of an ethnic community, its application to an individual may fall under article 27 of the Covenant.

The Committee acknowledged, as did both parties, that the purpose of the domestic legislation was to 'restrict the number of reindeer breeders for economic and ecological reasons and to secure the preservation and well-being of the Sami minority'.[63] It was also agreed that effective measures had to be taken; the question then was the impact of these measures upon the individual. The Committee, relying on its statement in *Lovelace v Canada*, that any restrictions upon the rights of an individual have to 'be necessary for the continued viability and welfare of the minority as a whole', felt that Kitok's rights had not been violated. A contributing factor to this outcome was the ability of Kitok to engage in reindeer husbandry and other aspects of the Sami culture, albeit not as of right.[64]

The impact of State policies for the exploitation of natural resources upon cultural practices in Finland has been the object of a number of challenges before the Committee. In *Ilmari Länsman et al v Finland* the applicants challenged a contract given to a private company to quarry stone and construct access roads in

61 Ibid, para 24.1.

62 *Kitok v Sweden*, above n 19, para 9.2.

63 Ibid, para 9.5.

64 Ibid, para 9.8.

an area used for reindeer herding. It was argued that the quarrying and transport would disrupt reindeer herding activities to a considerable degree. It was also claimed that the site of the quarry was a sacred place for the old Sami religion but traditional practices had not been carried out there for several decades. Finland argued that the commercial activities in the area had been insignificant in terms of stone quarried, the extent of the quarrying area and the transport network, with no negative effects on the applicants ability to pursue reindeer husbandry. The government invoked the Committee's views in *Lovelace v Canada* where it was stated that 'not every interference can be regarded as a denial of rights within the meaning of article 27 … [but] restrictions must have both a reasonable and objective justification and be consistent with the other provisions of the Covenant …'.[65] The Committee explained that States are free to encourage economic development or activity by private enterprises but this freedom is not absolute. Finland argued that the scope of this freedom is to be determined through a margin of appreciation where the local authorities are in a better position to decide what is best for society. The Committee disagreed, stating that where minority rights are at issue the scope of this freedom is to be assessed by reference to the obligations under article 27. In determining the extent of those obligations the Committee pointed out 'measures that have a certain limited impact on the way of life of persons belonging to a minority will not necessarily amount to a denial of the right under article 27'.[66] The Committee held that the activity in question was not substantial as to impact upon the right of the applicants to enjoy their own culture. The Committee also gave a clear warning that future developments on a larger scale may impact upon the rights of individuals to enjoy their culture and that the State party must keep this in mind.

Finland's treatment of the Sami minority came before the Committee again in *Jouni Länsman et al v Finland.* This application concerned logging activities in territory used for reindeer husbandry, as well as the exploitation of other economic resources. The applicants used the Committee's statements in *Ilmari Länsman* concerning the obligation to consider fully the impact the exploitation of resources would have upon the Sami's ability to enjoy their culture. Again the Committee held that the exploitation of the natural resources did not have a substantial negative impact upon the ability of the applicants to enjoy their culture. It was recognized that the economic viability of reindeer husbandry was in jeopardy but that this was not directly attributable to the activities of the State but was a result of factors beyond the State's control. The Committee felt that the long-term survival of reindeer husbandry was under threat but that the legislative measures being taken were not detrimental to the future of the Sami.[67]

The matter of logging activities by the State was once again before the Committee in the application of *Jouni and Eino Länsman et al v Finland.* The

65 *Lovelace v Canada*, above n 13, para 16.

66 *Ilmari Länsman et al v Finland*, above n 16, para 9.4.

67 *Jouni Länsman et al v Finland*, above n 29, para 10.6.

basis of the complaint was that the continuation of the logging activities that were the subject of the above two applications was jeopardizing the ability of the applicants to engage in reindeer husbandry as part of their cultural practices. It was argued with regard to the State's position on logging in the Sami area 'that the impact of logging operations are long-term, practically permanent, and that the measures employed create new damage, [and] exacerbate existing damage'.[68] The Committee repeated its view that 'measures with only a limited impact on the way of life and livelihood of persons belonging to a minority will not necessarily amount to a denial of the rights under article 27'. It further explained that an infringement of article 27 may 'result from the combined effects of a series of actions or measures taken by a State party over a period of time'.[69] The Committee concluded that in this particular application there was not sufficient evidence to demonstrate that the actions of the State were serious enough to amount to a denial of article 27 rights.

When it comes to the issue of the impact the exploitation of economic resources has upon minority rights there is often extensive disagreement among the parties as to facts upon which the application is based. In the Jouni and Eino Länsman application, the applicants supported their argument with substantial evidence showing that the ability to carry on with reindeer husbandry was seriously threatened by a range of factors, but primarily attributable to the actions of the State. The State in turn provided evidence showing that the detrimental impact on the activities related to article 27 rights were not attributable to the actions of the State or in any way under its control. The State also appeared to argue that the practices and demands of the Herdsmen Committee were in themselves damaging their ability to carry on with their cultural practices.[70] A similar situation arose in *Howard v Canada* where both parties submitted detailed information on the condition of fishing stocks as the applicant was arguing that the fishing rights he possessed on reserve lands were inadequate for the effective exercise of his cultural practices. Determinations of the viability, or not, of economic resources appear to hinge on appropriate facts, which the Committee holds are matters for the domestic courts to resolve. This is undoubtedly the correct position as the Committee cannot engage in its own fact-finding exercises. However, it remains necessary for the Committee to remain open as to the interpretation of the facts as in these circumstances perspectives and understandings of the facts will vary dramatically.

In *Apirana Mahuika et al v New Zealand* the government had negotiated a fisheries settlement with the Maori which the applicants claimed prevented them from exercising their traditional fishing rights, resulting in negative economic consequences and a denial of their right to enjoy their culture. The settlement had the purpose of benefiting the Maori as a whole allowing for the enjoyment of

68 *Jouni and Eino Länsman et al v Finland*, above n 17, para 8.7.

69 Ibid, para 10.2.

70 Ibid, para 7.10.

cultural activities directly related to fishing activities and to protect customary food gathering activities. The government noted that minority rights in these situations are not absolute and it is necessary to balance competing needs in ensuring the long-term sustainability of natural resources. The Committee was concerned that the applicants did not feel their rights were being adequately protected but felt that the State's obligations under article 27 were met as specific attention had been given to the sustainability of Maori fishing activities as whole.[71]

The applicants in *Diergaardt v Namibia* argued that Namibia had expropriated and privatized the group's communal land which 'robbed the community of the basis of its economic livelihood' undermining its cultural, social and ethnic identity. The Rehoboth Baster community had been living in the area since 1872 and had developed their own way of life and social systems. It was put forth that their use of the land for cattle grazing was directly related to their cultural existence. The Committee disagreed on this point stating:[72]

> … the link of the Rehoboth community to the lands in question dates back some 125 years, it is not the result of a relationship that would have given rise to a distinctive culture. Furthermore, although the Rehoboth community bears distinctive properties as to the historical forms of self-government, the authors have failed to demonstrate how these factors would be based on their way of raising cattle. The Committee therefore finds that there has been no violation of article 27 of the Covenant in the present case.

It appears from the facts of the application that the Rehoboth Baster community met all the necessary requirements for being recognized as a minority but did not possess distinctive cultural elements that the indigenous groups discussed above did in relation to the use of the territory and its resources. Even though it was argued that there was a 'traditional existence of the community as a collective of mainly cattle raising farmers', in the Committee's view there was no essential natural link between the natural resources in question and the cultural identity of the group.

Two individual members of the Committee expanded upon the difficult issue this application raised as to what role economic activities have in the enjoyment of culture.[73] They admitted that with indigenous communities the question is more easily resolved as these groups:

> … can very often show that their particular way of life or culture is, and has for long been, closely bound up with particular lands in regard to both economic and other cultural and spiritual activities, to the extent that the deprivation of or

71 *Apirana Mahuika et al v New Zealand*, above n 23, para 9.8.

72 *Diergaardt v Namibia*, Communication 760/1997, UN Doc CCPR/C/69/D/760/1997 (2000), para 10.6.

73 Individual opinion of Elizabeth Evatt and Cecilia Medina Quiroga.

> denial of access to the land denies them the right to enjoy their own culture in all its aspects.

But with regard to the present application these Committee members felt:

> … the authors have defined their culture almost solely in terms of the economic activity of grazing cattle. They cannot show that they enjoy a distinct culture which is intimately bound up with or dependent on the use of these particular lands, to which they moved a little over a century ago, or that the diminution of their access to the lands has undermined any such culture. Their claim is, essentially, an economic rather than a cultural claim and does not draw the protection of article 27.

A separate opinion in *Lubicon Lake Band v Canada* provided a warning about the complexity of linking the protection of culture and the exploitation of economic resources. In the opinion it was admitted that the enjoyment of culture is closely linked to the practice of a particular way of life and that the exploitation of natural resources can impact this way of life. However, it was warned that 'the right to enjoy one's own culture should not be understood to imply that the Band's traditional way of life must be preserved intact *at all costs*'. It was noted that technology brings change and that it would be inappropriate for an indigenous group to refuse to change its way of life if doing so would 'hamper the economic development of society as a whole'.[74]

Consultation/Participation

Many of the disputes discussed above involved contending claims concerning decision-making processes and the extent to which those impacted had participated and/or been consulted. The Committee has stated that when it comes to issues of economic resources '[t]he enjoyment of those rights may require positive legal measures of protection and measures to ensure the effective participation of members of minority communities in decisions which affect them'.[75] The necessity of consulting minority groups and ensuring some form of participation in matters directly affecting the group also applies to matters outside the question of economic resources but there is not much detail in the Committee's jurisprudence dealing with this aspect. It is possible, however, to see the Committee's position on consultation and participation as being of general applicability demonstrating the impacted groups should have a direct and active role in the decision-making process. As article 27 does not create more rights this does not mean that the right of individuals belonging to minorities to participate in matters impacting them is over and above article 25, but rather it ensures that when a minority group's

74 *Lubicon Lake Band v Canada*, above n 39, individual opinion of Nisuke Ando.

75 General Comment 23, above n 1, para 7.

essential way of life is impacted the group or its representatives should be part of the decision-making processes. In many of the applications involving this aspect there often exists a factual dispute as to whether or not the applicants had been adequately consulted in the decision making and whether or not the consultation/participation was effective.

In *Lubicon Lake Band* authors contended they were not party to the negotiations of the settlement but Canada claimed that that Band's representatives had been consulted and had met with government officials, including the Prime Minister. Canada felt that it was providing an effective remedy to the Band as a result of these consultations but recognized that such a remedy could not be imposed on the Band, underlining the importance of consultation. The applicants made the point that the negotiations were not substantive as it was left to the government to make the final decision on a number of major issues. The matter was further complicated by the government's claim that a new sub-group emerged from the Band which accepted the government's offer. The applicants raised serious objections on this point claiming the new group was a government creation in order to frustrate its position regarding the right to consultation or participation. The Committee did not address these points in its final views but did accept that the Government's remedy was sufficient, indicating it was satisfied with the level of consultation that had taken place.

In the various applications concerning Sami cultural practices the effectiveness of consultation and participation has been heavily disputed. In *Ilmari Länsman* the Committee noted that the particular interests of those impacted were considered and emphasized that the applicants were consulted on these matters.[76] In *Jouni Länsman* Finland argued that the government and the Herdsmen's Committees were in continual negotiations and that the negotiations were effective in considering the rights of the Sami. The applicants responded that the meetings did not constitute effective participation as the government refused to cooperate with the Herdsmen Committees.[77] The Committee held that the Herdsmen's Committee to which the applicants belonged was consulted and that it did not react negatively to the proposed plans. The Committee continued:[78]

> That this consultation process was unsatisfactory to the authors and was capable of greater interaction does not alter the Committee's assessment. It transpires that the State party's authorities *did* go through the process of weighing the authors' interests and the general economic interests in the area specified in the complaint when deciding on the most appropriate measures of forestry management …

76 *Ilmari Länsman et al v Finland*, above n 16, para 9.6.

77 In *Jouni and Eino Länsman et al v Finland*, above n 17, it was argued that the consultations relevant to this application were not effective as they were only opinion-gathering exercises undertaken by the State; a point the Committee did not address.

78 *Jouni Länsman et al v Finland*, above n 29, para 10.5 (emphasis in original).

In *Äärelä and Näkkäläjärvi v Finland* the applicants argued that a decision to allow logging in a specific area impacted their right to enjoy their culture. Finland responded that the applicants had been properly consulted in the decision-making process and the Committee agreed, pointing out that the original government plans had been amended following these consultations.[79] In the application the Committee was faced with conflicting facts and this prevented the Committee from determining that the logging would prevent the enjoyment of culture, and no violation of article 27 was found, primarily due to the point that effective consultations had taken place.

The inadequacy of the consultation process was also at issue in *Mahuika et al v New Zealand.* The government set up a process of negotiation with the Maori in order to create a settlement over fishing rights. In doing so the Maori representatives engaged in their own process of consultation in line with the organization of the Maori groups. The applicants argued that the process of consultation was not adequate as a full understanding of the settlement was not conveyed and not all tribes and sub-tribes were fully consulted. New Zealand invoked the Committee's views in *Marshall et al v Canada* where it was held that not all sub-groups have a right to participate directly in the consultation process. The Committee did not address this point but did explain:[80]

> … the State party undertook a complicated process of consultation in order to secure broad Maori support to a nation-wide settlement and regulation of fishing activities. Maori communities and national Maori organizations were consulted and their proposals did affect the design of the arrangement.

The Committee recognized that individual and group interests may clash but in this particular application it was held that the consultation process gave sufficient attention generally to the cultural rights of the Maori. The Committee was concerned that the end result of the consultations did create divisions within the Maori but this was not incompatible with the State's obligations under article 27.[81] In *Hopu and Bessert v France* the final decision pointed to the fact that France had not appropriately considered the impact the development would have upon the indigenous groups and accordingly felt this was a violation of their rights under the Covenant.[82]

In *Diergaardt v Namibia* the applicants claimed that they had been denied their historical arrangement for self government and that changes in the electoral

79 *Äärelä and Näkkäläjärvi v Finland,* Communication 779/1997, UN Doc CCPR/C/73/D/779/1997 (2001), para 7.6.

80 *Apirana Mahuika et al v New Zealand,* above n 23, para 9.6.

81 Ibid, para 9.8.

82 *Hopu and Bessert v France,* above n 7, para 10.3. As discussed above the Committee could not address the issue of minority rights but the views expressed demonstrate the need to have the impacted minority group involved in the decision-making process.

boundaries had dispersed the Community lessening its influence in any one region. The Committee responded to this argument with the position that the right to participate in government was an individual right and that the Rehoboth Baster community had not substantiated any significant impact upon their rights under article 25 as each individual of the community was free to participate.[83] The point of the applicants was they were a distinct community with a history of self-government and some recognition of this was necessary. Martin Scheinin provided a separate opinion with regard to the issue of minority participation. He felt that the Committee's views in this application unnecessarily emphasized the individual nature of article 25 participation rights. He explained:

> ... there are situations where article 25 calls for special arrangements for rights of participation to be enjoyed by members of minorities and, in particular, indigenous peoples. When such a situation arises, it is not sufficient under article 25 to afford individual members of such communities the individual right to vote in general elections. Some forms of local, regional or cultural autonomy may be called for in order to comply with the requirement of effective rights of participation.

The application of *Howard v Canada* raised an interesting issue about the validity of historical consultation processes. The applicant, a member of the Hiawatha first nations, contended that a treaty between the government and first nations groups signed in 1923 was invalid. The treaty in question resulted in aboriginal groups giving up hunting and fishing rights over specific tracts of land while maintaining traditional rights over other designated land tracts. The applicant argued that the terms of the 1923 treaty were unclear and as a result the first nations' signatories did not fully understand it. The domestic courts undertook what appears to have been a lengthy examination of the historical context and rejected the applicant's claim on this point.[84] The State party went on to explain that the 1923 treaty was negotiated at the request of the first nations groups who were seeking recognition of rights to traditional territories in Ontario. The State party asserted that the applicant's group, the Rice Lake Band, was familiar with the treaty process and there existed historical evidence showing that the treaty had been discussed by the Band before it was approved.[85]

The Committee did not make any determinations of the historical record or the nature of the process that resulted in the 1923 treaty. Given that the consultation process took place well before the Covenant entered into force for the State party, the Committee would be prevented from dealing with this particular issue *rationae temporis*. At the same time it appears the applicant was attempting to argue that the historical agreement was having an ongoing impact upon his ability to exercise his

83 *Diergaardt v Namibia*, above n 72, para 10.8.
84 *Howard v Canada*, above n 20, para 9.5.
85 Ibid, para 11.2.

minority rights. If this was the case the Committee would be entitled to examine a historical arrangement or at least the contemporary consequences of it. However, this has the potential for taking the Committee into a controversial area as the historical record is never wholly clear and the parties involved are likely to be continually arguing over the true meaning of any agreement. But if the Committee felt that a historical agreement was inhibiting the ability of individuals to exercise their rights this would essentially require a State party to reopen negotiations on the historical agreement; something that in most cases would not be in the interest of the State or the minority group.

The Committee's views in this area make clear that minority groups are to be consulted or provided with the means to participate in decisions impacting upon their way of life or existence. It appears the Committee has developed this into a strong obligation upon States, especially in relation to indigenous groups and economic issues. The views expressed by Martin Scheinin suggest that the nature of this obligation should extend further into public affairs and the process of government within a State. Such views do go against the Committee's decision in *Marshall v Canada* where it was held that not all minority groups have a right to participation.[86] The *Marshall* decision was clearly restrictive, whereas the views discussed above demonstrate the Committee taking a more expansive approach when it comes to the involvement of minorities in decisions impacting upon them. This expansive approach comes at a price as the main issue for the applicants in *Marshall* and *Mahuika* was that the general processes did not address their own perceived individual needs. The task for the Committee is to try to find an appropriate balance not only between the needs of the minority group and the State, but also between the differing needs within the minority group.

Language

With regard to the use of language by individuals belonging to minorities, General Comment 23 explains that this right is distinct from other language rights in the Covenant.[87] The Committee has been presented with a number of cases on language rights in France concerning the use of the Breton language by the Breton minority[88] but has been prevented from considering the implications for article 27 due to the State's reservation to that article. Concerning the other allegations made in these applications the Committee has not found any other violation of the rights in the Covenants and this has been due to the fact that the applicants could speak French as well and, therefore, could not claim to be unduly affected. In each case the Committee has made a point of asking the applicant if they could speak

86 *Marshall v Canada*, Communication 205/1986, UN Doc CCPR/C/43/D/205/1986 (1991), paras 5.4–5.5.

87 General Comment 23, above n 1, para 5.3.

88 *TK v France, HK v France, SG v France, RLM v France, CLD v France*, above n 7.

and understand French, even before notifying the State of the application. This appears to be a very insensitive position taken by the Committee as it prejudged the outcome of the application on the basis that if the applicants can speak French then their particular minority rights are not engaged. The Committee failed to recognize that the individuals wished to exert and enjoy a particular and central aspect to their identity as individuals belonging to a minority group.

In *Ballantyne et al v Canada* the applicants claimed that provincial laws in the province of Quebec requiring all business signs to be in French impacted upon their minority rights to language. As discussed above this part of the application was dismissed since it was held the applicants belonged to the majority language group of the State and could not claim minority status in a sub-State territory. The Committee did find a violation of article 19 rights to freedom of expression but this was disputed by Committee member Biraime Nidaye. Nidaye argued that the rationale of article 27 was to preserve and protect minority groups. The domestic law in question requiring all public business communication to be in French had this very purpose in relation to the French-speaking minority of Canada so it could not be seen as contrary to the Covenant. As discussed above, a dissenting view[89] felt that minority groups in sub-State units should be able to enjoy the protection of the Covenant as well, demonstrating that particular language rights for certain minority groups should be respected regardless of the national position in relation to their language. A major issue in this application was that all minority languages in Quebec were subjected to the same treatment, so the English speaking minority could not claim to be unfavourably impacted.

It was disputed in *Diergaardt v Namibia* that Namibia's constitutional provisions making English the official State language prevented the applicants from using their own language, Afrikaans, in all public matters. The applicants provided evidence of instructions from the government to civil servants which said they were not to reply to the applicants in Afrikaans, even if the civil servant could use that language. The majority finding of the Committee did not find a violation of article 27 but did claim that it was discrimination under article 26.[90] A number of members of the Committee[91] dissented on this point on the basis that 'the right to use one's mother tongue cannot take precedence, in relations with official institutions, over the official language of the country, which is, or which is intended to be, the language of all and the common denominator for all citizens'.[92] The dissent felt that 'a few people' cannot make demands for the use of language when there is an official language in place.

89 Individual opinion of Elizabeth Evatt, co-signed by Nisuke Ando, Marco Tulio, Bruni Celli and Vojin Dimitrijevic.

90 *Diergaardt v Namibia*, above n 72, para 10.10.

91 Individual opinions of Abdalfattah Amor, P.N. Bhagwati, Lord Colville, Maxwell Yalden and Nisuke Ando.

92 Ibid, individual opinion of Abdalfattah Amor, para 4.

The Committee's treatment of language issues under the OP has been particularly restrictive with the Committee appearing to accept the appropriateness of set official languages and the need of minorities to use an official language in the public sphere. In the Breton language applications the majority of the Committee appeared to be satisfied that since the applicants could speak French the compulsory and exclusive use of that language in all public affairs was not detrimental to their rights.[93] The same position was expressed by the dissent in *Diergaardt* where it was held that since Afrikaans was treated on the same level as all other minority languages there was no issue of obstructing the rights of a minority. In *Ballantyne* the Committee explained '[a] State may choose one or more official languages, but it may not exclude, outside the spheres of public life, the freedom to express oneself in a language of one's choice'.[94] This reinforces the point that official languages can be set for the conduct of public affairs but raises questions as to the extent of the positive obligations upon a State to respect minority rights.

Religion

General Comment 23 does not provide any further details on the issue of religion for minority groups and only one application under the OP has dealt with the issue. *Waldman v Canada* consisted of a challenge to constitutional arrangements providing for special educational arrangements for the Roman Catholic society in Canada. When Canada adopted its constitution in 1867 provisions were made to protect Roman Catholic schools from the Protestant majority by creating their own school boards and allowing them to be deemed public schools able to receive public funding. Private schools, including schools of other religious denominations,

93 *Ignatane v Latvia*, Communication 884/1999, UN Doc CCPR/C/72/D/884/1999 (2001) did not directly invoke article 27 but the issues at stake concerned language laws and minority groups. The applicant was a Latvian citizen of Russian origin and was prevented from running in local elections on the basis that she did not have sufficient aptitude in the Latvian language. Latvia argued that 'participation in public affairs requires a high level of proficiency in the State language and a language requirement for standing as a candidate in elections is hence reasonable and objective', para 7.3. The Committee held there was a violation of article 25 as the applicant had been unreasonably denied the right to participate in public affairs. The Committee did not elaborate on language rights but its views make it clear that the imposition of an official language cannot unreasonably prevent individuals from minorities participating in public affairs.

94 *Ballantyne et al v Canada*, above n 40, para 11.4. The application of *Michal Klečkovski v Lithuania*, Communication 1285/2004 UN Doc CCPR/C/90/D/1285/2004 (2007) involved a claim where the author, an ethnic Pole born in Lithuania, asserted that the requirement of his name be spelt in Lithuanian denied him a critical element of his identity and was contrary to the obligations under the Covenant, including those in article 27. The Committee declared the application inadmissible on the basis that the author failed to substantiate any of his claims under the Covenant, at para 8.3.

receive certain tax exemptions and other arrangements but do not receive public funding in the way Roman Catholic schools do. The applicant sent his children to schools of the Jewish religion and had to pay a significant amount in tuition. It was argued that denominational schools are:[95]

> … crucial to the practice of religion, that these schools form an essential link in preserving community identity and the survival of minority religious groups and that positive action may be required to ensure that the rights of religious minorities are protected.

Canada responded that article 27 does not require the State to fund private religious schools as positive action under article 27 'should be required only in rare circumstances'. The Committee rejected the Constitutional justification put forth by Canada and felt that there was nothing which demonstrated that the Roman Catholic community was in a disadvantaged position requiring specific elements of protection. The Committee found that the arrangements for public and private school funding was discriminatory under article 26 as only Roman Catholic schools could receive the public funding and no other private school could achieve this status by any means, eliminating any reasonable or objective reasons for the arrangement.[96] The Committee did not consider article 27 directly as the majority felt that no additional issues needed to be addressed.

However Martin Scheinin provided a separate opinion explaining the applicability of article 27 to religious education. He pointed out that the substance of the application concerned a historical arrangement for minority protection and therefore should have been considered under article 27. He stated 'article 27 imposes positive obligations for States to promote religious instruction in minority religions, and that providing such education as an optional arrangement within the public education system is one permissible arrangement to that end'. He continued with a warning that care must be taken where distinctions arise as to who is funded and that a strong indicator will be 'constant demand' for education based on a particular religion or language and whether or not there existed 'a sufficient number of children to attend such a school so that it could operate as a viable part in the overall system of education'.[97] This position is significant for it calls upon the State to take positive action for the protection of minority rights when there is a significant minority presence in a State and reasonable demands for particular aspects of protection. Scheinin's views on religious education also directly addressed the use of language rights. If a significant minority group exists in a State and there is substantial demand for education in the minority language then it appears the State is under an obligation to provide for the particular language. This conflicts with the views taken by the Committee with regard to language rights as

---

95 *Waldman v Canada*, above n 27, para 3.5.

96 Ibid, paras 10.4–10.6.

97 Ibid, individual opinion of Martin Scheinin, para 5.

it appears that an official language in all public affairs, including education, may be acceptable under the Covenant.

Conclusions

The Committee's treatment of minority rights under article 27 is far from ideal; given the contentious nature of minority rights protection generally this is hardly surprising. The Committee has made significant advances in ensuring minority groups are consulted about or able to participate in decision-making processes impacting upon them. The Committee's views in this area do not create a requirement that every individual or sub-group of a minority is able to choose the method of consultation/participation but the State does have to provide some sort of mechanism for the airing of views and opinions. The Committee also gives significant weight to the preservation of culture and economic resources as a means of preserving the overall identity of the minority group, but it has been less forceful when language issues are involved.

In all of these areas the rights of the minority group will not always be paramount as the rights of others in society are also taken into account. Naturally this leads to tensions over whether or not minority rights have been given too much protection or not enough protection, and it appears unlikely the Committee will ever be able to satisfy all concerned parties. There are a few black spots in the Committee's view where it appears much less concern is given to minority rights which are central to the group's identity, such as language rights. Another area of worry is the selectivity the Committee appeared to posses in the application of *Diergaardt v Namibia* where it has held that a distinct group was not entitled to the protection of article 27. It is suspected that the Committee's views in this application were influenced by the fact that it was a group of European descent, with links to an apartheid regime, living in an African State.

Perhaps the most interesting aspect of the Committee's views under article 27 is that they clearly demonstrate the rights protected under the OP are not purely individual in nature. This occurs at multiple levels. In considering the rights of individuals belonging to a minority, the Committee clearly is, in most cases, also considering the rights of the minority group as a whole. At the very least, most decisions under article 27 that find in favour for the individual application will have a knock-on impact for the remainder of the minority group. Also, in the applications involving article 27 the Committee has had to pass judgment on competing claims within minority groups and between the minority group and the wider society. While all human rights have to be considered in the wider context, it is with article 27 that the interrelationship between individuals and collectives is particularly stark.

Chapter 11
Equality and Non-Discrimination

Richard Burchill[1]

Equality of treatment and the prohibition of discrimination is a pervasive theme of the Covenant to which reference can be found in articles 2(1), 3, 4(1), 14(1), 20, 23, 24, 25 and 26. Article 2(1) contains a general obligation for States parties to respect and ensure to all individuals the rights recognized in the Covenant 'without distinction of any kind, such as race, colour, sex, language, religion, political or other opinion, national or social origin, property, birth or other status'. Article 3 requires States to ensure the equal rights of men and women in their enjoyment of the rights set forth in the Covenant. Article 4(1) prohibits discrimination when States are exercising their right of derogation under the Covenant. Here, measures of derogation must not involve 'discrimination solely on the ground of race, colour, sex, language, religion or social origin'. It is noticeable that the list of grounds upon which discrimination is prohibited in article 4(1) is more limited than those contained in article 2(1). The reason for this is that very often during war or national emergency it is permissible to discriminate against enemy aliens and their property.[2] Articles 23, 24 and 25 require equality of treatment and prohibit discrimination in relation to the exercise of particular rights, namely marriage and family, the rights of the child and the exercise of political rights. article 26 requires that all persons should be equal before the law and that the law should afford protection and guarantee to all persons equal and effective protection against discrimination. The grounds of discrimination against which such protection must be afforded replicates the list contained in article 2(1), that is, it prohibits discrimination on grounds 'such as race, colour, sex, language, religion, political or other opinion, national or social origin, property, birth or other status'. It will be noted in passing that the lists of prohibited grounds of discrimination are not exclusive, but illustrative; there may be discrimination on other grounds which are not immediately apparent from those specifically enumerated in the Covenant provisions.

---

1 This chapter is based substantially upon its first edition equivalent, written by Professor Scott Davidson of the University of Canterbury in New Zealand.

2 Manfred Nowak, *UN Covenant on Civil and Political Rights* (2nd revised edn, Kehl, Germany: NP Engel, 2005) pp 99–100.

Definition of Discrimination

There is no definition of discrimination in the text of the Covenant, but the Committee as in General Comment 18 elucidated its understanding of the concept. It states:[3]

> The Committee believes that the term 'discrimination' as used in the Covenant should be understood to imply any distinction, exclusion, restriction or preference which is based on any ground such as race, colour, sex, language, religion, political or other opinion, national or social origin, property, birth or other status, and which has the purpose or effect of nullifying or impairing the recognition, enjoyment or exercise by all persons on an equal footing of all rights and freedoms.

The General Comment goes on to explain that not all differences in treatment will constitute discrimination 'if the criteria for such differentiation are reasonable and objective and if the aim is to achieve a purpose which is legitimate under the Covenant'.[4]

General Comment 18 by referring to 'purpose or effect' comprehends the two categories of discrimination which are usually known as direct and indirect discrimination. Direct discrimination is generally easy to identify since a rule will usually single out a particular group which is subject to treatment that is less favourable than it would be for another group. Thus a law preventing black people from entering particular public buildings will constitute direct discrimination. On the other hand, a rule which is neutral on its face may have the effect of discriminating in fact against a particular group. Take for instance a rule which allowed only people who were taller than 1.70 metres to join the police force. Such a rule, while not discriminatory on its face, may none the less impact disproportionately on other groups such as women and certain ethnic minorities who are, on the whole, shorter than this. While the example of direct discrimination given above is clearly morally odious, it is irrelevant whether or not indirect discrimination is similarly offensive. In *Simunek et al v Czech Republic*,[5] which concerned the requirement that applicants who sought a return of property expropriated by the former communist authorities had to be resident nationals, the Committee held that

3 *General Comment 18: Non-discrimination*, UN Doc HRI/GEN/1/Rev.6 at 146 (2003), para 6.

4 General Comment 18, ibid, para 13.

5 *Simunek et al v The Czech Republic*, Communication 516/1992, UN Doc CCPR/C/54/D/516/1992 (1995), para 11.7. Also *Broeks v The Netherlands*, Communication 172/1984, UN Doc CCPR/C/OP/2 at 196 (1990) where the Committee noted that the Netherlands had not intended to discriminate against Mrs Broeks on grounds of sex and 'noted with appreciation' that the discriminatory provisions in the law had been repealed, para 16.

the Czech Republic's argument that since no discriminatory effect was intended the provision did not contravene article 26 was wrong. The Committee said:[6]

> The State party contends that there is no violation of the Covenant because the Czech and Slovak legislators had no discriminatory intent at the time of the adoption of Act 87/1991. The Committee is of the view, however, that the intent of the legislature is not alone dispositive in determining a breach of article 26 of the Covenant. A politically motivated differentiation is unlikely to be compatible with article 26. But an act which is not politically motivated may still contravene article 26 if its effects are discriminatory.

It has to be said that the Committee has not always been adept at distinguishing between direct and indirect discrimination. In *Ballantyne et al v Canada*,[7] a law adopted by the Quebec legislature prohibited the outdoor display of commercial signs in a language other than French. A number of English-speaking merchants complained that they were being discriminated against because they were prohibited from using English signs. The Committee rejected this part of the communication on the grounds that French speakers were also prohibited from using signs in English. This position seems untenable since it is quite clear that English speakers as a group were discriminated against by the law in question since it was primarily directed at them. While French speakers might want to use signs written in English, this would only appear to be a theoretical possibility. Even if this cannot be regarded as a case of direct discrimination, it is arguable that it is a case of indirect discrimination since there can be little doubt that the law in question would impact disproportionately upon English speakers as a group in Quebec. The question then would be whether it could be saved by objectively justifiable criteria. The only criterion which could be applied would be the protection of the French language in that particular province, but there would arguably be less restrictive – or discriminatory – ways of achieving such an end.[8]

The Committee has explained that discrimination may occur from the 'effect of a rule or measure that is neutral at face value or without intent to discriminate'.[9] However there may still be a violation of the Covenant[10]

> … if the detrimental effects of a rule or decision exclusively or disproportionally affect persons having a particular race, colour, sex, language, religion, political or other opinion, national or social origin, property, birth or other

6 *Simunek et al v Czech Republic*, ibid, para 11.7.

7 *Ballantyne et al v Canada*, Communications 359 and 385/1989. UN Doc CCPR/C/47/D/359/1989 and 385/1989/Rev.1 (1993).

8 The Committee did reject the State's arguments along these lines, ibid, para 11.2.

9 *Althammer v Austria*, Communication 998/2001, UN Doc CCPR/C/78/D/998/2001 (2003).

10 Ibid, para 10.2.

> status. Furthermore, rules or decisions with such an impact do not amount to discrimination if they are based on objective and reasonable grounds.

A clear example of indirect discrimination is to be found in *Singh Binder v Canada*. Here, the applicant, a Sikh, complained that a Canadian National Railway Company's rules requiring workers in certain jobs to wear protective helmets indirectly discriminated against Sikhs because their religion required them to wear turbans. In other words, the law impacted upon Sikhs more heavily than other groups because of their religious obligations. Although this was clearly a case of indirect discrimination, the Committee found that there were legitimate and objectively justifiable reasons in the form of workers' safety which nullified the discriminatory effect.[11]

While the Committee has been clear in its condemnation of indirect discrimination, it has not been entirely consistent in its treatment of such discrimination in its final views. A number of examples will serve to illustrate this point. In *Vos v The Netherlands* Mrs Vos was an estranged wife who was entitled to receive a disability allowance. Upon the death of her husband she was entitled to receive a widow's pension but this disqualified her from receiving a disability allowance. The value of the pension was less than the allowance. Although the Committee found that Mrs Vos did suffer less favourable treatment, the majority held that this result was justifiable on objective and reasonable criteria, namely the application of a uniform rule to avoid overlapping in the allocation of social security benefits.[12] While this rationale was repeated in a number of similar cases involving the Netherlands,[13] it has also been the subject of some vigorous dissent. In *Vos*, Committee Members Aguilar Urbina and Wennergren argued that the Dutch legislation created a class of persons, namely disabled widows, who were treated less favourably than disabled women who were not widows. They thus contended:[14]

> A differentiation with regard to full [social security] benefits among disabled women on the sole ground of marital status as a widow cannot be said to be

11 *Singh Binder v Canada*, Communication 208/1986. UN Doc CCPR/C/37/D/208/1986 (1989), para 6.2. Also *Wackenheim v France* Communication 854/1999, UN Doc CCPR/C/75/D/854/1999 (2002).

12 *Vos v The Netherlands*, Communication 218/1986, UN Doc CCPR/C/35/D/218/1986 (1989), para 12.

13 *PPC v The Netherlands*, Communication 212/1986, UN Doc CCPR/C/OP/2 at 70 (1990), para 6.3; *HAEdJ v The Netherlands*, Communication 297/1988, UN Doc CCPR/C/37/D/297/1988 (1989), para 8.2; *Oulajin and Kaiss v The Netherlands*, Communication 406 and 426/1990, UN Doc CCPR/C/46/D/406/1990 and 426/1990 at 117 (1992), para 8.2; *APLvdM v The Netherlands*, Communication 478/1991, UN Doc CCPR/C/48/D/478/1991 (1993), para 6.4; *JAMB-R v The Netherlands*, Communication 477/1991, UN Doc CCPR/C/50/D/477/1991 (1994), para 5.

14 *Vos v The Netherlands*, above n 12, para 5.

> based on reasonable and objective criteria. It therefore constitutes discrimination within the meaning of article 26.

Similarly, in *Araujo-Jongen v The Netherlands*, an unemployed married woman was denied unemployment benefits in circumstances in which an unemployed married man would have received such benefits. Although the State undertook remedial legislative action to correct this situation, it was a condition that in order to receive retrospective benefits covering the period in which discrimination had taken place, a married woman had to be unemployed at the time of the application. The Committee found that despite the indirect discrimination between employed and unemployed women at the date of application, this requirement was objectively justifiable.[15] What the Committee failed to see was that the provision was discriminatory as between men and women, since the condition of unemployment did not apply to men at any stage in the recovery of benefits.

The obligation upon States to prevent discrimination extends to the conduct of private parties. In General Comment 18 the Committee makes reference to this point with regard to the reporting procedures under the Covenant.[16] In General Comment 28 the Committee expands upon this:[17]

> State parties are responsible for ensuring the equal enjoyment of rights without any discrimination. Articles 2 and 3 mandate States parties to take all steps necessary, including the prohibition of discrimination on the ground of sex, to put an end to discriminatory actions both in the public and the private sector which impair the equal enjoyment of rights.

The same General Comment makes a further reference to private parties:[18]

> The right to equality before the laws and freedom from discrimination, protected by article 26, requires States to act against discrimination by public and private agencies in all fields.

In *Nahlik v Austria* the applicant brought forth an article 26 claim challenging benefits to retired persons that differed from those available to active employees as a result of a collective bargaining agreement. Austria argued that the agreement

---

15 *Araujo-Jongen v The Netherlands*, Communication 418/1990, UN Doc CCPR/C/49/D/418/1990 (1993), para 7.4.

16 General Comment 18, above n 3, para 9.

17 *General Comment 28: Equality of rights between men and women*, UN Doc CCPR/C/21/Rev.1/Add.10 (2000), para 4.

18 Ibid, para 31.

was a private law matter over which the State had no influence. This argument was not accepted:[19]

> The Committee observes that under articles 2 and 26 of the Covenant the State party is under an obligation to ensure that all individuals within its territory and subject to its jurisdiction are free from discrimination, and consequently the courts of States parties are under an obligation to protect individuals against discrimination, whether this occurs within the public sphere or among private parties in the quasi-public sector of, for example, employment.

Article 26 as an Autonomous Right

The Committee both in General Comment 18 and in its jurisprudence has identified article 26 as an autonomous right, that is, a general right of non-discrimination which exists independently and not, as in the case of article 2(1), a parasitic right which is dependent upon the existence of other substantive rights in the Covenant. The terms of article 26 make this clear:

> All persons are equal before the law and are entitled without any discrimination to the equal protection of the law. In this respect, the law shall prohibit any discrimination and guarantee to all persons equal and effective protection against discrimination on any ground such as race, colour, sex, language, religion, political or other opinion, national or social origin, property, birth or other status.

Thus, although the Covenant does not provide for a right to own property, if a State decided to enact laws which discriminated in favour of some people being able to own property while denying this right to others on the basis of racial origin, this would violate article 26. This position has been cogently expressed by the Committee in General Comment 18 where it says:[20]

> While article 2 limits the scope of the rights to be protected against discrimination to those provided for in the Covenant, article 26 does not specify such limitations. That is to say, article 26 provides that all persons are equal before the law and are entitled to equal protection of the law without discrimination, and that the law shall guarantee to all persons equal and effective protection against discrimination on any of the enumerated grounds. In the view of the Committee, article 26 does not merely duplicate the guarantee already provided for in article 2 but provides in itself an autonomous right. It prohibits discrimination in law

---

19 *Nahlik v Austria*, Communication 608/1995, UN Doc CCPR/C/57/D/608/1995 (1996), para 8.2.

20 General Comment 18, above n 3, para 12.

> or in fact in any field regulated and protected by public authorities. Article 26 is therefore concerned with the obligations imposed on States parties in regard to their legislation and the application thereof. Thus, when legislation is adopted by a State party, it must comply with the requirement of article 26 that its content should not be discriminatory. In other words, the application of the principle of non-discrimination contained in article 26 is not limited to those rights which are provided for in the Covenant.

The Committee addressed the particular issue of the interdependence between property rights and discrimination being covered by the Covenant in *Blancov v Nicaragua*. The applicant alleged that he had been deprived of his property because of his political opinions. Although the Committee did not find that the claim was substantiated, it none the less held:[21]

> With regard to the author's allegation concerning the confiscation of his property, the Committee recalls that the Covenant does not protect the right of property, as such. However, an issue under the Covenant may arise if a confiscation or expropriation is based on discriminatory grounds prohibited in article 26 of the Covenant.

The Committee in a number of cases has confronted the question of whether article 26 is an autonomous right that applies to substantive matter which does not fall within the Covenant *ratione materiae*. One of the first cases to raise this question was *Broeks v The Netherlands*. In this case, Mrs Broeks was employed as a nurse until 1979, when she was dismissed for reasons of disability. She had become ill in 1975, and from that time she received both unemployment and disability benefits. From 1980 onwards, although Mrs Broeks continued to receive a disability allowance, she was deprived of her unemployment benefit. The reason for this was that in the eyes of Dutch law Mrs Broeks remained a married woman, despite the fact that she had been separated from her husband for many years. Mrs Broeks argued that if she were a man, married or unmarried, the law in question would not have deprived her of unemployment benefits. Because she was a woman, and was married at the time in question, however, Dutch law prevented her from continuing to receive unemployment benefits. She argued that this violated the rule against discrimination in article 26 of the Covenant.

The Dutch government denied that there was any violation of article 26 arguing that issues relating to social security were a not a matter which fell to be governed by the Covenant *ratione materiae*, but that social security matters were to be dealt with exclusively by the International Covenant on Economic, Social and Cultural Rights (ICESCR), to which the Netherlands was also party. Furthermore, the Dutch government pointed out that the implementation obligations of the two Covenants

21 See *Blancov v Nicaragua*, Communication 328/1988 UN Doc CCPR/C/51/D/328/1988 (1994), para 10.1.

were different. While the Covenant was to be implemented immediately and unconditionally, the ICESCR was to be implemented progressively and subject to the availability of appropriate resources. It also argued that the methods of supervising the implementation of the two Covenants were different, in particular, the ICESCR was to be supervised by a system of periodic reports indicating the measures which States parties had taken and the progress which they had made in the areas in question. The Committee emphatically rejected the Netherlands' arguments, holding:[22]

> Although article 26 requires that legislation should prohibit discrimination, it does not of itself contain any obligation with respect to the matters that may be provided for by legislation. Thus it does not, for example, require any State to enact legislation to provide for social security. However, when such legislation is adopted in the exercise of a State's sovereign power, then such legislation must comply with article 26 of the Covenant.

The Committee noted that in this case Dutch law imposed equal rights and obligations on both spouses with regard to their joint income, but that a married woman, in order to receive unemployment benefits, had to prove that she was a 'breadwinner' – a condition that did not apply to married men. Thus a differentiation which appeared to be one which referred to the status of the individual was, in fact, one of sex that placed married women at a disadvantage in comparison to married men. The Committee held that such a differentiation was unreasonable and could not therefore be justified.

Broeks v Netherlands was the first in a line of communications in which the Committee has held that when a State adopts legislation which is discriminatory on its face or has discriminatory effects (that is, if it is either directly or indirectly discriminatory) it will be governed by article 26. The Committee has found this to be the situation in a number of cases involving States parties' social security laws,[23] as well as in a variety of other areas which do not, at first sight, fall within the Covenant *ratione materiae*.[24] While the Committee's jurisprudence in this

22 *Broeks v The Netherlands*, above n 5, para 12.4.

23 Examples includes *Araujo-Jongen v The Netherlands*, above n 15; *Danning v The Netherlands*, Communication 180/1984, UN Doc CCPR/C/OP/2 at 205 (1990); *García Pons v Spain*, Communication 454/1991, UN Doc CCPR/C/55/D/454/1991 (1995); *Gueye et al v France*, Communication 196/1985, UN Doc CCPR/C/35/D/196/1985 (1989); *Hoofdman v The Netherlands*, Communication 602/1994, UN Doc CCPR/C/64/D/602/1994 (1998); *Oulajin and Kaiss v The Netherlands*, above n 13; *Pauger v Austria*, Communication 716/1996, UN Doc CCPR/C/65/D/716/1996 (1999); *Sprenger v The Netherlands*, Communication 395/1990, UN Doc CCPR/C/44/D/395/1990 (1992); *Vos v The Netherlands*, Communication 786/1997, UN Doc CCPR/C/66/D/786/1997 (1999).

24 These include education subsidies as between private and public schools *Blom v Sweden*, Communication 191/1985, UN Doc CCPR/C/OP/2 at 216 (1990); *Waldman v Canada*, Communication 694/1996, UN Doc CCPR/C/67/D/694/1996 (1999); discrimination

area is now well established, there has been some criticism of this approach by a minority of Committee members in two subsequent cases. In *Sprenger v The Netherlands* Committee members Nisuke Ando, Kurt Herndl and Birame Ndiaye while acknowledging that article 26 constituted an autonomous right prohibiting discrimination none the less advocated a more sensitive and nuanced approach to the implementation of rights having and economic, social or cultural character. They suggested:[25]

> Surely, it is … necessary to take into account the reality that the socio-economic and cultural needs of society are constantly evolving, so that legislation – in particular in the field of social security – may well, and often does, lag behind developments. Accordingly, article 26 of the Covenant should not be interpreted as requiring absolute equality or non-discrimination in that field at all times; instead, it should be seen as a general undertaking on the part of the States parties to the Covenant to regularly review their legislation in order to ensure that it corresponds to the changing needs of society. In the field of civil and political rights, a State party is required to respect Covenant rights such as the right to a fair trial, to freedom of expression and freedom of religion, immediately from the date of entry into force of the Covenant, and to do so without discrimination. On the other hand, with regard to rights enshrined in the International Covenant on Economic, Social and Cultural Rights, it is generally understood that States parties may need time for the progressive implementation of these rights and to adapt relevant legislation in stages; moreover, constant efforts are needed to ensure that distinctions that were reasonable and objective at the time of enactment of a social security provision are not rendered unreasonable and discriminatory by the socio-economic evolution of society. Finally, we recognize that legislative review is a complex process entailing consideration of many factors, including limited financial resources, and the potential effects of amendments on other existing legislation.

This position was supported by a slightly larger minority in *Oulajin and Kaiss v The Netherlands*. Here, Committee members Kurt Herndl, Rein Müllerson,

---

in employment because of political opinion *Bwalya v Zambia*, Communication 314/1988, UN Doc CCPR/C/48/D/314/1988 (1993); confiscation of property on grounds of political belief *Blancov v Nicaragua*, above n 21; conscientious objection to military service *Brinkhof v The Netherlands*, Communication 402/1990, UN Doc CCPR/C/48/D/402/1990 (1993); right to property *Simunek et al v The Czech Republic*, above n 5; and termination of employment *Valenzuela v Peru*, Communication 309/1988, UN Doc CCPR/C/48/D/309/1988 (1993). Also see Sarah Joseph, Jenny Schultz and Melissa Castan, *The International Covenant on Civil and Political Rights: Cases, Materials and Commentary* (2nd edn, Oxford: Oxford University Press, 2004) pp 686–7.

25 *Sprenger v The Netherlands*, above n 23, individual opinion of Nisuke Ando, Kurt Herndl and Birame Ndiayepara.

Birame N'Diaye and Waleed Sadi argued that in the application of article 26 of the Covenant in the field of economic and social rights it was for the legislature of each country, which best knew the socio-economic needs of its own society, to try to achieve social justice in its own context. They went on to say that unless any distinctions made in the socio-economic field were manifestly discriminatory or arbitrary, it was not for the Committee to attempt to re-evaluate the complex socio-economic conditions of each society and to substitute its judgment for that of the legislatures of States parties.

At least one communication dealt with by the Committee since these criticisms were voiced seems to have implicitly acknowledged them. In *JHW v The Netherlands*, the General Child Benefit Act required contributions to be levied on the same basis as income tax. The purpose of the contributions was to fund benefits to assist parents in the maintenance of their children. Under the Act contributions had to be paid up to the age of 65, regardless of whether a contributor ever applied for a benefit or not. However, an exemption was made for unmarried childless women over the age of 45. The exemption was based on the expectation that women over 45 would remain childless. No similar exemption was made for unmarried childless men over the age of 45, presumably on the ground that they could still father children beyond that age. In 1989, however, the exemption for women was subsequently withdrawn. The author, a man, claimed that he was a victim of discrimination based on sex, since he had been denied an exemption which he would have enjoyed had he been a woman. He further argued that there was no objective, reasonable and proportionate justification for the distinction made in the Act between men and women.

While the complainant's arguments appear to be justified at first sight, the Committee nevertheless found, despite the Netherlands' failure to contest admissibility, that the communication was inadmissible, holding:[26]

> ... the Committee notes that the State party, in 1989, adopted measures to abolish the exemption at issue in the present communication. The Committee considers, taking into account that social security legislation and its application usually lag behind socio-economic developments in society, and that the purpose of the abrogated exemption was at its time not generally considered discriminatory, that the issue which the author raises in his communication is moot and that he has no claim under article 2 of the Optional Protocol.

This is an interesting proposition which seems to run counter to the Committee's earlier jurisprudence and appears to endorse the views of the minority in *Sprenger* and *Oulajin and Kaiss*. Views which have been adopted by the Committee since *JHW* in *Vos v The Netherlands* and *Waldman v Canada* have reasserted what might be called the 'traditional' approach to the interpretation of article 26 leaving *JHW*

---

26 *JHW v The Netherlands*, Communication 501/1992, UN Doc CCPR/C/48/D/501/1992 (1993), para 5.2.

standing out as rather anomalous. It seems therefore that *JHW* should probably be viewed as a decision on the particular facts and circumstances of the case and not as a departure from the Committee's established jurisprudence. The Netherlands did not contest the communication and had, by the time it was heard, remedied the situation to which the complaint referred. France did attempt to challenge the Committee's approach to article 26 in *Wackenheim v France* arguing that it regarded 'the non-discrimination clause in that article as the counterpart to article 2, paragraph 1, and as with article 2, the scope of application of article 26 is limited to the rights protected by the Covenant'.[27] The Committee succinctly rejected this argument stating 'the application of the principle of non-discrimination contained in article 26 is therefore not limited to those rights which are provided for in the Covenant.'[28] The Committee's approach might therefore simply be regarded as recognition of the complex realities in dealing with changing social security issues.

Prohibited Grounds of Discrimination

As noted above, both articles 2(1) and 26 contain an identical list of prohibited grounds of discrimination under the Covenant. These are: race, colour, sex, language, religion, political or other opinion, national or social origin, property and birth or any other status. From the formulation of these provisions it is clear that the prohibited grounds of discrimination are not exclusive and are capable of extension. Furthermore, it is clear that the existing grounds of prohibited discrimination are susceptible to interpretation, thus potentially extending the ambit of the stated grounds. In *Toonen v Australia*, for example, the author complained that two provisions of the Tasmanian Criminal Code which criminalized all forms of sexual contacts between consenting adult homosexual men in private was discriminatory. During the proceedings before the Committee the Australian government sought guidance upon whether sexual orientation was subsumed by the word 'sex' in article 26 of the Covenant. Noting that the same issue could arise under article 2(1) of the Covenant, the Committee observed that, in its view, 'the reference to "sex" in articles 2, paragraph 1, and 26 is to be taken as including sexual orientation'.[29] Discrimination on the basis of age was held to fall within the ambit of article 26 in the application of *Love et al v Australia*. The majority view did not elaborate upon this point placing the application under the heading of

27 *Wackenheim v France*, above n 11, para 4.4.

28 Ibid, para 6.6.

29 *Toonen v Australia*, Communication 488/1992, UN Doc CCPR/C/50/D/488/1992 (1994), para 8.7.

'other status',[30] but Nisuke Ando provided an individual opinion raising question with the Committee's methodology in this respect.[31]

Examples of discrimination on the stated grounds of race, colour, sex, language, religion, political or other opinion, national or social origin and property can be found in a number of views adopted by the Committee. However, in addition to these more or less transparent cases of discrimination, discrimination based on 'other status' has been elaborated by the Committee in an *ad hoc* fashion on a case-by-case basis.

Gender

Discrimination on grounds of sex has been found in a number of communications considered by the Committee. In *Aumeeruddy-Cziffra and 19 other Mauritian Women v Mauritius*, the authors claimed that the enactment of the Immigration (Amendment) Act, 1977, and the Deportation (Amendment) Act, 1977, by Mauritius discriminated against Mauritian women on grounds of sex, because the effect of the these Acts was to deprive alien husbands of Mauritian women of their residence status in Mauritius. The alien husbands of these women had to apply for a residence permit, the grant of which was discretionary. If they failed to seek and obtain a residence permit, they could be removed at any time by the Mauritian Minister of Interior. The legislation did not, however, affect the status of alien women married to Mauritian husbands who retained their legal right to residence in the country. The Committee had little difficulty in finding that the relevant legislation constituted discrimination based on grounds of sex since the women with foreign husbands were 'suffering from the adverse consequences of the statutes ... only because they are women'.[32] The Committee also noted that discrimination on grounds of sex was not prohibited by the Mauritian constitution.

Similarly in *Graciela Ato del Avellanal v Peru*, the Committee found a clear case of discrimination based on grounds of sex. Here, the author became the owner of two apartment buildings in Lima. On the change of ownership a number of tenants ceased paying rent for their apartments. After unsuccessful attempts to collect the overdue rent, the author sued the tenants. While the court of first instance found in her favour and ordered the tenants to pay her the rent due, the Superior Court reversed the judgment on the ground that the author was not entitled to sue, because, according to article 168 of the Peruvian Civil Code, only the husband of a married woman was entitled to act in respect of matrimonial property before the Courts. In other words, a married woman was not equal to her husband for the purposes of protecting matrimonial property. The Committee had little difficulty

30 *Love et al v Australia*, Communication 983/2001, UN Doc CCPR/C/77/D/983/2001 (2003), para 8.2.

31 Ibid, individual opinion of Committee Member Mr Nisuke Ando.

32 *Aumeeruddy-Cziffra et al v Mauritius*, Communication 35/1978, UN Doc CCPR/C/OP/1 at 67 (1985), para 9.2 (b) 2 (i) 6.

in finding that this distinction amounted to discrimination which was contrary to articles 3 and 26 of the Covenant.[33]

In *Müller and Engelhard v Namibia* the applicants claimed that Namibian law was discriminatory in imposing more strenuous obligations on a male spouse who wished to take his wife's name as opposed to a female spouse who wished to take her husband's name. Namibia argued that the difference in approach was to promote legal security and certainty of identity given the fact that it was a long-standing tradition in Namibia that women took their husbands name. Noting that a different treatment based on one of the specific grounds enumerated in article 26(2) of the Covenant places a heavy burden on the State party to explain the reason for the differentiation the Committee found that Namibia had not discharged this burden:[34]

> In view of the importance of the principle of equality between men and women, the argument of a long-standing tradition cannot be maintained as a general justification for different treatment of men and women, which is contrary to the Covenant. To subject the possibility of choosing the wife's surname as family name to stricter and much more cumbersome conditions than the alternative (choice of husband's surname) cannot be judged to be reasonable; at any rate the reason for the distinction has no sufficient importance in order to outweigh the generally excluded gender-based approach. Accordingly, the Committee finds that the authors have been the victims of discrimination and violation of article 26 of the Covenant.

Discrimination on grounds of sex has also been found in a number of communications involving indirect discrimination in respect of social security issues. In *Toonen v Australia* the State party called on the Committee to clarify whether or not sexual orientation was covered by the term 'other status' in article 26. The Committee responded that 'in its view the reference to "sex" in articles 2, paragraph 1, and 26 is to be taken as including sexual orientation'.[35] The decision in *Toonen* was ultimately decided on article 17 issues and the Committee did not expand upon the article 26 aspects. In *Young v Australia* the Committee was asked to address the matter of discrimination based on sexual orientation in a more direct fashion. In *Young* the applicant had been in a same-sex relationship for thirty eight years with a war veteran. Following his partner's death the applicant applied for pension benefit which was denied on the basis that he was not a dependant for the purposes of the domestic statute which defined a partner as an individual of the opposite

33 *Graciela Ato del Avellanal v Peru*, Communication 202/1986, UN Doc CCPR/C/34/D/202/1986 (1988).

34 *Müller and Engelhard v Namibia*, Communication 919/2000, UN Doc CCPR/C/74/D/919/2000 (2002), para 6.8.

35 *Toonen v Australia*, above n 29, para 8.7. Also *Young v Australia*, Communication 941/2000, UN Doc CCPR/C/78/D/941/2000 (2003), para 10.4.

sex. The applicant claimed that the denial of benefit due to sexual orientation was contrary to article 26 to which the Committee agreed:[36]

> The State party provides no arguments on how this distinction between same-sex partners, who are excluded from pension benefits under law, and unmarried heterosexual partners, who are granted such benefits, is reasonable and objective, and no evidence which would point to the existence of factors justifying such a distinction has been advanced.

The issue of sexual orientation was fundamental to the application of *Joslin et al v New Zealand*. Here, a number of lesbian couples complained that they had been discriminated against on grounds of sex because they had been refused a marriage licence on the grounds that under New Zealand law marriage could only take place between a man and a woman. Leaning heavily on the text of article 23(2) the Committee held:[37]

> Given the existence of a specific provision in the Covenant on the right to marriage, any claim that this right has been violated must be considered in the light of this provision. Article 23, paragraph 2, of the Covenant is the only substantive provision in the Covenant which defines a right by using the term 'men and women', rather than 'every human being', 'everyone' and 'all persons'. Use of the term 'men and women', rather than the general terms used elsewhere in Part III of the Covenant, has been consistently and uniformly understood as indicating that the treaty obligation of States parties stemming from article 23, paragraph 2, of the Covenant is to recognize as marriage only the union between a man and a woman wishing to marry each other.

As discussed in Chapter 8 the Committee's approach in this application was possibly designed to allow it to avoid having to make a pronouncement on a difficult social issue which would not have been appreciated even by moderately socially progressive States. But as the individual opinion in the application of *Young v Australia* explained, applications of this nature are likely to be more prevalent and will require the Committee to be clearer in its reasoning.[38]

Political Opinion

An example of apparent discrimination on grounds of political opinion can be found in *Valenzuela v Peru*. Here, the author was a member of the Peruvian bar

36 *Young v Australia*, ibid, para 10.4.

37 *Joslin et al v New Zealand*, Communication 902/1999, UN Doc CCPR/C/75/D/902/1999 (2002), para 8.2.

38 *Young v Australia*, above n 35, individual opinion by Committee members Mrs Ruth Wedgwood and Mr Franco DePasquale.

and had been a civil servant for 26 years. He had been counsel for the Chamber of Deputies and had served in the Peruvian Human Rights Commission for five years. Following a change of government in Peru in 1985, he was dismissed from his post at the Chamber of Deputies without any administrative proceedings. He claimed to be entitled to a civil servant's pension and sought to enforce this right in the courts. He further claimed that since he was opposed to the then government all attempts to obtain redress had been met by a politically motivated denial of justice. Since Peru did not provide information which contested these allegations, the Committee found that there had been a violation of article 26 because Valenzuela had not enjoyed equal protection of the law before the courts.[39] It will be noted that the Committee made no explicit finding of discrimination on grounds of political opinion, but it was clearly implicit from the tenor of its holding.

A communication in which the Committee did find explicitly that there had been discrimination on grounds of political opinion was *Bwalya v Zambia*.[40] In this case the author had been a political activist in Zambia who was opposed to the government of Kenneth Kaunda. He alleged that he had been subjected to intimidation, arbitrary detention and dismissal from employment because of his political opposition to the government. The Committee found, without elaboration, that the communication showed 'that the author has been discriminated against in his employment because of his political opinions, contrary to article 26 of the Covenant'.[41] A similar finding was made in *Oló Bahamonde v Equatorial Guinea* where the author alleged that since he did not share the views or adhere to the ruling party of the Guinean President, he was subjected to varying degrees of discrimination, intimidation and persecution, including arbitrary arrest. Equatorial Guinea was unable to provide compelling evidence with which to contradict these claims and as a result the Committee found that Bahamonde had been discriminated against because of his political opinions and his open criticism of, and opposition to, the government and the ruling political party, in violation of article 26.[42]

As noted above, since article 26 is an autonomous right, it applies to discrimination whether or not the actual subject matter of the complaint involves a right which is protected by the Covenant. Thus, although the right to property is not protected by the Covenant, if a person is deprived of that property because of their political opinion, it will constitute a violation of article 26. An example of this can be found in *Blancov v Nicaragua*. Here the author was arrested without a warrant and tried by a Peoples' Tribunal of the Sandinista Government for his outspoken criticism of the Marxist orientation of the Sandinistas. He was found

39 *Valenzuela v Peru*, above n 24, para 6.4.

40 *Bwalya v Zambia*, above n 24.

41 Ibid, para 6.7.

42 *Oló Bahamonde v Equatorial Guinea*, Communication 468/1991, UN Doc CCPR/C/49/D/468/1991 (1993), para 9.3.

guilty and sentenced to 30 years' imprisonment. Blancov also claimed that his property had been confiscated. On this latter point the Committee ruled:[43]

> With regard to the author's allegation concerning the confiscation of his property, the Committee recalls that the Covenant does not protect the right of property, as such. However, an issue under the Covenant may arise if a confiscation or expropriation is based on discriminatory grounds prohibited in article 26 of the Covenant. Although the author has stated that his property was confiscated as a consequence of his belonging to a category of persons whose political views were contrary to those of the Sandinista Government, and in a fashion that could be termed discriminatory, the Committee does not have sufficient facts before it to enable it to make a finding on this point.

It seems clear therefore that had the Committee possessed the evidence to support the author's claim there would have been no doubt that the confiscation of property because of the author's opinions being contrary to those of the incumbent government would have been in breach of article 26.

Religion

There have been few cases in which discrimination on grounds of religion has been found by the Committee.[44] In *Singh Binder v Canada*, the author, a Sikh, complained that the Canadian National Railway Company's rules requiring workers to wear protective helmets discriminated against Sikhs because their religion required them to wear turbans. Although there was clearly a case of indirect discrimination to answer since the regulations fell more heavily on Sikhs as a group, the Committee held that matters of health and safety provided an objective justification for the action taken.[45]

In *Waldman v Canada*, however, religious discrimination was found to exist. The matter being challenged in this communication was an Ontario law which gave the provincial government power to provide special funding for Catholic Schools while excluding other religious schools from such funding. The historical reason for this was to protect the position of the Catholic minority in a predominantly Protestant province. The author, who, because of the absence of a subsidy to schools of other religions, had to pay more for his children to attend a Jewish school argued that this law created a distinction or preference which was based on religion and which had the effect of impairing the enjoyment or exercise by

43 *Blancov v Nicaragua*, above n 21, para 10.1.

44 Communications to the Committee dealing with religious matters are commonly dealt with under article 18, but as Martin Scheinin has pointed out, there is a significant degree of interdependence between article 18 and article 26, see *Waldman v Canada*, above 24, individual opinion by Martin Scheinin, para 3.

45 *Singh Binder v Canada*, above n 11, para 6.2.

all persons, on an equal footing, of their religious rights and freedoms. He argued that the conferral of a benefit on a single religious group could not be justified and that when a right to publicly financed religious education was recognized by a State party, no differentiation should be made among individuals on the basis of the nature of their particular beliefs. The Committee agreed with the author's contentions. It found that if a State party chose to provide public funding to religious schools, it should make that funding available without discrimination or justify the funding of schools for one religious group and not for another on reasonable and objective criteria.[46] In the instant case, the Committee found that there was no evidence before it to show that the favourable treatment to the Roman Catholic faith and the correspondingly less favourable treatment to the author's religious denomination was based on such criteria. It consequently found that there had been a violation of the author's rights under article 26 of the Covenant to protection against discrimination.

Language

The application of *Ballantyne et al v Canada* involved a challenge to a provincial law in Quebec which required all commercial signs to be in French. The applicants were English speakers who carried out their business activities in English to a primarily English-speaking customer base. The applicants argued that the Quebec law put them at a disadvantage in comparison to businesses who conducted their commercial activities in French. The State responded that the law in question applied to all businesses, regardless of the language used by the proprietors and that its aims were legitimate and reasonable as the law was[47]

> … deliberately limited to the sphere of external public and commercial advertising, because it is there that the symbolic value of the language as a means of collective identification is strongest and contributes most to preserving the cultural identity of French speakers ….

The Committee held that the laws in question[48]

> … operate to prohibit the use of commercial advertising outdoors in other than the French language. This prohibition applies to French speakers as well as English speakers, so that a French speaking person wishing to advertise in English, in order to reach those of his or her clientele who are English speaking, may not do so. Accordingly, the Committee finds that the authors have not been discriminated against on the ground of their language, and concludes that there has been no violation of article 26 of the Covenant.

46 *Waldman v Canada*, above n 24, para 10.6.

47 *Ballantyne v Canada*, above n 7, para 8.7.

48 Ibid, para 11.5.

The Committee's reliance on the supposed impartiality of the law appears to overlook the actual impact of the law in the particular circumstances that existed in the State party making it clearly a matter of indirect discrimination due to the implications it had for the English-speaking part of society.[49]

In *Diergaardt v Namibia*, the authors claimed they were not allowed to use their Afrikaans mother tongue in court proceedings or in dealings with Namibian government officials, since English was designated the official language of the State. Namibia did not contest the allegations, so the majority of the Committee accepted the veracity of the facts and as a result of the Committee found that Namibia was in breach of article 26,[50] which appears to contradict the decision in *Ballantyne*. For this reason perhaps the decision prompted a number of dissenting opinions by Committee members. Abdalfattah Amor considered that there was no discrimination since all minority languages were placed on the same footing for the purposes of nation-building and to ensure that discrimination did not arise as between these languages. In granting speakers of Afrikaans the right to use their language, Mr Amor argued that the Committee was in fact granting them a privilege not accorded to other linguistic groups.[51] Nisuke Ando, however, took the view that Namibia's constitution put Afrikaans on precisely the same footing as any other native languages spoken in Namibia, thus guaranteeing Afrikaans equal treatment without discrimination. He went on to note that English was treated differently from all native languages including Afrikaans, but he argued that since each sovereign State may choose its own official language and that the official language may be treated differently from non-official languages, the differentiation in question constituted an objective and reasonable distinction and thus nullified any possible discrimination under article 26.[52] Committee members P.N. Bhagwati, Lord Colville and Maxwell Yalden were also strongly of the opinion that requiring Afrikaans speakers to use English, as the official language of the State, did not violate article 26. They observed that it was significant that nowhere in the communication was it alleged that the action of the State in declaring English as the official language and not allowing the use of other languages was directed only against the use of Afrikaans while permitting the other languages to be used. They thus took the view that in declaring English as the official language of the State and not allowing the use of other languages clearly did not violate article 26 because all languages other than English were treated on the same footing and

49 See Joseph et al, above n 24, who feel the situation in *Ballantyne* was potentially both direct and indirect discrimination, at p 699.

50 *Diergaardt v Namibia*, Communication 760/1997, UN Doc CCPR/C/69/D/760/1997 (2000), para 10.10.

51 Ibid, individual opinion of Abdalfattah Amor (dissenting), para 4.

52 Ibid, individual opinion of Nisuke Ando (dissenting).

were not allowed to be used for official purposes and there was no discrimination against Afrikaans *vis-à-vis* other languages.[53]

Other Status

The Committee has not been particularly explicit when discrimination on grounds of 'other status' arises, preferring instead to deal with the concept on a case by case basis. In fact, in most of the communications in which discrimination has been alleged on grounds of 'other status', the Committee has not found a violation, largely on the basis that the alleged discrimination was in fact a distinction between different classes of person which were based on objective and reasonable criteria. Nonetheless, some guidance can be found in these cases. In *B.d.B. et al v The Netherlands*, a group of physiotherapists alleged that they had been discriminated against by the Industrial Insurance Board for Health and for Mental and Social Interests and the Central Appeals Board. They argued that social security contributions payable by them were levied in a discriminatory manner because they became responsible for contributions for part-time contractors to their practice. The Committee, while finding that the group had been treated differently, was of the opinion that they could not demonstrate that this differential treatment was 'attributable to their belonging to any identifiably distinct category which could have exposed them to discrimination on account of any of the grounds enumerated or "other status" referred to in article 26 of the Covenant'.[54] This seems to suggest that other status must clearly encompass something more than a professional grouping, but it does not reveal what elevates a certain group of people to this protected category. There must clearly be some distinction which isolates a protected group from a non-protected group such as those in *B.d.B et al.* This point was made implicitly in *van Oord v The Netherlands*, where the authors complained that, as residents of the USA, they received a lower pension than Dutch citizens who were resident in Canada, Australia and New Zealand. The Committee found, however, that the categories of persons being compared in the communication were distinguishable because the bilateral agreements between the Netherlands and other States were based on reciprocity and thus constituted a reasonable and justifiable distinction.[55] It seems therefore that in order to fall within the definition of 'other status', one must belong to a group which is marked out by some inherent identifying factor which is not susceptible to change. Disabled persons would thus presumably constitute persons of an 'other status' deserving of protection from discrimination. We have already seen that a person's sexual

53 Ibid, individual opinion of PN. Bhagwati, Lord Colville and Maxwell Yalden (dissenting), paras 7–8.

54 *B.d.B et al v The Netherlands*, Communication 273/1988, UN Doc CCPR/C/35/D/273/1988 (1989), para 6.7.

55 *van Oord v The Netherlands*, Communication 658/1995, UN Doc CCPR/C/60/D/658/1995 (1997), para 8.5.

orientation falls within the concept of discrimination on grounds of sex, but if it did not, then, presumably, it would fall within the category of 'other status'.

Two cases which have acknowledged discrimination on grounds of nationality are, however, instructive. In *Gueye v France*, the complainant and 742 other retired Senegalese members of the French Army residing in Senegal complained of racial discrimination in French legislation, which provided for different treatment in the calculation of pensions of retired soldiers of Senegalese nationality who had served in the French Army prior to the independence of Senegal from France in 1960 and who receive pensions that are inferior to those enjoyed by retired French soldiers of French nationality. Although the Committee found that there was no evidence to support the allegation that France had engaged in racially discriminatory practices, none the less it was prepared to accept that there had been a differentiation by reference to nationality and that this fell within the reference to 'other status' in the second sentence of article 26.[56] Similarly, in *Adam v Czech Republic*, the author's father, Vlatislav Adam, was a Czech citizen whose property was confiscated by the Czechoslovak Government in 1949. Adam fled to Australia, where his three sons, including the author of the communication, were born. In 1985, Vlatislav Adam died and left his Czech property to his sons in his will. The sons had attempted, without success, to recover this property. In 1991, the Czech Republic enacted a law providing for restitution of the property or compensation for Czech citizens who had fled the country. On 6 December 1991, the author and his brothers submitted a claim for restitution of their property. Their claim was rejected on the grounds that they did not fulfil the requirement of the new law that applicants should have Czech citizenship and be permanently resident in the Czech Republic. Although the Committee noted that the author's claims related to property rights, which are not protected by the Covenant, it held that the facts of the communication appeared to raise an issue under article 26 of the Covenant since the confiscations themselves were alleged to be discriminatory, as was the new legislation of the Czech Republic which appeared to discriminate against persons who were not Czech citizens.[57]

A reliance on the provision of 'other status' has occurred in a number of cases involving military service and conscientious objection to such service in France;[58] in these cases, the authors were recognized conscientious objectors to military service who were assigned to civilian service duty. After one year of civilian service, they left their duty stations arguing that French law relating to civilian national service was discriminatory. Whereas people were required to perform military

56 *Gueye v France*, above n 23, paras 9.4–9.5.

57 *Adam v The Czech Republic*, Communication 586/1994, UN Doc CCPR/C/57/D/586/1994 (1996), paras 12.5 and 12.8.

58 *Foin v France*, Communication 666/1995, UN Doc CCPR/C/67/D/666/1995 (1999); *Maille v France*, Communication 689/1996, UN Doc CCPR/C/69/D/689/1996 (2000); *Venier and Nicolas v France*, Communication 690/1996 and 691/1996, UN Doc CCPR/C/69/D/690/1996 & 691/1996 (2000).

service for only one year, those who undertook civilian service were required to serve for two years. As a result of these actions, the authors were charged with, and convicted of, desertion in peacetime. France attempted to demonstrate that there were objective and reasonable justifications for extending the period of civilian service for conscientious objectors. Its argument was that doubling the length of service was the only way to test the sincerity of an individual's convictions in such circumstances. The Committee was not convinced by this argument and found that a violation of article 26 occurred, since the authors had been discriminated against on the basis of their conviction of conscience.[59]

The question of whether age constitutes a potential ground of discrimination within the category of other status has been considered in *Love et al v Australia* in which a number of Qantas pilots had been obliged to retire on reaching the age of 60. While the majority of the Committee found that age was a category of discrimination under the rubric of 'other status', the requirement that workers could be subject to compulsory retirement was justifiable on reasonable and objective grounds, in pursuit of an aim that was legitimate under the Covenant.[60] In this case it was the Committee's view that retirement age could include a dimension of workers' protection by limiting the life-long working time, in particular when comprehensive social security schemes secured the subsistence of retirees. Furthermore, at the time the compulsory retirement age was applied, it was general practice in the industry that retirement at 60 was necessary for aircraft safety. It is interesting to note, however, that Committee member Ando did not think that age could be comprehended as a ground of discrimination under the heading 'other status' because while all the other grounds enumerated in article 26 'are applicable only to a portion of the human species, however large it may be, age is applicable to the entire human race'. What Professor Ando's critique fails to address, however, is the application of circumstances which might render age a distinguishing characteristic.

Justifiable Differentiation

In General Comment 18 the Committee observes that:[61]

> … not every differentiation of treatment will constitute discrimination, if the criteria for such differentiation are reasonable and objective and if the aim is to achieve a purpose which is legitimate under the Covenant.

---

59 See *Venier and Nicolas v France*, ibid, para 10.4.

60 *Love et al v Australia*, above n 30, para 8.2.

61 General Comment 18, above n 3, para 13.

This approach has become the consistent jurisprudence of the Committee,[62] and most claims of discrimination have, in fact, been dismissed by the Committee on this ground. In fact, a review of the cases suggests that this particular hurdle is particularly difficult to overcome if the author of a communication wishes to demonstrate that they are the victim of discrimination under article 26 of the Covenant.

While it might be thought that General Comment 18 suggests a tripartite test of reasonableness, objectivity and legitimacy of purpose, it is apparent from the Committee's jurisprudence that such is not the case. Only in *Oulajin and Kaiss* has the Committee explicitly differentiated between the criteria of reasonableness and objectivity.[63] In other communications, the Committee has contented itself with stating in a general sense whether it considers differentiation to be objective and reasonable. The criterion of 'legitimacy of purpose' appears to be relegated to a subsidiary role, if, indeed, it appears at all. As with other areas of the Committee's activities, its jurisprudence in this area seems to have developed on an *ad hoc*, case by case basis.

In *Danning v The Netherlands*, the author complained that he was the victim of discrimination because, being in a 'common law' relationship with his fiancé, he continued to receive social security payments at a single person's rate rather than a married person's rate. The Committee held that this was an objective and reasonable differentiation. By choosing not to enter into marriage, Danning and his fiancé had not, in law, assumed the full extent of the duties and responsibilities incumbent on married couples. As a consequence of this, Danning was not entitled to receive the full benefits provided for in Netherlands law for married couples.[64] On the other hand, in *Sprenger v The Netherlands* the author's application for benefits was rejected on the grounds that she cohabited with a man whose income was higher than that permitted under the relevant regulations. The State explained that in matters of social security in this field there had been no general abolition of the distinction between married persons and cohabitants. The Committee found this argument compelling and thus held it to be differential treatment based on reasonable and objective grounds.[65] In *Vos v The Netherlands*, another case involving social security issues in the Netherlands, the author complained that her transfer from a disability pension to a lower widow's pension on the death of her husband amounted to discrimination under article 26. The Committee concluded that although Mrs Vos was indeed receiving lower benefits, it was persuaded in the

62 For example see *Zwaan de Vries v The Netherlands*, Communication 182/1984, UN Doc CCPR/C/OP/2 at 209 (1990), para 12.4; *Vos v The Netherlands*, above n 12, para 11.3; *Pauger v Austria*, Communication 415/1990, UN Doc CCPR/C/44/D/415/1990 at 122 (1992), para 7.2; *Sprenger v The Netherlands*, above n 23, para 7.2; *Oulajin and Kaiss v The Netherlands*, above n 13, para 7.3.

63 *Oulajin and Kaiss v The Netherlands*, above n 13, para 7.4.

64 *Danning v The Netherlands*, above n 23, para 14.

65 *Sprenger v The Netherlands*, above n 23, para 7.4.

light of the explanations given by the Netherlands that the unfavourable result of which she complained was the result of the application of a uniform rule to avoid overlapping in the allocation of social security benefits. The Committee found that this rule was thus based on objective and reasonable criteria, especially bearing in mind that the statutes under which Mrs Vos qualified for benefits were aimed at ensuring subsistence level income to all persons covered by them.[66] In *Araujo-Jongen v The Netherlands*, the Committee found that a requirement that the author be unemployed at the time of making an application for an unemployment benefit was reasonable and objective, in view of the purposes of the legislation in question, which was to provide assistance to persons who are unemployed.[67] Again, in *Neefs v The Netherlands*, a social security beneficiary who lived with his mother entered into a contract with her to be a sub-tenant. Neefs still, however, received benefits at a lower level because Netherlands law provided that where a beneficiary lived with a member of his or her family, they should be considered as a single household for benefit purposes. In this case the Committee observed that benefits under the Social Security Act were granted to people with low or no income in order to provide for their costs of living, and that the author had conceded that his costs of living were reduced by sharing a house with his mother. The Committee found therefore that the different treatment of parents and children contained in the regulations under the Social Security Act was neither unreasonable nor arbitrary, and its application did not constitute a violation of article 26 of the Covenant.[68] Social security legislation in the Netherlands was once again questioned in *Oulajin and Kaiss* where there was a distinction in the grant of support for a person's own natural children and foster children. In order to receive a grant for foster children, the child had to be living with the foster parent. Oulajin and Kaiss complained that this distinction bore more heavily on migrant workers and was therefore indirectly discriminatory. The Netherlands argued that the rationale underpinning the Child Benefit Act was to ensure that foster parents were practically involved in the raising of foster children. The Committee noted that the distinction between natural and foster children was objective and that it only needed to rule on the reasonableness of the situation. Here, the Committee ruled, in somewhat oracular fashion:[69]

> Bearing in mind that certain limitations in the granting of benefits may be inevitable, the Committee has considered whether the distinction between one's own children and foster children under the Child Benefit Act, in particular the requirement that a foster parent be involved in the upbringing of the foster children, as a precondition to the granting of benefits, is unreasonable. In the light of the explanations given by the State party, the Committee finds that the

66 *Vos v The Netherlands*, above n 12, para 12.

67 *Araujo-Jongen v The Netherlands*, above n 15, para 7.4.

68 *Neefs v The Netherlands*, Communication 425/1990, UN Doc CCPR/C/51/D/425/1990 (1994), para 7.4.

69 *Oulajin and Kaiss v The Netherlands*, above n 13, para 7.4.

> distinctions made in the Child Benefit Act are not incompatible with article 26 of the Covenant.

It will be noted here that the Committee stated that the distinctions made between foster and natural children were not 'incompatible' with article 26; what it did not say explicitly was that such distinctions were 'reasonable'. None the less, it would seem that this can be inferred from the general tenor of the Committee's ruling. The Committee used a similar formula in *Schmitz-de-Jong v The Netherlands*. In this case, the author was married to a Dutch citizen over the age of 65. Under Netherlands law, every Dutch citizen aged 65 years and older had the right to a pensioner's pass which allowed them to pay reduced fees for public transport, social and cultural activities, library services and museum entries. Partners of pass-holders also enjoyed a subsidiary right to the pass, on the condition that they were required to be 60 years or older. Here, however, the author was 44 years of age and had been denied a pass. Without providing any reasoning the Committee found that the age limitation of allowing only partners who had reached the age of 60 years to obtain an entitlement to entrance fee reductions as a partner to a pensioner above the age of 65 years was an objective criterion of differentiation and that the application of this differentiation in the case of the author was not unreasonable.[70] This finding seems difficult to justify, unless there is an implicit assumption on the part of the Committee that a claim such as this is essentially trivial.

The Committee has also found a number of distinctions in fields not involving social security law in the Netherlands which fulfil the requirements of objectivity and reasonableness and thus nullify any *prima facie* discrimination. In *Julian and Drake v New Zealand*, the authors, who had been civilian prisoners of the Japanese during the Second World War claimed that New Zealand by entering into a 1952 Peace Treaty with Japan and releasing Japan from the obligation to pay further reparation had violated international law and that this had adverse effects on the rights of New Zealanders, since New Zealand relied on the Peace Treaty as a basis for its lack of support for the claim of compensation for New Zealand citizens in international fora. They further claimed that New Zealand had discriminated against the authors because it had not provided compensation for the disabilities and incapacities suffered by the authors as a result of their mistreatment at the hands of the Japanese. On the other hand, ex-service personnel who had been incarcerated in German concentration camps during the Second World War had received an *ex gratia* payment by New Zealand in 1988. The Committee held, however, that the distinction was objective and reasonable and thus did not violate article 26. It found that the purpose of the relevant legislation was specifically to provide pension entitlements for disability and death of those who were in the service of New Zealand in wartime overseas and not to provide compensation

70 *Schmitz-de-Jong v The Netherlands*, Communication 855/1999, UN Doc CPR/C/72/D/855/1999 (2001), para 7.2.

for incarceration or for human rights violations.[71] In other words if the disability in question had arisen from war service it was irrelevant to the entitlement to a pension whether the person suffered imprisonment or cruel treatment by captors.

The Committee's final views in *Lestourneaud v France* will be of interest to lawyers. In this communication the author, an *avocat*, had been appointed under the State legal aid scheme to defend the interests of a minor who was the civil claimant in a criminal case involving rape and other sexual abuse. Under this scheme the defendant's lawyer was remunerated at a higher rate than that of the claimant's lawyer. The latter claimed that this was discriminatory because he had spent as much time on the case as the defendant's lawyer. The Committee, reiterating its jurisprudence that differences in treatment do not constitute discrimination when they are based on objective and reasonable criteria, held that representation of a person presenting a civil claim in a criminal case cannot be equated to representing the accused. The Committee did not explain why it came to this conclusion, but it did suggest that the evidence and arguments produced by the author had not persuaded them of the merit of his claim.[72]

In *Singh Binder v Canada*, a Sikh complained that rules requiring him to wear protective helmets indirectly discriminated against Sikhs because their religion required them to wear turbans. The Committee found, however, that these rules were reasonable and objectively justifiable in that they were designed to protect the health and safety of workers on Canada's railways.[73] In *Blom* and *Lindgren*, questions about the level of subsidies between State and private schools were raised. Here, subsidies were paid by the Swedish authorities at a lower rate to private schools than they were to public schools. The Committee found that 'the State party cannot be deemed to be under an obligation to provide the same benefits to private schools; indeed, the preferential treatment given to public sector schooling is reasonable and based on objective criteria'.[74] Again, there is little explanation in the Committee's views to support its reasoning, but it seems implicit that the State is under an obligation to support public schooling as a matter of social obligation, whereas private schooling is a matter of individual choice.

It appears the Committee will accept justifiable differentiations when the basis for such discrimination is essential for achieving particular social and political objectives. In *Stalla Colsta v Uruguay* the Committee accepted that a domestic law which was passed with the intention of redressing past wrongs resulting from the political situation in the State was not discriminatory as its objective

71 *Julian and Drake v New Zealand*, Communication 601/1994, UN Doc CCPR/C/59/D/601/1994 (1997), paras 8.4–8.8.

72 *Lestourneaud v France*, Communication 861/1999, UN Doc CCPR/C/67/D/861/1999 (1999), para 4.2.

73 *Singh Binder v Canada*, above n 11.

74 *Lindgren et al v Sweden*, Communication 298/1988 and 299/1988, UN Doc CCPR/C/40/D/298/1988 at 84 (1990), para 10.3; *Blom v Sweden*, above n 24, para 10.3.

was in line with the goals of the Covenant.[75] In *Gillot*, the authors complained that their prohibition from participating in referenda on self-determination in New Caledonia was discriminatory in nature since the electoral law in question bore more heavily on those of French citizenship, excluding them from participating in certain elections. The Committee noted that, given the special nature of the self-determination referenda, the criteria which allowed the strong ties to the territory of those taking part were objectively justifiable.[76]

In *O'Neill and Quinn v Ireland* the two applicants were serving jail sentences for an attempted robbery carried out in 1996 on behalf of the Irish Republican Army and where an Irish police officer was killed. In 1998 the Good Friday Agreement was agreed, setting out the basis for an end to the conflict involving Northern Ireland. Under the Agreement there were provisions for the release of prisoners who had committed certain offences and/or who acted on behalf of certain organizations. Both of the applicants met the criteria as set out in these provisions but the Irish government did not approve their release. The applicants argued that they were the only individuals who were excluded from the release scheme which was contrary to the obligations of Ireland under the Covenant. The Committee recognized the sensitivity of the circumstances surrounding this application, explaining:[77]

> The Committee notes that the State party justifies the exclusion of the authors (and others involved in the incident in which Garda McCabe was murdered) from the scheme, by reason of the combined circumstances of the incident in question, its timing (in the context of a breach of a cease-fire), its brutality, and the need to ensure public support for the GFA. In 1996 when the incident occurred, the government assessed the impact of the incident as exceptional. For this reason, it considered that all those involved would be excluded from any subsequent agreement on the release of prisoners. This decision was taken after the incident in question but before the conviction of those responsible, and thus, focused on the impact of the incident itself rather than on the individuals involved. All those responsible were made aware, from the outset, that if they were convicted of having had any involvement in the incident, they would be excluded from the scheme. … The Committee considers that it is not in a position to substitute the State party's assessment of facts with its own views, particularly with respect to a decision that was made nearly ten years ago, in a political context, and leading up to a peace agreement. It finds that the material in front of it does not disclose arbitrariness and concludes that the authors' rights

75 *Stalla Colsta v Uruguay*, Communication 198/1985, UN Doc CCPR/C/OP/2 at 221 (1990), para 10.

76 *Gillot et al v France*, Communication 932/2000, UN Doc CCPR/C/75/D/932/2000 (2002), paras 13.5–13.8.

77 *O'Neill and Quinn v Ireland*, Communication 1314/2004, UN Doc CCPR/C/87/D/1314/2004 (2006), para 8.4.

> under article 26 to equality before the law and to the equal protection of the law have not been violated.

The Committee's deferral to the State in this matter is not wholly unsurprising. During the negotiations and acceptance of the Good Friday Agreement there had been a number of public statements that the applicants would not be released due to the nature of their crimes and the impact their release would have on the overall peace process. One member of the Committee, Hipólito Solari-Yrigoyen, disagreed with the majority's deference in this respect explaining the Committee had to assess whether or not the decision not to release the applicants was based on fair and reasonable criteria regardless of the wider context of the peace process.[78]

A controversial case which raised questions about the relationship between objective justifications for differential treatment and issues of human dignity was *Wackenheim v France*. In this communication the applicant, who suffered from dwarfism, complained about a law which prohibited dwarf tossing. He alleged that this law prevented him from working and was thus an affront to his human dignity. France responded arguing that the ban on dwarf throwing was necessary to protect public order (one element of which was the protection of public morals) and due respect for the individual concerned. The Committee found that these justifications were based on objective and reasonable criteria which were compatible with the objectives of the Covenant, namely, the protection of public order and human dignity.

One argument which the Committee rejected in the *Wackenheim Case* is of broader interest. Here, the applicant argued that there were other (unspecified) activities which were as objectionable as dwarf tossing but which had not been banned by the authorities. Given the absence of a prohibition on these activities, the applicant argued that the banning of dwarf tossing was therefore discriminatory. The Committee responded stating:[79]

> … the Committee is of the opinion that, given that the ban on dwarf tossing is based on objective and reasonable criteria and the author has not established that this measure was discriminatory in purpose. The mere fact that there may be other activities liable to be banned is not in itself sufficient to confer a discriminatory character on the ban on dwarf tossing.

As other commentators have noted, the Committee's jurisprudence in the area of justifiable differentiation is far from consistent and determining what is reasonable and objective is a highly subjective process.[80]

---

78 Ibid, dissenting opinion by Hipólito Solari-Yrigoyen, para 3.

79 *Wackenheim v France*, above n 11, para 7.5.

80 Joseph et al, above n 24, p 700.

Affirmative Action

Although, as noted above, a number of provisions within the Covenant require the elimination of discrimination on various grounds, the question arises as to whether States parties are prevented from engaging in positive discrimination or adopting affirmative action programmes in order to benefit certain disadvantaged groups. On one reading, failure to take affirmative action to elevate such groups to a level of equality with other members of society could be regarded as the perpetuation of systemic discrimination and thus States would not be complying with their obligation to ensure equal and effective protection against discrimination as required by article 26. This obligation also exists in article 3 which requires States parties to ensure the equal right of men and women to all the Covenant rights. The Committee has discussed the need for affirmative action in a number of its General Comments. In General Comment 18 it is explained:[81]

> The Committee also wishes to point out that the principle of equality sometimes requires States parties to take affirmative action in order to diminish or eliminate conditions which cause or help to perpetuate discrimination prohibited by the Covenant. For example, in a State where the general conditions of a certain part of the population prevent or impair their enjoyment of human rights, the State should take specific action to correct those conditions. Such action may involve granting for a time to the part of the population concerned certain preferential treatment in specific matters as compared with the rest of the population. However, as long as such action is needed to correct discrimination in fact, it is a case of legitimate differentiation under the Covenant.

Further in General Comment 3 which deals with the general obligations of States parties under the Covenant it is explained:[82]

> The Committee considers it necessary to draw the attention of States parties to the fact that the obligation under the Covenant is not confined to the respect of human rights, but that States parties have also undertaken to ensure the enjoyment of these rights to all individuals under their jurisdiction. This aspect calls for specific activities by the States parties to enable individuals to enjoy their rights. This is obvious in a number of articles (e.g. art. 3 which is dealt with in General Comment 4 below), but in principle this undertaking relates to all rights set forth in the Covenant.

81 General Comment 18, above n 3, para 10.

82 *General Comment 3: Implementation at the national level*, UN Doc HRI/GEN/1/Rev.6 at 125 (2003), para 1.

And in General Comment 4 which deals with equality between men and women in the enjoyment of rights in the Covenant the Committee continues along similar lines:[83]

> Firstly, article 3, as articles 2 (1) and 26 in so far as those articles primarily deal with the prevention of discrimination on a number of grounds, among which sex is one, requires not only measures of protection but also affirmative action designed to ensure the positive enjoyment of rights. This cannot be done simply by enacting laws.

The circumstances involved in the application of *Ballantyne et al v Canada* involved the passage of laws to preserve French culture as the French society of Canada was a minority in the State as a whole and perceived to be under threat. The Committee rejected this argument when addressing freedom of expression issues saying the prohibition on commercial advertising in languages other than French was 'not necessary, in order to protect the vulnerable position in Canada of the francophone group'.[84]

The Committee did find in *Stalla Colsta v Uruguay* that the positive measures taken by the State to reinstate public officials who had lost their jobs during changes in the ruling regime were acceptable. The applicant had argued that since only former public officials who had been removed as a result of laws passed by the previous regime were being hired for public sector jobs, he was being denied access to the public service in a discriminatory way. The Committee took into account the overall purpose of the domestic law that was attempting to redress past wrongs. The Committee viewed the law as an 'effective remedy' to those individuals who had been denied their rights due to past actions and did not elaborate on its effect as an affirmative action measure.[85]

While the Committee has not addressed the question of affirmative action to any great degree, it is none the less arguable that where legislation or other measures of affirmative action are adopted they should be consistent with the Committee's jurisprudence in the area of justifiable differentiation. Thus the grounds for taking affirmative action should fulfil the tripartite test of General Comment 18 and should be therefore reasonable, objective and be directed towards the achievement of a purpose that is legitimate under the Covenant. These should be easily demonstrable if a disadvantaged section of society can be identified by reference to such factors as economic poverty or under-representation in areas such as government, employment, education and so on.

---

83 *General Comment 4: Equality between the sexes*, UN Doc HRI/GEN/1/Rev.6 at 126 (2003), para 2.

84 *Ballantyne v Canada*, above n 7, para 11.4.

85 *Stalla Colsta v Uruguay*, above n 75, para 10.

Appendix 1
International Covenant on Civil and Political Rights[1]

PREAMBLE

The States Parties to the present Covenant,

Considering that, in accordance with the principles proclaimed in the Charter of the United Nations, recognition of the inherent dignity and of the equal and inalienable rights of all members of the human family is the foundation of freedom, justice and peace in the world,

Recognizing that these rights derive from the inherent dignity of the human person,

Recognizing that, in accordance with the Universal Declaration of Human Rights, the ideal of free human beings enjoying civil and political freedom and freedom from fear and want can only be achieved if conditions are created whereby everyone may enjoy his civil and political rights, as well as his economic, social and cultural rights,

Considering the obligation of States under the Charter of the United Nations to promote universal respect for, and observance of, human rights and freedoms,

Realizing that the individual, having duties to other individuals and to the community to which he belongs, is under a responsibility to strive for the promotion and observance of the rights recognized in the present Covenant,

Agree upon the following articles:

PART I

Article 1

1. All peoples have the right of self-determination. By virtue of that right they freely determine their political status and freely pursue their economic, social and cultural development.

2. All peoples may, for their own ends, freely dispose of their natural wealth and resources without prejudice to any obligations arising out of international economic

1 International Covenant on Civil and Political Rights, opened for signature 16 December 1966, 999 UNTS 171 (entered into force 23 March 1976). As at 22 July 2008, there are 162 States parties to the ICCPR (together with eight further States who are signatories only): see Office of the United Nations High Commissioner for Human Rights 'Status of Ratifications of the Principal International Human Rights Treaties'.

co-operation, based upon the principle of mutual benefit, and international law. In no case may a people be deprived of its own means of subsistence.

3. The States Parties to the present Covenant, including those having responsibility for the administration of Non-Self-Governing and Trust Territories, shall promote the realization of the right of self-determination, and shall respect that right, in conformity with the provisions of the Charter of the United Nations.

PART II

Article 2

1. Each State Party to the present Covenant undertakes to respect and to ensure to all individuals within its territory and subject to its jurisdiction the rights recognized in the present Covenant, without distinction of any kind, such as race, colour, sex, language, religion, political or other opinion, national or social origin, property, birth or other status.

2. Where not already provided for by existing legislative or other measures, each State Party to the present Covenant undertakes to take the necessary steps, in accordance with its constitutional processes and with the provisions of the present Covenant, to adopt such legislative or other measures as may be necessary to give effect to the rights recognized in the present Covenant.

3. Each State Party to the present Covenant undertakes:

(a) To ensure that any person whose rights or freedoms as herein recognized are violated shall have an effective remedy, notwithstanding that the violation has been committed by persons acting in an official capacity;

(b) To ensure that any person claiming such a remedy shall have his right thereto determined by competent judicial, administrative or legislative authorities, or by any other competent authority provided for by the legal system of the State, and to develop the possibilities of judicial remedy;

(c) To ensure that the competent authorities shall enforce such remedies when granted.

Article 3

The States Parties to the present Covenant undertake to ensure the equal right of men and women to the enjoyment of all civil and political rights set forth in the present Covenant.

Article 4

1. In time of public emergency which threatens the life of the nation and the existence of which is officially proclaimed, the States Parties to the present Covenant may take measures derogating from their obligations under the present Covenant to the extent strictly required by the exigencies of the situation, provided that such measures are not inconsistent with their other obligations under international law and do not involve discrimination solely on the ground of race, colour, sex, language, religion or social origin.

2. No derogation from articles 6, 7, 8 (paragraphs 1 and 2), 11, 15, 16 and 18 may be made under this provision.
3. Any State Party to the present Covenant availing itself of the right of derogation shall immediately inform the other States Parties to the present Covenant, through the intermediary of the Secretary-General of the United Nations, of the provisions from which it has derogated and of the reasons by which it was actuated. A further communication shall be made, through the same intermediary, on the date on which it terminates such derogation.

Article 5

1. Nothing in the present Covenant may be interpreted as implying for any State, group or person any right to engage in any activity or perform any act aimed at the destruction of any of the rights and freedoms recognized herein or at their limitation to a greater extent than is provided for in the present Covenant.
2. There shall be no restriction upon or derogation from any of the fundamental human rights recognized or existing in any State Party to the present Covenant pursuant to law, conventions, regulations or custom on the pretext that the present Covenant does not recognize such rights or that it recognizes them to a lesser extent.

PART III

Article 6

1. Every human being has the inherent right to life. This right shall be protected by law. No one shall be arbitrarily deprived of his life.
2. In countries which have not abolished the death penalty, sentence of death may be imposed only for the most serious crimes in accordance with the law in force at the time of the commission of the crime and not contrary to the provisions of the present Covenant and to the Convention on the Prevention and Punishment of the Crime of Genocide. This penalty can only be carried out pursuant to a final judgement rendered by a competent court.
3. When deprivation of life constitutes the crime of genocide, it is understood that nothing in this article shall authorize any State Party to the present Covenant to derogate in any way from any obligation assumed under the provisions of the Convention on the Prevention and Punishment of the Crime of Genocide.
4. Anyone sentenced to death shall have the right to seek pardon or commutation of the sentence. Amnesty, pardon or commutation of the sentence of death may be granted in all cases.
5. Sentence of death shall not be imposed for crimes committed by persons below eighteen years of age and shall not be carried out on pregnant women.
6. Nothing in this article shall be invoked to delay or to prevent the abolition of capital punishment by any State Party to the present Covenant.

Article 7

No one shall be subjected to torture or to cruel, inhuman or degrading treatment or punishment. In particular, no one shall be subjected without his free consent to medical or scientific experimentation.

Article 8

1. No one shall be held in slavery; slavery and the slave-trade in all their forms shall be prohibited.
2. No one shall be held in servitude.

3.(a) No one shall be required to perform forced or compulsory labour;

(b) Paragraph 3 (a) shall not be held to preclude, in countries where imprisonment with hard labour may be imposed as a punishment for a crime, the performance of hard labour in pursuance of a sentence to such punishment by a competent court;

(c) For the purpose of this paragraph the term 'forced or compulsory labour' shall not include:

(i) Any work or service, not referred to in subparagraph (b), normally required of a person who is under detention in consequence of a lawful order of a court, or of a person during conditional release from such detention;

(ii) Any service of a military character and, in countries where conscientious objection is recognized, any national service required by law of conscientious objectors;

(iii) Any service exacted in cases of emergency or calamity threatening the life or well-being of the community;

(iv) Any work or service which forms part of normal civil obligations.

Article 9

1. Everyone has the right to liberty and security of person. No one shall be subjected to arbitrary arrest or detention. No one shall be deprived of his liberty except on such grounds and in accordance with such procedure as are established by law.
2. Anyone who is arrested shall be informed, at the time of arrest, of the reasons for his arrest and shall be promptly informed of any charges against him.
3. Anyone arrested or detained on a criminal charge shall be brought promptly before a judge or other officer authorized by law to exercise judicial power and shall be entitled to trial within a reasonable time or to release. It shall not be the general rule that persons awaiting trial shall be detained in custody, but release may be subject to guarantees to appear for trial, at any other stage of the judicial proceedings, and, should occasion arise, for execution of the judgement.
4. Anyone who is deprived of his liberty by arrest or detention shall be entitled to take proceedings before a court, in order that court may decide without delay on the lawfulness of his detention and order his release if the detention is not lawful.

5. Anyone who has been the victim of unlawful arrest or detention shall have an enforceable right to compensation.

Article 10

1. All persons deprived of their liberty shall be treated with humanity and with respect for the inherent dignity of the human person.

2.(a) Accused persons shall, save in exceptional circumstances, be segregated from convicted persons and shall be subject to separate treatment appropriate to their status as unconvicted persons;

(b) Accused juvenile persons shall be separated from adults and brought as speedily as possible for adjudication.

3. The penitentiary system shall comprise treatment of prisoners the essential aim of which shall be their reformation and social rehabilitation. Juvenile offenders shall be segregated from adults and be accorded treatment appropriate to their age and legal status.

Article 11

No one shall be imprisoned merely on the ground of inability to fulfil a contractual obligation.

Article 12

1. Everyone lawfully within the territory of a State shall, within that territory, have the right to liberty of movement and freedom to choose his residence.

2. Everyone shall be free to leave any country, including his own.

3. The above-mentioned rights shall not be subject to any restrictions except those which are provided by law, are necessary to protect national security, public order (ordre public), public health or morals or the rights and freedoms of others, and are consistent with the other rights recognized in the present Covenant.

4. No one shall be arbitrarily deprived of the right to enter his own country.

Article 13

An alien lawfully in the territory of a State Party to the present Covenant may be expelled therefrom only in pursuance of a decision reached in accordance with law and shall, except where compelling reasons of national security otherwise require, be allowed to submit the reasons against his expulsion and to have his case reviewed by, and be represented for the purpose before, the competent authority or a person or persons especially designated by the competent authority.

Article 14

1. All persons shall be equal before the courts and tribunals. In the determination of any criminal charge against him, or of his rights and obligations in a suit at law, everyone shall be entitled to a fair and public hearing by a competent, independent and impartial tribunal established by law. The press and the public may be excluded from all or part of a trial for reasons of morals, public order (ordre public) or

national security in a democratic society, or when the interest of the private lives of the parties so requires, or to the extent strictly necessary in the opinion of the court in special circumstances where publicity would prejudice the interests of justice; but any judgement rendered in a criminal case or in a suit at law shall be made public except where the interest of juvenile persons otherwise requires or the proceedings concern matrimonial disputes or the guardianship of children.

2. Everyone charged with a criminal offence shall have the right to be presumed innocent until proved guilty according to law.

3. In the determination of any criminal charge against him, everyone shall be entitled to the following minimum guarantees, in full equality:

(a) To be informed promptly and in detail in a language which he understands of the nature and cause of the charge against him;
(b) To have adequate time and facilities for the preparation of his defence and to communicate with counsel of his own choosing;
(c) To be tried without undue delay;
(d) To be tried in his presence, and to defend himself in person or through legal assistance of his own choosing; to be informed, if he does not have legal assistance, of this right; and to have legal assistance assigned to him, in any case where the interests of justice so require, and without payment by him in any such case if he does not have sufficient means to pay for it;
(e) To examine, or have examined, the witnesses against him and to obtain the attendance and examination of witnesses on his behalf under the same conditions as witnesses against him;
(f) To have the free assistance of an interpreter if he cannot understand or speak the language used in court;
(g) Not to be compelled to testify against himself or to confess guilt.

4. In the case of juvenile persons, the procedure shall be such as will take account of their age and the desirability of promoting their rehabilitation.

5. Everyone convicted of a crime shall have the right to his conviction and sentence being reviewed by a higher tribunal according to law.

6. When a person has by a final decision been convicted of a criminal offence and when subsequently his conviction has been reversed or he has been pardoned on the ground that a new or newly discovered fact shows conclusively that there has been a miscarriage of justice, the person who has suffered punishment as a result of such conviction shall be compensated according to law, unless it is proved that the non-disclosure of the unknown fact in time is wholly or partly attributable to him.

7. No one shall be liable to be tried or punished again for an offence for which he has already been finally convicted or acquitted in accordance with the law and penal procedure of each country.

Article 15

1. No one shall be held guilty of any criminal offence on account of any act or omission which did not constitute a criminal offence, under national or

international law, at the time when it was committed. Nor shall a heavier penalty be imposed than the one that was applicable at the time when the criminal offence was committed. If, subsequent to the commission of the offence, provision is made by law for the imposition of the lighter penalty, the offender shall benefit thereby.
2. Nothing in this article shall prejudice the trial and punishment of any person for any act or omission which, at the time when it was committed, was criminal according to the general principles of law recognized by the community of nations.

Article 16
Everyone shall have the right to recognition everywhere as a person before the law.

Article 17
1. No one shall be subjected to arbitrary or unlawful interference with his privacy, family, home or correspondence, nor to unlawful attacks on his honour and reputation.
2. Everyone has the right to the protection of the law against such interference or attacks.

Article 18
1. Everyone shall have the right to freedom of thought, conscience and religion. This right shall include freedom to have or to adopt a religion or belief of his choice, and freedom, either individually or in community with others and in public or private, to manifest his religion or belief in worship, observance, practice and teaching.
2. No one shall be subject to coercion which would impair his freedom to have or to adopt a religion or belief of his choice.
3. Freedom to manifest one's religion or beliefs may be subject only to such limitations as are prescribed by law and are necessary to protect public safety, order, health, or morals or the fundamental rights and freedoms of others.
4. The States Parties to the present Covenant undertake to have respect for the liberty of parents and, when applicable, legal guardians to ensure the religious and moral education of their children in conformity with their own convictions.

Article 19
1. Everyone shall have the right to hold opinions without interference.
2. Everyone shall have the right to freedom of expression; this right shall include freedom to seek, receive and impart information and ideas of all kinds, regardless of frontiers, either orally, in writing or in print, in the form of art, or through any other media of his choice.
3. The exercise of the rights provided for in paragraph 2 of this article carries with it special duties and responsibilities. It may therefore be subject to

certain restrictions, but these shall only be such as are provided by law and are necessary:

(a) For respect of the rights or reputations of others;
(b) For the protection of national security or of public order (ordre public), or of public health or morals.

Article 20

1. Any propaganda for war shall be prohibited by law.
2. Any advocacy of national, racial or religious hatred that constitutes incitement to discrimination, hostility or violence shall be prohibited by law.

Article 21

The right of peaceful assembly shall be recognized. No restrictions may be placed on the exercise of this right other than those imposed in conformity with the law and which are necessary in a democratic society in the interests of national security or public safety, public order (ordre public), the protection of public health or morals or the protection of the rights and freedoms of others.

Article 22

1. Everyone shall have the right to freedom of association with others, including the right to form and join trade unions for the protection of his interests.
2. No restrictions may be placed on the exercise of this right other than those which are prescribed by law and which are necessary in a democratic society in the interests of national security or public safety, public order (ordre public), the protection of public health or morals or the protection of the rights and freedoms of others. This article shall not prevent the imposition of lawful restrictions on members of the armed forces and of the police in their exercise of this right.
3. Nothing in this article shall authorize States Parties to the International Labour Organisation Convention of 1948 concerning Freedom of Association and Protection of the Right to Organize to take legislative measures which would prejudice, or to apply the law in such a manner as to prejudice, the guarantees provided for in that Convention.

Article 23

1. The family is the natural and fundamental group unit of society and is entitled to protection by society and the State.
2. The right of men and women of marriageable age to marry and to found a family shall be recognized.
3. No marriage shall be entered into without the free and full consent of the intending spouses.
4. States Parties to the present Covenant shall take appropriate steps to ensure equality of rights and responsibilities of spouses as to marriage, during marriage and at its dissolution. In the case of dissolution, provision shall be made for the necessary protection of any children.

Article 24

1. Every child shall have, without any discrimination as to race, colour, sex, language, religion, national or social origin, property or birth, the right to such measures of protection as are required by his status as a minor, on the part of his family, society and the State.

2. Every child shall be registered immediately after birth and shall have a name.

3. Every child has the right to acquire a nationality.

Article 25

Every citizen shall have the right and the opportunity, without any of the distinctions mentioned in article 2 and without unreasonable restrictions:

(a) To take part in the conduct of public affairs, directly or through freely chosen representatives;

(b) To vote and to be elected at genuine periodic elections which shall be by universal and equal suffrage and shall be held by secret ballot, guaranteeing the free expression of the will of the electors;

(c) To have access, on general terms of equality, to public service in his country.

Article 26

All persons are equal before the law and are entitled without any discrimination to the equal protection of the law. In this respect, the law shall prohibit any discrimination and guarantee to all persons equal and effective protection against discrimination on any ground such as race, colour, sex, language, religion, political or other opinion, national or social origin, property, birth or other status.

Article 27

In those States in which ethnic, religious or linguistic minorities exist, persons belonging to such minorities shall not be denied the right, in community with the other members of their group, to enjoy their own culture, to profess and practise their own religion, or to use their own language.

PART IV

Article 28

1. There shall be established a Human Rights Committee (hereafter referred to in the present Covenant as the Committee). It shall consist of eighteen members and shall carry out the functions hereinafter provided.

2. The Committee shall be composed of nationals of the States Parties to the present Covenant who shall be persons of high moral character and recognized competence in the field of human rights, consideration being given to the usefulness of the participation of some persons having legal experience.

3. The members of the Committee shall be elected and shall serve in their personal capacity.

Article 29

1. The members of the Committee shall be elected by secret ballot from a list of persons possessing the qualifications prescribed in article 28 and nominated for the purpose by the States Parties to the present Covenant.

2. Each State Party to the present Covenant may nominate not more than two persons. These persons shall be nationals of the nominating State.

3. A person shall be eligible for renomination.

Article 30

1. The initial election shall be held no later than six months after the date of the entry into force of the present Covenant.

2. At least four months before the date of each election to the Committee, other than an election to fill a vacancy declared in accordance with article 34, the Secretary-General of the United Nations shall address a written invitation to the States Parties to the present Covenant to submit their nominations for membership of the Committee within three months.

3. The Secretary-General of the United Nations shall prepare a list in alphabetical order of all the persons thus nominated, with an indication of the States Parties which have nominated them, and shall submit it to the States Parties to the present Covenant no later than one month before the date of each election.

4. Elections of the members of the Committee shall be held at a meeting of the States Parties to the present Covenant convened by the Secretary General of the United Nations at the Headquarters of the United Nations. At that meeting, for which two thirds of the States Parties to the present Covenant shall constitute a quorum, the persons elected to the Committee shall be those nominees who obtain the largest number of votes and an absolute majority of the votes of the representatives of States Parties present and voting.

Article 31

1. The Committee may not include more than one national of the same State.

2. In the election of the Committee, consideration shall be given to equitable geographical distribution of membership and to the representation of the different forms of civilization and of the principal legal systems.

Article 32

1. The members of the Committee shall be elected for a term of four years. They shall be eligible for re-election if renominated. However, the terms of nine of the members elected at the first election shall expire at the end of two years; immediately after the first election, the names of these nine members shall be chosen by lot by the Chairman of the meeting referred to in article 30, paragraph 4.

2. Elections at the expiry of office shall be held in accordance with the preceding articles of this part of the present Covenant.

Article 33

1. If, in the unanimous opinion of the other members, a member of the Committee has ceased to carry out his functions for any cause other than absence of a temporary character, the Chairman of the Committee shall notify the Secretary-General of the United Nations, who shall then declare the seat of that member to be vacant.

2. In the event of the death or the resignation of a member of the Committee, the Chairman shall immediately notify the Secretary-General of the United Nations, who shall declare the seat vacant from the date of death or the date on which the resignation takes effect.

Article 34

1. When a vacancy is declared in accordance with article 33 and if the term of office of the member to be replaced does not expire within six months of the declaration of the vacancy, the Secretary-General of the United Nations shall notify each of the States Parties to the present Covenant, which may within two months submit nominations in accordance with article 29 for the purpose of filling the vacancy.

2. The Secretary-General of the United Nations shall prepare a list in alphabetical order of the persons thus nominated and shall submit it to the States Parties to the present Covenant. The election to fill the vacancy shall then take place in accordance with the relevant provisions of this part of the present Covenant.

3. A member of the Committee elected to fill a vacancy declared in accordance with article 33 shall hold office for the remainder of the term of the member who vacated the seat on the Committee under the provisions of that article.

Article 35

The members of the Committee shall, with the approval of the General Assembly of the United Nations, receive emoluments from United Nations resources on such terms and conditions as the General Assembly may decide, having regard to the importance of the Committee's responsibilities.

Article 36

The Secretary-General of the United Nations shall provide the necessary staff and facilities for the effective performance of the functions of the Committee under the present Covenant.

Article 37

1. The Secretary-General of the United Nations shall convene the initial meeting of the Committee at the Headquarters of the United Nations.

2. After its initial meeting, the Committee shall meet at such times as shall be provided in its rules of procedure.

3. The Committee shall normally meet at the Headquarters of the United Nations or at the United Nations Office at Geneva.

Article 38

Every member of the Committee shall, before taking up his duties, make a solemn declaration in open committee that he will perform his functions impartially and conscientiously.

Article 39

1. The Committee shall elect its officers for a term of two years. They may be re-elected.

2. The Committee shall establish its own rules of procedure, but these rules shall provide, inter alia, that:

(a) Twelve members shall constitute a quorum;

(b) Decisions of the Committee shall be made by a majority vote of the members present.

Article 40

1. The States Parties to the present Covenant undertake to submit reports on the measures they have adopted which give effect to the rights recognized herein and on the progress made in the enjoyment of those rights:

(a) Within one year of the entry into force of the present Covenant for the States Parties concerned;

(b) Thereafter whenever the Committee so requests.

2. All reports shall be submitted to the Secretary-General of the United Nations, who shall transmit them to the Committee for consideration. Reports shall indicate the factors and difficulties, if any, affecting the implementation of the present Covenant.

3. The Secretary-General of the United Nations may, after consultation with the Committee, transmit to the specialized agencies concerned copies of such parts of the reports as may fall within their field of competence.

4. The Committee shall study the reports submitted by the States Parties to the present Covenant. It shall transmit its reports, and such general comments as it may consider appropriate, to the States Parties. The Committee may also transmit to the Economic and Social Council these comments along with the copies of the reports it has received from States Parties to the present Covenant.

5. The States Parties to the present Covenant may submit to the Committee observations on any comments that may be made in accordance with paragraph 4 of this article.

Article 41

1. A State Party to the present Covenant may at any time declare under this article that it recognizes the competence of the Committee to receive and consider communications to the effect that a State Party claims that another State Party is not fulfilling its obligations under the present Covenant. Communications under this article may be received and considered only if submitted by a State Party which has made a declaration recognizing in regard to itself the competence of the

Committee. No communication shall be received by the Committee if it concerns a State Party which has not made such a declaration. Communications received under this article shall be dealt with in accordance with the following procedure:

(a) If a State Party to the present Covenant considers that another State Party is not giving effect to the provisions of the present Covenant, it may, by written communication, bring the matter to the attention of that State Party. Within three months after the receipt of the communication the receiving State shall afford the State which sent the communication an explanation, or any other statement in writing clarifying the matter which should include, to the extent possible and pertinent, reference to domestic procedures and remedies taken, pending, or available in the matter;

(b) If the matter is not adjusted to the satisfaction of both States Parties concerned within six months after the receipt by the receiving State of the initial communication, either State shall have the right to refer the matter to the Committee, by notice given to the Committee and to the other State;

(c) The Committee shall deal with a matter referred to it only after it has ascertained that all available domestic remedies have been invoked and exhausted in the matter, in conformity with the generally recognized principles of international law. This shall not be the rule where the application of the remedies is unreasonably prolonged;

(d) The Committee shall hold closed meetings when examining communications under this article;

(e) Subject to the provisions of subparagraph (c), the Committee shall make available its good offices to the States Parties concerned with a view to a friendly solution of the matter on the basis of respect for human rights and fundamental freedoms as recognized in the present Covenant;

(f) In any matter referred to it, the Committee may call upon the States Parties concerned, referred to in subparagraph (b), to supply any relevant information;

(g) The States Parties concerned, referred to in subparagraph (b), shall have the right to be represented when the matter is being considered in the Committee and to make submissions orally and/or in writing;

(h) The Committee shall, within twelve months after the date of receipt of notice under subparagraph (b), submit a report:

   (i) If a solution within the terms of subparagraph (e) is reached, the Committee shall confine its report to a brief statement of the facts and of the solution reached;

   (ii) If a solution within the terms of subparagraph (e) is not reached, the Committee shall confine its report to a brief statement of the facts; the written submissions and record of the oral submissions made by the States Parties concerned shall be attached to the report. In every matter, the report shall be communicated to the States Parties concerned.

2. The provisions of this article shall come into force when ten States Parties to the present Covenant have made declarations under paragraph I of this article. Such

declarations shall be deposited by the States Parties with the Secretary-General of the United Nations, who shall transmit copies thereof to the other States Parties. A declaration may be withdrawn at any time by notification to the Secretary-General. Such a withdrawal shall not prejudice the consideration of any matter which is the subject of a communication already transmitted under this article; no further communication by any State Party shall be received after the notification of withdrawal of the declaration has been received by the Secretary-General, unless the State Party concerned has made a new declaration.

Article 42

1.(a) If a matter referred to the Committee in accordance with article 41 is not resolved to the satisfaction of the States Parties concerned, the Committee may, with the prior consent of the States Parties concerned, appoint an ad hoc Conciliation Commission (hereinafter referred to as the Commission). The good offices of the Commission shall be made available to the States Parties concerned with a view to an amicable solution of the matter on the basis of respect for the present Covenant;

(b) The Commission shall consist of five persons acceptable to the States Parties concerned. If the States Parties concerned fail to reach agreement within three months on all or part of the composition of the Commission, the members of the Commission concerning whom no agreement has been reached shall be elected by secret ballot by a two-thirds majority vote of the Committee from among its members.

2. The members of the Commission shall serve in their personal capacity. They shall not be nationals of the States Parties concerned, or of a State not Party to the present Covenant, or of a State Party which has not made a declaration under article 41.

3. The Commission shall elect its own Chairman and adopt its own rules of procedure.

4. The meetings of the Commission shall normally be held at the Headquarters of the United Nations or at the United Nations Office at Geneva. However, they may be held at such other convenient places as the Commission may determine in consultation with the Secretary-General of the United Nations and the States Parties concerned.

5. The secretariat provided in accordance with article 36 shall also service the commissions appointed under this article.

6. The information received and collated by the Committee shall be made available to the Commission and the Commission may call upon the States Parties concerned to supply any other relevant information.

7. When the Commission has fully considered the matter, but in any event not later than twelve months after having been seized of the matter, it shall submit to the Chairman of the Committee a report for communication to the States Parties concerned:

(a) If the Commission is unable to complete its consideration of the matter within twelve months, it shall confine its report to a brief statement of the status of its consideration of the matter;
(b) If an amicable solution to the matter on tie basis of respect for human rights as recognized in the present Covenant is reached, the Commission shall confine its report to a brief statement of the facts and of the solution reached;
(c) If a solution within the terms of subparagraph (b) is not reached, the Commission's report shall embody its findings on all questions of fact relevant to the issues between the States Parties concerned, and its views on the possibilities of an amicable solution of the matter. This report shall also contain the written submissions and a record of the oral submissions made by the States Parties concerned;
(d) If the Commission's report is submitted under subparagraph (c), the States Parties concerned shall, within three months of the receipt of the report, notify the Chairman of the Committee whether or not they accept the contents of the report of the Commission.

8. The provisions of this article are without prejudice to the responsibilities of the Committee under article 41.

9. The States Parties concerned shall share equally all the expenses of the members of the Commission in accordance with estimates to be provided by the Secretary-General of the United Nations.

10. The Secretary-General of the United Nations shall be empowered to pay the expenses of the members of the Commission, if necessary, before reimbursement by the States Parties concerned, in accordance with paragraph 9 of this article.

Article 43

The members of the Committee, and of the ad hoc conciliation commissions which may be appointed under article 42, shall be entitled to the facilities, privileges and immunities of experts on mission for the United Nations as laid down in the relevant sections of the Convention on the Privileges and Immunities of the United Nations.

Article 44

The provisions for the implementation of the present Covenant shall apply without prejudice to the procedures prescribed in the field of human rights by or under the constituent instruments and the conventions of the United Nations and of the specialized agencies and shall not prevent the States Parties to the present Covenant from having recourse to other procedures for settling a dispute in accordance with general or special international agreements in force between them.

Article 45

The Committee shall submit to the General Assembly of the United Nations, through the Economic and Social Council, an annual report on its activities.

PART V

Article 46
Nothing in the present Covenant shall be interpreted as impairing the provisions of the Charter of the United Nations and of the constitutions of the specialized agencies which define the respective responsibilities of the various organs of the United Nations and of the specialized agencies in regard to the matters dealt with in the present Covenant.

Article 47
Nothing in the present Covenant shall be interpreted as impairing the inherent right of all peoples to enjoy and utilize fully and freely their natural wealth and resources.

PART VI

Article 48
1. The present Covenant is open for signature by any State Member of the United Nations or member of any of its specialized agencies, by any State Party to the Statute of the International Court of Justice, and by any other State which has been invited by the General Assembly of the United Nations to become a Party to the present Covenant.
2. The present Covenant is subject to ratification. Instruments of ratification shall be deposited with the Secretary-General of the United Nations.
3. The present Covenant shall be open to accession by any State referred to in paragraph 1 of this article.
4. Accession shall be effected by the deposit of an instrument of accession with the Secretary-General of the United Nations.
5. The Secretary-General of the United Nations shall inform all States which have signed this Covenant or acceded to it of the deposit of each instrument of ratification or accession.

Article 49
1. The present Covenant shall enter into force three months after the date of the deposit with the Secretary-General of the United Nations of the thirty-fifth instrument of ratification or instrument of accession.
2. For each State ratifying the present Covenant or acceding to it after the deposit of the thirty-fifth instrument of ratification or instrument of accession, the present Covenant shall enter into force three months after the date of the deposit of its own instrument of ratification or instrument of accession.

Article 50
The provisions of the present Covenant shall extend to all parts of federal States without any limitations or exceptions.

Article 51

1. Any State Party to the present Covenant may propose an amendment and file it with the Secretary-General of the United Nations. The Secretary-General of the United Nations shall thereupon communicate any proposed amendments to the States Parties to the present Covenant with a request that they notify him whether they favour a conference of States Parties for the purpose of considering and voting upon the proposals. In the event that at least one third of the States Parties favours such a conference, the Secretary-General shall convene the conference under the auspices of the United Nations. Any amendment adopted by a majority of the States Parties present and voting at the conference shall be submitted to the General Assembly of the United Nations for approval.

2. Amendments shall come into force when they have been approved by the General Assembly of the United Nations and accepted by a two-thirds majority of the States Parties to the present Covenant in accordance with their respective constitutional processes.

3. When amendments come into force, they shall be binding on those States Parties which have accepted them, other States Parties still being bound by the provisions of the present Covenant and any earlier amendment which they have accepted.

Article 52

Irrespective of the notifications made under article 48, paragraph 5, the Secretary-General of the United Nations shall inform all States referred to in paragraph I of the same article of the following particulars:

(a) Signatures, ratifications and accessions under article 48;

(b) The date of the entry into force of the present Covenant under article 49 and the date of the entry into force of any amendments under article 51.

Article 53

1. The present Covenant, of which the Chinese, English, French, Russian and Spanish texts are equally authentic, shall be deposited in the archives of the United Nations.

2. The Secretary-General of the United Nations shall transmit certified copies of the present Covenant to all States referred to in article 48.

Appendix 2

Optional Protocol to the International Covenant on Civil and Political Rights[1]

The States Parties to the present Protocol,

Political Rights (hereinafter referred to as the Covenant) and the implementation of its provisions it would be appropriate to enable the Human Rights Committee set up in part IV of the Covenant (hereinafter referred to as the Committee) to receive and consider, as provided in the present Protocol, communications from individuals claiming to be victims of violations of any of the rights set forth in the Covenant.

Have agreed as follows:

Article 1
A State Party to the Covenant that becomes a Party to the present Protocol recognizes the competence of the Committee to receive and consider communications from individuals subject to its jurisdiction who claim to be victims of a violation by that State Party of any of the rights set forth in the Covenant. No communication shall be received by the Committee if it concerns a State Party to the Covenant which is not a Party to the present Protocol.

Article 2
Subject to the provisions of article 1, individuals who claim that any of their rights enumerated in the Covenant have been violated and who have exhausted all available domestic remedies may submit a written communication to the Committee for consideration.

Article 3
The Committee shall consider inadmissible any communication under the present Protocol which is anonymous, or which it considers to be an abuse of the right of

1 Optional Protocol to the International Covenant on Civil and Political Rights, opened for signature 16 December 1966, 999 UNTS 302 (entered into force 23 March 1976). As at 18 April 2008, there are 119 States parties to the Protocol: see Office of the United Nations High Commissioner for Human Rights 'Status of Ratifications of the Principal International Human Rights Treaties'.

submission of such communications or to be incompatible with the provisions of the Covenant.

Article 4

1. Subject to the provisions of article 3, the Committee shall bring any communications submitted to it under the present Protocol to the attention of the State Party to the present Protocol alleged to be violating any provision of the Covenant.

2. Within six months, the receiving State shall submit to the Committee written explanations or statements clarifying the matter and the remedy, if any, that may have been taken by that State.

Article 5

1. The Committee shall consider communications received under the present Protocol in the light of all written information made available to it by the individual and by the State Party concerned.

2. The Committee shall not consider any communication from an individual unless it has ascertained that:

(a) The same matter is not being examined under another procedure of international investigation or settlement;

(b) The individual has exhausted all available domestic remedies. This shall not be the rule where the application of the remedies is unreasonably prolonged.

3. The Committee shall hold closed meetings when examining communications under the present Protocol.

4. The Committee shall forward its views to the State Party concerned and to the individual.

Article 6

The Committee shall include in its annual report under article 45 of the Covenant a summary of its activities under the present Protocol.

Article 7

Pending the achievement of the objectives of resolution 1514(XV) adopted by the General Assembly of the United Nations on 14 December 1960 concerning the Declaration on the Granting of Independence to Colonial Countries and Peoples, the provisions of the present Protocol shall in no way limit the right of petition granted to these peoples by the Charter of the United Nations and other international conventions and instruments under the United Nations and its specialized agencies.

Article 8

1. The present Protocol is open for signature by any State which has signed the Covenant.

2. The present Protocol is subject to ratification by any State which has ratified or acceded to the Covenant. Instruments of ratification shall be deposited with the Secretary-General of the United Nations.
3. The present Protocol shall be open to accession by any State which has ratified or acceded to the Covenant.
4. Accession shall be effected by the deposit of an instrument of accession with the Secretary-General of the United Nations.
5. The Secretary-General of the United Nations shall inform all States which have signed the present Protocol or acceded to it of the deposit of each instrument of ratification or accession.

Article 9

1. Subject to the entry into force of the Covenant, the present Protocol shall enter into force three months after the date of the deposit with the Secretary-General of the United Nations of the tenth instrument of ratification or instrument of accession.
2. For each State ratifying the present Protocol or acceding to it after the deposit of the tenth instrument of ratification or instrument of accession, the present Protocol shall enter into force three months after the date of the deposit of its own instrument of ratification or instrument of accession.

Article 10

The provisions of the present Protocol shall extend to all parts of federal States without any limitations or exceptions.

Article 11

1. Any State Party to the present Protocol may propose an amendment and file it with the Secretary-General of the United Nations. The Secretary-General shall thereupon communicate any proposed amendments to the States Parties to the present Protocol with a request that they notify him whether they favour a conference of States Parties for the purpose of considering and voting upon the proposal. In the event that at least one third of the States Parties favours such a conference, the Secretary-General shall convene the conference under the auspices of the United Nations. Any amendment adopted by a majority of the States Parties present and voting at the conference shall be submitted to the General Assembly of the United Nations for approval.
2. Amendments shall come into force when they have been approved by the General Assembly of the United Nations and accepted by a two-thirds majority of the States Parties to the present Protocol in accordance with their respective constitutional processes.
3. When amendments come into force, they shall be binding on those States Parties which have accepted them, other States Parties still being bound by the provisions of the present Protocol and any earlier amendment which they have accepted.

Article 12

1. Any State Party may denounce the present Protocol at any time by written notification addressed to the Secretary-General of the United Nations. Denunciation shall take effect three months after the date of receipt of the notification by the Secretary-General.

2. Denunciation shall be without prejudice to the continued application of the provisions of the present Protocol to any communication submitted under article 2 before the effective date of denunciation.

Article 13

Irrespective of the notifications made under article 8, paragraph 5, of the present Protocol, the Secretary-General of the United Nations shall inform all States referred to in article 48, paragraph I, of the Covenant of the following particulars:

(a) Signatures, ratifications and accessions under article 8;

(b) The date of the entry into force of the present Protocol under article 9 and the date of the entry into force of any amendments under article 11;

(c) Denunciations under article 12.

Article 14

1. The present Protocol, of which the Chinese, English, French, Russian and Spanish texts are equally authentic, shall be deposited in the archives of the United Nations.

2. The Secretary-General of the United Nations shall transmit certified copies of the present Protocol to all States referred to in article 48 of the Covenant.

Appendix 3

Party Status to the International Covenant on Civil and Political Rights and its Optional Protocol (as at 18 April 2008)[1]

States and Self-Governing Territories	ICCPR	Optional Protocol
Afghanistan	24 January 1983 (a)	–
Albania	4 October 1991 (a)	4 October 2007 (a)
Algeria	12 September 1989 (r)	12 September 1989 (a)
Andorra	22 September 2006 (r)	22 September 2006 (r)
Angola	10 January 1992 (a)	10 January 1992 (a)
Argentina	8 August 1986 (r)	8 August 1986 (a)
Armenia	23 June 1993 (a)	23 June 1993 (a)
Australia	13 August 1980 (r)	25 September 1991 (a)
Austria	10 September 1978 (r)	10 December 1987 (r)
Azerbaijan	13 August 1992 (a)	27 November 2001 (a)
Bahrain	20 September 2006 (a)	–
Bangladesh	6 September 2000 (a)	–
Barbados	5 January 1973 (a)	5 January 1973 (a)
Belarus	12 November 1973 (r)	30 September 1992 (a)
Belgium	21 April 1983 (r)	17 May 1994 (a)
Belize	10 June 1996 (a)	–
Benin	12 March 1992 (a)	12 March 1992 (a)
Bolivia	12 August 1982 (a)	12 August 1982 (a)
Bosnia and Herzegovina	1 September 1993 (d)	1 March 1995 (r)
Botswana	8 September 2000 (r)	–
Brazil	24 January 1992 (a)	–
Bulgaria	21 September 1970 (r)	26 March 1992 (a)
Burkina Faso	4 January 1999 (a)	4 January 1999 (a)
Burundi	9 May 1990 (a)	–
Cambodia	26 May 1992 (a)	27 September 2004 (s)

1 See Office of the United Nations High Commissioner for Human Rights 'Status of Ratifications of the Principal International Human Rights Treaties'. Key: (a) signifies the date of accession; (d) signifies the date of succession; (r) signifies the date of ratification; (s) signifies the date of signature, where only signature has been made.

States and Self-Governing Territories	ICCPR	Optional Protocol
Cameroon	27 June 1984 (a)	27 June 1984 (a)
Canada	19 May 1976 (a)	19 May 1976 (a)
Cape Verde	6 August 1993 (a)	19 May 2000 (a)
Central African Republic	8 May 1981 (a)	8 May 1981 (a)
Chad	9 June 1995 (a)	9 June 1995 (a)
Chile	10 February 1972 (r)	27 May 1992 (a)
China	5 October 1998 (s)	–
Colombia	29 October 1969 (r)	29 October 1969 (r)
Congo	5 October 1983 (a)	5 October 1983 (a)
Costa Rica	29 November 1968 (r)	29 November 1968 (r)
Côte d'Ivoire	26 March 1992 (a)	5 March 1997 (a)
Croatia	12 October 1992 (d)	12 October 1995 (a)
Cuba	28 February 2008 (s)	–
Cyprus	2 April 1969 (r)	15 April 1992 (r)
Czech Republic	22 February 1993 (d)	22 February 1993 (d)
Democratic People's Republic of Korea	14 September 1981 (a)	–
Democratic Republic of Congo	1 November 1976 (a)	1 November 1976 (a)
Denmark	6 January 1972 (r)	6 January 1972 (r)
Djibouti	5 November 2002 (a)	5 November 2002 (a)
Dominica	17 June 1993 (a)	–
Dominican Republic	4 January 1978 (a)	4 January 1978 (a)
Ecuador	6 March 1969 (r)	6 March 1969 (r)
Egypt	14 January 1982 (r)	–
El Salvador	30 November 1979 (r)	6 June 1995 (r)
Equatorial Guinea	25 September 1987 (a)	25 September 1987 (a)
Eritrea	22 January 2002 (a)	–
Estonia	21 October 1991 (a)	21 October 1991 (a)
Ethiopia	11 June 1993 (a)	–
Finland	19 August 1975 (r)	19 August 1975 (r)
France	4 November 1980 (a)	17 February 1984 (a)
Gabon	21 January 1983 (a)	–
Gambia	22 March 1979 (a)	9 June 1988 (a)
Georgia	3 May 1994 (a)	3 May 1994 (a)
Germany	17 December 1973 (r)	25 August 1993 (a)
Ghana	7 December 2000 (r)	7 September 2000 (r)
Greece	5 May 1997 (a)	5 May 1997 (a)
Grenada	6 September 1991 (a)	–
Guatemala	5 May 1992 (a)	28 November 2000 (a)
Guinea	24 January 1978 (r)	17 June 1993 (r)
Guinea-Bissau	12 September 2000 (s)	12 September 2000 (s)

States and Self-Governing Territories	ICCPR	Optional Protocol
Guyana	15 February 1977 (r)	10 May 1993 (a)
Haiti	6 February 1991 (a)	–
Honduras	25 August 1997 (r)	7 June 2005 (r)
Hungary	17 January 1974 (r)	7 September 1988 (a)
Iceland	22 August 1979 (r)	22 August 1979 (a)
India	10 April 1979 (a)	–
Indonesia	23 February 2006 (a)	–
Iran	24 June 1975 (r)	–
Iraq	25 January 1971 (r)	–
Ireland	8 December 1989 (r)	8 December 1989 (r)
Israel	3 October 1991 (r)	–
Italy	15 September 1978 (r)	15 September 1978 (r)
Jamaica	3 October 1975 (r)	3 October 1975 (r)
Japan	21 June 1979 (r)	25 September 2007 (s)
Jordan	28 May 1975 (r)	–
Kazakhstan	24 January 2006 (r)	–
Kenya	1 May 1972 (a)	–
Kuwait	21 May 1996 (a)	–
Kyrgyzstan	7 October 1994 (a)	7 October 1994 (a)
Lao People's Democratic Republic	7 December 2000 (s)	–
Latvia	14 April 1992 (a)	22 June 1994 (a)
Lebanon	3 November 1972 (a)	–
Lesotho	9 September 1992 (a)	6 September 2000 (a)
Liberia	22 September 2004 (r)	22 September 2004 (s)
Libyan Arab Jamahiriya	15 May 1970 (a)	16 May 1989 (a)
Liechtenstein	10 December 1998 (a)	10 December 1998 (a)
Lithuania	20 November 1991 (a)	20 November 1991 (a)
Luxembourg	18 August 1983 (r)	18 August 1983 (a)
Madagascar	21 June 1971 (r)	21 June 1971 (r)
Malawi	22 December 1994 (a)	11 June 1996 (a)
Maldives	19 September 2006 (a)	19 September 2006 (a)
Mali	16 July 1974 (a)	24 October 2001 (a)
Malta	13 September 1990 (a)	13 September 1990 (a)
Mauritania	17 November 2004 (a)	–
Mauritius	12 December 1973 (a)	12 December 1973 (a)
Mexico	23 March 1981 (a)	15 March 2002 (a)
Monaco	28 August 1997 (r)	–
Mongolia	18 November 1974 (r)	16 April 1991 (a)
Montenegro	23 October 2006 (d)	23 October 2006 (d)
Morocco	3 May 1979 (r)	–
Mozambique	21 July 1983 (a)	–

States and Self-Governing Territories	ICCPR	Optional Protocol
Namibia	24 November 1994 (a)	28 November 1994 (a)
Nauru	12 November 2001 (s)	12 November 2001 (s)
Nepal	14 May 1991 (a)	14 May 1991 (a)
Netherlands	11 December 1978 (r)	11 December 1978 (r)
New Zealand	28 December 1978 (r)	26 May 1989 (a)
Nicaragua	12 March 1980 (a)	12 March 1980 (a)
Niger	7 March 1986 (a)	7 March 1986 (a)
Nigeria	29 July 1993 (a)	–
Norway	13 September 1972 (r)	13 September 1972 (r)
Pakistan	17 April 2008 (s)	–
Panama	8 March 1977 (r)	8 March 1977 (r)
Paraguay	10 June 1992 (a)	10 January 1995 (a)
Peru	28 April 1978 (r)	3 October 1980 (r)
Philippines	23 October 1986 (r)	22 August 1989 (a)
Poland	18 March 1977 (r)	7 November 1991 (a)
Portugal	15 June 1978 (r)	3 May 1983 (r)
Republic of Korea	10 April 1990 (a)	10 April 1990 (a)
Republic of Moldova	26 January 1993 (a)	23 January 2008 (r)
Romania	9 December 1974 (r)	20 July 1993 (a)
Russian Federation	16 October 1973 (r)	1 October 1991 (a)
Rwanda	16 April 1975 (a)	–
Saint Vincent and the Grenadines	9 November 1981 (a)	9 November 1981 (a)
Samoa	15 February 2008 (a)	–
San Marino	18 October 1985 (a)	18 October 1985 (a)
Sao Tome and Principe	31 October 1995 (s)	6 September 2000 (s)
Senegal	13 February 1978 (r)	13 February 1978 (r)
Serbia and Montenegro	12 March 2001 (d)	6 September 2001 (r)
Seychelles	5 May 1992 (a)	5 May 1992 (a)
Sierra Leone	23 August 1996 (a)	23 August 1996 (a)
Slovakia	28 May 1993 (d)	28 May 1993 (d)
Slovenia	6 July 1992 (d)	16 July 1993 (a)
Somalia	24 January 1990 (a)	24 January 1990 (a)
South Africa	10 December 1998 (r)	28 August 2002 (a)
Spain	27 April 1977 (r)	25 January 1985 (a)
Sri Lanka	11 June 1980 (a)	3 October 1997 (a)
Sudan	18 March 1986 (a)	–
Suriname	28 December 1976 (a)	28 December 1976 (a)
Sweden	6 December 1971 (r)	6 December 1971 (r)
Switzerland	18 June 1992 (a)	–
Syrian Arab Republic	21 April 1969 (a)	–
Tajikistan	4 January 1999 (a)	4 January 1999 (a)

States and Self-Governing Territories	ICCPR	Optional Protocol
Thailand	29 October 1996 (a)	–
The Former Yugoslav Republic of Macedonia	18 January 1994 (d)	12 December 1994 (r)
Timor-Leste	18 September 2003 (a)	–
Togo	24 May 1984 (a)	30 March 1988 (a)
Trinidad and Tobago	21 December 1978 (a)	14 November 1980 (a)
Tunisia	18 March 1969 (r)	–
Turkey	23 September 2003 (r)	24 November 2006 (r)
Turkmenistan	1 May 1997 (a)	1 May 1997 (a)
Uganda	21 June 1995 (a)	14 November 1996 (a)
Ukraine	12 November 1973 (r)	25 July 1991 (a)
United Kingdom of Great Britain and Northern Ireland	20 May 1976 (r)	–
United Republic of Tanzania	11 June 1976 (a)	–
United States of America	8 June 1992 (r)	–
Uruguay	1 April 1970 (r)	1 April 1970 (r)
Uzbekistan	28 September 1995 (a)	28 September 1995 (a)
Vanuatu	29 November 2007 (s)	–
Venezuela	10 May 1978 (r)	10 May 1978 (r)
Viet Nam	24 September 1982 (a)	–
Yemen	9 February 1987 (a)	–
Zambia	10 April 1984 (a)	10 April 1984 (a)
Zimbabwe	13 May 1991 (a)	–
Total (full parties; signatories only)	**(162; 8)**	**(119; 6)**

Appendix 4
Model Complaint Form

For communications under:

- Optional Protocol to the International Covenant on Civil and Political Rights
- Convention against Torture, or
- International Convention on the Elimination of Racial Discrimination

Please indicate which of the above procedures you are invoking: ....
Date: ....

I. Information on the complainant:

Name: ....   First name(s): ....
Nationality: ....   Date and place of birth: ....
Address for correspondence on this complaint: ....

Submitting the communication:
on the author's own behalf: ....
on behalf of another person: ....

[If the complaint is being submitted on behalf of another person:]
Please provide the following personal details of that other person

Name: ....   First name(s): ....
Nationality: ....   Date and place of birth: ....
Address or current whereabouts: ....

If you are acting with the knowledge and consent of that person, please provide that person's authorization for you to bring this complaint: ....
Or
If you are not so authorized, please explain the nature of your relationship with that person: ....
and detail why you consider it appropriate to bring this complaint on his or her behalf: ....

II. State concerned/Articles violated

Name of the State that is either a party to the Optional Protocol (in the case of a complaint to the Human Rights Committee) or has made the relevant declaration (in the case of complaints to the Committee against Torture or the Committee on the Elimination of Racial Discrimination):

…………

Articles of the Covenant or Convention alleged to have been violated:

…………

III. Exhaustion of domestic remedies/Application to other international procedures

Steps taken by or on behalf of the alleged victims to obtain redress within the State concerned for the alleged violation – detail which procedures have been pursued, including recourse to the courts and other public authorities, which claims you have made, at which times, and with which outcomes:

……………………

> If you have not exhausted these remedies on the basis that their application would be unduly prolonged, that they would not be effective, that they are not available to you, or for any other reason, please explain your reasons in detail: ……………………………

Have you submitted the same matter for examination under another procedure of international investigation or settlement (e.g. the Inter-American Commission on Human Rights, the European Court of Human Rights, or the African Commission on Human and Peoples' Rights)? ……………

> If so, detail which procedure(s) have been, or are being, pursued, which claims you have made, at which times, and with which outcomes: ……………………………

IV. Facts of the complaint

Detail, in chronological order, the facts and circumstances of the alleged violations. Include all matters which may be relevant to the assessment and consideration of your particular case. Please explain how you consider that the facts and circumstances described violate your rights.

……………………………

……………………………

……………………………

Author's signature: ....

[The blanks under the various sections of this model communication simply indicate where your responses are required. You should take as much space as you need to set out your responses.]

V. Checklist of supporting documentation (copies, not originals, to be enclosed with your complaint):

- Written authorization to act (if you are bringing the complaint on behalf of another person and are not otherwise justifying the absence of specific authorization): ....
- Decisions of domestic courts and authorities on your claim (a copy of the relevant national legislation is also helpful): ....
- Complaints to and decisions by any other procedure of international investigation or settlement: ....
- Any documentation or other corroborating evidence you possess that substantiates your description in Part IV of the facts of your claim and/or your argument that the facts described amount to a violation of your rights: ....

If you do not enclose this information and it needs to be sought specifically from you, or if accompanying documentation is not provided in the working languages of the Secretariat, the consideration of your complaint may be delayed.

Index

Note: page numbers in *italics* indicate subjects referred to in the footnotes.